The Ohio State Buckeyes Class of '68

No.	Name	Pos.	Wgt.	Hgt.	Age	Class	Hometown
63	Adams, Douglas	LB	215	6-0	18	So	Xenia, OH
85	Aldrin, Charles	ORE	207	6-3	19	So	Glenview, IL
26	Anderson, Tim	DRH	194	6-0	19	So	Follansbee, WV
86	Aston, Daniel	DRE	208	6-2	20	Jr	Cincinnati, OH
57*	Backhus, Thomas	OLG	207	5-11	19	Jr	Cincinnati, OH
33*	Bartley, Thomas	LB	198	5-11	21	Sr	Springfield
19	Bender, Edward	ORH	172	6-0	21	Sr	Akron
48*	Bombach, Jay	ORH	201	6-1	20	Jr	Dayton
42	Brockington, John	ORH	210	6-1	20	So	Brooklyn, NY.
12*	Brungard, Dave	OLH	184	5-10	20	Jr	Youngstown
21	Burton, Arthur	LB	193	6-1	20	Jr	Fostoria
75	Cheney, David	OLG	230	6-3	19	So	Lima
47	Coburn, James	DLH	190	5-11	19	So	Maumee
36	Cunningham, Richard	FB	188	5-10	19	So	Portsmouth
83	Debevc, Mark	DRE	210	6-1	19	So	Geneva
78	Dombos, John	DLT	205	6-0	19	So	Garfield Heights
66	Donovan, Brian	OLG	206	6-3	19	So	Columbus
90	Ecrement, Thomas	DLE	195	6-0	19	So	Canton
28**	Ehrsam, Gerald	S	194	6-0	21	Sr	Toledo
70**	Foley, David [cc]	ORT	246	6-5	20	Sr	Cincinnati
39	Gentile, James	LB	210	6-2	20	Jr	Poland
11*	Gillian, Ray	OLH	194	5-11	20	Jr	Uniontown, Pa.
44	Greene, Horatius	OLH	180	5-11	19	Jr	Jersey City, N.J.
51	Hackett, William	LB	204	6-1	20	Jr	London
65	Hart, Randy	ORT	220	6-2	20	Jr	Willoughby
22	Hayden, Leophus	OLH	204	6-2	20	So	Dayton
67	Holloway, Ralph	MG	222	6-1	19	So	Oberlin
34*	Huff, Paul	FB	217	6-3	20	Jr	Dover
72*	Hutchison, Charles	OLT	240	6-3	19	Jr	Carrollton
61*	Jack, Alan	ORG	215	6-0	20	Jr	Wintersville
82	Jankowski, Bruce	OLE	192	5-11	19	So	Fair Lawn, N.J.
10	Kern, Rex	QB	180	6-0	19	So	Lancaster
81	Kuhn, Richard	ORE	208	6-2	19	So	Louisville
64	Kurz, Ted	ORG	222	6-2	19	So	Struthers
24**	Long, William	QB	180	6-1	21	Sr	Dayton
18	Maciejowski, Ronald	QB	186	6-2	19	So	Bedford
73**	Mayes, Rufus	OLT	250	6-5	20	Sr	Toledo
53**	Muhlbach, John	C	194	5-10	21	Sr	Massillon
77*	Nielsen, Brad	DRT	222	6-3	20	Jr	Columbus
76	Oppermann, James	OLT	240	6-4	18	So	Bluffton
35*	Otis, James	FB	208	6-0	20	Jr	Celina
15*	Polaski, Michael	DLH	170	5-10	19	Jr	Columbus
46*	Provost, Ted	DLH	182	6-3	20	Jr	Navarre
58	Qualls, Larry	C	190	6-0	19	So	Dayton
43	Quiling, Richard	S	190	6-1	20	Jr	Celina
55*	Radtke, Michael	LB	200	6-1	20	Jr	Wayne, N.J.
52**	Roman, James	C	211	6-0	20	Sr	Canton
89**	Roman, Nicholas	DRE	221	6-4	21	Sr	Canton
59	Roush, Gary	ORT	200	6-4	21	Sr	Springfield
23*	Rusnak, Kevin	ORH	190	6-1	20	Jr	Garfield, N.J.
74*	Schmidlin, Paul	DLT	222	6-1	19	Jr	Toledo
3***	Sensibaugh, Michael	S	187	6-0	19	So	Cincinnati
50*	Smith, Butch	DRT	224	6-2	20	Jr	Hamilton
87	Smith, Robert	ORE	221	6-4	21	Sr	Lakewood
91*	Sobolewski, John	DRE	192	6-1	20	Jr	Steubenville
54**	Stier, Mark	LB	202	6-1	21	Sr	Louisville
68	Stillwagon, James	MG	220	6-0	19	So	Mt. Vernon
69**	Stottlemyer, Victor	MG	200	6-0	21	Sr	Chillicothe
92	Stowe, John	OLE	200	6-2	21	Sr	Columbus
62	Strickland, Phillip	ORG	217	6-1	19	So	Cincinnati
32	Tatum, John	LB	204	6-0	19	So	Passaic, N.J.
17	Trapuzzano, Robert	DRH	187	6-0	19	Jr	McKees Rocks, Pa.
71	Troha, Richard	ORT	227	6-3	19	So	Cleveland
79*	Urbanik, William	DLT	238	6-3	21	Jr	Donora, PA
41	Wagner, Tim	DRH	175	5-10	19	So	Columbus
80	White, Jan	OLE	214	6-2	19	So	Harrisburg, Pa.
88*	Whitfield, David	DLE	184	6-0	20	Jr	Massillon
56**	Worden, Dirk [cc]	LB	198	6-0	22	Sr	Lorain
16	Zelina, Lawrence	ORH	195	6-0	19	So	Cleveland

*Indicates letter   CC— co-captain

DECEMBER 1998

JAMES HISER

ENJOY THIS WONDERFUL TRIP DOWN 'MEMORY LANE'

Class of '68
a season to remember...

by Harvey Shapiro

Witness Productions
P.O. Box 34, Marshall, IN 47859

Class of '68

a season to remember...

ISBN 1-891390-01-5

Cover Design/ Harvey Shapiro.
Front Cover photo/ Courtesy Dr. James Otis.
Back Cover photo: Reprinted with permission of
Mike Major and The Columbus Dispatch.

Published by: Witness Productions
Box 34, Church Street
Marshall, IN 47859
765-597-2487

The Class of '68

INTRODUCTION

I had been a full-time journalist for almost 10 years by the Fall of 1968, starting out in Grand Junction, Colorado in December 1958. I was a combination police reporter and one-man sports department for the long-defunct Morning Sun.

By the summer of '68, I had worked for four newspapers in Colorado, Illinois, Ohio and Pennsylvania. My career was moving in an upward direction, from the 3,800-daily Morning Sun to the 'big time' Pittsburgh Press.

That summer, I became general assignment reporter for United Press International, also based in Pittsburgh. Little did I know what was in store for me.

After only two months on the job, I was asked by Eastern Division bureau chief Ed DiPietro if I would consider a transfer to Columbus, Ohio as UPI Sports Editor.

I had lived and worked in Akron, Ohio for four years [1963-67]. I enjoyed it there and the thought of returning to the Buckeye State was attractive enough. But when I was told I could cover the Ohio State University home football games, I was sold hook-line-and-sinker. My first chance to cover a major college team.

It was the Fall of '68. The Woody Hayes-coached Buckeyes were about to launch their 'season to remember' against Southern Methodist. I knew nothing about Ohio State, but I didn't mind playing catch-up, learning as much as I could in the shortest possible time.

Sitting in the Ohio Stadium press box sure beat those high school days when I not only walked the sidelines in all kinds of weather, but also had to take pictures as well. Occasionally, a ball carrier came close enough to my lens. Occasionally, a shot in focus.

I covered Ohio State's home games for two seasons. That means I didn't see Ohio State lose a game. As sportswriter at the Dayton [Ohio] Daily News, I covered Ohio State home and away from 1976-1978.

Back in '68, the wire service demands that first season were too much for this reporter. How can you boil down the Buckeyes' 35-14 season opening victory against pass-happy SMU in 300 words???

That's about 30 lines.

That might be OK for a ho-hum game, but there were no ho-hummers in 1968. Chuck Hixson and his replacement at SMU combined for an NCAA-record 76 passes, completing 40 for some 437 yards. Ohio State, bent but never broke, intercepting five Hixson passes. SMU wide receiver Jerry Levias caught 15 of those passes. My 300 word limit, I'm sure that game, must have amounted to 3,000 words. But a cool customer back in our bureau, John Kady, calmly re-tooled my 'epic' into 300 choice words.

Covering an Ohio State game was really a four-man operation. While Ohio State furnished reams of material, including play-by-play, quotes, statistics, I kept my own running play-by-play. I'd done it for some 10 years and I simply preferred it that way.

At halftime, I 'banged out' a quick add to the lead that was yet to come. In that way, I got a head start as speed was really the name of the game. One guy went down to both locker rooms after the game for coaches and player quotes. Another sat along side of me in the press box and dictated my game story back to John Kady.

Kady, a real character out of a Hollywood movie, once climbed out of a hospital bed with a bleeding ulcer to cover a plane crash. He had a small refrigerator next to his desk. He'd munch on his fried chicken, take the dictation and craft it into an acceptable wire service piece.

A born competitor, I played three years of varsity soccer at Long Island University, 'ballooning' to 120 pounds as a senior starting left halfback. As far as I was concerned, it was a war...UPI versus The Associated Press.

AP Ohio Sports Editor Hal Paris, in all honesty, was restricted by his company's policy. My story would be transmitted across the country to client newspapers complete. The AP story, however, was transmitted in pieces. First the lead, and then eventually the rest of the story. Sports editors in Ohio and elsewhere were fighting a deadline. They had sports sections to fill, and the first story coming across would be the choice. Yeah, UPI.

By my second year, I had calmed down and limited my stories to the mandated 300 words. But because Ohio State had won the national championship in 1968, there was more demand for Buckeye stories and I was also allowed to write sidebars.

Every Monday at noon during the football season, I'd attend the weekly Ohio State luncheons. Woody Hayes was always there as was Esco Sarkinnen, defensive end coach and chief scout.

As a sportswriter for the Akron Beacon Journal, I had attended my share of banquets. I'd seen the funny, human, delightful side of Wayne Woodrow Hayes. Same at the luncheons.

During my career, I covered 12 Indianapolis 500s from 1965-1982. I was there when A.J. Foyt won No. 3 in 1967. I was there 10 years later when he became the first in Indy history to capture four 500s. I always called A.J. Foyt 'the Woody Hayes of Auto Racing'. Likewise, I called Woody Hayes 'the A.J. Foyt of College Football'. Same type of personality. That intensity. That charming nature when things went right. That volatility when things went wrong. Two peas in a pod. TWO WINNERS.

I attended Ohio State's post-season banquets in both 1968 and 1969. I proudly keep two glasses from those shindigs.

In the past few years, 'THE CLASS OF '68' would surface when a John Cooper-led team would move closer to an unbeaten and untied season and a national championship. And just when it appeared they would move shoulder-to-shoulder with the '68 edition, they'd self-destruct. Usually at the hands of 'that team up North.' AKA Michigan.

Now 30 years later, that feat of 1968 with it's improbable cast of characters, meaning 13-17 sophomores in the starting lineup, becomes even more impressive.

For me, it was a wonderful trip 'down memory lane.' Interviewing 14 Ohio State players, including three All-Americans as well as four OSU assistant coaches, opponents the likes of Leroy Keyes [Purdue] and Chuck Hixson [SMU].

Few realize that Lou Holtz spent one memorable season at Ohio State. He was a 31-year-old backfield coach in 1968.

Holtz left Ohio State the next year to become head coach at William and Mary. His memories of Woody Hayes and that experience are still vivid.

After two months of letter-writing, the then famous Notre Dame head football coach agreed to give me 10 minutes for a phone interview. His secretary would call me with the day and time. It was June of 1996.

At 11 a.m., on July 8, I placed my call to South Bend, Indiana where the same Lou Holtz was waiting for my call. To make a long story very short, some 30 minutes later Holtz said, 'Harv, I've gotta run.' I replied, 'God bless.'

All of those interviewed have their own story to tell. Inside stuff, that 'CLASS OF '68', not just another rehash.

I tried to explore the many sides of Woody Hayes through the words of his players, his coaches, those who knew him best. Such as a then 18-year-old freshman end at Denison University by the name of Robert Shannon. Shannon, who carved out his own distinguished 40-year coaching career at Denison, was the driving force in reuniting almost 40 of 'Woody's Boys' from his 1946-47-48 Denison squads. It was a joyous gathering attended by Woody's widow, Anne Hayes who died in January 1998 at the age of 83. It was her last public appearance.

The Woody Hayes Section contains 17 chapters. The entire book—55 chapters—well exceeds 100,000 words.

Now, enjoy the journey. Return with us to those days of yesterday. A time of turmoil as American boys were shedding blood in a land far away and protests at home made the front pages. A time when a spanking new car cost less than $3,000. A magical time when dreams came true.

ACKNOWLEDGMENTS

Writing a book of this scope can't be done alone. It takes a lot of help. So many contributing. To all of them, my heartfelt thanks. If I've left someone off this Honor Roll, please forgive.

THE PLAYERS: Tom Backhus, Dave Brungard, Mark Debevc, Dave Foley, Ron Maciejowski, Jim Otis, Mike Polaski, Ted Provost, Jim Roman, Paul Schmidlin, Mark Stier, Jan White, Dirk Worden, Larry Zelina.

THE COACHES: George Chaump, Lou Holtz, Bill Mallory, Lou McCullough.

SUPPORTING CAST: Sports Illustrated, The Sporting News, Columbus [Ohio] Dispatch, Cincinnati [Ohio] Enquirer, Cincinnati [Ohio] Post, Dayton [Ohio] Daily News, The Newcomerstown [Ohio] News, Granville [Ohio] Sentinel-Booster, New Philadelphia [Ohio] Times-Reporter, The Register-Guard [Eugene, Oregon], Journal and Courier [Lafayette, Indiana], Wisconsin State Journal/Capital News [Madison, Wisconsin], The News-Gazette [Champaign, Illinois].

Steve Snapp, Sports Information Director, Ohio State University; Sue Ferguson, The Varsity O Alumni, Ohio State University; Ohio State University Archives; Southern Methodist University, Iowa State University, University of Southern California, University of Iowa, University of Notre Dame, Indiana University, University of Texas, Denison University [Granville, Ohio], United States Naval Academy, Miami University [Oxford, Ohio], University of Oklahoma, Michigan University, University of Alabama, College Football Hall of Fame [South Bend, Indiana], New Philadelphia [Ohio] High School, Celina [Ohio] High School, Cincinnati [Ohio] Roger Bacon High School, Ron Shay, Columbus [Ohio] Watterson High School.

National Football League: Chicago Bears, Indianapolis Colts, Oakland Raiders, Detroit Lions. Canadian Football League: Toronto Argonauts, Saskatchewan Rough Riders; Saskatchewan Sports Hall of Fame.
Tom Farbizo, president, Quaker Club, New Philadelphia, Ohio; Phyllis and Robert Shannon, Rix Yard, Dr. Richard Mahard, Keith Piper, Leroy Keyes, Bob DeMoss, Chuck Hixson, Jan Ebert, Mike Major, Dr. James Otis, Vicki Otis, John Hlay, Barbara and Vane Scott, Temperance Tavern Museum, Newcomerstown, Ohio; Tuscarawas County Convention and Visitors Bureau, New Philadelphia, Ohio.

And special, special thanks to Bill Ashworth, Laurie Vernay and Mauricio Almeida.

Ohio Stadium
Home of the Buckeyes

PROLOGUE

'AIN'T NOTHING EASY'

Once upon a time there was a crafty old TV lawyer by the name of Ben Matlock. Seems like in each episode, he was on his own one yard line with time running out.

Defeat seemed inevitable.

But with wisdom that comes from age, experience, and a great script writer, Ben would say time-and-time again, 'As Momma used to say, ain't nothing easy.'

Right on, Ben Matlock.

Just ask 'that team up North.' The late Woody Hayes never mentioned his arch-rival Michigan by name.

Way back in 1947-48, Michigan registered back-to-back unbeaten and untied seasons, claiming the national crown in '48. But it wasn't until January 1, 1998 that the Wolverines had done it again. It took 'ONLY' 49 years.

'Ain't nothing easy.'

Michigan, under head coach Lloyd Carr, won 12 in a row, climaxing the dream season with a 21-16 conquest of Washington State in the Rose Bowl.

Yet, 'that team up North' had to be content with only a share of the national championship. Michigan was The Associated Press [writers' poll] winner while Nebraska took the USA Today/ESPN [coaches' poll] balloting.

Thus, Michigan became the first Big Ten team in the last 30 years to finish unbeaten, untied, capture the Rose Bowl and share the national title.

The last team? Why Woody Hayes' 1968 crew.

Funny thing, the Buckeyes haven't finished unbeaten since.

During his long and legendary reign at Michigan, Hayes disciple Glenn "Bo" Schembechler compiled a 194-48-5 record at that school and won 13 Big Ten titles...outright or shared. Yet this National Football Foundation Hall of Fame inductee [1993] never enjoyed an unblemished season.

'Ain't nothing easy.'

Darrell Royal led the University of Texas to a record of 267-47-5 during his highly-successful career. His Longhorns took the national title in 1969. Two of his teams posted perfect records, 11-0 in both 1963 and 1969.

That was 29 years ago.

Texas hasn't done it since.

'Ain't nothing easy.'

Once upon a time, as the story goes, a mighty college football team from the nation's heartland slashed through 47 straight opponents like an Oklahoma tornado and in the process claimed consecutive national championships in 1955 and 1956.

That glorious streak began at Dallas on October 10, 1953 with a 19-14 win over Texas. It finally ended, 7-0, against visiting Notre Dame on November 16, 1957.

You probably guessed it by now. The University of Oklahoma was that very special team. Charles "Bud" Wilkinson was that legendary head coach. Wilkinson coached 17 years at that Norman, Oklahoma school [1947-1963], compiling a record of 145-29-4. A gaudy winning percentage of .826. His Sooners won three national crowns, 14 Big Eight championships, finished in the Top Ten for 11 straight years.

Quite a legacy to pass on.

Oklahoma prospered through the mid-90s. It's been a bumpy road the last three seasons.

Oklahoma's last national title dates back to 1985, the last unbeaten season to 1974. Both under the direction of Barry Switzer.

Switzer left after 16 seasons, producing an even gaudier record of 157-29-4 and three national championships. Oklahoma hasn't been unbeaten in 24 years.

'Ain't nothing easy.'

Ohio native Lou Holtz was Woody Hayes' backfield coach in 1968. A year later, he began his head coaching career at William and Mary. His head coaching career would span 27 years at four schools, the last 11 at fabled Notre Dame.

He took over at Notre Dame in 1986 and remained through the 1996 season, becoming the second winningest coach in Irish history. Second only to Knute Rockne. During a six-year span [1988-1993], Notre Dame posted a 52-9-1 record, including five victories in the Cotton, Sugar, Orange and Fiesta Bowls. His 1988 team [12-0] won the national title. That was Notre Dame's last unbeaten/untied season.

'Ain't nothing easy.'

John Robinson served two tours of duty as Southern Cal head coach, compiling a 104-35-4 record in 12 seasons from 1976-1982 and 1993-1997. His Trojans struggled to a 12-11 record the last two campaigns after going 9-2-1 in 1995, including a 41-32 Rose Bowl victory against Northwestern. In December of 1997, following his team's 6-5 performance, Robinson was fired and replaced by Paul Hackett, offensive coordinator for the NFL Kansas City Chiefs.

Robinson's shining moments took place in the 1977-78-79 seasons. Southern Cal posted records of 12-1-0, 11-0 and 11-0-1, copping the national title in 1978. Three times John Robinson was named Coach of the Year. It's been 18 years since the Trojans' last unbeaten season.

'Ain't nothing easy.'

The 1978 Sugar Bowl in New Orleans was billed as Woody Versus Bear. The great 'chess match' between two masters. Ohio State against Paul "Bear" Bryant's Alabama Crimson Tide.

It turned out to be a mismatch. 'Bama buried the Buckeyes, 35-7. That victory is listed among the most important in school history.

Bryant coached from 1945-1982. He died January 23, 1983. He compiled an imposing 323-85-17 career record at Maryland, Kentucky, Texas A and M and Alabama. Bryant kicked off his career at Alabama in 1958, posting a 232-46-9 record, six national championships, unbeaten teams in 1961 [11-0], 1966 [11-0] and 1979 [12-0]. It took 13 more seasons, under Gene Stallings, for another unbeaten campaign. That was in 1992.

'Ain't nothing easy.'

I think you get the idea.

Nebraska and Penn State, however, have managed to operate on eight cylinders year-in-and-year-out, or so it seems. Joe Paterno has amassed a 298-77-3 record at Penn State, claiming two national crowns [1982, 1986] and six perfect seasons, the last coming in 1994 [12-0]. Tom Osborne, who retired after 25 years at Nebraska after his Huskers' 42-17 destruction of Tennessee and QB Peyton Manning in the 1998 Orange Bowl, claimed three national titles as did Bob Devaney, the man he succeeded. Nebraska won 60 of 63 games since 1993, posting unbeaten seasons in three of the last four years. Osborne's record: 255-49-3.

Some think, including Lou McCullough, that Ohio State should have won 29 in a row from 1968-69-70 and three national championships. Instead, the Buckeyes had 'to settle' for a 27-2 record, the one championship [1968] and back-to-back one-loss seasons in 1969 and 1970. McCullough, who served as Ohio State's defensive coordinator during those glory years, now enjoys retirement in Athens, Georgia. "In those three years I felt we shouldn't have lost a game. We played a lot better defense in 1969 and 1970 as those sophomores matured. Ohio State hasn't been unbeaten since, and I consider John Cooper a very fine coach.

"John's had a lot of material, a lot of good players. Sometimes it just doesn't jell. Sometimes it could be key injuries, or kids leaving school early to enter the NFL draft. It was just a dream season in 1968. Everything jelled. We didn't have many injuries. It was a special group of kids, probably one of the greatest sophomore classes in college football history. They were a perfect mix with our juniors and seniors.

"We were pretty deep at virtually every position. Senior linebacker Mark Stier looked like he would miss the Rose Bowl. We didn't wear pads on Thursday and Stier hit on his shoulder diving for the ball. It was only two days before the Rose Bowl. We didn't know if he was gonna play until he walked onto the field on Saturday and played one heckuva game.

"I had two days to get Mike Radtke ready to play linebacker. He had played it in 1967, but we moved him to defensive end the next year. I'm sure that Mike could have done the job for us had Mark Stier been unable to play.

"The game has changed so much the past 30 years. Players have changed. The passing game is so much better now. It's much tougher to go through a season unbeaten.

"It's not only been tough for Ohio State. It's been tough for Purdue, Michigan State, Michigan. All of 'em."

Photos courtesy University of Texas, University Southern California and University of Oklahoma.

Darrell Royal

John Robinson

Bud Wilkinson

Table of Contents

Table of Contents

Class of '68

a season to remember...

by Harvey Shapiro

A FALL RITUAL

It is a Fall ritual that captures the hearts and souls of millions of Americans. Age is no barrier. Wealth is no barrier. The young...the old...the rich...the poor. It is a game of strategy played on a rectangular-shaped battlefield. Men pounding men. Seizing territory. Overcoming every obstacle. Marching bands prancing proudly across the field. Cheers echoing throughout these man-made caverns. 'Go, Team, Go'...'Hold That Line'...'Two, Four, Six, Eight, Who Do We Appreciate?'

Young men become heroes, then legends for all time. Gipp...Grange... Thorpe...Nagurski...Cassady...Simpson.

Sportswriters create prose. 'The Four Horsemen'...'The Seven Blocks of Granite.'

Wiley 'old' coaches become folk-heroes. 'Hurry Up Yost', 'Pop' Warner, Knute Rockne, Bud Wilkinson, Woody Hayes, Joe Paterno.

It is a game called football. It is played from sea-to-shining sea. From California-to-Maine. From Florida-to-Alaska. In magnificent cathedrals. In tiny arenas. Please keep our warriors safe from harm. Those Buckeyes, those Trojans, those Nittany Lions, those Cornhuskers, those Gators. Bless 'Em All.

photo courtesy Mark Stier

CHAPTER 1

'HIT 'EM HARD, SEE 'EM FALL

Football tradition runs long and deep at Ohio State University. It began way back in 1890. Ohio State defeated Ohio Wesleyan 20-14 in it's first ever game. Alexander S. Lilley and Jack Ryder served as coaches.

Ohio State lost three of four decisions in its first intercollegiate season. Seven years later, Ohio State and Michigan met for the first time. The Wolverines 'tasted flesh' 34-0.

In 1899, with John B. Eckstrom as head coach, Ohio State's Buckeyes outscored their 10 opponents, 184-5, enroute to a sparkling 9-0-1 record. Only a 5-5 standoff with Case marred an otherwise perfect season.

By 1904, Ohio State had hired it's first 'year round' coach. He was E.R. Sweetland. Ticket prices ranged from 25 cents to a dollar for 'deluxe' games against Michigan and Carlisle.

Eight years later, Ohio State joined the Western Conference which became known as The Big Ten.

In 1915, varsity manager William A. Dougherty wrote the fight song 'Across The Field'. The song was dedicated to coach John Wilce and first performed at the Michigan game.

ACROSS THE FIELD
Fight that team across the field,
Show them Ohio's here
Set the earth reverberating with a mighty cheer
Rah! Rah! Rah!
Hit them hard and see how they fall;
Never let that team get the ball,
Hail! Hail! The gang's all here,
So let's win that old conference now.

The fight song must have worked. Ohio State lost only one of six games in 1915 and rollicked to the schools' second unbeaten season 8-0-1 in 1916. The Buckeyes won their first Western Conference title and back Chic Harley was named the school's first All-American. The team set a school scoring record in humiliating Oberlin, 128-0.

Ohio Stadium opened in 1922, and the Buckeyes responded with a 5-0 win over Ohio Wesleyan. The horseshoe-shaped stadium was officially dedicated two weeks later against Michigan.

Fourteen years later, the Ohio State Marching Band performed the famous formation 'Script Ohio' for the first time.

By December of 1941, Americans would be marching off to war. But football would still be played on college campuses across the land.

Paul Brown, Massillon High School's legendary coach, took over at Ohio State in 1941. A year later, the Buckeyes won their first national championship with a season record of 9-1.

Three years later, Les Horvath became the school's first Heisman Trophy winner, rushing for 924 yards and passing for 344 more. Ohio State's third unbeaten edition 9-0-0 would be coached by Carroll C. Widdoes.

After three head coaches within a span of six years, there appeared to be stability under the command of Wesley E. Fesler who compiled a 21-13 record from 1947-1950.

In 1949, Ohio State beat California 17-14, for its first Rose Bowl victory. A year later, junior back Vic Janowicz captured the Heisman Trophy. Fesler's last game was the famous 'Snow Bowl' against Michigan.

Despite those achievements, Wes Fesler would be gone. Ohio State would unveil the 28th coach for the 1951-52 season.

A man well-known in Ohio, but a 'Who's He?' on the national level.

A man who would be the most colorful, most ornery, but the most successful head football coach in Ohio State history.

That man: Wayne Woodrow Hayes.

Ohio born-and-bred, Hayes came onto the coaching scene like a meteor, leading little Denison University of Granville, Ohio to back-to-back unbeaten seasons in 1947 [9-0] and 1948 [8-0], then spun his magic at Miami of Ohio.

Limping through a 5-4 record in his first season at Miami, the Woody Hayes-led Redskins went on the warpath in 1950.

Once-beaten Miami reeled off eight straight victories, including a 34-21 decision over Arizona State in the Tangerine Bowl.

The 9-1 'Skins' amassed 356 points while yielding only 113.

Next stop...Ohio State.

A tough man who saw combat duty in World War II, Woody Hayes would survive every skirmish until he lost his temper one time too often during the 1978 Gator Bowl.

But in those tumultuous 28 years, he set a standard that may never be duplicated.

He compiled a 205-61-10 record at Ohio State, won two national championships, 13 Big Ten titles, and scored four Rose Bowl triumphs.

Add to that more than 50 All-Americans and two Heisman Trophy winners.

By 1966, the natives were restless. Banners flying over Ohio Stadium echoed the sentiments of disgruntled Buckeye fans.

'Bye, Bye, Woody.'

But Woody Hayes would not go easily.

The seeds were being planted for the greatest three-year period in Ohio State football history.

And those seeds were Buckeye grown.

Each year the finest schoolboy football players in Ohio strut their stuff at the North-South game at Canton. A total of 13 players from that showcase event would select Ohio State.

That talented group, led by Lancaster, Ohio, High School All-American quarterback Rex Kern would be varsity-ready by 1968.

A total of 59 Ohio-born youngsters earned varsity roster spots that magical season.

Thirteen sophomores would start regularly for a team considered 'one year away.' Sometimes, as many as 17 sophs would be in the starting offensive and defensive lineups. It would truly be a season to remember.

21

Class of '68

Unbeaten. Untied. No. 1 in the nation. Conqueror of O.J. Simpson and Southern Cal in the Rose Bowl.

The top team, the top coach.

Two All-Americans in senior offensive tackles Dave Foley and Rufus Mayes. Four All-Big Ten selections in Foley, Mayes, plus sophomore defensive backs Jack Tatum and Ted Provost.

Somehow overlooked by the All-American pickers, senior linebacker Mark Stier was awarded the highest honor by his teammates. He was named the Buckeyes' Most Valuable Player.

The 1968-69-70 class carved out the most successful three year period in OSU football history. How about 27-2 and one national title.

It could just have easily been 29-0 and three straight national crowns. But the Buckeyes proved human after all, stumbling in the season finales the next two years.

During that three-year span 23 were named to the all-Big Ten team. An astounding 13 were accorded All-American Honors. They were: 1968—Offensive tackles Dave Foley and Rufus Mayes, 1969—Nose guard Jim Stillwagon, quarterback Rex Kern, fullback Jim Otis, defensive backs Jack Tatum and Ted Provost. 1970—Tight end Jan White, Stillwagon, fullback John Brockington, Tatum, defensive backs Mike Sensibaugh and Timmy Anderson.

Tatum and Stillwagon were named two-time All-Americans. Stillwagon, a 6-0, 220-pounder from Mt. Vernon, Ohio, was named recipient of the prestigious 'Outland Trophy' his last two years, as well as winner of the 'Lombardi Award.' He scored that rare double in 1970.

Presented by the College Football Writers Association since 1946, the 'Outland Trophy' recognizes the "outstanding interior lineman" in college football.

The 'Lombardi Award', named for the late Green Bay Packers' coaching legend Vince Lombardi, has been presented each year by the Rotary Club of Houston to the "outstanding college lineman."

In addition to down linemen, the 'Lombardi Award' also includes linebackers.

It seems like only yesterday since the "CLASS OF '68' fulfilled the impossible dream. But it was 30 years ago.

The quest began on September 28, 1968 with a 35-14 verdict of pass-happy Southern Methodist and ended January 1, 1969 at the Rose Bowl.

Ten opponents. Ten victories.

During those thirty years, Ohio State has continued to produce great football players and great teams, but none has captured the same excitement as the very special "CLASS OF '68."

CHAPTER 2

ONE OF THE HERD

Only twice in 28 years had Ohio State finished under .500 during the long reign of taskmaster Woody Hayes. But after 3-5-1 records in 1959 and 4-5 in 1966, the Buckeyes bounced back. Two years after that disastrous '59 season, Ohio State posted an 8-0-1 record, took the Big Ten crown and in the process destroyed arch-rival Michigan, 50-20, in the season's finale.

Would history repeat itself in 1968?

The '67 campaign ended on a high note with the Buckeyes reeling off four straight victories at the expense of Michigan State [21-7], Wisconsin [17-15], Iowa [21-10] and Michigan [24-14].

Southern Methodist... Oregon... Purdue... Northwestern... Illinois... Michigan State...Wisconsin...Iowa...Michigan...Southern Cal...an odyssey that would begin on September 28 at Ohio Stadium. No one in the Ohio State camp would dare to dream aloud. Southern Cal was the defending national champion, and with quarterback Steve Sogge and tailback O.J. Simpson heading a veteran cast, the Trojans weren't about to give up the top spot without a fight.

Notre Dame would come out of the gate with Terry Hanratty throwing and All-American Jim Seymour catching. The Fighting Irish offense seemed unstoppable. However, Notre Dame did not own exclusive bragging rights in the Hoosier State. Arch-rival Purdue would have it's own 'dynamic duo' in quarterback Mike Phipps and triple threat back Leroy Keyes.

Joe Paterno's Nittany Lions of Penn State had snared the Lambert Trophy in 1967, symbolic of the East's top major power. The national title certainly seemed within their grasp.

Sophomore-laden Ohio State was included in a long list of 'wannabes.' Teams that could be capable of successful seasons. Teams the likes of Army, Syracuse, Yale, Alabama, Tennessee, Florida, Louisiana State, Georgia, Mississippi, Clemson, Miami, Oklahoma, Nebraska, Missouri, Indiana, Minnesota, Texas, Texas A and M, Arkansas, Houston, Oregon State, UCLA, Arizona State, and Wyoming.

Those battles would be waged on the field. The rulemakers would add some new wrinkles. Or in the case of the punt return rule, an old wrinkle.

For 1965, despite the protests of the vast majority of head coaches, the NCAA Football Rules Committee deemed that the five interior linemen could not cross the line of scrimmage until the ball was kicked. The idea was to cut down on the number of fair catches and hopefully pave the way for long, exciting punt returns. What looked good on paper turned out to be a disaster.

As it turned out, the returns became minimally longer— only 1.3 yards a kick and there were increased injuries to players on the punt team who ran downfield to cover kicks.

Notre Dame's Ara Parseghian put it this way, "The men who covered punts were sitting ducks."

The restoration of the old rule meant that any member of the kicking team could run downfield once the ball was snapped for a punt.

Other rule changes:

The tackle-eligible play, in which a tackle lined up as an end and became eligible to catch a pass, was outlawed. It created too much confusion.

The rule on legal clipping was tightened to eliminate crack-back blocks. Clipping [blocking from behind] had always been allowed four yards to either side of the ball and three yards in front or in back of it. But in 1968, a split end or flanker could not race in and clip legally.

A defensive man who signals for a fair catch of a punt no longer can block on the play. In the past, a safety often would indicate a fair catch near the goal line, then let the ball bounce while he blocked an opponent trying to down the ball before it went into the end zone.

The 'sucker shift,' in which a defensive player is tricked to move offside, is outlawed. Now, when an offensive lineman has a hand set on or near the ground, he cannot straighten up. [The 'sucker shift' would play a prominent role in the Ohio State-Michigan State game].

When a first down is achieved, the clock is stopped until the sideline chains are moved. The idea is to avoid stealing playing time from a team on the move. In addition, a time out, formerly two minutes, would be cut to 90 seconds.

Ohio State was anxious to start the season. The 1:20 P.M. kick off against SMU couldn't come soon enough.

"We've had five scrimmages this Fall," said Woody Hayes, "and we haven't had a single serious football injury."

The only serious injury, to senior defensive end Nick Roman of Canton, Ohio, didn't even happen on the football field. He hurt his knee on an obstacle course during summer military training.

Six days before the curtain-raiser, Hayes, his coaches, his top players, were introduced at the Quarterback Club luncheon, held at the school's Ohio Union. A jam-packed crowd of 700 was on hand.

Woody Hayes assured the group that Ohio State would have a good team. "We've got to get off to a good start," he stressed.

Defensive coordinator Lou McCullough introduced 15 defensive starters, or alternate starters. The 15 had played a total of 14 years and had 31 more years of eligibility.

Offensive tackle/end coach Hugh Hindman introduced 14 potential starters who had 11 years of experience and 31 more years of eligibility. And of those 29 players, only six were seniors, offensive tackles Dave Foley and Rufus Mayes, center John Muhlbach, quarterback Billy Long, linebackers Dirk Worden [Buckeyes' MVP in 1967] and Mark Stier.

First, the offense.

Hayes couldn't help but smile when he began talking about sophomore quarterback Rex Kern of Lancaster, Ohio.

"For the first time in years and years, we've got a quarterback who can run.

Last spring, Kern was a will-of-the-wisp. He hasn't been that good this Fall, but he's getting better. He can run and he can pass. He's an exceptional athlete."

A three-sport prep star, Kern had undergone back surgery in June of '68 and had been brought around slowly. Although he wore a special back 'corset', Kern had successfully survived full-scale scrimmages.

Waiting in the wings would be Bill Long, OSU's starting signal caller in '67 and soph Ron Maciejowski of Bedford, Ohio. Sophomore John Brockington [Brooklyn, New York] and Junior Dave Brungard [Youngstown, Ohio] rated the edge at halfback. Juniors Jim Otis [Celina, Ohio] and Paul Huff [Dover, Ohio] would battle it out at fullback.

Hayes called Brungard "an all-round football player. He can run, he can catch and he can block your head off."

But he pointed out, "don't count out soph Larry Zelina [Cleveland, Ohio] who missed much of Fall practice because of an injury. He's a darn good football player."

Concerning the fullback tandem of Otis and Huff: "Our fullbacks complement each other," meaning Otis with speed and Huff with power. "Huff is as strong as anything in the world."

Woody Hayes called soph tight end Jan White [Harrisburg, Pennsylvania] a gem. "We haven't had an end this strong, not even Jim Houston."

Bruce Jankowski, a sophomore speedster from Fair Lawn, New Jersey, had the nod at wide receiver. Foley, a two-year starter from Cincinnati, and Mayes, a converted tight end from Toledo, both stood 6-5 and weighed in the 260-270 range. They were Ohio State's 'Twin Towers.'

Mulhbach, a two-year starter from Massillon, Ohio, was back at center. Tom Backhus, a junior from Cincinnati, and junior Alan Jack [Winterville, Ohio] had the edge at offensive guard. But waiting in the wings were talented sophs Dave Cheney [Lima, Ohio], Brian Donovan [Columbus, Ohio] and Paul Strickland [Cincinnati].

Defensively, it shaped up this way:

Ends— Junior Dave Whitfield [Massillon] and soph Mark Debevc [Geneva, Ohio]. Tackles— Juniors Brad Nielsen [Columbus], Paul Schmidlin [Toledo], or Bill Urbanik [Donora, Pennsylvania]. Middle Guard— Sophomore Jim Stillwagon [Mt.Vernon, Ohio], senior Vic Stottlemyer [Chillicothe, Ohio]. Linebackers— Seniors Dirk Worden [Lorain, Ohio], Mark Stier [Louisville, Ohio], and soph Doug Adams [Xenia, Ohio]. Backs— Juniors Ted Provost [Navarre, Ohio] and Mike Polaski [Columbus], sophomores Jack Tatum [Passaic, New Jersey], Mike Sensibaugh [Cincinnati], Tim Anderson [Follansbee, West Virginia]. Tatum, a 6-0, 202-pounder, had been the starting fullback on Ohio State's super talented freshman team. As a high school senior, he gained some 1,400 yards rushing. But with Otis and Huff already on the scene and Brockington in the picture, Jack Tatum would have to seek his glory on the defensive side of the ball.

And defensive coordinator Lou McCullough couldn't have been happier. "Tatum has the speed to get the job done and he's a tooth-rattling tackler."

Anderson had gained some 2,000 yards as a high school halfback and fullback, while Sensibaugh was an All-Ohio quarterback. Provost, a 6-3, 182-pounder, had intercepted a team-leading seven passes as a sophomore in 1967. Polaski led the Buckeyes' in punt returns in '67. He could play every defensive backfield position. Sensibaugh would handle the punting chores while junior walk-on Dick Merryman would start the season as Ohio State's No.1 place kicker.

Ohio State kicked off the '68 season with a modest four-game winning streak, surprisingly the longest in the Big Ten.

"We want to get in that win column again," said Woody Hayes, "and stay in that win column."

Even though Ohio State would start the season against two non-conference opponents, Hayes vowed "we'll show everything we've got and hope it's enough. This team coming in here—SMU—has a lot of good football players."

Lou McCullough agreed. "SMU has a fine offensive football team. Really good. There are a few teams in our league they could score 40 points against. I hope we're not one of them."

Despite his lack of varsity experience, Kern would be allowed to run his own show. "We're going to let Rex call most of the plays," said Hayes. He said it was partially to conserve time "because we want to get in more plays."

Three days before the season opener, Woody Hayes was in a talkative mood. He talked with reporters for more than an hour after practice, then headed for the shower. His subjects ranged from Vietnam, military strategy, Pearl Harbor, patriotism, the problems of youth... and some football, too.

While Ohio State had the luxury to scout SMU's opening season upset victory over Auburn, the visiting Mustangs didn't have the same opportunity.

They were, as the saying goes, 'flying blind.'

According to SMU head coach Hayden Fry, "Coach Woody Hayes declined to permit us to scout his Spring training game or to exchange films. So we faced the Buckeyes not knowing what to expect."

What they faced:

[Alphabetical]

No.	Name	Pos.	Wgt.	Hgt.	Age	Class	Hometown
63	Adams, Douglas	LB	215	6-0	18	So	Xenia, OH
85	Aldrin, Charles	ORE	207	6-3	19	So	Glenview, IL
26	Anderson, Tim	DRH	194	6-0	19	So	Follansbee, WV
86	Aston, Daniel	DRE	208	6-2	20	Jr	Cincinnati, OH
57*	Backhus, Thomas	OLG	207	5-11	19	Jr	Cincinnati, OH
33*	Bartley, Thomas	LB	198	5-11	21	Sr	Springfield
19	Bender, Edward	ORH	172	6-0	21	Sr	Akron
48*	Bombach, Jay	ORH	201	6-1	20	Jr	Dayton
42	Brockington, John	ORH	210	6-1	20	So	Brooklyn, NY.
12*	Brungard, Dave	OLH	184	5-10	20	Jr	Youngstown
21	Burton, Arthur	LB	193	6-1	20	Jr	Fostoria
75	Cheney, David	OLG	230	6-3	19	So	Lima
47	Coburn, James	DLH	190	5-11	19	So	Maumee
36	Cunningham, Richard	FB	188	5-10	19	So	Portsmouth
83	Debevc, Mark	DRE	210	6-1	19	So	Geneva
78	Dombos, John	DLT	205	6-0	19	So	Garfield Heights
66	Donovan, Brian	OLG	206	6-3	19	So	Columbus
90	Ecrement, Thomas	DLE	195	6-0	19	So	Canton

No.	Name	Pos.	Wgt.	Hgt.	Age	Class	Hometown
28**	Ehrsam, Gerald	S	194	6-0	21	Sr	Toledo
70**	Foley, David [cc]	ORT	246	6-5	20	Sr	Cincinnati
39	Gentile, James	LB	210	6-2	20	Jr	Poland
11*	Gillian, Ray	OLH	194	5-11	20	Jr	Uniontown, Pa.
44	Greene, Horatius	OLH	180	5-11	19	Jr	Jersey City, N.J.
51	Hackett, William	LB	204	6-1	20	Jr	London
65	Hart, Randy	ORT	220	6-2	20	Jr	Willoughby
22	Hayden, Leophus	OLH	204	6-2	20	So	Dayton
67	Holloway, Ralph	MG	222	6-1	19	So	Oberlin
34*	Huff, Paul	FB	217	6-3	20	Jr	Dover
72*	Hutchison, Charles	OLT	240	6-3	19	Jr	Carrollton
61*	Jack, Alan	ORG	215	6-0	20	Jr	Wintersville
82	Jankowski, Bruce	OLE	192	5-11	19	So	Fair Lawn, N.J.
10	Kern, Rex	QB	180	6-0	19	So	Lancaster
81	Kuhn, Richard	ORE	208	6-2	19	So	Louisville
64	Kurz, Ted	ORG	222	6-2	19	So	Struthers
24**	Long, William	QB	180	6-1	21	Sr	Dayton
18	Maciejowski, Ronald	QB	186	6-2	19	So	Bedford
73**	Mayes, Rufus	OLT	250	6-5	20	Sr	Toledo
53**	Muhlbach, John	C	194	5-10	21	Sr	Massillon
77*	Nielsen, Brad	DRT	222	6-3	20	Jr	Columbus
76	Oppermann, James	OLT	240	6-4	18	So	Bluffton
35*	Otis, James	FB	208	6-0	20	Jr	Celina
15*	Polaski, Michael	DLH	170	5-10	19	Jr	Columbus
46*	Provost, Ted	DLH	182	6-3	20	Jr	Navarre
58	Qualls, Larry	C	190	6-0	19	So	Dayton
43	Quiling, Richard	S	190	6-1	20	Jr	Celina
55*	Radtke, Michael	LB	200	6-1	20	Jr	Wayne, N.J.
52**	Roman, James	C	211	6-0	20	Sr	Canton
89**	Roman, Nicholas	DRE	221	6-4	21	Sr	Canton
59	Roush, Gary	ORT	200	6-4	21	Sr	Springfield
23*	Rusnak, Kevin	ORH	190	6-1	20	Jr	Garfield, N.J.
74*	Schmidlin, Paul	DLT	222	6-1	19	Jr	Toledo
3***	Sensibaugh, Michael	S	187	6-0	19	So	Cincinnati
50*	Smith, Butch	DRT	224	6-2	20	Jr	Hamilton
87	Smith, Robert	ORE	221	6-4	21	Sr	Lakewood
91*	Sobolewski, John	DRE	192	6-1	20	Jr	Steubenville
54**	Stier, Mark	LB	202	6-1	21	Sr	Louisville
68	Stillwagon, James	MG	220	6-0	19	So	Mt.Vernon
69**	Stottlemyer, Victor	MG	200	6-0	21	Sr	Chillicothe
92	Stowe, John	OLE	200	6-2	21	Sr	Columbus
62	Strickland, Phillip	ORG	217	6-1	19	So	Cincinnati
32	Tatum, John	LB	204	6-0	19	So	Passaic, N.J.
17	Trapuzzano, Robert	DRH	187	6-0	19	Jr	McKees Rocks, Pa.
71	Troha, Richard	ORT	227	6-3	19	So	Cleveland
79*	Urbanik, William	DLT	238	6-3	21	Jr	Donora, PA
41	Wagner, Tim	DRH	175	5-10	19	So	Columbus
80	White, Jan	OLE	214	6-2	19	So	Harrisburg, Pa.
88*	Whitfield, David	DLE	184	6-0	20	Jr	Massillon
56**	Worden, Dirk [cc]	LB	198	6-0	22	Sr	Lorain
16	Zelina, Lawrence	ORH	195	6-0	19	So	Cleveland

*Indicates letter   CC— co-captain

Section II

The Players

Even as a 19-year-old junior, Mike Polaski was well aware of his place in history. "I remember when I was in high school, reading about teams in the Rose Bowl, seeing pictures and television of them. When we marched down the street at Disneyland, it suddenly came to me... Now I'm in the Rose Bowl and some kid is going to be watching me."

What kid wouldn't become a fan of this 5-10, 158-pound package of dynamite? He was the 'little engine that could.'

Now Mike Polaski, as well as other proud members of Ohio State's last unbeaten, untied and No. 1 rated Buckeyes, are delighted to tell their stories and share their fondest memories.

Some All-Americans. Some not so highly publicized. All part of the fairytale season that began on September 28, 1968 with a 35-14 victory over pass-happy Southern Methodist and ended at the Rose Bowl in Pasadena, California on New Year's day with a decisive 27-16 conquest of O.J. Simpson and USC.

Let's hear a cheer for Polaski...Otis...Foley...Provost...Backhus... Roman...Schmidlin...Brungard...Worden...Maciejowski...Zelina...Stier...Debevc and White.

photo courtesy Mark Stier

Chapter 3

IN MEMORIUM

DOUG ADAMS, NO.63, LINEBACKER
6-0, 215 Pounds, 18 Years Old, Sophomore.

*** *** ***

RUFUS MAYES, NO.73, OFFENSIVE TACKLE
6-5, 250 Pounds, 20 Years Old, Senior.

*** *** ***

BRAD NIELSEN, NO.77, DEFENSIVE TACKLE
6-3, 222 Pounds, 20 Years Old, Junior.

*** *** ***

Ohio State Photo Archives

Class reunions are a wonderful time to renew old friendships. A time to hug. A time to laugh. A time to turn back the hands of time. For the Ohio State Buckeyes, it will be a wonderful time to celebrate their fairytale season. Unbeaten. Untied. Big Ten and Rose Bowl champions. The TOP national college football power. Hail 1968. But it will also be a time to bow their heads in a moment of silence for three teammates whose lives were cut short long before their time. Doug Adams...Rufus Mayes...Brad Nielsen. Adams, the oldest at age 47. Nielsen, the youngest in his early 30s.

Adams, a dentist from Mt. Orab, Ohio, was riding a bicycle along a berm of Ohio 32 in Brown County on August 9, 1997 when he was hit by a car driven by a driver who was asleep at the wheel. He was thrown from the bicycle, according to Brown County Sheriff's Department. A native of Xenia, Ohio, Adams was the greatest linebacker to ever graduate from that school. As a sophomore at Ohio State, he was ticketed for backup duties behind senior Dirk Worden. But when Worden was hurt early in the season, Adams took over. A three-year starter, he was named defensive co-captain his senior year along with All-American nose guard Jim Stillwagon.

During his varsity career, Ohio State lost only two of 29 contests and claimed the national title at 10-0 in 1968. Drafted by the National Football League Cincinnati Bengals, Doug Adams played until 1974 when a career-ending knee injury forced his retirement. He returned to Ohio State to earn his degree as a dentist.

Ohio State All-American quarterback Rex Kern called Adams "One of the great people and football players that we ever had at Ohio State. He was quiet and unassuming, but very loyal, dependable and productive. He let his actions speak for his words, and that's how he led."

Bengals' president Mike Brown called him "a bright-eyed, energetic young man. He seemed to be successful in all his endeavors."

Adams went out riding with his close friend, Mike Hood. Such was the case the day he died. "He was one of the few men I loved," said Hood. "I loved him like a brother. I'm sure many people did as well. He was one in a billion."

Lou McCullough, linebacker coach as well as defensive coordinator at Ohio State back then, fondly remembers Doug Adams. "He was a great player in high school. Quick and strong. Doug had all the tools. He was one of our No.1 players in the state. Tiger Ellison did the most work on him. Tiger was from Middletown, Doug Adams from Xenia, Ohio.

"I came in at the end. Doug wanted to take dentistry. We had an All-American basketball player who helped a lot in the recruitment. In fact, Jimmy Hull was one of Ohio State's first All-Americans. He was also a dentist. He and Tiger Ellison did most of the work.

"I never saw Doug play in high school, but I saw quite a few pictures of him, enough to know he was what we call a blue-chipper. Doug was a very good student. He was one of the finest young men I've ever been associated with in football. He was outgoing. He had a purpose in mind, both in the classroom and on the football field. I can't remember any one incident involving Doug Adams. It's just been too long. He was a great player in every game. You didn't have to tell him but once."

Doug Adams was pegged for back-up duties his sophomore season, as understudy for senior Dirk Worden. Worden, the team's MVP in 1967, injured his knee during the third game against Purdue. Except for a few token appearances, his career was over.

"I don't think Doug had a chance to be nervous," says Worden. "He didn't have the time. I can remember my first start as a sophomore. It was against TCU. Believe me, there were plenty of butterflies before the game. But once you get that first hit, you settle down and just concentrate on what you have to do.

"Doug had seen some action in our first two games against SMU and Oregon. I strained my hamstring in the Oregon game, so he did see some action. My injury happened at the end of the first quarter or the start of the second quarter. I hurt my knee bad, came off the field and headed straight for the locker room. They taped me up. I came out and Lou McCullough asked me how I felt. I said, 'Well, let me see if I can give it a go.'

"We had man-to-man pass coverage on a third-and-long. A back came out of the backfield. I made a cut and just fell down. It turned out to be ligament damage."

From that point on, Dirk Worden could only become a cheerleader and unofficial coach.

"I knew very little about Doug Adams, or the other highly-recruited freshmen. All I knew is that it was supposed to be a very strong class. Doug's name was mentioned in there, along with Stillwagon, Kern, and so forth.

"Back then, Ohio State ran a pretty segregated practice. The varsity defense practiced against the freshman offense. The varsity offense practiced against the freshman defense.

"I had very little contact with Doug his freshman year. I was going up against the Rex Kerns and the John Brockingtons. It wasn't until the spring of 1968 that he began practicing with the varsity defense.

"By today's standards, he would be small. But so would a lot of us.

"Doug was about 6-feet and 210, a well-built kid. He was a great athlete, not afraid to hit people. It looked like he had a future at major college football. He was fundamentally sound. His role was as my backup until I destroyed my knee.

"He took my place. He was pretty much introverted, but he had a real nice personality. He was real humble, real reserved. But he seemed confident in his abilities.

"Doug used to hang out with Jim Stillwagon if I remember right. They were kinda inseparable in those days. I can remember as a sophomore we had very little rapport with the seniors. I vowed when I became a senior I was gonna try hard to build a bridge between the under-and-upper classmen.

"I would go out of my way, not only to help Doug Adams, but basically all the younger guys. You could tell that sophomore group was going to vie for a lot of playing time. There was a lot of competition, but no resentment. There really was a team concept, a team spirit. Everybody understood that the best kid was gonna play.

"When you play at a place like Ohio State, you're always battling for playing time. You look upon it as a challenge. I never considered Doug Adams as a threat to my closed-side linebacker position. He was my teammate.

"I could see Doug Adams mature his sophomore year. Believe me, if he couldn't do the job, someone else would.

"We weren't deep at linebacker, but we had so many great athletes. For instance, Stillwagon could have been shifted from nose guard to linebacker. Mike Radtke was a linebacker in 1967, but was moved to defensive end in '68. He could have been moved back to linebacker had Doug Adams not done the job, or been hurt.

"Over the years, we really didn't keep in touch much. I'd see Doug at a Fourth of July party, or one of our reunions. I played with Jim Nein in 1967. He wasn't on our national championship team. It was Jim who called to tell me about Doug's tragic death. I was stunned, sick-to-my-stomach. I went to the funeral home. His parents greeted all of Doug's ex-teammates.

"I hope over time I can fondly remember the good times with Doug Adams, remembering a young, smiling athlete instead of how I last saw him.

"I went by that road where he got killed. It's a divided four-lane highway. The berm is probably 12-foot wide. It's not a berm that's two-foot wide. It's an extra lane. I guess his friend was in front. The guy who killed Doug fell asleep at the wheel, woke up just before he hit Doug. He tried to swerve back onto the road. Doug's buddy stopped his bike, doubled back, but Doug was gone.

"I think it happened on a Saturday. Doug was cremated according to his own wishes. His ashes were spread on his Mt. Orab farm. It was just a heart-wrenching scene, something I don't want to see again."

*****

Rufus Mayes died of bacterial meningitis on January 9, 1990 at the age of 42. He left a wife and son.

Mayes, who was a marketing rep for Hewlett-Packard, lived in Redmond, Washington. Born-and-raised in Toledo, Ohio, Mayes played for Macomber High School. He was one of the cogs in Macomber's 1964 City League championship team.

Dave Witkowski, an offensive/defensive halfback on that team, called Mayes "an All-American guy. He was the nicest person you'd ever want to meet. He was a top-notch individual as a friend, and as a decent person."

photo courtesy Chicago Bears

Steve Contos, Mayes' high school coach, said of the 6-5, 250-pound offensive tackle, "He was just a great guy, a very bright, very concerned, happy, easy-to-get-along-with-type-of-guy.

"I remember one time Rufus had a tooth pulled at the Ohio State clinic, and they pulled the wrong tooth. Before they pulled the impacted tooth two months later, he had gained 25-to-30 pounds. I told him if I had known that was going to happen, I would have had them pull a tooth at Macomber.

"He was a competitor and a gentleman at Macomber. He was the kind of guy you'd like to have in your home and visit."

The late Hugh Hindman, an assistant coach under Woody Hayes at Ohio State before he became the school's athletic director, came to visit Mayes at Macomber during his junior year. Said Hindman: "I'll be back to get him when he's a senior." He told Mayes, "You'll come to Ohio State. You'll start in your sophomore year. You'll play on great teams for three years, be an All-American, and a professional player." Hugh Hindman's predictions all came true.

Rufus Mayes was a starting offensive lineman in all 28 games during his three-year varsity career. He was a tight end as a sophomore and junior, then shifted to left tackle for the 1968 season. He and Dave Foley, Ohio State's other starting offensive tackle, were known as 'The Twin Towers.' The Buckeyes won the national title in '68. Mayes and Foley were both named first team All-Americans.

Drafted by the Chicago Bears in the first round of the 1969 National Football League draft, Mayes played only one season in Chicago. He was traded to the Cincinnati Bengals, playing left tackle for the next eight seasons. He then played out his option, became a free agent, and played his last season with the Philadelphia Eagles. Mayes retired in 1979, moved to the West Coast and became a marketing rep with various companies.

Mike McCormick was his coach in Cincinnati. Upon hearing of Mayes' death, he simply said, "I'm shocked."

The late Woody Hayes, his head coach at Ohio State, called Rufus Mayes one of the best offensive tackles he had ever coached. "He was quicker than most of them, and, of course, very powerful."

"I met Rufus when we both arrived at Ohio State," recalls Dave Foley. "Rufus would probably be described as a guy who was everybody's friend. Always upbeat, and very congenial. Everybody enjoyed being around him. Everybody liked Rufus. He had no enemies.

"He was a tackle in high school, but he played tight end for two years at Ohio State until they shifted him to offensive tackle as a senior. We had a lot of great tackles at Ohio State. Doug Van Horn played for years with the New York Giants. Mike Current played 13 years with the Denver Broncos. In my junior year, we had Dick Himes who played about 10 years with the Green Bay Packers.

"Rufus might have been stuck at tight end as a senior had not a great sophomore named Jan White arrived. Jan could not only block, but he could catch the ball. On the other hand, Rufus never could catch the ball very well. That's the truth. Woody made him carry a football around campus. He said if Rufus got the feel for the ball, he'd be able to catch it better. So every place on campus you'd see Rufus Mayes, he'd be carrying that darned football.

"Rufus was a tremendous blocker. He had great balance and great range. The transition from tight end to tackle was easy for him. At that time, we had the tight ends and tackles practice together with one coach.

"Our coach was Hugh Hindman who really stressed fundamentals. The blocking techniques were the same for both positions. We practiced on our individual drills, such as cut-off blocks.

"The tight end would do exactly what the tackles were doing. There really wasn't that much of a transition."

Dave Brungard, who started as a sophomore tailback in 1967 will always remember Rufus Mayes' smiling face.

"He always smiled. He was always positive, never griped. Sometimes we'd run an unbalanced line, with Rufus Mayes, Dave Foley and Jan White on the same side of the line. Man, it was a wonderful sight to behold if you were an Ohio State running back.

"Rufus was an excellent athlete. We played a lot of basketball in the off-season to keep in shape. He was a big, rangy kid with huge, huge hands.

"You'd think he would have been able to catch the ball. On the contrary. I guess there's just some guys who freeze up when they try to catch the ball.

"It wasn't until he was a senior that they let him blow up, put a bunch of weight on him, and let him play tackle.

"He didn't have to catch the ball...just knock people down."

*****

photo courtesy Columbus Bishop Watterson High School

Paul Schmidlin was starting left defensive tackle. Brad Nielsen and Bill Urbanik shared the right tackle spot.

"I first met Brad when we were both freshmen at Ohio State. We played four years together. I even roomed with him during our pre-season, two-a-day drills.

"We called him 'Buckeye Brad' because he always had such enthusiasm," Schmidlin fondly recalls.

"He had lots of energy. He was lots of fun.

"Brad loved to play hard."

'Reckless Abandon' was the phrase Lou McCullough—defensive coordinator—used to like to say we should play with.

"Brad definitely fit that. Both on-and-off-the-field.

"Brad Nielson was a bit reckless, a bit wild. He'd get into trouble, but nothing like they do today. He'd go out, wander down High Street, sometimes pick a fight in a bar. That type of thing.

"But you just couldn't stay mad at the guy. He was so likeable. He'd always smile easily. He'd always get you talking, but as I said, he would also get himself into trouble.

"Our coach, Bill Mallory, would get pretty upset with him. But if you'd ask Bill Mallory about Brad, I think the first thing he'll do is laugh. He will enjoy remembering Brad.

"We were small tackles, even by the standards of my day. We both went about 220, but we had a lot of quickness. Brad was good at rushing the passer. There were a number of games where he did that.

"As I said, Brad was so aggressive. I think we were playing Illinois. I can't remember who it was who hit the ball. It went straight up in the air. It was coming down. I was right underneath it.

"I was reaching up to grab it. All of a sudden, Brad came flying through the air. He was grabbing for the ball, scrambling to get it.

"He was pulling at it so hard.

"I had control of it.

"I vividly recall knowing that if we continued to fight over the ball, it was gonna be fumbled. So I just took it and shoved it into his gut.

"Brad started running. It was just one of those experiences you never forget."

Says Bill Mallory: "I didn't recruit Brad Nielsen. I think Esco Sarkkinen did. Brad was from Columbus, from Bishop Watterson. He was a highly sought-after kid, a good football player. He wasn't a blue-chipper. He came from a real good program. Football was important to him, and he played hard. He was a kid who gave 110 percent.

"Let's just say Brad Nielsen was the kind of kid who enjoyed life. He had a sort of good-time attitude. He really wasn't a bad kid. You couldn't help but like him. He wasn't an outlawish kid. You had to stay with him. You had to stay in his ears. At times he'd get his butt in trouble. It was maturity, a growing-up processs.

"People sometimes don't understand that these are young men despite their size. They're going through growing pains, the whole ball of wax. People think these guys are men. Well, there's still a lot of boy in 'em.

"Brad kept things lively. He was an energetic individual. He would challenge you, but not to the point of being defiant. I'd have to be firm with him, but he'd respond. He was coachable. He'd do what you'd want, but sometimes you had to repeat it.

"He was just the kind of kid you had to spend a little time with. It's just like raising a family. You raise kids and they're all different. It's the same way with coaching players. You've gotta get the key to 'em.

"Deep down, you want to see them all do well. That was always my approach. That's what I made them understand. If I was on their so-called ass, it was because I wanted to see them shape up and not screw up. That's how I approached it. Woody cared about his kids. I guarantee I cared about mine.

"You had to be strong with Brad or he'd overpower you. He knew who was in control. But when they did good things, you'd compliment them. But you couldn't get carried away with Brad. If you said too many nice things, you're gonna eat your crow the next day. There was a fine line. It was knowing how to handle him.

"If he was an Outlaw and you couldn't handle him, he wouldn't have been in the program. Woody wasn't gonna tolerate that kind of person. I know I wouldn't.

"He was quick and he was tall. He'd get his hands up and he'd be very effective as a pass rusher. He did a good job with his hands. He had pretty good movement. He was pretty elusive for a tall kid. When Brad was in there, he'd harass the quarterback.

"Brad certainly kept me on my toes. The position coaches were responsible for their players, both on-and-off-the-field. One time he cut class, Woody's football class of all things.

"Woody was mad and got on my case good.

"I went back to see Brad. The door to his room was locked. I pounded until he finally opened the door. I took him to see Woody. Woody met with the both of us.

"It was the kind of a maturing that he had to go through. But through it all, you had to respect him, If there's one thing about Brad, it was his pride. He was a kid with a lot of pride. He wanted to do well.

"You could find his so-called 'hot button', get him cranked up and get him going. He had a little bit of wildness in him. He was kind of a party kid. That was simply Brad Nielsen."

Ron Shay was assistant football coach at Columbus Bishop Watterson High School when Brad Nielsen transferred to that school.

"Brad went to Aquinas High School for two years, then transferred to Watterson. He wasn't that big. He ran well. He was really quick, aggressive. He made those kind of plays that a kid of that stature makes in high school.

"He played offensive tackle in high school, but when he got to Ohio State they moved him to defense. He was a good kid."

Brian Doyle was Brad Nielsen's best friend, dating back to the fourth grade at Immaculate Conception School in Columbus. They remained best of friends until Nielsen's tragic auto crash in 1981. Brad Nielsen was only 33.

"We just spent a lot of time in each other's homes. We both felt so welcome. I had a relationship with Bradley as close as I've ever had with any male in my life. We played side-by-side throughout high school. I was offensive left guard, Brad left tackle. We started off at a school called Columbus Aquinas, which was a Dominican all-boys school.

"That school announced they were closing. So we transferred to Watterson. Brad was about 6-3 and 215 and he never got much bigger. I was 5-10 and played at 185 max.

"I was strictly a high school player. Some might even doubt that Bradley was All-State. Back then they didn't have a playoff system. We were undefeated in our senior year.

"All the Big Ten schools were after him. I think it boiled down to Purdue, Indiana or Ohio State. He picked Ohio State because he wanted to stay at home.

"We grew up in Columbus. We used to go to Ohio Stadium and sell Coke and newspapers. At times, we tried to sneak into the games, or bum a ticket off of a policeman. Things like that.

"Brad went on to Ohio State. I went to Xavier. I didn't play any football in college.

"He was a free spirit, very outgoing. He was quite popular with the ladies. He was very popular in the fraternity scene. He dated a lot of girls. He was real good looking. Could have been a model.

"Bradley always put more effort into the social aspects of his life than he would the academics or working out. He was always a bit lazy in the weight room. Sort of the prodigal son of the coaching staff.

"Brad had quickness. Most of the guys he lined up against were 30-40 pounds heavier, but they rarely got a clean shot at him.

"He was a fun-loving kid who was always kinda mischievous, wouldn't walk away from an altercation. Maybe he'd get involved in a pushing match at a bar. Nothing serious. No weapons. No police record.

"He spent a lot of time trying to beat the system as opposed to conforming to it and going through the regular channels to get from A to B.

"Brad never regained consciousness after his crash. He died 7-10 days later. I had time for some closure as opposed to BAM...BAM...BAM... putting him in the ground.

"For a long time I thought about keeping his memory alive, but it wasn't until

37

about 10 years ago I finally decided to do something about it. I started The Brad Nielsen Scholarship Fund at Watterson.

"I kicked it off with a $3,000 personal donation. I wanted it to be for the kind of kid Brad would have liked to go to Watterson. Sort of an underdog. A kid that wouldn't have had the financial ability to go there himself. A kid who loved to play football.

"Tuition at Watterson is now about $2,200 a year. We'd have some 10-14 young men go all the way through the program. I think I did it for Brad's family as much as I did it for Brad. It was very hard for them to lose him. He was kinda the pride of their family.

"Bradley had to be nudged and motivated. Dick Walker [his high school coach] and Woody Hayes were the two people who really challenged him.

"You had to challenge Brad sometimes to get his attention, to get him focused. But once you got him focused, he was fine. Sometimes his attention span would wane on you for a pretty girl or some other thing.

"He kinda reminds me a little of Bo Belinsky. Bo was a happy-go-lucky major league pitcher who was here and then gone in the twinkling of an eye.

"There's not a day goes by that I don't think about Bradley. He's influenced my life in so many ways. I'm not so sure they're all positive.

"But then again, I don't think I'd have it any other way."

Chapter 4

GO SOUTH, YOUNG MAN

DAVE BRUNGARD, NO.12, OFFENSIVE HALFBACK
5-10, 184 Pounds, 20 Years Old, Junior.

photo courtesy University of Alabama

"It was called 'A Blast' play, which is up the middle. Kern turns, spins out of the way and I would follow the fullback. The linebacker blitzed, and actually ran past the fullback. I scored a touchdown on a long run [41] yards."

Class of '68

Dave Brungard was born-and-raised in Youngstown, Ohio. A three-sports star in football, basketball and track, Brungard was not only named All-Ohio in football, but a schoolboy All-American by Scholastic Magazine. As a sophomore at Ohio State, he was starting left half in 1967. Starting out strong in 1968, Brungard's playing time virtually disappeared. Rather than sit on the bench his senior year, he transferred to Alabama and became a red-shirt. He was starting fullback and offensive co-captain his senior year. Drafted by the NFL Pittsburgh Steelers, he was cut during training. Dave Brungard is now an insurance salesman and lives in Birmingham, Alabama.

My father, George Brungard, played football at Ohio State from 1932-1936. He was on the 1935 Big Ten championship team. We were about the same size— 5-10 and 184. He played guard and fullback. But he never tried to steer me to Ohio State. He did a reverse kind of thing. The only school I know he didn't want me to go to was Notre Dame.

That goes back to his playing days. Ohio State met Notre Dame in 1935 or 1936. That was the last time the two teams had faced each other until a few years ago.

He just didn't like Notre Dame.

Come to think of it, he wouldn't have been too happy had I gone to Michigan.

I started playing football when I was 11 years old. We didn't have junior high football. I didn't play it again until my sophomore year in high school. I played basketball as a sophomore, but quit playing my junior year. I was also a sprinter on the track team. My top time was 9.9 in the 100.

As a senior, I rushed for more than 1,000 yards, was named All-City, All-State and All-American. My best single game was 275 yards and five touchdowns against Youngstown East.

I was about the same size in high school that I was in Ohio State. I had good speed, with a 4.5 clocking for the 40. We were 9-0 my final year, the first unbeaten untied team in school history. We played the Wing T.

The recruiting process was a little different back then. As I recall, you could visit as many schools as you wanted. You didn't have to make a commitment until March or April.

While I played left halfback on offense and cornerback on defense, all the interest in me was as a running back. My goal was to play at a major school. I thought I was good enough.

I was contacted by a lot of schools, including Arizona, Arizona State, Duke, Wake Forest, Georgia, Florida State, Ohio State, Michigan, Penn State.

My short-list narrowed down to Ohio State, Michigan and Penn State. In fact, I favored Penn State. The year I was recruited was the year that Penn State changed from Rip Engle to Joe Paterno as head coach. It may sound strange but I think I would have gone to Penn State if Engle had stayed. It would have had a bigger influence on me.

I think more than anything else, the transition was a big negative to me. I signed my national letter of intent to Ohio State in the Spring of 1966. Even though Ohio State had struggled since it's last Big Ten Championship season of 1961, even a freshman like me sensed that something was in the air. The '66 varsity team lost five of nine games. There was a sense that things had better get better.

I was starting left halfback my sophomore year. I worked out with the first team during the Spring, so I felt the position was mine to lose. Bo Rein had been the starting left half in '66, but he graduated. The position was wide open. It came down to a choice of me or Ray Gillian. We were both sophomores, about the same size. I think I got the edge on speed.

I'd played a few games my senior year in high school with crowds of 10,000. Once 15,000. But playing at Ohio Stadium...that's totally different. During warm-ups you look around. You're a little bit in awe. You have a million things going through your mind about what might happen in the game.

We opened against Arizona, a team we were supposed to beat. We lost that game [14-7], but came back to bury Oregon [30-0]. Purdue beat us the next week [41-6]. It was brutal. They had us 34-0 at the half.

We managed to survive against Northwestern [6-2]. Clearly, we were struggling early in the 1967 season. It was Homecoming the next week against Illinois. We were supposed to win, but we lost 17-13. We're 2-3 and playing Michigan State the next Saturday.

Duffy Daugherty was at the tail end of those big-time teams. They were still supposed to be good. We were definitely the underdog. We played our tails off and beat 'em, 21-7.

Hayes said something like this after the game. 'You guys will never know what this means to me.' I think it saved his job.

We ran off four straight wins to finished at 6-3. It could have been 8-1 just as easily.

The Michigan State game was definitely the turning point of our season. It wasn't a real great team. It wasn't a bad team. The offense focused around our fullback. That was Woody's thing. Paul Huff started early in the season, but then Jim Otis took over. Billy Long was the starting quarterback. He was a good quarterback who ran the offense they let him run. He did things well that they asked him to do.

You weren't there to pass. You were there to run and then you passed a little. It was a fairly simple, basic passing attack. Billy executed the offense very well.

I led the team in rushing with 500-something yards. My best game was against Illinois. I rushed for 174 yards and one touchdown. That was a 67-yarder on a sweep.

I don't recall Hayes talking about a national championship before the start of the 1968 season. Maybe the Big Ten title. He talked a lot about game-to-game winning.

We'd won four in a row at the end of last season and let's see if we can continue on the positive note. Something of that tone.

Our 1968 team was a young team, comprised mostly of sophomores and juniors. I think the consensus would have been we were a year away from something really big. There's no doubt that the sophomore group was very talented. We [the varsity] scrimmaged against them a bit when they were freshmen. They gave us fits. Guys like Stillwagon and Tatum.

We didn't have a lot of full scrimmages, certainly not once the season started. We had a couple in the Summer. Once the season started, there wasn't a lot of full-speed stuff, like tackling, during the week. It would be a lot of full-speed blocking with no tackles. Obviously, that would be for injury reasons. As John McKay of Southern Cal once said, 'You don't beat anybody on Tuesday.'

From a personal standpoint, the group of running backs was head-and-shoulders better in 1968 than it had been the previous year. I knew it would be tough to remain No.1 on the depth chart at left half. I had a good Spring and Summer practice. At that point, I was the better running back.

We opened up against SMU and I probably played my best all-around game. They were real quick, real fast defensively. As I recall, we struggled early in the game. It was called a 'blast play,' which is right up-the-middle. Kern turns, spins out of the way and I would follow the fullback.

Funny thing is the play didn't work that way. The linebacker blitzed and actually ran right past the fullback. He got through without being touched. There was a fairly violent collision about a yard deep in the backfield. I kinda bounced from there to the outside and went around left end.

Two guys had a shot at me on the sideline, but I outran them. The touchdown run was 41 yards. I also caught touchdown passes from Rex Kern of 18 and 20 yards. [Brungard had 101 yards rushing on 11 carries, three pass receptions for another 38 yards].

Rex was a good short passer, an amazing scrambler. Ron Maciejowski was a drop-back passer, a better thrower. Add Billy Long to that mix and we're three-deep at quarterback. In fact, we're three-deep at just about every backfield spot.

We had a play where the quarterback would roll to the right. I'd swing out of the backfield to the left. The idea was to get mismatched with a linebacker. I don't recall the particulars of the first touchdown pass. On the second, we caught them with the defensive end trying to cover me.

The three pass catches for a running back was as much as you're gonna get in Hayes' passing attack. It's my guess the plays weren't big-time in the game plan.

I also remember it was a long, long day that never seemed to end. They threw a ton of passes. I think their only running play was a draw.

Our next game was against Oregon. We won 21-6. It was a tough game. It was the game before Purdue and I think that played a role. We played just good enough to win.

I recall being in a meeting in the early part of the week we were to meet Oregon. It could have been tongue-in-cheek, but I think Hayes said something like 'God, this is amazing. Oregon does so much similar to Purdue.'

It was one of those deals where you try to get through because the game of the year is next week. We survived. I didn't come close to duplicating the opener [35 yards rushing in 18 attempts]. You don't always have career-type days. For the first two games, Hayes started John Brockington at wingback. But against Purdue, he was at tailback and I was on the bench. You look at the depth chart that's posted every week. Hayes never spoke to me about it.

Brockington got hurt either at the end of the first quarter or the start of the second. I played the rest of the game. We had a 6-0 lead on Ted Provost's interception and TD run.

I thought I had scored a touchdown. It was a trap play up-the-middle. I busted loose for 45 yards, but the touchdown was called back because of a clipping penalty downfield. It was a very questionable call. So, the touchdown was nullified.

We went on to beat Purdue, 13-0. I felt great for the guys. We beat the No.1 team in the country. As it turned out, we were on our way to the national championship. But for me, the season was virtually over. Maybe I'd get in for a couple of plays at the end of a game that had already been decided. At that point, football played a very important role in my life.

I didn't want to spend the last year of my college career on the bench. I felt I could still do it, but not at Ohio State. The hardest part was leaving the guys. We had a lot of fun together. They're some of my best friends in the world.

It was tough to start fresh. You're kinda going into the unknown. But it was the only way it was gonna happen. It was either that or sit there and be miserable.

I had a friend from Youngstown who was several years older than me. We went to the same high school. He played at Alabama the same time Joe Namath was there. He said he'd contact a bunch of coaches around the country and help me find a school. He's the one who called Tuscaloosa, Alabama.

Coach [Bear] Bryant must have liked what he heard because he told my friend to tell me, 'C'mon down.'

I was red-shirted my first year and was starting fullback as a fifth-year senior. By then, I was up to 195-200. A sophomore named Johnny Musso was the starting left half. We weren't real good. We finished 6-5-1, but we went to the Bluebonnet Bowl.

Musso led the team with more than 1,000 yards rushing. I had about 500 and led the SEC with a 6.3 average per carry.

The whole thing turned out great because I was able to play. I was able to enjoy college football. I had good feelings. I proved my point that I could do it, if only to myself.

I proved that I could play.

How many other guys can say they played for both Woody Hayes and Bear Bryant? They were legendary coaches. Both winners, both Hall of Famers.

But they had a totally different philosophy.

Hayes coached the offense. That was his thing. If you did not start the game on offense, you didn't play much unless somebody got hurt.

Coach Bryant's philosophy was that Alabama was going to win in the fourth quarter. Alabama was going to be fresh in the fourth quarter. So, he would play a lot of people. I mean 60-70 a game.

We had six or seven running backs at Ohio State who could have played anywhere in the country. We had three excellent quarterbacks.

What if you were interchanging those people as the game went on? Suppose Mace got a hot hand while he was in? So go with the hot hand.

You're not hurting anyone. Look how much better it would have been, not only for morale, but for performances also.

It would have created a better atmosphere.

But that was not Woody Hayes' style. It never changed.

What happens over a period of time if you're not on the starting team?

First of all, you lose interest. You lose enthusiasm. You also start to lose skills.

43

There was no reason for that to happen at Ohio State.

I saw it from a different perspective at Alabama.

Maybe you didn't play for 40 minutes. Maybe you were on the kickoff team and was in there for a couple of series.

That kind of thing.

But when you left the stadium on Saturday, you felt good. You were part of the team, part of the game.

Chapter 5

LITTLE GUY WHO PLAYS BIG

MIKE POLASKI, NO.15, DEFENSIVE HALFBACK
5-10, 170 Pounds, 19 Years Old, Junior

Ohio State Photo Archives

"I wasn't exceptionally fast. I knew in order to get playing time, I had to make myself a valuable commodity."

Class of '68

Mike Polaski was born-and-raised in Columbus, Ohio. A three-sports star at Brookhaven High School, he played football, basketball and baseball. All-Ohio in football and All-City in baseball, he played three seasons as a defensive halfback at Ohio State. A shortstop on the varsity baseball team, Polaski earned All-American honors his senior year. He played several years of minor league baseball. Mike Polaski has been a fireman in Columbus for 25 years.

In our championship season, I started eight of 10 games in the defensive secondary. Considering Jack Tatum, Timmy Anderson and Mike Sensibaugh were first round NFL draft picks and Ted Provost was selected in the fourth round, I was indeed in very select company. All four were college All-Americans.

I sure wasn't big. They always listed me at 170, but it was a lot closer to 158. I wasn't exceptionally fast. I knew in order to get playing time, I had to make myself a valuable commodity.

I learned all the positions. I was able to play closed-side halfback, wide-side halfback, safety, and Monster or Roverback. That was Jack Tatum's position. Today, that would be considered a cross between a strong safety and linebacker.

During my career, I played closed-side, wide-side and safety. I would have played Monster, but only in an emergency. I didn't, mainly because of my size. I also returned punts.

I had three backfield coaches in as many years. Lou Holtz was my coach during our championship season. I'd have to say, he was the best coach I played for at Ohio State.

He's an extremely fair man. He tells you up front what he wants. It's up to you to deliver. If you do, you play. If you don't, you've got six guys who can't wait to play your position.

It didn't matter if your name was Tim Anderson, Jack Tatum, Mike Sensibaugh, or Mike Polaski. You can't ask a coach to be any more fair than that.

Offensively, we were as big as anybody, especially at tackles with Dave Foley and Rufus Mayes. Defensively, we played small. A lot smaller than any team we faced.

We probably had combinations of 6-7 zone coverages. We had man-to-man coverage when we played man with a free safety. We played what we called 'bump-and-run' coverage on the outside receiver, the tight end.

We'd also have two guys split the field in half, playing zone coverage behind 'em. That was our 'Buckeye' coverage.

If we were in regular man, we're lining up 4-7 yards off the ball, either on the receiver's inside or outside shoulder depending on how close he was to the sidelines.

If we ran our 'Buckeye' coverage, then you go up and bump-and-run on him. You play him on the line of scrimmage. You were supposed to get help.

You try to disrupt the receiver from getting into his route right away. Then you get on his hip and shadow him underneath.

We had a lot of different coverages and used 'em effectively. We tried to disguise 'em as much as possible. That was one of the things we did against Purdue.

The pass that Teddy Provost intercepted and scored on was a change-up call off of our normal zone that we were using to that side.

Phipps thought his receiver was gonna be open because the guy he was reading was running away from him. When he released the ball, he had no idea Provost was coming.

Calls in the secondary were keyed on what formation they were in. We like to know their tendencies, what 3 or 4 running and passing plays they favored. We called our coverages accordingly.

We had a ton of fun in practice, I mean the defensive secondary. I attribute that in part to Lou Holtz. He told us 'Guys, this is just a game. There are two billion Chinese people who don't even know we do this.

'This is supposed to be fun. We're gonna play great football, don't get me wrong. We won't settle for anything less than that. We'll have fun while we're doing it. As soon as it's not fun, I'm gonna be the first one to walk off the practice field.'

We got everything done. We did it well. We managed to laugh about it while we were doing it.

Monday was usually a light practice day. We were still getting over our bumps-and-bruises from the game. If there was any contact, it was done on Tuesday and Wednesday. You start to slow down on Thursday. Friday was just run-throughs in the stadium in nothing but sweats and a helmet.

We'd watch films every day. We were well-prepared come game time. We knew exactly what to expect.

I can remember going to watch film in Lou's office. We were gonnna play Oregon that week. Coach Holtz said to me, 'You're going to block a punt this week.'

'How am I gonna do that, Coach?' It's usually hard to block punts from 35-40 yards down the field. I've been runnin 'em back."

He said, 'You're not going to return punts this week. We think we've seen something in the films and we're gonna go after it this week. We're gonna block it and you're the guy who's gonna do it.'

I looked at him. 'Okay, whatever you want.'

So we started looking at the films and he's showing me a flaw he thought he found.

'It's gonna be real simple,' he explained. 'When they snap the ball, I want you to be ready for it. Take off like a rocket for seven yards, throw your hands up in the air and make sure you come across in front of the punter. You've gotta be going to the point where the ball's going, and know where the punter is.'

We worked on it all week. The more we did it, the more comfortable I felt about the whole operation. I told Lou later in the week, 'I'm not only gonna block it, I'm gonna score.'

He looked at me. 'Just make sure you block the damn thing. We'll worry about the scoring part when we get the football back.'

The first time they went to punt, we ran the play and it worked perfectly. I ran seven yards, put my hands in the air in front of the punter. The guy kicked it right into my arms.

The ball popped into the air. The only thing I could see was the football. It looked as big as the moon. It dropped into my arms, I caught it and ran into the end zone.

I didn't have to run very far, probably about 12 yards. That was my only touchdown in my whole career. Defensive players don't get to score very often.

I'd say from a personal standpoint, the Oregon game or the SMU game was my best performance. Funny thing, those games were back-to-back. We opened the '68 season at home against SMU, then played at Oregon.

We beat SMU 35-14. In the secondary that day, we did the greatest job of scrambling that you could ever see. Chasing Jerry Levias around in the open field is like chasing a jack rabbit.

Levias was probably the best receiver I saw in college from the standpoint of speed, moves, and the ability to catch the ball. He's not a big guy, about my size. I don't think he went over 165.

SMU had the best passing attack of anybody we saw. It was certainly the most sophisticated. Like putting three guys on one side, two to the other side, and nobody in the backfield except the quarterback. Hixson just went in and threw.

Chuck Hixson couldn't run. He probably could have run a rollout, only if the other team thought he was calling time out and going to the sidelines.

That's probably a major reason why he didn't make it in the pros. That and his height. I don't think he was much over six feet tall, maybe 6-1.

But man, he could throw the ball.

Southern Cal had a good passing game, but theirs was predicated differently. SMU put so many potential receivers out. Southern Cal ran all their routes from three different depths.

They ran their outs and slants five yards. They ran 'em 12 yards. They ran 'em 17-18 yards.

I can remember covering Levias on a slant pattern. I was man-to-man on him, bump-and-run. I'm on him like a blanket. I bump him at the line. He turns upfield. I'm doing everything I'm supposed to do. I'm in perfect position on him. He turns to the sidelines.

Chuck Hixson delivers the ball in the only place I couldn't get to it, but Jerry Levias could. He caught it and we both go out-of-bounds. We get up. I look at him and say 'That's a helluva catch.'

What else could I do? You don't see that in today's game. They all want to stand over the guy and all that kind of stuff. There's times when the other guy is allowed to be great.

It was the longest game I ever played because of the amount of times the clock stopped. The game seemed like it lasted forever. We were physically exhausted at the end of it. When you're chasing guys like that around all day long, that wears on you.

Of course, our defensive linemen had to be even more drained. That's a lot of pass rushing. That's much more than playing the run, fighting off the double-team, or anything like that because it's a 7-to-10-yard sprint to get to the quarterback.

Hixson threw the ball 69 times. He had to leave the game because he was tired. Then they brought in a southpaw who threw it seven more times.

I went to Brookhaven High School in Columbus, Ohio, playing football, basketball and baseball. I was All-Ohio in football and All-City in baseball.

Until about the third game of my senior year, I was a wide receiver on offense as well as a defensive back. Well, our coach decided we weren't running the ball enough. He wanted a balanced attack, so he moved me to tight end.

It was a lesson in learning how to block. Learning different ways to block and not get hurt. The first game I played, I got matched up with a defensive end who was 6-4 and 220. I learned real quick.

I knew I wasn't going to blow this guy off the line of scrimmage. I figured a lot of ways to get down and kinda tie up his legs, try to make him think I was releasing to catch a pass, but then double back on him. Ambush-type blocking. Obviously, I wasn't going to take this guy head on.

Ohio State wasn't on my 'wish list.' I had a letter from Florida State. They were interested in me as a wide receiver. I also received letters from Wake Forest, Northwestern, Yale, and some of the Mid-American Conference schools.

They were all interested in me as a football player. Never got into talks regarding baseball. Recruiting wasn't nearly as intense as it is today. None of this contact came until well into my senior year.

Ohio State entered the game only by chance. It turned out to be my good luck.

Hugh Hindman actually came to see us play against Columbus DeSales because he was interested in a couple of tackles and two of our running backs, as well as a few players from DeSales. I was not on his shopping list.

I played very well that game and when Hindman came back and gave his report, Ohio State decided to show interest in me.

What it all boiled down to was this. Ohio State was right here in town. I was gonna end up living on campus which meant I was gonna be as far away from home as I wanted to be, but I was also gonna be as close to home as I wanted to be.

My parents basically would be able to see all my home games. If I had gone to Florida State, Wake Forest, or someplace like that, then my Mom and Dad maybe would have been able to see me play one game a year.

I liked Esco Sarkkinen. He was the gentleman responsible for recruiting in Central Ohio. Woody made a very good impression. He was an awesome recruiter. In fact, he and Lou McCullough probably should have been outlawed. They did such a great job in their home state.

The only thing Woody Hayes said about football was that I'd get a chance to play. He emphasized the fact that I'd get a great education, that a scholarship would be granted to me for four years.

Back then a lot of schools granted a one-year scholarship that was renewable the following year at the discretion of the university. He told me and my parents, 'When you sign this scholarship, we honor our scholarships.' No matter what.

Woody also promised me that I could play baseball, and I held him to his promise. Every Spring we'd argue about it. He really wanted me to concentrate on football, but he had told me as long as I could help the baseball team I could play.

He kept his word. In my senior year I was fortunate enough to be named to the All-American team.

CHAPTER 6

'Z WHIZ'...MR. VERSATILITY

LARRY ZELINA, NO.16, WINGBACK
6-0, 195 Pounds, 19 Years Old, Sophomore

Ohio State Photo Archives

"When you make a decision to go to a major school, you go there to answer one question in your mind. 'Can I compete with the best?'"

Larry Zelina was born-and-raised in Cleveland, Ohio. All-State in both football and baseball at Benedictine High School, Zelina was a starting offensive halfback for three years at Ohio State. Drafted by the NFL Cleveland Browns in the eighth round, he survived the final cut, but injured his hamstring five games before the season opener. He tried in 1971-73 to make it in Canada, but injuries ended his playing career. He is now an insurance executive in Columbus.

When you make a decision to go to a major school the caliber of Ohio State, you go there to answer one question in your mind. 'Can I compete with the best?'

I could have gone to a smaller school and been Big Man On Campus. But it would have always bothered me as to whether or not I could play on a big-time level.

They brought me in as a tailback. That was my dream. But during the course of my freshman year, they found out I could catch the ball. They found out I could run reverses. They found out I was probably the best blocking back they brought in.

So they moved me from tailback to wingback.

I gave up my dream to go to a position that helped our offense. If you're a team player, you do what you have to do for the good of the team. Our offense was better with me at wingback than it would have been with me at tailback.

I played right halfback when we played our full-house backfield. I was wingback when we ran from the I formation.

I was at a position where I did a little bit of everything and not much of anything. I'd carry the ball 4-5 times a game. I'd catch 4-5 passes a game. I'd return 2-3 punts and as many kickoffs. I'd handle the ball 10,12,15 times a game. I was always involved.

I was All-Ohio in both football and baseball at Cleveland Benedictine High School. I was All-State my junior and senior years in football. We finished in the Top Ten in the state, both in 1965 and 1966. There was only one division back then.

We finished 9-1 both years, and the only losses were to Massillon. We played them every year.

I was a center fielder in baseball and hit .500 my junior year to lead all of the Cleveland area players. I could have signed right out of high school. The Pittsburgh Pirates and San Francisco Giants were both interested in signing me.

But honest, I didn't want to miss the chance to get an education. I didn't want to take the chance of spending 5,6,7 years in the minors and not make the major leagues.

It was a tough decision, but one I've never regretted.

I was supposed to have the opportunity to play baseball at Ohio State, but chose not to once I got there. I decided to put all of my efforts into football.

I would say 100 or more colleges were interested in recruiting me. Every major college, including Southern Cal, UCLA, Yale, Alabama, Notre Dame, Nebraska, just to name a few.

At that time I believe we were allowed to make six recruiting visits. I had 12 years of Catholic school education. I went to a Catholic high school, an all-boys Catholic High School.

My high school coach, Auggie Bossu, played at Notre Dame in the late 1930s. He retired just a few years ago after coaching for five decades. He's a member of both the Ohio Hall of Fame and the National High School Hall of Fame.

So, if I had a favorite school, it would have been Notre Dame.

When I visited Ohio State, I liked the way Woody treated me. I liked the way the University treated me. I wanted to get into some type of business after college and the late John Galbraith played a big role in my going to Ohio State.

Mr. Galbraith was not only owner of the Pittsburgh Pirates, but he was a big Ohio State supporter. He didn't talk so much about football as he pointed out the potential advantages of doing business and having a career in Ohio. And, of course, he pointed out the benefits of playing for Ohio State. He was a great man.

I had a good feeling about Ohio State from the start. I was very familiar with at least a dozen other recruits. I played with and against them in the annual North-South All-Star game at Canton.

I was on the North team. The score was South 40, North 12. I had a 65 or 70 yard punt return for a touchdown that game. There was another halfback from Cathedral Latin who also scored for the North. We were the only two guys who scored in that massacre.

Rex Kern, from Lancaster, was the South quarterback. Leo Hayden, from Dayton, was a running back. We became teammates at Ohio State.

It takes a while to get used to everybody. You knew this was a special group of guys. It all stems from chemistry. I think the key to any special team is the comraderie. It was phenomenal. There was no conflict. It was a brotherhood. It really was.

During the first week of summer practice in 1968, I twisted my ankle real bad and went down to No. 4 in the depth chart.

At that time, Woody Hayes was still playing around with different positions. In the first game against SMU, John Brockington started at wingback. Ray Gillian was second team and I was third team.

I got some playing time in the opener, and I moved up to second team for the second game. By the third game, my ankle was a lot better.

I'll never forget it. Hugh Hindman came to see me the Monday of the Purdue game. He said 'Z, you've earned it, you're starting.' He put me at wingback and had Ray Gillian behind me. That's when they moved Brockington to tailback.

When we were freshmen in '67, Purdue came into town and blew us away, 41-6. It was Mike Phipps and Leroy Keyes. We were freshmen sitting up in the stands and they're kicking our ass.

Purdue was our third game of the season. We had won our first two games. We went into that game against the No.1 team in the country.

I think Purdue came in a little big headed. We were ready. We were ready to play. We went out there and did what had to be done. It was a springboard for our magical season.

I had a good game, but it wasn't my best game of the season. From a personal standpoint, my best game was against Michigan. We beat 'em 50-14. I had almost 200 yards in kickoff and punt returns. I rushed for 92 yards on only eight carries. Yeah, I had a good game.

From an offensive standpoint, we had no weakness. We were 2-3 strong at every position.

Back then people didn't realize that we averaged about 19 passes a game.

When you go with one quarterback, you go with him and don't switch except when the quarterback gives you a reason to switch. Rex Kern never gave Woody a reason. He was a winner.

That meant that Ron Maciejowski didn't see much action in his three years. When Rex got hurt, Ronnie came in and the offense didn't suffer one bit. As far as I'm concerned, he was every bit as good as Rex Kern.

Mace won a number of games for us as a sophomore. He won the Michigan State and Illinois games when Rex got hurt. He started against Wisconsin, ran for three touchdowns and passed for a fourth.

We did the 'Three Yards And A Cloud Of Dust' when we had to with Jim Otis at fullback, Brockington and Leo Hayden at tailback and me at right half.

We had Jan White at tight end and Bruce Jankowski at wide receiver. Jan was an excellent blocker and a sure-handed receiver. Jankowski was a long-ball threat.

There were so many weapons on that national championship team. Every game it seemed somebody else was stepping up and making big plays.

You couldn't key on anybody. If you did, we'd burn you someplace else. Absolutely. It was always the case.

I got hurt in the Rose Bowl against Southern Cal. Ray Gillian came in, played a great game and almost won the MVP award.

I got my ribs broken the last play of the first quarter. I tried to kick a field goal on the opening play of the second quarter. Nobody at that point knew I had three cracked ribs. That was my last play of the game.

People may not realize it but we had a lot of close games in 1968. We beat Michigan State, 25-20. We blew a big lead against Illinois to win, 31-24. We went up to Iowa and barely survived, 33-27.

Contrast that to my junior year, 1969. That was an awesome year. It was incredible. This was a better team than our national championship team.

We breeze through eight straight opponents, then lose to Michigan 24-12 in the last game of the season. I still don't understand what happened.

I'm thrilled to have been a part of it. I'm thrilled to have had the opportunity to contribute. It was as fine an experience as I've ever had from an athletic standpoint.

I was drafted in the eighth round by Cleveland. It was a dream come true. I'm a Cleveland boy. I was in contention for a backup running back position behind Leroy Kelly and Bo Green.

I was with them for nine weeks and made the final cut, but I tore my hamstring five days before the start of the season. They let me go. When you're a third or fourth running back, you've got to be ready.

Actually, it was the recurrence of an old injury. I injured my hamstring my senior year at Ohio State, missed three games, and yet I was selected in the top half of the draft.

I was going to play pro ball in Canada in 1972. A week before I was supposed to leave, I was working out and tore a cartilage in my knee. I wound up with phlebitis, was in the hospital for a few weeks and almost died.

I came back and tried one more time in '73. I went to Canada. I was there for three weeks with the Saskatchewan Rough Riders when I tore my hamstring again.

I went to an orthopedic specialist who said it was time to quit trying. So, I quit trying.

Chapter 7

IN THE BULLPEN

RON MACIEJOWSKI, No.18, QUARTERBACK
6-2, 186 Pounds, 19 Years Old, Sophomore.

During the "Dream Season" Mace directed Ohio State to victories against Illinois and Michigan State. In his only start he scored three TD's and passed for another against Wisconsin.

Ron Maciejowski was born-and-raised in Bedford, Ohio. A basketball and football star at Bedford High School, he earned All-Northeast Ohio honors in football as a running/passing quarterback. Maciejowski went to Ohio State and became one of the best known 'relief pitchers' in college football, saving two games in the 1968 'dream' season. He failed in NFL tryouts with the Chicago Bears and Cincinnati Bengals. Ron Maciejowski is now a high-ranking executive with Worthington Industries in Toledo, Ohio. He lives in nearby Holland.

I was really excited before my first varsity game at Ohio State, but I managed to get some sleep. Running onto the field at Ohio Stadium was everything I thought it would be. It was awesome.

There's no college stadium like it. I mean, it's a shrine. There's bigger stadiums, but there's nothing as defined as Ohio Stadium.

You look at Michigan's stadium from the outside. Hell, it's nothing. Just a bunch of girders. You look at Ohio Stadium from the outside and it's architecture. It's absolutely gorgeous. I mean, you don't see stadiums like that any more.

We opened up against SMU. I'm third string quarterback behind Rex Kern and Billy Long. Larry Zelina and I are sitting next to each other on the bench. We're both sophomores. Larry was a fine halfback from Cleveland.

There was a key series in the game when Rex waves the punter off the field. It's fourth down and something like 10 yards to go for a first down. I think we're on the SMU 40.

He calls the play at the line of scrimmage, goes back to pass, but the whole play breaks down. He's got nothing. Kern sprints right. He's hemmed in. He's trying to make the best of a terrible situation. He's running like hell. This guy hits him and about the same time, Rex jumps, spins in the air, does a 360, lands on his feet and runs 15 yards for a crucial first down.

Zelina's next to me. He looks over and yells, 'Well, Mace, it's gonna be a long three years [for you].' It wasn't too much after that play when John Brockington catches a pass and goes about 60 or 70 yards, breaking four or five tackles.

Brockington's a wingback, the same position that Zelina plays. I yelled back to Larry, 'It's nice to know I'll have some company.'

As a kid, I was more interested in Ohio State basketball than I was in Ohio State football. When I was 11 or 12, Jerry Lucas and John Havlicek played for Ohio State. I lived-and-died when they lost two straight years to Cincinnati in the NCAA finals.

Don't get me wrong. I liked both football and basketball in high school. But basketball was just more fun to play. Football was work. You played basketball in the Summer to have fun and to keep in shape. You can't play football to have fun.

I mean, football is a serious game. Like Woody used to say, 'You never see a guy make a tackle with a smile on his face.' It doesn't happen. But you can make a three-pointer with a huge smile on your face.

I was recruited by a number of schools in both sports. I was a 6-2 shooting guard. We had a real good basketball team my senior year.

In football, we ran a wide-open offense. It was Sprint Out Right, Sprint Out Left. We threw the ball 15 times a game on the average. In one game, I threw 37 times.

I felt I had a better future in college as a football player. Bill Mallory of Ohio State showed a lot of interest. Ohio State tried to get me down, but I couldn't make it on a weekend. I was playing basketball on Friday and Saturday nights.

Finally they said, 'Why don't you come down on a week night?' I came down on a Monday. Coach Mallory had Northeast Ohio for his recruiting area. Only problem is, he sent me to the wrong airport.

He sent me to Burke Lakefront instead of Hopkins. By the time I got to St. John Arena, it was halftime. It was also finals week at Ohio State. I stayed with a couple of guys and really didn't do anything.

For some reason I still can't put my finger on, I liked Ohio State. I was tired of the recruiting game. One day I told my coach I was going to Ohio State. He said, 'Fine, let's call Woody.' We called Woody Hayes.

I figured maybe I'd go to Baldwin-Wallace or Marietta. Some smaller school. But it became apparent to me by the end of my junior year that I was gonna play Division I football. I just knew that.

Once I made the decision, I started checking up on who was also going. I realized it would be a hell of a freshman class. My class included John Brockington, Mike Sensibaugh, Doug Adams, Timmy Anderson, Leo Hayden, Mark Debevc. I could go on-and-on.

We had 14 guys drafted by the pros out of that freshman class. We had 11 All-Americans. We had 19 guys who made All-Big Ten.

As a freshman, I ranked behind Kern and Sensibaugh. We scrimmaged against the varsity primarily, but we also played two freshman games against Pitt and Indiana.

Mike Sensibaugh was an All-Ohio quarterback. He became, of course, an All-American safety at Ohio State and all-NFL. At Ohio State, he was a punter and free safety. He was the only guy to lead both the NCAA and NFL in interceptions.

Tiger Ellison was our freshman coach. They wanted us to play offense and also play some defense. Two quarterbacks would stay with the offense, and one would be shifted to the defense.

Sensibaugh never came back to the offense. He couldn't throw very well and he decided quarterback wasn't where he could make his name. And he did.

When we came in 1967, we were in camp for four days. The fifth day was a dress rehearsal against the varsity. It was a week before the varsity season began. We still had tape on our helmets with our names so that the coaches knew who we were.

We were running plays off cards in the huddle. At halftime, we were tied with the varsity. It was 14-14. This was a group of 30 kids who had been there for just four days. Rex and I took our units and scored. We had the ball twice and scored both times.

Some of our full-scale scrimmages turned kinda ugly. We had fights. We were playing hard. We were trying to prove something. They [the varsity] wanted to get through practice so they could make it to the opener. But this was OUR GAME. This was our Saturday.

I got in for two plays against SMU. Woody thought we'd be a really good football team. He was really excited because our freshman team was exceptional. I think he felt we could beat anybody, but he wasn't saying that.

He had always felt for every sophomore he started, he lost a football game. That's how he felt. Well, that year we started 13 on a regular basis, and as many as 17 sophomores at one time or another.

The next game was against Oregon. Rex got hurt. Bill went in and threw an interception. Rex went back in. He was OK, but he got hurt again. Bill went in again and threw another interception. I was in the next series and played the rest of the game.

It might have been the fourth quarter. It was a 14-6 game when I came in. My first play was called '99 Jet Cut.' It was only a 10-15 yard outcut. Bruce Jankowski broke a tackle, went down the sidelines for a 55-yard touchdown. Bruce was a strong kid.

Woody used to say 'It was the longest pass in history...from Pole to Pole.' That's Woody.

In the three years that Rex and I played at Ohio State, I started only two games. Rex was a natural athlete, a great runner, but he was a little fragile. I was a good runner.

As a sophomore, I started against Wisconsin, ran for three touchdowns and passed for another. I started one game as a senior. I rushed for more than 100 yards in each game.

There was no jealousy on my part. Rex and I were good friends in college. Now, we're great friends.

One game will always stick out in my mind. We were beating Illinois, 24-0, at halftime in 1968. Illinois wasn't very good that year, but it was their Homecoming. The fans were yelling 'Go Illini, Hold 'Em to 50.' Things like that. We had quite a few guys who didn't make the trip because of injuries, but we were breezing.

All systems were GO. Everything seemed fine.

We start the second half and Rex throws the ball to Jim Otis. Otis gets hit and fumbles. They go in and score a touchdown and make the two-point conversion. It's 24-8 at the end of the third quarter.

Beginning of the fourth quarter they drive 80 yards in 15 or 18 plays. They get another two-point conversion and it's 24-16. There's almost eight minutes to go in the game.

They stop us cold. We punt. They go 65 yards for a touchdown and make a third two-point conversion. It's 24-24 with two-and-a-half minutes to play.

Rex goes out there. The first play, he rolls right. He's trying to find somebody to throw to. He can't find anyone, so he starts to run and gets knocked out.

On top of that, he loses seven yards on the play. It's second-and-17. Woody yells 'Gimme Billy Long.' Woody's talking to Billy. I'm sitting on the bench with my cape on. Clouds start moving in. The wind picks up. It was horrible...all those bad omens.

As Billy tells it, Woody's holding him by his jersey to push him into the game. Woody looked at him with this incredible look on his face and yells, 'No goddamit, gimme Maciejowski.'

I said 'Oh shit.' So I get up. I don't have my helmet on. I've gotta find my helmet. Finally, I get my helmet. Woody says to me, 'Are you ready to go?' I said 'Sure, sure.' In his gruff voice he says, 'Okay, get in and do the job for us.'

So he pushed me in. I go running out onto the field and go into the huddle. Dave Foley is our All-American tackle. The first thing he said is 'Don't screw it up. Don't you throw an interception.'

The first play I hit Zelina for 10 yards. It's third-and-seven. I'm feeling pretty good about completing that first pass. A play comes in from the sidelines.

In the meantime, I'm calling an automatic at the line. I've got the 12th guy standing next to me, and I'm calling an automatic. I get him off the field and call this play.

It was a terrible play. I go back to pass. The whole thing breaks down. I break out, roll right and gain about 25 to midfield.

I call the next play and hit Zelina on a post pattern for 46 yards to the Illinois four. We go in for the winning touchdown.

I had no clue I was going into the game. I didn't have a chance to be nervous. The fans were going nuts by that time. We were in deep trouble. We were a little panicked in the huddle.

I'm calling the play. This guy's coming in, this guy's coming out. Then in the paper I read 'A well-oiled Ohio State machine drove 80 yards in the waning moments to win.' I'm thinking 'There was nothing but chaos in the huddle.'

People thought of Ohio State as strictly 'three yards and a cloud of dust.' It wasn't that at all. We thought of ourselves as a multi-faceted offense. We threw the ball 20 times a game. Against Michigan, we had four backs gain 90 yards or more. I think Otis had 110. We only threw seven times because we ran so well.

We ran only from a couple of formations. We never ran the full-house backfield unless it was third-and-a-yard, or we were close to the goal line. We were basically spread out. It was a very diversified team with great speed at the wide receivers. Jan White and Bruce Jankowski. Both played pro ball for a long time.

In 1993, we had a big blowout. It was our 25th year reunion. It was really interesting. A group got together that wanted to do a big thing. They wanted to have a party on a Friday night.

We took the Ohio State indoor practice facility. We sold 2,400 tickets to that banquet. It was an amazing blowout. Twenty-four-hundred tickets to an appreciation banquet. That was part of the Woody and Anne Hayes Scholarship Fund.

The next day, we were honored at halftime at Ohio Stadium. We were introduced one-by-one. Ninety-six thousand people cheered us. It doesn't get any better than that.

Chapter 8

BORN TO BE A FULLBACK

JIM OTIS, NO.35, FULLBACK
6-0, 208 Pounds, 20 Years Old, Junior.

"I always made the quarterback give me the ball as deep as possible and as quickly as possible because my cuts were always gonna be after the first two steps."

Class of '68

Jim Otis was born-and-raised in Celina, Ohio. A three-sports star at Celina High School—football, basketball, track—Otis was All-Ohio in football his senior year. A highly sought-after fullback, he played three seasons at Ohio State, leading his team in rushing his sophomore, junior and seniors years, earning All-Big Ten and All-American honors. Named MVP of a summer college All-Star game at Lubbock, Texas, Otis was selected in the seventh round by the NFL New Orleans Saints. He had a productive nine year career with the Saints, Kansas City Chiefs and St. Louis Cardinals. Now a real estate developer, Jim Otis lives in Chesterfield, Missouri.

I didn't want to be a fullback for Ohio State until I was about four. Guess I was a little slow. I always dreamed about it. Bob Ferguson, Bob White and Hop Cassady were my heroes. As a sophomore in high school, I was 5-6 and weighed 165. A year later, I was six-feet tall and weighed about 195. They stuck me at offensive tackle my junior year. My best friend was the starting quarterback. After practice, we'd stay on the field and I'd run plays from fullback.

About the fourth game of my junior year, our fullback was injured. The backup fullback was sick and out of school. So, my friend-the quarterback-goes up to the coach and says 'Let Jim play fullback.'

I was inserted into the lineup in the second half and started running over people that night. Celina came from behind to beat Wapakoneta, Neil Armstrong's home town.

I rushed for more than a mile as a senior, scored something like 30 touchdowns. I was the first kid ever from Celina to be chosen for the Ohio High School All-Star game in Canton. That game was a unique experience and one that motivated me more than anyone will ever know.

My Dad and Mom drove me over to Canton. After the first practice I said to my Dad, 'I'm not gonna get to play in this game.'

He said, 'Oh, you can't tell that after one practice.' Dick Walker of Columbus Waterson was our coach. He had a real good fullback who was going to Notre Dame. Then, there was another fullback, so he relegated me to playing defense. I don't think Coach Walker ever heard of Celina.

I didn't get into the game until the last two minutes. I think they put me in at defensive tackle. I hadn't even practiced at that position.

There were 200-250 people that came from Celina for the game. I felt like I had really let all my friends down. Celina is a real quiet football town, and also a town that looks after their kids.

I'm in the locker room after the game and guess who walks in? Woody Hayes. He goes over to Dick Walker and he says 'Coach, I'm gonna tell you something in front of Jim. I just want you to know you made a big mistake out there by not playing him at fullback. We think he's gonna be a great one at Ohio State.'

With that comment, he walked out. He didn't say goodbye. He didn't say anything. He just turned and walked out. That was the way he was. He always showed up when you needed him. Nobody knew I needed my spirits lifted about that time and as always his timing was perfect.

Two things really helped me as a fullback. I took tumbling lessons and I was a diver on the swim team. I only lost one diving meet in all of the times I dove in

60

competition. I did my diving from the one meter board. More than anything, I learned how to leave my feet and maintain body balance.

When you get up in the air, you have to be able to turn and maintain perfect balance. I learned that diving. I knew how to fall and never get hurt. Certainly I wasn't a 9.3 sprinter, but by the time I took my second step I was making my turn. I'd say my Number One asset was my quickness.

What did I enjoy most about playing fullback?

Getting in my stance, putting my fingers down in the turf and knowing I was gonna get the ball many times in the course of a game. So did everybody else in the stadium, as well as the other team.

There was never a time on third or fourth down when I didn't think I was gonna make the first down. Never. Never did I doubt that the play called wasn't the right play, regardless of what type of defense we were up against.

I just loved to run. I was blessed with guys up in front of me at Celina High, Ohio State, and in the pros. I just seemed to be blessed playing with good people.

Norm Decker was my high school coach. He was out of the Ohio State mold. He was a tough guy who ran the fullback all the time. I liked that.

He was also the guy who tried to stay between me and all the recruiters. He was the guy who intercepted a lot of that stuff, but he wasn't always successful.

In my senior year, I didn't play basketball. I mean those people would come up into our arena. Hell, they'd come up right into the stands where I was sitting.

Bo Schembechler, who was then at Miami of Ohio, was the only other coach I told I would go to his school if I didn't go to Ohio State.

Throughout my football career, I always felt like I had to prove myself. Each and every game. In high school, Ohio State, and the National Football League.

As I said, my first game at fullback at Celina High, was against our arch-rivals. We were down 12-0 in the middle of the third quarter. In college and the pros, each quarter was 15 minutes. In high school, it was 12 minutes.

In the last quarter-and-a-half, I scored two or three touchdowns and ran for something like 170 yards. The local newspaper sent a reporter and photographer to our school. They named me Player of the Week.

They take your picture and write a few paragraphs. My coach was also there. Do you know what Coach Decker told me? He said 'I just wanna let you know one thing. You haven't sewn up the top position yet.'

I started nine games my junior year, led the league in rushing and was picked all-conference. I was All-Ohio my senior year. At Ohio State, I had to constantly prove I wasn't playing fullback simply because Woody Hayes and my Dad were best friends in college. Not to myself, but to a lot of other people. In the pros, it took me three years to finally get a chance for a starting position. That was, I guess, the easy part. It's a lot tougher to keep the No. 1 spot.

Those challenges made me a better player and person. Paul Huff and I altered at fullback my sophomore year at Ohio State. That is until I fumbled twice in one game. I didn't play in the second half of the Illinois game, and for the next two games against Wisconsin and Michigan State.

It was my fault. I probably carried the ball 500-600 times in three years at Ohio State. I had only three fumbles my whole career.

Class of '68

After the benching, I honestly didn't think I was ever gonna play at Ohio State again. Standing on the sidelines just plain killed me.

Woody came to see me the night before we played Iowa. At that point, he wasn't my favorite person. He said, 'Jim, do you sleep much before games?'

I said 'Well, generally I don't, but I've been sleeping like a baby the last two weeks.'

He looked at me. 'I want to let you know you're gonna start tomorrow.'

I didn't ask him why he changed his mind. He didn't volunteer an answer. He said what he had to say.

I had 149 yards against Iowa. Then we went up to Michigan and I had something like 120 yards rushing. We won both games. Maybe that was my personal turning point. Maybe it was just a difference in confidence. Maybe the team was maturing.

Or maybe I just got mad and said to myself, 'By God, no one's ever gonna take this position again.' And they didn't. I'd like to say Woody never sat me down again. He did it at Minnesota my senior year. We were in the locker room before the game and Woody said there would be a change in the starting lineup.

He looked over to John Brockington. Brock started.

When Woody tells us, I'm thinking to myself. The sports section is running almost a full-page picture of me and I won't even be in the game.

More than that, I'm trying to figure out in my head why Woody made the change. I don't think I was the first person to try to figure Woody Hayes out.

I don't know if I was getting cocky. I just don't know. I do know we received the opening kickoff. Brock carried the ball and gained five. Then we threw a short pass over-the-middle to Jan White and it was third-and-one.

We ran the ball again and they stopped us. Woody turns around. I'm on the bench wearing my sideline cape. It was chilly enough in Minnesota that day to wear a cape.

He motions for me to come to him. I go over to Woody. He barks, 'Goddam you, why aren't you in there?' I said, 'Coach, you didn't start me.'

He said, 'Get in there.' It's hard to single out my most memorable game during our championship season. We played so many good games.

I remember we were scoreless at halftime against Purdue. Purdue was ranked No.1 in the country. We were No.4. We chewed up a lot of real estate, but we just didn't score.

Our defense kept us in the game all day long. The defense made the big play of the game. Ted Provost picked off a Mike Phipps pass and ran 35 yards to score. That touchdown would have been enough. Later, Billy Long came in for Rex Kern and scored on a keeper. Ohio State 13, Purdue 0. When you play a position like I did, people forget how many times you carried the ball and how many yards you gained over the course of the game.

In the second half against Purdue, I wanna say I carried almost every running down. I gained an awful lot of yards, more than a hundred the second half.

We were both real good teams. I don't know if we were nervous in the first half, or just didn't execute well enough. But I know we played much better in that second half.

We blew a 24-0 halftime lead against winless Illinois. The score was tied at 24-all, and we had only a couple of minutes to score.

I'm saying 'Gimme the ball, gimme the ball,' but hell you can't give me the ball when we were so far away from scoring territory.

We've got two minutes to go and we're 60-65 yards away from the field goal. Anyhow, we moved the ball down the field. We threw some passes and got down inside the five where it was time for me to run the ball. We won a real squeaker and learned a valuable lesson.

I scored a school record-tying four touchdowns in our 50-14 win over Michigan, but the story of the last touchdown is worth re-telling.

We had a 44-14 lead. I was out of the game, as were most of the starters. The game was out of reach for Michigan.

Ray Gillian got the ball and made a big run. I mean 40 or 50 yards. Until then, we were running the clock down.

Well, we get to the Michigan three. It's first-and-goal. But before you know it, it's fourth-and-goal. I'm standing behind Woody. I said, 'Coach, you want the score?'

He turned to me and said, 'Go in and get it.' I asked 'What play?'

'You call the play.'

So, I get in the huddle. I'm looking around and there's a lot of new faces. Dave Cheney, who became a great player, was a sophomore. He was at left tackle.

I looked at Dave. 'Woody wants this touchdown and he wants it over you. So you'd better make it.' I called out 'Twenty-seven.' We went in for the final touchdown.

When I went back into the game, there was pandemonium. The place was shaking. After we scored the touchdown, the kicker never came onto the field.

Woody got blamed for what happened next. Woody never said what really happened. He never made an excuse. Kevin Rusnak was at quarterback.

He just said 'let's run a play.' I don't remember what play it was. To everyone it looked like we were going for two points. That was the farthest thoughts in our minds.

Woody didn't know a damn thing about it. He was probably excited himself when we scored the last touchdown. Looking back, we should have called time to get the kicker onto the field. We never thought about how Woody would be criticized. We were all so excited.

I ran three basic plays. Off tackle right—twenty-six. Off tackle left—Twenty-seven. Right up-the-middle. Once in awhile, I'd run a wide play, or I'd go out for a delay pass.

Rufus Mayes and Dave Foley were our two big tackles. Those guys were big, big people in those days, but actually they weighed only 250.

Dave had such good technique. He had this big bruise and swelling on his forehead all the time. This guy did it right every time.

Mayes had played tight end for two years, then switched to tackle. He was probably quicker and a little rangier. Both of them were great players and leaders. We just lined up and said 'Look, we're gonna run at you.' And we did.

I couldn't have done it without tackles like Dave and Rufus. We did not have big guards—Tom Backhus and Alan Jack—or a big center—John Muhlbach. Offensively, we were small except for our tackles and tight end Jan White.

We ran from the I formation and the old-fashioned straight T, but only in short yardage situations, as well as from the Slot and modified T.

I was always the same distance from the line of scrimmage. My feet would be four-and-a-half-yards from the center.

Great running backs have great eyes. They can immediately see the entire defense. If you look at films of me after I've taken two steps, I'm cutting.

I always made the quarterback give me the ball as deep as possible and as quickly as possible because my cuts were always gonna be after the first two steps.

I'm either coming back behind the center, or I'm taking it outside the tackles. We just ran the off-tackle play so many different ways, and always ran to daylight.

We could double team down on the defensive tackle. We could double team on the guy that's playing over the tackle with the tight end. We could block everybody down and let the guard pull down. We could block the linebacker. I think you get the picture.

Vince Lombardi said 'Run to daylight.' That's what we did. We never asked our linemen to take a man in a direction he didn't want to go.

In other words, if Dave Foley was supposed to block the guy over him down and he was taking an outside rush, Foley would put his head in the middle and drive him where he wanted to go. Dave would expect me to make the proper cut inside of him.

If it were a double-team block with the tight end and tackle taking the opponent outside, I would expect the halfback to read that so he would lead outside.

One of my favorite plays, even though I didn't carry the ball, was the belly fake to me. We had that play where Rex Kern or Mace [Ron Maciejowski] would actually stick the ball in the pocket I gave him and pull it out. I would always lower my inside shoulder, making it impossible to see whether or not I had the ball.

There was no way that the people across the line could see whether I had the ball or not. They had to respect the fact that I went into the air. They had to respect the fact because I carried the ball so much.

Rex would just tuck the ball on his hip and literally walk into the end zone. He and Mace were tremendous ball handlers.

When you run that play, the quarterback and fullback have to have a lot of confidence in each other. I'm charging up there awfully hard and it has to be a perfect mesh.

You can't hit the quarterback or you'll knock him down. The quarterback has got to come to you. He can't be afraid that you're gonna hit him. So there has to be confidence in both players. And of course, having a coach like Woody Hayes, you know we practiced that a lot.

Rex had a bad back. In fact, we didn't think he was gonna play the first game against SMU in '68. He did seem to be a little injury prone. But I'll tell you something. Rex Kern ran with reckless abandon. He probably should have gone down a few times when he was still up. He did take some hard hits. Rex was 185 pounds. He wasn't a very big quarterback.

We were blessed in the fact that we had such a talented team. We could replace Kern with Maciejowski, or Billy Long, and not miss a beat. Mace, as far as I'm concerned, could have been a starting quarterback for just about every major college team in the country. He was that good.

We had this guy named Brockington playing behind me and swinging at halfback, Ray Gillian playing behind our wingback Larry Zelina, who was probably the best all-around back on the team.

It was the same way on defense.

No one would argue the fact that we were really better in 1969. We blew everyone out until that Michigan game. Somehow we just couldn't get untracked and it cost us the Big Ten title, an unbeaten season, No.1 ranking and the national championship.

Which reminds me of this crazy story. Mace and I were roommates for the Michigan game at Ann Arbor. They kept changing the TV time on us which meant they changed the time the bus would leave for the stadium. Somehow, Mace and I missed the team bus.

Do you know what it's like trying to get to Michigan Stadium? Traffic is a nightmare. It's bumper-to-bumper. It's insane. We managed to get the manager at the hotel we were staying at to drive us to the game.

I told him to start driving down the other side of the highway. There wasn't much traffic coming the other way. But we got stopped by the police. We explained who we were, but he didn't really believe us.

He said, 'I'm gonna do this. I'm gonna take you guys in there but if you're lying, you're going to jail.' I don't remember if he gave us an escort or put us into his police cruiser. Anyway, we made it to the stadium and made it into the locker room without Woody ever finding out. His whole life, he never knew about it or we'd still be running laps.

As I look back, maybe it was an omen of bad things to come. In my whole career, I didn't miss many first downs. That day against Michigan, I missed one on fourth down. It still gnaws at me to this day. I don't think I missed it.

When a runner is going down, he can look to the sidelines. He can see the sideline markers. We needed that first down to sustain a drive. I had a lot of yards that day. I had a lot of carries, but that 'missed' first down will always be with me.

I was listed at 207 or 208 at Ohio State. I was really 218. I carried 225 in the pros. My Number 35 jersey still proudly hangs on a wall in my home.

When you're living it, you don't know how much it means to you, how great it is. Not just winning the national championship, but the friendships you develop.

You only have a certain amount of good friends in the world. And even if you haven't seen them for awhile, when you do, it seems like yesterday. They're a great bunch. They know me as well as anyone in the world.

Jim Roman got tagged with the nickname 'Pork.' Dave Foley was 'Duke' and they called me 'The King.' To this day, I don't know why. When I was in the pros, they called me 'Shake.' My old teammates with the Cardinals still do.

Even when Rex Kern calls up at my office, he'll shout out 'King, how are you doing?' I like that.

Chapter 9

RIGHT OFF THE FARM

Ted Provost, No.46, Defensive Halfback
6-3, 182 pounds, 20 years old. Junior.

Ohio State Photo Archives

"I'm a small town guy who grew up on a thirty acre farm. We had both milk and beef cattle... It was fun growing up. I kinda miss it today. In college I was tall and kinda skinny. I weighed about 183. I managed to bulk up to 205 as a pro. I didn't have blazing speed, but I had pretty good speed with a 4.5 or 4.6 for the 40."

Ted Provost was born-and-raised in Navarre, Ohio. A three sports star at Fairless High School, Provost was starting cornerback for three years at Ohio State. An All-American as a senior, Provost intercepted 17 passes during his college career. He went on to play eight years of pro ball, including five as safety with the Canadian Football League Saskatchewan Rough Riders. Ted Provost is in the construction business and lives in Columbus, Ohio.

I'm a small town guy who grew up on a 30-acre farm in rural Northeast Ohio. We had both milk and beef cattle. My grandparents and my uncle had farms across the street.

It was fun growing up. I kinda miss it today, but I don't know if I could put the time in that they do. You've gotta milk the cows twice a day, or they go dry on you. My cousin runs my grandparents' farm and he also holds down a full-time job.

I went to Fairless High School which was a consolidation school. Kids from three towns went there. We lived about three miles from Navarre, which had a population of about 2,000. I think my graduation class numbered 144.

I ran track, played football and basketball. During the Summer I played baseball. Hot Stove League, or something like that.

I lettered in each sport for three years. In track, I ran the high and low hurdles as well as the 220-yard dash. I was a forward in basketball and played quarterback in football the last two years.

Actually, in a small school, once you get on the field you don't get off. I played defensive halfback. I also ran back kickoffs and punted.

We were a member of the Federal League. They were small schools, but some pretty good players like [quarterback] Cleve Bryant, who went to Ohio University, and [lineman] Dan Dierdorf who went to Michigan, then was an NFL standout for many years. He now does the Monday Night NFL game on television.

I didn't make All-County. Until schools started showing interest in me as a senior, I never thought about playing football in college. Basketball was my best sport.

I'd say there were about 10 schools interested in me, not as a quarterback but as a defensive back. I'd call me more of a running quarterback. I didn't have the greatest throwing arm.

I kinda narrowed it down to Michigan State, Ohio State and Ohio University. The Naval Academy was also after me.

I was leaning towards Ohio University, but I didn't want to make my decision until after the basketball season. Ohio U couldn't wait that long and backed out.

That left it between Michigan State and Ohio State. As a kid, I was a big Ohio State fan, especially in basketball with [John] Havlicek and [Jerry] Lucas.

Coach Bruce put in a good word for me. Coach [Lou] McCullough came down to see me. I didn't get to meet Woody Hayes until I came down to Columbus.

All the schools were interested in me as an athlete. They knew I was a good basketball player. They knew I had a lot of speed. They knew I didn't get a lot of publicity, coming from a small school. They knew I was an excellent student.

Some schools offered me only a half-scholarship. Ohio State offered a full ride. I was interested in engineering and Ohio State had an excellent engineering program.

My parents left it up to me to make a choice. It was done more out of a gut feeling. I was from Ohio and had been a big Ohio State fan since I was a kid.

I certainly enjoyed my visit to Michigan State. I even got to meet Bubba Smith who was still there.

I was recruited at the same time with Chuck Hutchison. Woody Hayes took us out to dinner at the Jai Alai. He basically took me for a drive and told me what position I was gonna play.

They called it wide-side defensive halfback. We always played our defense to the strength of the field. I always played to the wide side of the field. I was more of a cornerback.

Woody mentioned Paul Warfield. That was the position he played at Ohio State. An All-Pro wide receiver, Warfield didn't play much offense in college.

Ohio State was down a bit and Woody wanted to get back on top. He said he could do it with three straight strong recruiting classes.

His plan began with the group that included [All-American tackles] Dave Foley and Rufus Mayes. They were a year ahead of me.

My class included [fullback] Jim Otis, and [offensive guard] Tom Backhus. My class was followed by the super group that included Rex Kern.

I don't know if it was by design or what, but I lucked out. They threw three small-town kids together. Me, Chuck Hutchison and Alan Jack.

I'd heard of Chuck before we met. He was from Carrollton which is near Canton. I'd never heard of Alan. You were around the team most of the time.

Earle Bruce was my backfield coach in 1967 and Lou Holtz in '68. Dick Walker coached the defensive backs my senior year.

Lou knew the passing game, so he knew all the schemes. We had a lot more man-to-man coverage. We disguised our defenses so well that the opposition didn't know what we were gonna do, which is really what you have to do.

In 1967 we played a zone. We really didn't have the talent to even think about playing man-to-man. I intercepted seven passes as a sophomore, including three against Northwestern. Most of those came early in the season.

That was the year they started giving out the Buckeye Leaf. I got a bunch of 'em in the first three games. That's when they tagged me with the nickname 'The Tree.'

We started out slow but gained momentum and won our last four games. We finished at 6-3 and with a little luck it could have been 8-1. We had some real close games.

As a sophomore we scrimmaged against the freshmen. We know how talented they were. The week before our season opener, the freshmen were reading off cards. They scored two touchdowns against our first defense.

We had a drill where the freshmen backs would try to score against us. It was one-on-one. We'd plant our feet on the one yard line.

[John] Brockington and [Jack] Tatum would run over you. They were that strong. Tatum was a great high school running back, but when he came to Ohio State we were loaded at that position. So, they moved him to defense.

I'm digressing for a moment. Dave Brungard had been our top rusher in '67, but by the fourth or fifth game in 1968, he was third string. That was the talent level. Dave was a heck of a good player. He transferred to Alabama, was not only a starter but was elected offensive captain by his teammates.

Rex [Kern] would come up in that goal-line drill, side step so quick that you couldn't even touch him. Towards the end of the year, Coach

Bruce would offer an orange drink to anyone who would even touch Rex. He was an unbelieveable athlete.

Billy Long had been our starting quarterback in 1967. He alternated with Jerry Ersham, but Billy played most of the time. He had a good arm, was smart, but didn't have the mobility of Rex or Mace [soph Ron Maciejowski]. Nobody had Rex's mobility.

Mace had a better arm than Rex. He would have started at any other school in the country. No doubt about it. He bailed us out a couple of times in 1968 when Rex was hurt.

Lou Holtz was very demanding, yet he had his funny times. He insisted that you paid attention to detail and didn't screw up. He was very adamant about that.

When you're playing man-to-man you know what you're doing. There are different reads. You've got that man and that's it.

I was always as wide as the widest guy. That's against the wide receiver. I played 7-8 yards deep. In man-to-man, you're usually getting help somewhere. That's usually the free safety.

Sometimes we'd go man with two safeties. Sometimes if you're running a blitz, you've got no safety to help you.

When you're in a zone, there's a lot of little things you've got to read. You've got to know what drops you've got and who's helping you underneath. Stuff like that.

In 1967, the defensive backfield basically consisted of three seniors and a sophomore. That all changed in '68. Jack Tatum, Timmy Anderson and Mike Sensibaugh were sophomores. Me and Mike Polaski were both juniors.

We played together as a unit for the first time against Chuck Hixson, Jerry Levias and SMU. They came out firing from the locker room. By the time it was over, they threw 76 times. We had five interceptions.

All their passes were short. Short outs, quick cuts, quick pops up-the-middle. They really didn't have a running game. They came out with multiple formations but they didn't have a back in the backfield.

They were predictable to the point that we knew it was gonna be short passes. We were playing some man, but mostly zone. We tried to keep everything in front of us.

Levias caught something like 12 passes [actually it was 15]. He was a pure athlete, the best receiver we faced.

Woody just buttoned it down [the offense] in our second game against Oregon. We played well enough to win [21-6].

Woody pointed to Purdue for a year. In 1967, they scored at will against us. It was embarrassing. You don't forget it. Even while practicing against Oregon, we worked a little bit against Purdue.

I think one of the reasons we brought in Lou Holtz was because of his knowledge of the passing game. It really paid off against No.1-rated Purdue. We were so well-prepared. We mixed up our defenses on 'em. Tatum and I would switch assignments. I'd take the inside guy and he'd take the outside. Or we'd switch it around.

On the play I intercepted and ran 35 yards for a touchdown, [Purdue quarterback Mike] Phipps thought the outside guy was open. That meant I didn't have to cover anything deep.

It was a sideline pass. It was probably a 10-yard pass, but he threw it across the field. I'm playing the right side of the field. Our defense was called, so I didn't have to worry about anything deep. I'm just laying in the flat.

They had two wide receivers on the play. The flanker and the wide receiver were lined up on the same side. The outside guy ran a curl pattern. The inside guy ran an outcut.

They saw Tatum taking the inside guy so they thought the outside was open.

Phipps disguised things pretty well, but we practically knew what formation they were in, what they were gonna run. He basically threw it right at me. I was right there.

It happens so quick, you don't even think about it. You see it coming at you. It hits you right in the middle of the chest. You're off-and-running.

It was a 35-yard touchdown. It could have gone for 80 just as well. It was one of those plays where everybody's going the other way and you've got nothing in front of you but daylight.

That was my only touchdown in three years at Ohio State. It gave us a 6-0 lead. There was bedlam right after the TD. Everybody was jumping on me. I got up and threw the football into the stands.

I got the idea from Lou Holtz.

I think we watched films of Northwestern play Iowa a few weeks before. After every touchdown, they'd throw the ball into the stands. I guess Holtz thought it was pretty cool, so he suggested we [defensive backs] do it if we scored a touchdown.

After beating Purdue [13-0], we were in the national spotlight. We knew we had something special. We had just beaten the best team in the country.

Woody told us not to get too smug because once you're on top, everybody's gonna try to knock you off.

We didn't have the same intensity against Northwestern, Illinois and Michigan State. Thank goodness we had Mace. He came in after Rex was hurt and bailed us out.

Even with several defensive starters out of the lineup against Illinois, we breezed to an easy 24-0 lead at halftime. Then the roof fell in and it was tied.

I really wasn't involved the second half. The ball was on the other side of the field. All you're doing is chasing. They're knocking off 5, 6 yards at a crack marching down the field.

You've got to give Illinois credit. They kept hitting away at our weakness. We were deeper offensively than we were defensively. We were deepest in the secondary.

I was basically healthy the entire season, but I hurt my foot in practice for the Rose Bowl and played only the first quarter.

You work so hard to get there and then all of a sudden you get hurt. Actually, I'd missed a couple of days of practice. My foot got better and I resumed practice. Southern Cal was marching down to our goal line. They didn't score a touchdown. I think they had to settle for a field goal.

I was in the end zone and it just popped. It was a tear in the arch of the foot. I couldn't push off.

Defensively, we were much smaller than Southern Cal. They were huge, but we were quicker. Our quickness, our speed, really neutralized O.J. [Simpson] and that massive offensive line.

We spent so much time preparing for him. It was a relief to know we could even be on the same field with those guys. I wasn't out there when O.J. broke his 80-yard touchdown run.

But I saw enough of him while I was in. He was real deceptive. He wasn't a real punishing runner when you hit him. He had a real gliding motion. We played against Ron Johnson of Michigan. He was more of a slasher and a punishing runner.

I made a couple of tackles on him. No doubt about it, O.J. was the best running back I faced in college. He was scary.

I'd like to brag a little bit about our defensive backfield. Tatum, Anderson, Sensibaugh and I were named All-Americans during our college career. Only reason Polaski didn't make it was because four of us did. He really deserved the honor.

Jack Tatum was a quiet guy. Never said much. He just went about his business. He was a smart guy. He was a super running back in high school who was switched to defense. He picked up the system real easy.

He was a punishing tackler. There were a lot of times our opponents would throw a little dump pass to a running back. Jack would just annihilate the guy. The next time the guy's going out for a pass, he's not even looking for the ball. He's looking for Jack.

Timmy Anderson was a lot like Jack. I don't think he was as quick, but he was a great hitter. He played our closed side halfback. A lot of teams tried to run to our closed side because we just put our strength to the wide side of the field.

Mike Sensibaugh was a great athlete with great hands. He had the ability to read the quarterback. He was really a smart player that way.

Mike Polaski could play any defensive backfield position, even though he never played Tatum's 'Rover back' spot in a game. Jack was really more like a linebacker. Mike wasn't that big. What about Ted Provost?

I was tall and kinda skinny. I weighed about 183. I managed to bulk up to 205 as a pro.

I didn't have blazing speed, but I had good speed. Did a 4.5 or 4.6 for the 40. I was a good open-field tackler, but not the punishing type like Jack Tatum.

I was pretty good at reading the quarterback. I'm looking at his eyes. You read a little bit through the linemen. You can tell whether they're setting up. If you're playing safety it's different. You can read through the guards. Where I was playing you took your step backwards and read the quarterback.

I didn't play safety until I got to the pros. I could have been playing there if Sensibaugh wasn't there. I was probably a little quicker.

My high at Ohio State was winning the Rose Bowl, being on that national championship team. My most disappointing moment came in our last game in 1969. My last game.

Man, we were so much better in 1969. We steamrolled over everyone going into that Michigan game, the final game of the season. We were unbeaten and headed for a second straight national title.

Maybe we left it all on the field the week before against Purdue. We manhandled Purdue. Why does something like that happen? I still don't know.

It was totally unbelieveable in the locker room after the game. Nobody said a word. We had to drive from Ann Arbor to Detroit to get the plane.

The worst thing for me was that I was a senior. I wouldn't be back for revenge the next year. It was over with. It's a taste that never seems to go away.

Chapter 10

HE GOT HIS KICKS

JIM ROMAN, NO. 52, CENTER/KICKER
6-0, 211 Pounds, 20 Years Old, Senior.

Ohio State Photo Archives

"I scored nine points with my right leg. I kicked two field goals and three extra points. Not bad for a fat kid from Canton."

Jim Roman outscored Heisman Trophy winner O.J. Simpson in the 1969 Rose Bowl.

Jim Roman was born-and-raised in Canton, Ohio. A two-sports star at Canton McKinley High School, he was All-Ohio and All-American in football and All-Conference in baseball. A three-year letterman at Ohio State, Jim Roman was the Buckeyes' most consistent kicker during the 1968 season. After a year as Graduate Assistant to head coach Woody Hayes, he accepted a teaching position at New Philadelphia [Ohio] High School. He has been there ever since...almost 30 years. Jim Roman has served as both assistant and head football coach.

Everyone knows that O.J. Simpson was 'all world' in college and in the pros. He was college football's top player and the first NFL running back to gain 2,000 yards in a single season. But how many people remember who outscored O.J. in the 1969 Rose Bowl? Not many I'll bet. O.J. had that memorable 80-yard TD run in the first half. That's six points.

I scored nine points with my right leg. I kicked two field goals and three extra points. Not bad for a fat kid from Canton.

Growing up in Ohio, Henry Vafides and I were the best of friends. We lived a block from each other. My grandparents came to the United States from Romania and his from Greece. We both played on the McKinley football team. I was our center. Henry was defensive tackle and place kicker.

As a senior, Henry scored 50 points as a kicker. He went to Cincinnati on a full ride, but he got into an accident with a lawn mower and cut off the toes of his kicking foot.

We spent a lot of time during the summer kicking. I'd hold the ball for Henry and he'd hold the ball for me. He was serious about it. I was really foolin' around.

McKinley and Massillon went into the last game of the 1964 season both unbeaten at 9-0. They finished 10-0 and first in the state. We finished 9-1 and second.

Until the Massillon game we had only one scare. We beat Canton Lincoln 10-7, on Henry's field goal. During the season my coach let me try three extra point attempts. I made one and had one blocked. I never got off the third kick because of a bad snap from center.

I was second team All-Ohio and third team All-American my senior year. I think it would have been different had we beaten Massillon. Massillon center John Muhlbach finished one spot ahead of me in State and on the Parade Magazine All-American team.

Funny thing, we would be teammates at Ohio State and again he'd be one spot ahead of me. I had about 30 college offers. I visited Michigan, Michigan State, Ohio State, Illinois, Pittsburgh, Notre Dame, Navy.

I might have gone to Navy had I not done so poorly on the math section of the test. They wanted me to go to a prep school in Arizona, but I didn't want to do that. I scored high in everything else except math. They thought I could make it at Navy. Prep school didn't appeal to me.

As it got down closer to making my final decision, I still hadn't made up my mind. I was still being kinda selfish, riding the gravy train, wanting to take all those trips.

My first visit was to Michigan. When I came back home I told my Dad, 'Cancel the rest of the trips. That place is out of this world. That's where I'm going.' It sounds funny hearing me say that now. My Dad just looked at me and said, 'Slow down. Slow down. You've got a lot more trips to make.'

73

I went to Illinos and went out with Dick Butkus. Watched him drink beer all weekend. That was entertaining as hell, drinking a pitcher at a time. But I liked the school real well. Went to Notre Dame. Loved it. I was 17 years old. I suppose I was overwhelmed.

Don Nehlen was my high school coach in my senior year. Then he went to Bowling Green. Bowling Green wanted 4 or 5 kids from our class. Coach Nehlen got madder than hell with me and my cousin Nick because we didn't even want to visit the school.

I asked him, 'What bowl does Bowling Green go to?'

He said 'Grantland Rice Bowl.'

Then I asked, 'What bowl does Ohio State go to?'

He said, 'Alright, you might go down there and just sit. I promise you when you come up here you'll start as a sophomore.'

I said, 'Well, I'd rather sit on a Rose Bowl team.'

Nick was 6-4 and I was 6-0. He weighed 221 to my 211. He was a defensive end. We both went to Ohio State and were members of the national championship team.

Lou McCullough and Hugh Hindman were the guys who recruited us for Ohio State. They came to see us play three times. They approached us after the second game of the season.

There were 11 guys from our high school team who got full rides. It was probably Woody as much as anyone who made the difference. When Woody came to my home and talked to my Mom and Dad, he didn't talk about football. He talked about the educational opportunities at Ohio State.

I was from Ohio. I was an offensive lineman so Woody's famed 'three yards and a cloud of dust' certainly appealed to me. Columbus was only two hours from home. My family could see the games.

Another deciding factor was the fact that I got married to my childhood sweetheart before my freshman year of college. I needed to stay closer to home.

She stayed at home with her parents the first year. Then she came down to Columbus. We lived at Buckeye Village my last three years. It was a housing complex for married students. In fact, when we went to the Rose Bowl there were nine guys on the team who were married. Their wives also made the trip at the University's expense.

There were 33 guys in our recruiting class but only a handful of us started when we got to the Rose Bowl—Foley, Mayes, Stier, Worden, Urbanik, Muhlbach. It was the Year of the Sophomore.

I had three goals when I came to Ohio State. I wanted to make the traveling squad as a sophomore, earn a letter as a junior and be a starter my senior season.

As a sophomore, I was backup center to two-time All-American Ray Pryor. I didn't feel bad about that. I made the traveling team and actually played in three games when Pryor went down. I played enough to earn a varsity letter. We finished 4-5. It really wasn't that bad a team. We were a few points from being real good.

Michigan State was out of this world and we gave them a real battle [losing 11-8]. We lost to Illinois by one point [10-9], to Iowa by four [14-10] and by seven to Texas Christian [14-7] and Indiana [7-0].

The following Spring, I went into practice listed as first string center. But all of a sudden there's staff changes and John Muhlbach is playing ahead of me.

When Muhlbach came to Ohio State, he was a defensive end and defensive back. But when Earl Bruce, his coach at Massillon, was switched from defense to coach the guards and centers, John became first team.

To be honest, I was a little bit upset and disappointed. Don't get me wrong. John Muhlbach is a great guy. We called him 'The Deacon.' He was in the Fellowship of Christian Athletes. He did all the team prayers.

At times, I was sorta rough around-the-edges. If I got kicked in the shins, I'd let out an expletive. Woody would be all over me. I wasn't the All-American boy John was. He was a hell of a player. I've always respected him. We remain good friends. It became apparent to me that I had better do something to get some more playing time. In practice we didn't go first team, second team.

We went what we call 'Half Line.' You took the right guard, center and the entire left side against a half of line of defense and a set of backs. And vice versa.

We always needed two centers and two sets of guards. I made myself learn the guard assignments. I was backup center and backup long snapper. I thought the more I could do, the more I might play.

I lettered as a junior and started against Northwestern when Muhlbach was injured. During the Winter of 1967, I began working out with the kickers. Back in those days, we had only two Universal weight machines. We didn't have the 10,000-square foot weight rooms with machines and strength coaches that they have today.

The weight room was in French Field House. The kickers used to work out on the baseball field that was inside a screen at one end of the field house.

Having done a little kicking in high school, it's not like I was starting from scratch. When you're looking for a kicker you don't necessarily look for a big guy or a strong guy.

You look for your athletes because it's a timing sort of thing. I was a good enough athlete. I couldn't play basketball at McKinley because I was too slow and too short. But I was a good football player. I was a good baseball player.

There was a full field of kickers and during the season, Woody would try 'em all. Dick Merryman started out as the No.1 kicker. He was a walk-on. All he did was kick.

We also had Jim Opperman, who was an offensive lineman, Larry Zelina and me. There's probably someone else I've forgotten about.

I was a straight-up kicker. We all were. In those days I don't remember seeing a sidewinder [soccer-style kicker].

Our kicking coach was Ernie Godfrey who coached Lou Groza back in the 1940s. The only films I watched of kicking were of Ernie working with Groza. It was a two-step approach.

We won our first two games in 1968 and I never got a chance to kick. Our third game was against No.1 ranked Purdue. Opperman kicked off and almost missed the ball. He hit a divot and darn near missed the ball.

The first half was scoreless. As I recall, Zelina missed two field goals.

We beat Purdue, 13-0. After we missed our first extra point attempt, I went up to Woody. 'Coach, is it my turn yet? Everybody in the world has missed so far.'

Woody said, 'Okay. It's your turn next time. You're up next.'

After we scored the second touchdown, I already had on my kicking shoe. I ran out onto the field before the team lined up. Before we had a chance to call for a time out.

Sure I was excited. I could have been kicking in a closet. I don't know if I did it intentionally or what. I was completely unaware of the surroundings. I looked at Muhlbach's butt and Billy Long's hands. The timing was perfect. The kick was good.

Man, I'm feelin' real good as I run off the field. Woody just gave me this look. He didn't say a word. I knew what he was thinking. In that situation you go for two points.

But then again, I wouldn't have gotten the chance now would I?

My nickname was Pork. Someone came over to me and said, 'Pork, Hugo wants you on the phone.' Hugo was coach [Hugh] Hindman who was up in the press box.

He said, 'Nice job you egghead. You know damn well we should have gone for two.'

I said, 'It was my turn and the stadium was gonna have to fall down to keep me off the field.'

I didn't have a super leg but against Michigan State I barely missed a 50-yarder. I never even practiced a field goal from that distance.

It was at the end of the first half. Woody looked around and said, 'It's gonna be a long field goal.'

I piped up, 'Coach, I can kick it into the end zone. That's what your punter is gonna do anyway. I can kick it in the end zone.'

Woody said, 'Just make sure the damn thing goes in the end zone. Don't get the damn thing blocked.'

I hit it. It was towards the open end of the stadium. It went under the bar, but out of the end zone. It was only a few feet short of clearing the crossbar. Surprised the heck out of me.

I had two perfect games during the season. Against Michigan to clinch the Big Ten championship and against Southern Cal in the Rose Bowl.

In our 50-14 destruction of Michigan, I had a 32-yard field goal and five extra points.

We left Columbus for California and the Rose Bowl on December 20. Woody worked our butts off. We had two-a-days for two weeks. That means middle guard Jim Stillwagon beating the heck out of me for two weeks.

By the time we got to California, I was physically beat.

Two days before the Rose Bowl, we had a kick-off to see who would do the kicking against Southern Cal. I was terrible. I'm just exhausted.

Larry Zelina hadn't practiced for a week, resting his bruised ribs. He's fresh and just pounding the hell out of the ball. Early in the game, Zelina gets popped. He can't stand up straight. He misses two field goals.

I went up to Woody in the second quarter and said 'Coach, Z's hurt. He can't even stand up straight.' As it turned out, he suffered three cracked ribs.

Woody said, 'All right, you take the rest of 'em.'

Again, I probably wouldn't have gotten in there to kick if I hadn't said something. A 32-yard field goal tied it at 10-10 with only three seconds left in the first half. A 25-yarder gave us a 13-10 lead in the third period. I also kicked three extra points.

When Muhlbach went down in the fourth quarter, I went in at center. He got chopped on a punt and suffered a broken leg.

I was in during our last touchdown drive, but I wasn't exactly a hero. I missed my block badly, the middle guard stepped right around me and I sorta got lost. Fortunately, Rex [Kern] got rid of it fast enough and found Ray Gillian for a touchdown. No one seemed to notice my missed assignment.

Even before the Rose Bowl showdown, we felt in our hearts we were No.1. They had the best player in college football, but we had a lot of guys who must have been No.2.

In a three-year span, we'd gone from 4-5 to 10-0. Unbeaten. Untied. Number One is definitely better.

We had so much talent. We had so much depth. Both offensively and defensively.

Sports Illustrated named our 1968 team as the best of that decade. And to think I had a part in that achievement. Sometimes it's still hard to believe.

Chapter 11

IT JUST HAPPENED

MARK STIER, NO.54, OUTSIDE LINEBACKER
6-0, 225 Pounds, 21 Years Old, Senior.

"From a personal standpoint, the Iowa game probably stands out because I had a couple of interceptions. I picked off a pass in the flat. I tipped a ball then caught it in the end zone for a touchback."

Mark Stier was born-and-raised in Louisville, Ohio. A three-year-letterman at Louisville High School, he earned All-Ohio honors as a senior. Stier was a three-year starter at Ohio State as well as an Academic All-American. He was named the Buckeyes' Most Valuable Player as a senior in a vote of his fellow players. Despite a shoulder injury which labeled him as a question mark, Mark Stier not only started against Southern Cal in the Rose Bowl but played an inspiring game on defense. He is an executive for Worthington Industries and now resides in Columbus, Ohio.

Ohio State had a terrible season in 1966. By terrible I mean we lost five of nine games. Everyone wanted Woody Hayes' scalp. I can remember a small plane circling Ohio Stadium pulling a banner. The banner said something like 'Goodbye Woody.' And just think. Two years later, the same Woody Hayes wins the national championship.

As a kid I didn't dream of playing at Ohio State. It just happened. In high school, I was a pulling guard for awhile. I also played tight end. But I was always a linebacker. I was 6-foot and weighed 200-205.

My buddy was a great running back named Bob Gladieux. Bob and I had an agreement. We would go to the same college. It was one of those boyhood kind of things. It sounded good when we made that sacred pledge. It didn't turn out that way.

We were both recruited. We went on a visit to Notre Dame together. Ohio State was really interested in Bob and offered him a full-ride. But they showed absolutely no interest in me.

I was really thinking in terms of the military academies, the Ohio Conference, meaning teams like Baldwin-Wallace, Wittenberg, Otterbein. Also Kent State of the Mid-American Conference, simply because my coach at Louisville High School had taken a job at Kent as assistant to Leo Stange.

Gladieux decided to go to Notre Dame and had a fine career there. By turning down Ohio State, that meant a scholarship was available, but at the time it wouldn't have done me any good. Ohio State wasn't knocking at my door.

But then a crazy thing happened.

Woody Hayes came to our high school football banquet. He was the main speaker. As Woody watched the films of Bob [Gladieux], I kept popping up. And to make a long story very short, I got the last scholarship to Ohio State that year.

I liked Woody Hayes from the beginning. He was very dynamic. I can still remember him coming to my house. He probably spent two hours with my parents and about 15 minutes with me. He had them pretty well convinced that's where I should go academically. It wasn't a hard sell.

My Dad was a funeral director in Louisville. It's a small town of about 5,000. It was a one-man business. My Dad wanted to see me play in college, but he couldn't travel too far for a game.

Even if I had wanted to go to Notre Dame with Bob, I wouldn't have done it. South Bend, Indiana was too far away. Kent State seemed like the logical choice. But then Woody came to our banquet.

I was a three-year starter. I had a very good sophomore year, in fact, I was

Class of '68

named Sophomore of the Year on a very poor team. As a junior, I had a knee injury but it wasn't serious enough to miss a lot of games. I know I missed the Michigan game. I played gimpy a couple of games. We started slowly, finished hot, and went 6-3 in 1967.

We went into the '68 season a question mark. We had a great sophomore class coming up but we really didn't know how good we could be. We were either a year away, or it might be something very special.

I called the defensive signals since I was a sophomore. Dirk Worden was elected defensive captain my senior year, but Dirk got hurt. As a result, I was appointed captain.

The defensive setup came in from the sidelines, but I called the automatics. We played a 5-2. I was wide side. We always believed in flip-flopping the defensive sets.

I loved playing defense because there was always something going on. There was always a stunt. Very seldom did we sit. We just weren't big enough to just sit and catch people. Things were always happening.

The guys were quick and fast. We'd get there and pursue. We did a lot of running as a team. We ran sprint-after-sprint. We were probably one of the best conditioned teams ever.

Lou McCullough was our defensive coordinator. He would never tell us 'Okay, we're gonna run 30 sprints.' You'd run until he decides you've run enough. You might run 15 sprints. You might run 25 sprints. You might run 40 sprints [all 40 yards each], like we did the week of the Iowa game.

At the time I thought Lou was crazy, but it paid off. Except for O.J.'s 80-yard run in the Rose Bowl, and that was basically a case of over pursuit, we kept the other team's best running back contained.

Jim Stillwagon was our great middle guard. He made the linebackers look good. Jim was 240, extremely quick and extremely strong. They had to double-team him to keep him out.

Stillwagon was always in the middle. The tackle, the ends. Everybody flip-flopped. The hash marks were different back then. They were set closer to the sidelines.

Woody's philosophy was to put bigger, stronger people into the sidelines and lighter, quicker people to the open field because that's where they primarily ran sweeps. He would always say, 'The sideline is that extra 12th man on the field. Let 'em run to the sidelines.'

Most of the time, the linebackers played zone. It was a short zone. It was primarily a hook zone, but occasionally you'd catch a back out of the backfield, or a tight end man-to-man.

I had Jack Tatum out on my flank. He always was on the wide side, so a lot of the teams ran away from him, to the short side. With Tatum behind me, you didn't have to worry about getting outrun.

We opened up the '68 season with SMU and Chuck Hixson. We knew it would be pass...pass...pass. It was hard to get a feel on how good we were even after we won the season opener.

It really wasn't until the third game with Purdue that things really started coming together.

We could have folded a couple of times, but we kept hanging in. The longer

80

the game went you realized, 'Hey, you can play with these guys...they're not that good.' We upset 'em, 13-0.

The team grew closer as the season progressed. We became very close. Rex [Kern] and Jim [Otis] were getting a lot of press, but no one got swell-headed. There was no racial problem at the time race riots were spilling onto the streets. Everyone was really focused. There were no superstars. No heroes.

No.1 Ohio State and No.2 Southern Cal in the Rose Bowl was a Cinderella deal. Winner-take-all to decide the national championship.

It was the job of the coaches to keep us focused and they did a good job of it. We practiced hard. We were pretty tired of hitting each other. By the time the game was finally played, we looked forward to hitting someone else. The game was actually easier than the practice.

We didn't go to the Rose Bowl Parade. We didn't get to do a lot of the things that maybe some of the other teams do when they go to California. We were accustomed to playing in front of big crowds. Once the game starts you lose track of whether there's 103,000 or 1,300 people in the stands.

But what I do remember is the large contingency of Ohio State people. They all had those shaker things. It was just a sea of red. It was beautiful.

I can remember going up on the hotel elevator after the game. After all the crowds. My parents, my girlfriend and her parents had come out. But once I'm finally back in my room it was a real letdown.

It was like 'Is this it? Is this the end of it?' It was over. I had played my last game at Ohio State.

From a personal standpoint, the Iowa game probably stands out because I had a couple of interceptions that game. The weather was horrible. I picked off a pass in the flat. I tipped a ball and then caught it in the end zone for a touchback.

I started the season at 225. I finished it about 210.

Offensively, Southern Cal was huge. They looked like clones of each other. We were small even back then. It will sound like a cliche when I say we played like giants.

Chapter 12

ALL IN THE FAMILY

DIRK WORDEN, NO.56, LINEBACKER
6-0, 198 Pounds, 22 Years Old, Senior.

photo courtesy Dirk Worden

"I was really looking forward to my senior season. As a junior, I led the team with 130 tackles and was named Most Valuable Player. I made second team All Big Ten and got Honorable Mention All American."

Dirk Worden was born-and-raised in Lorain, Ohio. A two-sports star at Lorain Clearview High School, he went the prep school route before attracting the attention of Ohio State. A three-year letterman at Ohio State, he led the Buckeyes in tackles as a junior and was named team MVP. Named co-captain his senior year, Worden was injured for most of the season. A one-time teacher, Dirk Worden is now executive director in charge of training for 18,000 construction laborers in the state of Ohio. He lives in Huron.

I was born to play football. It's in the genes.

My Dad played in the National Football League. My older brother played professionally for 7-8 years in Canada.

We lived-and-breathed football for as long as I can remember. That's the way it was. My Dad never pushed his sons to play. He never bragged.

But my Mom let us know early on there was no better football player in the country than my father. She kinda promoted him in that way.

Both my Dad and brother are named Jim. Dad played his college ball at Waynesburg [Pa,] College. He was a defensive halfback. About my height. Weighed 180-185.

He told me he played against The Seven Blocks of Granite. Vince Lombardi and those guys at Fordham. In fact, my Dad was named to Fordham's all-opponent team.

Back in 1945, he was good enough to play for the old Cleveland Rams of the National Football League. They won the championship that year. He was a 29-year old rookie.

Unfortunately, he played only one season of pro ball. He tore up his knee against the Chicago Bears, shagging punts at Soldier Field at the end of the year. For years after college, Dad played semi-pro ball around Lorain, Cleveland, Pittsburgh. He worked at U.S. Steel weekdays and played on weekends.

Finally, a scout from the Cleveland Rams saw him play.

My brother went to Wittenberg and was actually drafted by the Dallas Cowboys, but he went up to Canada and played for the Saskatchewan Rough Riders. He was 6-2 or 6-3 and weighed 225-230. He played tight end. I think he played up there 7-8 years. Ironically, all three of us had our football careers ended with knee injuries. Talk about coincidence?

Maybe I'm wrong, but I don't think what we did has been duplicated. My Dad played on the NFL championship team. My brother played on the Canadian Grey Cup championship team. I played on the 1968 NCAA championship team.

I played three years of high school football at Clearview High School. It's a small school on the outskirts of Lorain. I played offensive end and linebacker. When I graduated, I was 5-11 and 175.

Players at small schools didn't get much publicity. I was All-Conference, but never even got All-Ohio mention.

As I said, I was small when I graduated. My brother was about that size when he graduated from high school. He really started growing after that.

Naturally, I thought the same thing would happen to me. Jim is four years older.

At that point, I hadn't heard from any big schools.

Class of '68

I had it on my mind that I'd spurt. Back in those days, a lot of kids were going to prep schools. Jim Grabowski stuck in my mind. He was small when he graduated from high school, went to a prep school, gained some height and weight. He got a shot to play at Illinois. Eventually, he moved into the NFL.

My high school coach knew a coach at a prep school in West Virginia. I went to Greenbrier Prep School, played in that league. I grew a little and made All-Conference.

At the time I was at prep school, an Ohio State recruiter visited Lorain Clearview. He was looking at a real good halfback named Leroy Peyton.

My coach said 'If you like him, you'd better take a look at this other kid at Greenbrier.' He called Greenbrier and my films were sent to Woody Hayes.

I was invited to Columbus. I was really an after thought. Ohio State was looking for some kids from Northern Ohio. Peyton and I both went to Ohio State, but he left after a few years.

Mine was the strongest recruiting class Ohio State had in awhile. Starting with my class, Ohio State made a conscious effort to put some numbers back into the program.

Now I can say it. Ohio State was always my dream. I can remember sitting in front of the TV set. It was a small set back in 1954, about 12 inches. I'm just a little guy and I'm yelling and screaming, watching Ohio State play in the Rose Bowl.

I told my parents that someday I was gonna play at Ohio State. No joke. I didn't tell too many others. But honestly, I didn't know how I was gonna do it. I just felt I would, that it was my destiny. Sure I was elated when Ohio State showed interest in me and then actually offered me a scholarship. But at the same time, I really wasn't surprised.

I played quite a bit as a sophomore. I probably started half the games. I can remember starting against Michigan State in 1966. They were No. 1 in the country. They had a tremendous team.

We had 'em beat, 8-3, until the last three minutes of the game. They put together a real good drive in the pouring rain to go up 9-8, then ran a two-point conversion.

We really weren't that bad a team. We lost a lot of close games and finished at 4-5. We really became a good football team in my junior year [1967]. We won our last four and finished at 6-3. It could have been 8-1 with a few breaks. I believe we set the stage for the next four years.

By the end of the year, we put the hammer down on Michigan and that was at their place. By the end of the year, we were pretty tough to handle.

By my senior year, we knew we were gonna be good. Not just because of the super sophomore class. We practiced against those kids when they were freshmen. We saw that raw talent.

You could just feel the whole atmosphere, just feel the whole thing shift. From a defensive standpoint, we were small.

Everybody on the team could run. I mean we were in excellent physical shape, especially defensively. Lou McCullough was our defensive coordinator. His philosophy was if you can get to the ball and hit, you can play for him.

That's exactly the way they coached us and we were quite successful. The defense was good enough to get the job done, game-in-and-game-out.

84

I played at about 195. I was what they call a short-side linebacker, which was a linebacker to the side of the field that was closest to the sidelines. Wherever the wide side of the field was, I was on the opposite side.

I was really looking forward to my senior season. As a junior, I led the team with 130 tackles and was named Most Valuable Player. I made second team All-Big Ten and got some honorable mention All-American.

I knew I had some work ahead of me, such as building my strength. I sure couldn't do anything about my size. Between my junior and senior years, Ohio State installed the old Universal gym. Those were the first wave of your true weight lifting machines. You had eight different stations on the same machine. Bench press. Knee press. Pull-down press, etc. At the time, that equipment was state-of-the-art.

Without weights I probably would have been a natural 175 pounds. With weights, however, I was able to bulk up to a solid 195-196.

I had decent speed, about 4.7 for the 40. I wasn't a burner, but I was quick enough for linebacker. I was also a big-time hitter.

I also had it in the back of my mind that I wanted to take a crack at pro ball, if not the NFL then the Canadian Football League which was a faster game.

During the winter of 1967, the team elected Dave Foley and me as co-captains for the next year, Dave for the offensive unit and me for defense.

I couldn't wait for the '68 season to begin.

In the opener against SMU, I pulled a hamstring and played on it most of the game. The next game was against Oregon. I only played towards the end. I just tried to get it loosened up a little bit. Until then, I had never been injured.

I felt good enough to start against Purdue the next game. Purdue was unbeaten and ranked No.1. They really hammered us the year before [41-6].

They had some great players, four or five, All-Americans like Leroy Keyes and Mike Phipps. They had great big people, especially on offense.

I was doing just fine until the second quarter. We were covering man-to-man. I had somebody coming out of the backfield. He caught a pass for a very short gain, maybe 2 or 3 yards.

I'm trying to cut him off to the sideline. He stops. I plant my foot and heard it pop. It just tore up my knee. I could feel it. I got sick to my stomach.

It was just the way I planted my foot. I planted it and tried to turn back towards the center of the field. I could tell something was very wrong, very bad. I tried to stay in for a few more plays. Then, I went to the sidelines.

They took me into the locker room, taped my knee. I started feeling a little bit better. I came to the sideline and Woody asked me if I wanted to go back in. I said I'd like to give it a try.

I went in. I had man-to-man coverage again. I went to plant my leg, to try to stay with the Purdue player. The knee just gave out. I knew I was gonna hurt the team at that point, so I took myself out. That was basically the end of my season.

Arthroscopic surgery was unheard of back then. They knew if I had major surgery I'd be gone for the rest of the season. They really didn't know the full extent of my injury until I did undergo surgery right after the Rose Bowl. It ended up being torn cartilage as well as some ligament damage.

Class of '68

In my heart, I thought I'd be able to play again. Maybe sit out for two or three games. Once the swelling went down, I'd start working on weights.

After the Purdue game, Lou McCullough came over to me. We're hugging. He's crying. 'We shut 'em out. I can't believe we shut 'em out. We're gonna get your knee better now.'

The next day I couldn't even walk. It was really blown up big.

I wanted to play. I wanted to contribute. As an athlete, you might have little injuries here-and-there. But when you have a major injury like that, you know right now it's gonna take a lot to get back.

But I was tickled pink that we had beaten Purdue.

I was never a holler type of guy until I was hurt. That's the only thing I could offer. I was always a quiet guy. I led by example. When I went to Ohio State, that's how Woody felt. You should practice what you preach.

By the amount of CCs they drained from my knee, they thought it was pretty bad but not terrible. They thought I might be able to return by the end of the year with no problems.

I started lifting weights, and towards the end of the year it got to the point where I started playing a little. I played a bit against Wisconsin and Michigan in the last game of the season.

By then, I'd say I was about 50 percent back. But that was pretty damn good compared to what I had been after the Purdue game.

I dressed for all the games. They wanted me dressed even though I wasn't going to play. Even the away games. At times, I felt like a mascot.

I was like a relief pitcher who was never gonna properly participate although my knee got better by the end of the year. As I said, I played a little. It felt great. Everybody likes to contribute. It's one thing to offer verbal support, especially when you've been a fairly large contributor for the past 2-3 years. Then, all of a sudden, you're relegated to just cheerleading. It's pretty hard to take.

Doug Adams took my place. He was a sophomore who went on to a real good career at Ohio State. He played 2-3 years with the Cincinnati Bengals.

I tried to help anyway I could. That included giving Doug some tips. I was happy he was there. I couldn't do the job. Much of it is learning by doing.

We buried Michigan, 50-14, so they really didn't need my help. But I got in for a few plays. It was a sentimental gesture on Woody's part, one I very much appreciated.

In fact, they gave me the game ball. I still have it. It meant a great deal to me because it was from all the guys.

I think it was Mike Polaski—junior defensive back—who gave me the ball. I can't remember the exact words, but I can remember I wasn't able to say much. It was very emotional.

By the end of December we flew to California to meet O.J. Simpson and Southern Cal in the Rose Bowl. My condition had improved. I was taking part in full-contact drills.

Maybe I wasn't 100 percent back, but it felt good. I could get in a game and not be a handicap. I could contribute. We were unbeaten, untied, No.1 and I really hadn't played a major role in that wonderful season.

Several days before the Rose Bowl, I injured my knee during practice. They ran an end sweep. I ran towards the sidelines, planted again to try to make a tackle. It just gave out. My knee was pretty bad. It had gotten to the point where it was pretty spongy.

Once I got hurt again, it was pretty much over for me. They even asked me if I wanted to dress for the Rose Bowl. I wanted to dress because I wanted to go out onto the field for the coin toss. I felt I had earned that right.

We had the game pretty well in hand in the fourth quarter. We were ahead 21-10 at that point. Lou McCullough came over to me. He asked me to go in. He told me, 'You deserve to play some in the Rose Bowl...just to say you played.'

So, I went in and played maybe a couple of series. I was just gimping around, really. Just trying to keep people from running into me. But, at least, I could say I played in the Rose Bowl.

It was such a great feeling just going onto that field. There was a lot of emotion. We tackled O.J. on one play and I was close enough where I managed to fall on the pile.

It was kinda memorable. I wasn't crying. I was happy. I was happy for the guys. I just didn't feel like I was a real participant, at least physically.

I can remember the guys hugging and that. I was hugging some guys. I was very happy that we had accomplished what we had as a team.

I remember Larry Catuzzi coming over to me in the locker room. He had been an assistant coach at Ohio State. He came to the Rose Bowl, came over to me and said 'You helped set the stage for this, being a solid leader for these guys.' That made me feel good.

We flew home the next day. I went right into the hospital. They had a big rally at St. John Arena for the team which I missed. A couple of my teammates came up to see me and offer their support. In a span of only three years, we'd come full cycle from our 4-5 record in 1966 to our 10-0 dream season in 1968.

In 1966 they were flying 'Goodbye, Woody' banners over Ohio Stadium. We had heard about him being given a win-or-else ultimatum. I don't know if that's a fact. There was a lot of turmoil in the program.

I think the program started turning around with that tough loss to Michigan State in 1966. It gained momentum in my junior season. I'm convinced that as good as the sophomore class was in 1968, we wouldn't have had that same kind of season had not the tone been set in 1967.

I didn't feel bitter back then because of my injury. It was one of those things that happened. The 'WHAT IFS' never entered my mind. You just have to go on with your life.

Chapter 13

QUICK AND POWERFUL

TOM BACKHUS, NO 57, OFFENSIVE GUARD
5-11, 207 Pounds, 19 Years Old, Junior.

Ohio State Photo Archives

"The only thing Woody Hayes ever promised me was a good education. Woody cared about us going to school and graduating. That was really the promise."

Tom Backhus was born-and-raised in Cincinnati, Ohio. A three-year varsity letterman at Moeller High School, he was not only first team All-Ohio but first team All-American as selected by Parade Magazine. A two-year starter at Ohio State, Backhus pursued a career in coaching with stops at Tampa, Iowa State, Wisconsin, Notre Dame, and Air Force Academy where he served as offensive coordinator. Tom Backhus now owns and operates his guest ranch, "Four Eagle Ranch," in Vail, Colorado.

As a kid growing up in Cincinnati, Ohio, my dream was to play football at Xavier. My mother was secretary to the university president. I went to every Xavier football game.

When I was being recruited by bigger schools, my aspirations became bigger. Ultimately, it boiled down to Michigan or Ohio State. I remember when I visited Michigan, it just didn't seem as personal as it had during my visit to Columbus.

I think the deciding factor was Dave Foley. I stayed with him during my recruiting trip. He was a freshman at Ohio State and I was a high school senior.

I knew Dave. I played against him in high school. He'd gone to Roger Bacon which was one of the big, powerful schools in the Cincinnati area before Moeller came along.

I played three years under Gerry Faust, who later became head coach at Notre Dame. In fact, I left the Air Force Academy to become an assistant at Notre Dame. But that's another story.

Dave was not only a very good football player, he was an excellent student. He graduated in four years and two quarters from a five-year program. He played for the New York Jets, then came back to school and graduated. Dave was the offensive captain on our national championship team. I guess I've always admired and respected him.

The only thing that Lou McCullough or Woody Hayes ever promised me was a good education. Woody cared about us going to school and graduating. That was really the promise.

I was born an optimist. I always believed that everything was gonna go right for me. I guess I realized I faced a challenge by going to Ohio State.

I believed I was going to play. I believe my strong point was my competitiveness. It was probably the best thing going for me. I had a good work ethic.

I was strong. I lifted weights in high school. I weighed 187, but I bench-pressed over 400 pounds. I think we probably had 10 kids on the team who pressed 300 pounds. That was before anybody even thought about weightlifting.

I also had pretty good quickness. I played center and linebacker in high school. I was named Parade All-American as a center. It was only after I got to Ohio State that I was switched to offensive guard. I never questioned or argued against the move. The transition was very easy. I played center and was long snapper on extra points, field goals and punts.

I played in every game and lettered as a sophomore, but I wasn't a starter until my junior year. I was on the varsity as a sophomore and practiced against the very-talented freshmen. Believe me, those were tough practices.

But you never know if this is going to be THE special team. You find that out as the season rolls along. You have to remember those times. They were turbulent.

Class of '68

There were race riots in the streets, protests on campus against the Vietnam War. It seems like everyone was having black-white problems. Everyone except Ohio State. Our team really got along well. Everyone was treated the same. Woody just kept the ship that way. It was a good group of guys.

We believed in each other. I think maybe that's the key. Everybody had a great work ethic. That's what Woody recruited. When we went on the field to practice, we'd get after it.

You could look at everybody else you were playing with and you knew they were gonna play hard. That's probably where the respect comes from.

Back in 1966—when I was a freshman—Woody had a losing season and the press was getting on him pretty good. It carried over to the '67 season. We started out 2-3. Our next game was at Michigan State which was coming off those great teams with Bubba Smith, George Webster and those guys.

We went up to Michigan State and beat that team. In fact, we won our last four games of the season. I can't explain it but something happened with that upset of Michigan State. It was like we rallied around Woody.

That carried over to '68 with the older players. The seniors provided the leadership. I don't think we went into that season with a 'we're gonna show you' kind of attitude. But we were confident. We knew what we had.

Check the record books. We didn't lose a game in '68. We went unbeaten until our final game of the 1969 season against Michigan. Until that game, our smallest margin of victory was 27 points. [The Buckeyes' 22-game win streak ended, 24-14].

Our 13-0 win over Purdue was probably the turning point of the season, even though it was only our third game. I guess it set the tone. They had All-American halfback Leroy Keyes who finished second to O.J. [Simpson] for the Heisman, and an excellent quarterback in Mike Phipps.

They beat the hell out of us the year before in Columbus, and they were picked to win the national title. One of my greatest memories of 1968 happened in that game.

Bill Long had been our starting quarterback in 1967. But the next year, as a senior, Rex Kern beat him out of the job. Ted Provost ran back an intercepted pass for our first touchdown. Billy came in when Rex was hurt and scored the other TD on a scramble.

God, when we got that one, we believed we could do it.

I was a little small for an offensive guard, but with Woody's offense it wasn't a handicap. We were always pulling, cross-blocking or trapping. We were always flip-flopping, meaning I'd either line up next to Dave Foley or Rufus Mayes, our two big tackles.

The game has changed so much since then. Not only in the size of the players but in the complexity of the game. Teams didn't use multiple defenses back then.

If a team was a 4-3 team, they played a 4-3 the whole game. If it was a 5-2 defense, which most teams played, I'd line up against a linebacker. If it was a 4-3 defense like Purdue, it would be against a big, big tackle.

I had 4.8 speed for the 40 which was considered good. It was quick for a down lineman.

I loved to pull, get out on the corner with the running back behind me. I distinctly remember one play in the Rose Bowl.

90

For some reason Southern Cal started playing their linebackers up real tight. We were driving. We were on their 20 or 25 at the time. I think we were trailing. At one point, we were behind 10-0.

As I said, they suddenly started playing their linebackers really up tight. I don't know if that was because they were so afraid of the run.

We called for a play-action pass and the linebacker bit on the run. I took him on as if it was a run block. Rex set up a little bit and decided to run off the pass play.

He took the ball down to about the three. I mean we opened up the big hole. It was a great play. Those kind of things are fun.

I remember the Southern Cal linebackers were big. I remember that.

I don't think anybody realizes the true impact of what we did at the time. It hits you when it's over and you have time in retrospect to look at it all.

There was so much emotion at the time. Woody worked our butts off. Woody watched your diet. He watched your life. Playing against Southern Cal was really a relief.

I was a junior that season, so I had my senior year to look forward to. It could well be that the '69 team was better than the Rose Bowl champion team.

My career ended in my third game against Michigan State. I never played again. I tore all the ligaments that controlled my toes.

If I had any thoughts of playing in the pros, I was gonna have to go from 208 to 250-260. Pro guards that were 5-11 at the time were weighing 250-260. I was really conscious of the fact that I didn't want to do that to my body.

Or it's possible I could have done it if I had gone to a Mid-American Conference school, been an outside linebacker, and played that position the whole time. But when I went to Ohio State, they moved me to guard.

I have no regrets in the way things turned out. The longer we're the last unbeaten, untied and No.1 team at Ohio State, the better we become.

Chapter 14

'YOUR DAY WILL COME'

DAVE FOLEY, NO.70, OFFENSIVE TACKLE
6-5, 250 Pounds, 21 Years Old, Senior.

photo courtesy Buffalo Bills

Big Dave Foley [No. 78] was one of the major reasons that Buffalo Bills' running back O.J. Simpson became the first in NFL history to gain 2,000 yards rushing in one season [1973]. Foley played left tackle.

Dave Foley was born-and-raised in Cincinnati, Ohio. A two-year starter for Roger Bacon High School, he was named All-Ohio, UPI Lineman of the Year as well as Parade Magazine All-American. A three-year starter at Ohio State at offensive tackle, Dave Foley was not only an Academic All-American but was named first team All-American as a senior, along with the other half of the 'Twin Towers,' offensive tackle Rufus Mayes. Foley played nine years in the NFL with the New York Jets and Buffalo Bills. He was named to the Pro Bowl in 1974. Dave Foley owns his own financial services company. He lives in Springfield, Ohio.

I was always a big kid. I was the biggest kid in grade school. I went to a little Catholic grade school. Playing sports at that school was a big deal when I was growing up.

The earliest you could go out for football was in the sixth grade. But there was a weight limit and it didn't matter which position you played. That limit was 120 pounds.

I went out for the sixth grade team. They had a weigh-in the first day. I weighed 140. This was about two weeks before the start of the season.

The coach told me, 'You're 20 pounds overweight, but we can sweat you down.' I thought that was great. I was going to play football.

I went home and told my Dad, 'I've got good news and I've got bad news for you. The bad news is that I'm 20 pounds overweight. The good news is that the coach said he can sweat me down.'

My Dad looked at me and said, 'Son, you're not going back there. Your day will come. Don't let anybody treat you like that.'

That was my entire athletic career as a grade schooler.

As a freshman at Roger Bacon High School, I was 6-feet tall and weighed 200-215. I came out my senior year at 6-5 and 245. I obviously matured and grew a little bit.

Back in those days, Roger Bacon was the top power in Cincinnati, along with Purcell. Roger Staubach went to Purcell. A lot of talented guys came out of Roger Bacon.

I didn't start until my junior year. I went both ways as a junior and senior. I think in the three years I was on the football team, we lost one game. We ranked high in the state, but didn't get nearly the same kind of publicity and support as Massillon or Canton McKinley. Northern teams like that.

Back then you weren't limited as to the number of trips you could make to colleges. I traveled eight or nine weekends to different schools.

Three trips stand out in my mind.

At Illinois, Dick Butkus took me around. He was the top college lineman in the country. He won the Outland Trophy and here he is spending time with a 17-year-old. Believe me, it was impressive.

The entire recruiting pitch focused on how much media attention I would get at Illinois. The media center was nearby Chicago. Illinois could really promote one or two players each year and they were interested in promoting me as their next Dick Butkus type of guy.

I liked that. I liked spending the time with Dick Butkus. It was kinda neat.

I was expecting a great trip to Notre Dame, to meet head coach Ara

Parseghian. Parseghian was named Coach of the Year that year and as a result, his schedule became more hectic. He had to attend a convention the weekend I came to Indiana.

The guy who hosted the recruits wasn't nearly as personable as Parseghian would have been. As a result, I was disappointed.

I really had no feelings about Ohio State. All I knew about Woody Hayes was that he ran a ball-control offense and that he was a disciplinarian. Ohio State was buried in the local papers.

Xavier, University of Cincinnati, Dayton which was still playing major college football and Miami of Ohio were carried on the front page of the Sunday sports section. Ohio State would be lumped in the back.

That wasn't true of the rest of the state, with the possible exception of Toledo. The University of Toledo and Michigan, because Toledo is so close to Ann Arbor, would get the major sports coverage. But throughout the state of Ohio, from Cleveland to Dayton, the Ohio State Buckeyes were front page news.

There wasn't much television coverage back then. You might see one Ohio State game a year, which would always be the Ohio State-Michigan game.

There was no real connection between Cincinnati athletes and Ohio State. There weren't a lot of guys that I know of who went to Ohio State.

Coach [Lou] McCullough was Ohio State's recruiter. He's an interesting guy. About two or three times a week I'd come home after school and it seemed his car would be sitting out in front of my house. He'd have something else to talk about. He would spend a lot of time hangin' around.

Every place I went the program was basically geared towards making you a football player, or so it seemed to me. In other words, they didn't stress the total experience.

After having enough of those trips, it really struck me how differently Woody recruited. When I got to Ohio State, he took me to his office.

He said 'I've noticed from your transcript that you're really good in math. What do you want to do for a living?'

I said 'Gee, I haven't thought about it.' I didn't even know I was going to go to college. I was just going through life, minding my own business.

He said 'I think you ought to consider being an engineer because engineering really requires a lot of math. You can always change from engineering to another major, but if you go the other way you'll miss too many science courses.'

Then, he took me to meet this engineering guy who showed me around the labs. That's what sold me on Ohio State.

He was the only coach that recruited me who was actually talking about going into a more difficult curriculum with the thought I would make the most out of what I could do.

In other words, everyone else said, 'We want you to come to school and you're going to become a great football player. You're gonna get an education and the football experience is gonna be the deal.'

Woody actually recruited me from the other side of the spectrum which was really kind of interesting. It certainly got Dave Foley.

After my visit to Columbus, Woody came to my home. He could really sell the parents. He sold the parents on the value of Ohio State football, on the value of an Ohio State education and how he was gonna be the parent away from home.

It was one of those things. When he left, you were almost forced to think about going to Ohio State even if you didn't want to because he sold the parents. It was remarkable how he related to the parents.

The entire recruiting experience was very confusing. Each school had a uniqueness that made it look like it was going to be the greatest experience in the world.

But all of a sudden you had to bring it back to the basics, on what you were really after. I think the education aspect that Woody stressed sold me on Ohio State.

I enrolled in engineering. I did very well. I think I was Academic All-American my sophomore and senior years. But about halfway through my sophomore year, it dawned on me that all my buddies were having a little more time in doing what they wanted to do.

I was always studying. You couldn't get through engineering without spending a lot of time, especially with the labs. I was home on break, either for Thanksgiving or Christmas, and I told my mother I was going to change majors from engineering to business.

Well, my mother called Woody. The day I returned to school, I got a call. I was supposed to report to Woody's office after classes.

He sits me down and goes through all of this stuff about how I should stay in engineering. If I quit engineering, it's like slapping my mother in the face. I graduated with a degree in Industrial Engineering, with some kind of honors.

We won four and lost five in my sophomore year [1966]. People didn't like Woody. They didn't like the Ohio State Buckeyes. Having that kind of public reaction, it makes you more determined than ever that it won't happen again. Success of a team comes from within the team. It doesn't come because everybody from the outside says, 'Man, you're great.'

Woody would always say, 'You've gotta watch out for anyone who pats you on the back. There's probably an ulterior motive by that guy telling you how great you are.'

In the three years I was at Roger Bacon High School, we lost only one game. We were very, very good. It took a little longer at Ohio State. We started to turn the corner my junior year. [Ohio State posted a 6-3 record].

It was a long winter. I had no clue as to how well we'd do that senior year. I felt we were gonna be better. I even said I think we've got a great chance the year after that.

I didn't have a crystal ball. I knew Woody Hayes well enough to know he'd be bringing in better athletes. No one takes defeat very well. Especially Woody.

I know we lost some games that made him really mad. Illinois at Ohio Stadium was one of them. Purdue was another. We got beaten badly. But we beat a good Michigan team at Michigan. Michigan had a pretty good team that year. We weren't expected to win that game.

The thing I most remember about our 41-6 loss to Purdue was a one-man wrecking crew named Chuck Kyle. He had the greatest game I've seen any defensive lineman have.

He was their nose guard. He would get down on the nose. He would also stand up as middle linebacker. He was a lot like our Jim Stillwagon.

It seems he made almost every tackle. Woody got so ticked off at halftime

[Ohio State trailed, 34-0]. He said, 'I want the guards and centers to chase Chuck Kyle around and don't let him make any more tackles.'

We had three guys trying to block one guy and he still made tackles all over the place. I mean this guy had THE GAME of a lifetime. Single-handedly, he manhandled our offense.

The next year [1968], Woody put in some plays to misdirect this guy, double-team him and so forth. As a result, he wasn't nearly as effective.

As a junior, I practiced against the freshmen every day. It didn't take a rocket scientist to figure out how talented this class really was.

But the pieces didn't start to fall into place until Spring practice, when the now sophomores became integrated with the rest of the guys.

For instance, Jack Tatum was a great running back, but he was moved to the defensive secondary his sophomore year. He became a two-time All-American and All-Pro with the Oakland Raiders.

Nobody thinks about an unbeaten, untied season and national championship. But you have a really good feeling about things to come.

We all knew the key to the season was our third game against Purdue. Woody prepared us a year for that game, even though we didn't always realize it.

We'd be practicing against our upcoming opponent but then Woody would have the defensive unit we're working against suddenly give us an entirely different look.

He'd always be doing that. During Spring practice or early in the season. After awhile, we realized we'd been practicing against Purdue or Michigan's defense all the while.

Woody wanted to see how his players lined up against these teams he really cared about beating. Except for Rufus [Mayes] and me, we really had a small offensive and defensive line. Neither one of us got much heavier than 255 or 260 until we got to the pros.

The game was so much different back then. Nobody used their hands. The rules were different. If I had to describe my ability, I would say I was much more of a power blocker who relied on the tough part of the game as far as hard-hitting, just playing football.

Rufus had more skill as far as balance, foot speed and so forth. He really was an excellent athlete. I was probably a marginally good athlete with size and determination. Looking back, I made the most of what I had.

When you're 6-5, weigh 255, work hard, lift a ton of weights, a lot of people will say 'That guy's got a lot of talent.' That's true, but when you get to the next level you see how much talent the other guys have too.

The 1968 national championship team got leadership from both the seniors and the juniors. We got the talent from the sophomores. We just blended so well together.

It really amazes me, looking back 30 years, that the team never repeated. The nucleus of real talent were the sophomores. It was just bad breaks. They got beat by Michigan [1969] and the next year by Jim Plunkett and Stanford in the Rose Bowl.

When the 1968 season began, we had reason for optimism. Everybody knew we had a lot of talent, more tools than we had in previous years. But I don't think anyone knew just how good we were gonna be.

We certainly had our scares, our anxious moments, but we came through on the top end. Sometimes you have an experience where the team grows the whole year but then has a letdown at the end of the season.

This team didn't do that. It seems like we grew and matured a little bit more with each game. It probably culminated at the Rose Bowl as opposed to some other time during the season.

I think the Michigan game was certainly a tremendous experience that year [Ohio State buried Michigan, 50-14, in Game 9]. The Rose Bowl was our best game. We all played our best game individually and collectively.

We had a bunch of guys who never had any previous college experience. I think we got the most out of the talent we had in most of our games.

What do I remember about that season?

It's not what I did on the playing field. It's not a block I made that set up a touchdown. Nothing like that.

There's something very special about being a co-captain at Ohio State. You feel it when you walk onto the field before the game, before the coin toss, and the crowd is cheering.

That in itself is a wonderful feeling. But the feeling I had right before the Michigan game was something special. We walked out onto that field at Ohio Stadium just before our marching band preformed Script Ohio.

The stadium was roaring. Our co-captains and the Michigan guys were shaking hands. I looked at their eyes and I KNEW we were gonna beat Michigan that day.

There was simply no way we were gonna lose. That was the neatest experience of my collegiate career.

Chapter 15

DOWN IN THE TRENCHES

**PAUL SCHMIDLIN, NO.74, DEFENSIVE TACKLE
6-1, 222 Pounds, 19 Years Old, Junior.**

Ohio State Photo Archives

*"We probably played three basic formations. We did the 4-
3 for a period of time. We called the 5-0 'Oklahoma'. We
also played what we called 'Irish'. My principle job as a
defensive lineman was to make sure I protected my territory
first and then rushed the passer and kept him contained."*

Harvey Shapiro

Paul Schmidlin was born-and-raised in Toledo, Ohio. A three-sports star at Rogers High School in football, wrestling, track and field, he was named first team All-Ohio in football as a defensive lineman his senior year. A highly sought-after player, Schmidlin was starting defensive tackle for three years at Ohio State. He also finished third as a heavyweight his senior year in the Big Ten wrestling tournament. He played two years of professional football in Canada for the Hamilton Tiger Cats before a knee injury ended his career. He is not only a State Farm insurance agent but an ordained minister. Paul Schmidlin leads a small congregation—King of Glory Lutheran Church—in Perrysburg, Ohio.

I played only one position in high school and college. I was a defensive tackle. I weighed about 200 pounds my senior year at Toledo Rogers High School. I was listed at 222 my junior year at Ohio State. I think I was playing at 224. Bill Urbanik was the heaviest defensive tackle at 227 or 228.

It sure wasn't the size. It was the quickness. I did the 40 in 4.6.

You'd have one or two quality athletes on your high school team. Once I got to Ohio State, everybody at every position had great skills.

We probably played three basic formations. We did the 4-3 for a period of time. We called the 5-0 'Oklahoma.' At times we also played what we called 'Irish.'

You'd move the tackles in over the guards and stack the linebackers behind their offensive tackles. We'd have four people in the middle with a lot of freedom to move. It was a little bit more difficult to defend.

We did a fair amount of blitzing. We had the 'Monster-rush', of course, which Jack Tatum became famous for. That was outstanding.

My principle job as a defensive lineman was to make sure I protected my territory first and then rushed the passer, keep him contained anytime I was on the closed side of the field.

I was on the freshman team in 1966. We practiced against the varsity. You would hear the comments about the varsity team and the comments about Woody. As freshmen we really worked hard to prepare the varsity. I can't remember the final score, but we almost upset Michigan State in '66, the top team in the country. I could see Ohio State had potential even though it might not have looked like it in the press.

I was starting defensive tackle for three years. We went 6-3 my sophomore season, with Billy Long at quarterback. I remember telling people that Summer of 1968 that we had a shot at the national championship. Why? Just knowing that the athletes, especially the sophomores, were quality athletes.

I believe that was the difference between 1967 and 1968. We had key skills in areas that just pushed us further ahead. And those of us who were juniors were really coming on strong, developing our abilities.

I didn't play a glamour position, but I played at the time when people were just beginning to recognize defensive linemen. I was left defensive tackle. Bill Urbanik and Brad Nielsen alternated at the other tackle. Jim Stillwagon was middle guard. Mark Debevc and Dave Whitfield played a lot at the defensive end positions.

Obviously, the key to our season was the 13-0 upset win over Purdue.

99

The defensive backs worked on controlling Leroy Keyes. The line worked on making sure [quarterback Mike] Phipps was contained. We tried to get in his face as much as possible and keep his throwing arm down.

Three or four plays stand out in my mind. One took place against Phipps and Purdue.

I had broken through. Phipps was trying to get up and scramble through the middle of the line. I was far enough away from him. There was no way I could get a hold of him.

So, I just dove out with my hands, my right arm outstretched trying to catch him. I grabbed his foot but my hand pulled off. It was such an odd sensation.

I felt his other foot hit my arm and I said to myself 'Alright.' He went down. It was one of those lucky trip-ups. It was probably a two or three yard loss.

I remember that Michigan Stated played us very tough that season. But in all honesty, for me the toughest game was the Rose Bowl. I was playing across from a big All-American offensive tackle from Southern Cal.

His name escapes me. He stood about 6-4 and weighed about 260. He was just big and strong. He outweighed me by almost 40 pounds.

When you're playing against a guy who's that much bigger, you want to get underneath, get your hands up underneath his shoulder pads, hold them at a distance and determine where the ball is. Then you just shuck him off and make the tackle.

If I wasn't able to get position on him, he would usually drive me out of my position.

Believe it or not, we weren't as concerned about O.J. Simpson as we were their quarterback Steve Sogge. We were concerned about his passing ability. We wanted to make sure we kept him under control. If we could do that, it would also cut down on his ability to scramble out of the pocket.

Obviously, everyone knew about O.J.

I was playing on the left side on his 80-yard touchdown run. He broke through the right. I've always joked that I had the best seat in the stadium for that run.

I wouldn't say we practiced any harder for the Rose Bowl, but we certainly practiced as hard. There was no letup. I was kinda lucky because I injured my knee and wasn't able to practice for several of those two-a-days at Ohio State. I considered myself very fortunate.

By the time we got out to California, I was ready to go full-bore again. We worked equally hard in California. The school gave us national championship rings. I still wear mine. I think most of the guys still wear theirs.

I was a junior in 1968. I still had one more season to look forward to. Most of the guys were returning in '69. We had a great team in '68, but I think we were even better my senior year.

I know. The record says we lost 24-12 to Michigan the last game of the season to end our 22-game winning streak. Looking back, I can pinpoint several reasons for that loss.

We played Purdue the game before we played Michigan. Purdue still had Mike Phipps. They had a tough team and our coaches thought if anyone could knock us off, it would be Purdue.

They were also counting on us to get emotionally ready for Michigan. We always got up for that one, so that shouldn't be a problem. They just drilled us so hard about how tough Purdue was going to be.

They just filled us with a lot of stuff. We went out and blew 'em out [42-14]. It was really anti-climactic when we went up to Ann Arbor.

We weren't as mentally sharp as we should have been. The first half was a real wake up call. In the second half we were shored up defensively, but we couldn't get the offense to where it could put points on the board.

That was a sad way to end my career, knowing we should have won and we didn't. Knowing we were a better team.

But the good memories far outweigh the bad. It's a mind-blower to think I was part of that magical season. I still have my jersey and I look at it every once in awhile.

Chapter 16

HE MADE HIS DAD PROUD

JAN WHITE, No.80, TIGHT END
6-2, 214 Pounds, 19 years Old, Sophomore.

photo courtesy Buffalo Bills

"This was a very close knit team. We all wanted to do well for ourselves and each other. I can't ever recall any kind of an ugly incident at Ohio State."

Jan White was born-and-raised in Harrisburg, Pennsylvania. A high school All-American in both football [wide receiver] and track [low hurdles], he was recruited by more than 100 schools for football. Converted to tight end his sophomore year, Jan White started every game at Ohio State during his three-year career. Drafted in the second round by the NFL Buffalo Bills, he was a starter for three years, then retired. With a background in social work, sociology and criminology, he is director of a Greene County juvenile court and lives in Clayton, Ohio.

I was heavily recruited by Joe Paterno of Penn State. You'd think a native Pennsylvanian would have jumped at the chance to play for him. Believe me, I was flattered.

While I didn't root for any particular college team, I had a favorite conference. It was the Big Ten. As far as I was concerned, it was THE conference if you wanted to go big time.

I was a 17-year-old kid. It seems so long ago. In the beginning, I was flattered by all the attention. But after awhile it became a distraction. Not just the trips across the country to visit different campuses, but the recruiters showing up at my high school. Pulling me out of class.

I remember going to George Chaump, my high school coach, asking him to intervene. Academics were very important to me. My parents instilled that in me and I'm glad they did.

I played football and track at John Harris High School. My high school football team never lost a game. I was All-State, a Parade All-American. I played in the annual Big 33 game pitting the best schoolboy players of Pennsylvania against Texas.

I had some 150 college offers in football but none for track. While I loved track, it was a conditioner for my football. I weighed 185 as a senior wide receiver but bulked up to about 200 for track.

I don't know what my high school stats were. But I was pretty prolific as a receiver. I had 4.35 speed for the 40.

I guess you could call me a momma's boy. I had never left home and that was the deciding factor as far as which college I would attend.

Southern Cal was very interested in me. They had a running back named O.J. Simpson. As it turned out, I played with him for three years with the Buffalo Bills.

Southern Cal flew me out and I loved the setting. I loved the weather. The major problem was that I wouldn't be able to make too many trips home and my parents wouldn't get a chance to see me play. They were my biggest fans.

Certainly Penn State would have been closer to home, but as I said, I was more interested in a Big Ten school. My folks were delighted when I made the determination. I have no regrets.

I was recruited by Ohio State as a wide receiver. At that time freshmen couldn't play varsity ball. We had a number of guys who could have played varsity. There was that much talent. We played a few freshman games but mostly we practiced against the varsity.

I was still a wide receiver at the start of my sophomore year. All that changed when our tight end, Richard Kuhn, got hurt. They needed somebody to step in for him. To this day I don't know why it was me.

I was designated first string wide receiver. Bruce Jankowski was my backup. When they moved me to tight end, Bruce became a starting wide receiver.

It was supposed to be temporary. It turned out to be my entire three-year college career. They liked what I could do over there and they left me at tight end.

The coaches explained it this way. This would be the best way for me to contribute to the team. To be honest about it, I wasn't real happy about the move.

I'd never blocked in high school. I was split wide and I liked that. I wanted to catch the ball and run. I never blocked. I really didn't want to get down in the trenches.

But as time went by, I became pretty good and my whole thought process changed. Maybe I'm not making the big catch, the big run, but I'm helping my team. I'm a part of it's success.

Hugh Hindman was my coach. He had a lot of patience with me. He was always encouraging me, always positive. 'C'mon, Jan, you can do it.' He'd say things like that.

As a wide receiver, I'm being hit in the open field, usually by a defensive back. As a tight end, I'm usually blocking a linebacker or one of those huge defensive tackles.

As a tight end, I always moved with the ball. I went to the strong side all the time. I was always protected by either Dave Foley or Rufus Mayes.

We called these big offensive tackles our 'Twin Towers.' They went around 270. They were pretty much the same kind of players. They were very strong, very confident, very talented.

When I first came to Ohio State, Rufus Mayes was a tight end. He couldn't catch the ball very well. He was real happy when they moved him to tackle.

The 1968 roster lists me at 214. I find that hard to believe. I was more like 205. I can't imagine Woody letting me balloon up to 214.

Most of the time we used double-team blocking. I moved around, meaning I could line up next to Dave or Rufus. The big guy would stand 'em up first. I'd take my stutter step and finish the block. I'd come in, hit 'em and knock 'em away.

Woody Hayes used the forward pass sparingly. He believed three things could happen when you threw the ball and two of them weren't good. Heck, as a sophomore it seemed as if we passed only four times a game. I'm sure it was more than that.

This was a very close-knit team. We all wanted to do well for ourselves and for each other. I can't ever recall any kind of an ugly incident at Ohio State.

I didn't have one particular roommate. Woody would move us around. I'd room with whites. I'd room with blacks. We all got along very well. There was a lot of comraderie. Some of the guys have photographic memories. Not me. I remember we beat SMU 35-14 in my first varsity game, but most of the details are hazy.

I do remember a couple of things though. I remember it was a frightening feeling for me running onto the field at Ohio Stadium. There were 80,000 people in the stands and I'd never seen that many people. The butterflies were fluttering in my stomach.

Woody Hayes was an offensive coach. When we huddled, he was always there with us. He was the 12th man. The first time the offense took the field we huddled up. But there was a gap in that huddle.

We automatically left a spot where the old man would stand. We all looked at each other and laughed. I remember that. Then we closed up the huddle.

Everyone says the 13-0 upset win over Purdue was the turning point for us. I agree. I knew they were ranked either first or second nationally and that they had a great quarterback in Mike Phipps and a super back in Leroy Keyes.

That happened early in the season. There was no way Woody Hayes or his coaching staff would let us get a swelled head. The only time we let up that season was against Illinois.

We were supposed to win by something like 50 points. We grabbed an easy 24-0 lead and then everything went wrong. Illinois came back and tied the game. It sure looked like the impossible was going to happen.

Lucky for us we had Ron Maciejowski. Mace replaced Rex Kern at quarterback and re-fired our engine. He was that kind of player.

From a personal standpoint, I'll always remember one play against Northwestern. We called for a post pattern to me. It's a very basic play.

I slant to the middle. It's a 10-15 yard play. But sometimes you can really break it. Rex connected and I caught it. A lot of thoughts flashed through my mind after that.

I said things to myself like 'Where's the guy [linebacker or defensive back]?'...'Don't let them catch me.' I'm running for my life. It's a long, long way to the end zone. As it turned out, nobody was able to catch me. It went for a 72-yard touchdown. Man, that was a great feeling.

I really didn't understand the enormity of what we had accomplished that season. I had always been connected with a winning program. I mean no losses in three years of high school.

We went unbeaten and untied in 10 games my sophomore year at Ohio State. We were unbeaten until the final game in '69. We won nine in a row in my senior year until we lost in the Rose Bowl. That's 27-2.

I think most of us probably read the newspapers. We thought it was nice. We got our names in the paper. They were saying good things about us and we were feeling good about that.

But our heads never got bigger than our helmets. If they did, Woody took us down. He had this thing called 'senioritis.' When the guys started to get too cocky, he'd do certain things to those guys to make sure they'd work hard.

I expected our Rose Bowl trip to be a fun trip. Boy was I nieve. We went straight to the practice field off the bus. Woody made a statement that this wasn't going to be a vacation. We had business to take care of.

Except for part of the Illinois game, I can't recall us ever being tight. I don't know why we were tight against Illinois. They hadn't won a game all season.

After the 1968 season, I gave my championship ring to my Dad so he could wear it. Partly because I really didn't comprehend the significance of what we'd accomplished. I didn't realize how important it was and what it meant to be national champions. Not then.

Class of '68

I also wanted to make my Dad proud and it gave him some bragging rights. He wore it until the day he died. When my last college game was over I was ready to see if I could progress to the next level.

I was picked fourth in the second round, 30th overall, by the Buffalo Bills. I was the starting tight end for three years and had the privilege of playing with O.J. With him you knew you didn't have to sustain a block. Just hold it for a fraction of a second and he was gone. He was a real gentleman, real appreciative of his offensive linemen. He'd let you know when you made a good block.

I went to training camp my fourth year but my heart wasn't in it. The ability was there but I wasn't the same person psychologically or emotionally. I was just going through the motions. My coach understood it. My agent understood it.

I had had enough. I didn't have the fire for the game anymore. It was fun in high school. I enjoyed it in college. But once it became a profession, it just wasn't the same. It was time to get on with my life.

Chapter 17

PLENTY GOOD ENOUGH

**MARK DEBEVC, NO.83, DEFENSIVE END
6-1, 210 Pounds, 19 Years Old, Sophomore.**

Ohio State Photo Archives

"All I knew about Woody Hayes was that he was a good coach. I was a little leery about playing at Ohio State."

Class of '68

Mark Debevc was born in Italy and raised in Geneva, Ohio. A three-sports star at Geneva High School—football, basketball, track—he earned honorable mention All-Ohio honors in football. He was a national high school discus champion. A three-year starter at Ohio State, Debevc was named to the All-Big Ten team in both his junior and senior years. Although drafted by the NFL Cincinnati Bengals, he never made it to the Opening Game roster after trying with the Bengals and the Calgary Stampeders in Canada. Mark Debevc runs the family winery in Geneva.

I didn't come to the United States until I was almost three years old. I spoke no English, but learned quickly. Actually, I hold citizenship in three countries.

I have Slovenian citizenship because my parents were both born in Yugoslavia. I have Italian citizenship because I was born in Italy. We are naturalized Americans.

My late father was a freedom fighter in the civil war in Yugoslavia. He fought against the Communists who wanted to overthrow the King and Queen. That war was a war within a war, pitting brother against brother.

The world was embroiled in World War II. With the blessing of the West, Tito took over my country and my family was forced to flee. I was born in Pagani, Italy. It's a small town near Rome. I was born in a rehabilitation camp.

We came to the United States in 1952. I started playing sports in the seventh grade. It came easy to me. I lettered in football, basketball and track in high school. We played in the Northeast Conference against the likes of Ashtabula, Madison, Conneaut. I was a running back and linebacker.

We played the I formation and I was tailback. I was 6-1 and about 190. I was considered a big kid and ran the ball 30 times a game.

In my big game against St. John, I had 320 yards, four or five touchdowns, in only 20 carries. It was one of those games you dream about. The holes were there and everything fell into place.

I probably ran the 40 in 4.8 with full pads, which wasn't bad in those days. It wasn't blazing speed, but as I found out when I went to Ohio State, it was slow for a running back.

I was recruited by all the schools in Ohio, including Ohio State. Hugh Hindman did the recruiting in my area. But until Woody Hayes came to my house, Ohio State was third on my list behind West Virginia and Miami of Ohio.

Ohio State was the only school that wanted me as a defensive player. I was gonna go to West Virginia as a running back.

Bo Schembechler was head coach at Miami. He also wanted me as a running back. In my heart, I wanted to be a running back.

Woody called and said he wanted to come over to meet me and my family. He came in the afternoon and stayed for dinner. He told me I'd probably start as a defensive player and probably in that second year we'd be playing for the national championship. He was absolutely right.

I really liked Morgantown, West Virginia. They wanted me real bad, but I decided I'd rather be a small bit player in the larger scheme of things.

Woody Hayes really impressed my parents. Me too. Believe it or not, I didn't know too much about him or Ohio State. I lived in Notre Dame country.

108

All I knew about him was that he was a good coach, a tough coach. I admit I was a little leery about the possibility of playing at Ohio State. That's as big league as you can get. I didn't know if I was good enough.

But like my high school coach told me, 'If they didn't think you were good enough, they wouldn't ask you.' That was kinda the way it was. When Woody came up, he bolstered my spirits.

He really didn't talk much about football. He stressed the academics, the lifestyle. He had a lot of credentials and trust. He had that sincerity, that charisma.

Woody knew I was a running back and he said I would get a chance. Everybody would get a chance, but more than likely because of the commitments he had, the people he had, I would probably be playing defense.

That didn't scare me.

When Woody came to my house, I figured Ohio State was building up for something big. I wanted to be a part of it. He rattled off the names of players he'd recruited, but to be honest, they really didn't ring a bell with me.

When I came to Columbus, I saw it for myself. I knew I couldn't beat out [fullback] Jim Otis. I couldn't beat out John Brockington.

I didn't have to be the star. I didn't have to be the top running back. 'I'm here. Whatever you want to do with me is fine. I'm a team player.'

Coach Mallory gave me the impression I was going to be a defensive back. I played that position my freshman year.

Actually, I played Jack Tatum's position. I was 'Rover' or 'Monster' back, but I had size working against me. I had problems keeping up with those quick receivers.

Tatum was recruited as a running back. You couldn't tackle him. His big problem, however, was holding onto the ball. He fumbled a lot and Woody wouldn't allow anybody to fumble.

I had a tough time as a defensive back. I had never played the position before. I was relieved when I was told in the spring of 1968 that I would be shifted to defensive end. Tatum moved into 'Rover.' Jack Tatum was probably the best athlete I ever saw.

As a freshman, I was a little bit in awe. I came from a small school, basically unheralded and I'm surrounded by Parade Magazine All-Americans.

There was a little bit of doubt. I said to myself, 'I'm gonna see it through and just do the best I can.' We played two of our own games as freshmen. Most of the time, we worked against the varsity. I knew we were an exceptional team the first time we went against the varsity. We pretty much held our own.

There were several reasons for my switch to closed-side defensive end. I had trouble covering one-on-one. But I was also moved to bolster the defensive end position. They had only one veteran returning and that was Nick Roman.

Nick Roman was a senior out of Canton McKinley. I was probably fourth in the depth chart when my position coach, Esco Sarkkinen, told me that Nick had injured his knee and it was between me and Mike Radtke.

Nick's injury happened during the summer. When we opened the season against Southern Methodist, I was fortunate enough to be the starting closed-side end.

Making that transition was easy. It was like playing linebacker and I was a linebacker in high school. I was more suited for that position. I was actually relieved when they made the switch. In August of 1968, I thought I was never gonna play. A month later, I'm in the starting lineup. Strange how things can happen.

'Sark' was a great guy, a great coach, a great motivator. He had his own style which was laid-back. But if you made a mistake, you'd be reprimanded. I liked his style. He was an older gentleman. He was more like a father figure. I owe whatever success I had to him because he made the decision to switch me to end. I was fortunate enough to have been named All-Big Ten my last two years.

Our basic defense was a 5-3. I lined up next to Paul Schmidlin or Bill Urbanik, our tackles. I'd flip-flop. I'd drop off on passes and occasionally blitz. I was small. Our defensive tackles were small. We made up for lack of size with quickness.

I played scared. I think it made me play better. I played scared for several reasons:

Number One—Ohio State.

Number Two—Starting.

Number Three—Remembering your assignment.

Number Four—Keeping your position, keeping your job.

It's hard enough to get there, but a lot harder to stay in the starting lineup.

A big crowd at Geneva High School was something like 1,500. I'll never forget stepping onto Ohio Stadium as a sophomore against Southern Methodist.

It was the only time I can recall being afraid of the crowd. I was very much in awe. I remember thinking during warmups, 'Wow.' I had butterflies in my stomach, but that feeling quickly disappeared after the second hit. Or maybe it was the first.

I ran my tail off, chasing Hixson [SMU soph quarterback Chuck Hixson]. We did a lot of one-on-one coverage. We tried some blitzes. We tried everything.

SMU had a tremendous attack. They had a pro attack, even more wide open than the pros would run. They passed on every down. They threw out of every formation.

Against a team like that, you disregard the run. They couldn't beat you with the run. We put a lot of pressure on Hixson and dumped him a few times.

They had a great wide receiver in Jerry Levias. He caught something like 15 passes that game. He was very, very tough. Quick as a cat.

Believe me, SMU was a darned good team.

Our second game was against Oregon. It was a rough, hard-hitting game. We picked off some passes. I intercepted a pass in that game, and picked off one later in the season against Michigan State.

It was a good test for us because Purdue was coming up next. I did better in some of the other games, but the 13-0 win over Purdue will always stand out in my mind. After we beat them, we kinda realized we had something going.

Woody wanted to beat Purdue real bad. In the summer, we were practicing against Mike Phipps, Leroy Keyes and Purdue. Purdue buried us 41-6 in 1967 and Woody wouldn't be happy until we returned the favor.

We knew we had to beat Purdue for us to be a factor for the Big Ten championship. And as it turned out, we couldn't have gone to the Rose Bowl or won the national championship without that victory.

Our coaches really won the Purdue game. They had us so well prepared. We knew what they were going to do. They were a very predictable team because they were just two-dimensional.

I don't know what they could have done with the personnel they had. They couldn't pass and they had only Leroy Keyes. Ohio State has always had the ability to stop one guy. Purdue was noted for their sweeps. They'd try one way and get stopped. Then they'd try the other way. They changed formations.

We played up to our full potential and made Keyes and those guys look worse than what they were.

Emotion also played a major role, not just against Purdue but against Michigan for the Big Ten title and the chance to face O.J. Simpson and Southern Cal in the Rose Bowl.

We were in such a frenzy for those games. I don't want it to sound like I'm bragging, but the defensive ends played a major factor in beating Southern Cal which also did a lot of sweeps.

Purdue and Southern Cal were very similar. They both ran from the I. But O.J. carried the ball a lot more often than Leroy Keyes.

Southern Cal handed the ball off to O.J. and let him pick his holes. My main thing was to keep O.J. head-up with me and make him run laterally, rather than up the field. Basically, it was cat-and-mouse.

Don't go in there and try to make that tackle because if you miss, you open up a hole in the defense. O.J. was a shifty runner. He would avoid the contact. He would try to get around you, rather than run you over. You know O.J. was gonna get the ball. But how do you stop him?

A great athlete like him gets his yards. Woody told us he probably would. But he said if we can limit him, make him work for the yardage he gets, then we should be alright.

Woody was right. We contained him except for his 80-yard touchdown run early in the game. He made a great run, but we opened the door.

Our basic defense is a 5-3. Every once in awhile, we'd switch to a 6-1 with Jim Stillwagon playing middle linebacker instead of middle guard. Just before the snap of the ball, we shifted to the 6-1.

My assignment in that formation is to force the ball carrier inside. In a 5-3, you try to make the runner go outside because the defense rotates and we have help on the outside. It's the only way he broke it.

Chandler [freshman tight end Bob Chandler] gets a good block on me, gets into my legs a little bit. I knew I had to make O.J. turn. I turned up and that was it.

The only only thing I remember was lying on the ground and looking up. Tatum was bearing down on O.J. He was coming at him straight. But O.J. dipped in, dipped out, and he was gone.

He made a good move on me and Tatum. He got everybody. He was a tremendous back, the best I've ever seen.

After that run, we stuck to the basic 5-3 and held him in check. Michigan State and Southern Cal had huge offensive lines. But we were quick and quickness will win out most of the time.

We're in our locker room celebrating after the Rose Bowl win when O.J. comes in. We just gather around him. He shakes everyone's hands and says something like 'You're the best damn football team in the land.'

111

Class of '68

Man, I was very, very impressed for somebody to do that. All the guys were. I think it took years for me to fully comprehend what we had accomplished that season. I was a 19-year-old sophomore and I thought the best was yet to come.

From a personal standpoint, my best game was probably against Michigan State. I had an interception, a safety and a touchdown and rated out at about 100 percent.

I think I got the quarterback for a safety. Jim Stillwagon got the quarterback by the arm, deep in Michigan State territory. He managed to throw a wobbly pass. The ball came to me and I had an easy touchdown.

Only one running back in 1968 rushed for 100 or more yards against us. That was O.J. We shut down Ed Podolak of Iowa and Ron Johnson a week after they set single-game Big Ten rushing records.

I'd simply call it unit pride. We had a unique combination of racehorses and workhorses. In other words, we had the slick players but we also had a few guys like myself who brought their lunch bucket every day. The workhorses had talent, but not the best of talent.

It was this combination that worked so well. We had deep respect for each other. As a team, we were very close.

There were a lot of hunters and fishermen on the team. In the off-season, there were other things to talk about besides football. Doug Adams, Stillwagon and I went fishing together a lot of times.

We were blessed with talent and as a result, some guys fell victim. I roomed with Ron Maciejowski. He was my man. Ron and Rex Kern were both sophomores in 1968. Billy Long was a senior and a former starter.

Ron and Billy saw very little playing time when Rex was healthy. I felt so bad for Ron. He could have been bitter about it, but he never bad mouthed Rex, or the situation he was in.

That showed me a lot of class and helped me a lot. I don't know if I would have taken it that well.

Billy Long was a real leader even though he was restricted at that position. In my opinion, we probably would have won without Rex or Mace. I think we would have won with Billy because he was a hell of a quarterback.

I'm sure Woody felt bad about that one for years. But he had to do what he felt was right. It's easy to second-guess. I choose not to do that.

If someone had told me that during my three years at Ohio State, we would have won 27 of 29 games and a national championship, I would have thought the guy was crazy.

But that's what we did. It could just as well been 29-0 with three straight national titles.

Woody tried to guard against complacency. I believe that played a role in our 1969 loss to Michigan. Michigan beat us with emotion. Bo [Michigan coach Bo Schembechler] had his team in a frenzy.

We'd beaten Michigan up pretty bad, 50-14, my sophomore year. We weren't emotionally ready and we paid the price. We thought the big gun was loaded, but we came up firing blanks.

At the Rose Bowl the next year, Stanford beat us with the pass. Jim Plunkett was a hell of a passer and they had a hell of an attack.

Most of the time, they rolled away from me. They didn't even block me half the time. They killed us with timing patterns. The quarterback takes 5-6 steps, looks and throws. If the receiver isn't there, he throws it away.

Do you think Michigan and Stanford were better teams? Not in my mind. But I think it was our time to get beat.

I played in two Rose Bowls, my sophomore and senior years. I thought we were a lot looser when we beat Southern Cal than we were against Stanford. We just didn't execute.

Over the years, I got to know some of the West Coast players. We've talked about their Rose Bowl superiority. I think there are several reasons for it.

Number One. They're on their home turf.

Number Two. They generally run a little bit more of an open offense.

Number Three. Their philosophy seemed like it was a reward for winning the season. It was gravy. It was extra. It seemed like they played very, very loose. With no pressure.

I'm very glad I went to Ohio State. Otherwise, I would never have been a part of a big thing that has lasted this long. I might have had more personal achievements, but I would never have had that national championship ring.

Section III

Wayne Woodrow Hayes

Wayne Woodrow Hayes never apologized for his competitive nature. "I don't think it's possible to be too intent on winning. If we played for any other reason, we would be totally dishonest. This country is built on winning and on that alone. Winning is still the most honorable thing a man can do."

He once told his squad, "When you start winning and somebody comes up to congratulate you, you kick them in the shins unless it's a little old lady over 80. Pats on the back soften you."

His 28-year coaching record at Ohio State speaks for itself. Woody Hayes is the winningest coach in Buckeyes' history. But he is also the most controversial. The general public saw only one side. A hand grenade ready to explode. A man gone wild. A man constantly sitting on the hot seat. A man who finally got what he deserved.

But there are the others. Those who knew him best. Those who loved Woody Hayes for his many acts of caring. A man who would literally give you the shirt off his back.

This section attempts to portray the total picture of a life filled with triumph and tragedy. MOSTLY TRIUMPH!

Ohio State Photo Archives

115

Chapter 18

THE DAY WOODY DIED

In its edition of Friday, March 13, 1987, the Columbus (Ohio) Dispatch ran a lead editorial about Woody Hayes' death. The prestigious daily has given permission to reprint that editorial.

Why do we love Woody Hayes?

He was irascible, brash, domineering, and intimidating.

He made mistakes and never apologized.

He had many qualities that people love to hate.

He knew it and sometimes flaunted it. But if you walked about Columbus yesterday, the day Woody died, you could hear his name everywhere.

On the streets and in the offices.

In fast-food restaurants and in courtrooms.

In gas stations and in City Hall. Woody was on the minds of the mighty and the meek, the professional and the laborer, the minister and the manager, those who knew him and those who only knew of him.

He was a hero to most, a man to be admired, a role model for children, a sage for adults. We loved him because he engendered in each of us the desire for greatness.

He taught that achievement required work, that success required sweat. He taught us to expect adversity and to believe in our ability to overcome it. His teachings were for each of us.

To confine his legacy to the football field does the man a great injustice. Though it is sometimes overlooked, he was also an educator, a professor in the College of Education.

He also was a history buff. He saw in history lessons that applied not only on the football field but to the day-to-day challenges of life. His football fame was, of course, of historic proportions.

His Ohio State teams were disciplined, determined squads that reflected the coach's passion for fitness, execution and for victory.

He became so closely identified with the university that his name was synonymous with OSU. His sense of loyalty to friends and decency to those in need were also well-known.

He was loyal to his players of whom he demanded academic achievement as well as athletic excellence; loyal to his former players staying in touch, counseling them with problems and personal decisions; and loyal to his staff. Three of his former assistants are now head coaches in the Big Ten.

"He was one of the greatest men I've ever known and one of the greatest humanitarians," said Jack Nicklaus, a former Ohio State golfer who went on to an incomparable professional career.

But he did not belong just to the famous, not to the athlete, nor to the history book. He did not stop living when his coaching career ended in 1978. He looked for other ways to inspire and contribute.

116

He was a frequent dinner speaker and talked to school classes. He visited many ill persons. What he called "the greatest day of my life" came when he addressed the winter commencement at Ohio State in 1986. There he called on the graduates to "pay forward," returning the help they had received by helping other people.

"So seldom can we pay back because those whom you owe, your parents and those people, will be gone," he said.

We loved Woody Hayes because he challenged us to be the best we could. We saw his faults and recognized our own.

But we saw his greatness and we recognized our own potential.

We'll remember the day Woody died, because that day a little bit of us died too.

Ohio State University Photo Archives.

Chapter 19

REMEMBERING 'THE FATMAN'

On March 23, 1987, Sports Illustrated paid tribute to Woody Hayes in a first-person story written by Rick Telander. Sports Illustrated has graciously given permission to reprint this article. The multi-decked headline read:

DEFINING A GRID LEGEND...
Woody Hayes was an apostle of primal struggle.

After I heard the news that Woody Hayes had died, my thoughts returned to an autumn afternoon in 1970 at Ohio Stadium in Columbus, when my team, Northwestern University, was leading Ohio State 10-3 just before the half. I was a cornerback and standing only a few yards from Hayes.

He looked at me and I could feel his loathing for me, my teammates and everything else that stood in the way of his Buckeyes.

The winner of this game would likely go to the Rose Bowl, a place Hayes' team seemed to visit every other year, but to which Northwestern hadn't seen since 1948. Hayes was at the peak of his fame then; the NU coaches referred to him as The Fatman, partly out of hatred, largely out of envy.

He won national championships in '54 and '68 and was well on the way to becoming the fifth-winningest college coach ever. He was already a legend for chewing out his players, snarling at the press, smashing projectors and cheap watches, and ripping up pretorn baseball caps.

And he already had issued his famous edict: "Three things can happen when you pass, and two of them are bad." I personally had proved him right that afternoon, having intercepted two of quarterback Rex Kern's passes.

For the half Ohio State would pass 10 times, completing only three, with three interceptions. Hayes was almost out of his mind with rage. And yet his passing attack was so primitive, so readable that there was little we defenders could do but catch the ball or bat it down. As I looked at Hayes just before the gun sounded it struck me that perhaps he had planned it this way.

Like a child he had guaranteed the failure of a system he hated.

"See, Mom, I told you it wouldn't work."

In the second half Ohio State threw just two passes. The offense came out in the tight T formation, the gridiron equivalent of the bulldozer, and plowed us into the ground.

"The most deceptive course in football is straight at the goal posts," Hayes had stated, "When the Germans went through the Argonne it wasn't an 18 Sweep, it was a 10 Trap."

Undefeated OSU 10-trapped us into submission that day, then went to the Rose Bowl and lost to an over achieving Stanford team which relied heavily on that deceptive thing, the forward pass. To me the point was clear. You can always crush a weakling; it takes guile and innovation to defeat an equal.

118

Hayes built his record by beating up on the "little Eight" in the Big Ten, saving his greatest fury for those season-ending tractor pulls against Michigan. His style of power football, conceived in simpler times, may have set the Big Ten back a decade in relation to other conferences. In the Rose Bowl alone, the PAC-10 has defeated the Big Ten 16 of the last 18 years.

Hayes' final rage at the vagaries of the forward pass occurred in the last moments of the 1978 Gator Bowl when he slugged Clemson noseguard Charlie Bauman who had just intercepted a last-gasp OSU pass.

Chicago Tribune columnist, and OSU grad, Bernie Lincicome has written of Hayes "that was the night that his life truly ended." The essential conflict of Hayes' life was neatly encapsulated in the run-pass dilemma.

The one form of attack personified the earth, primal struggle, stavism, simplicity, things that could be controlled; the other embodied air, lightness, modernity, freedom and risk. Hayes was of the earth, an old-fashioned toiler.

"I despise gimmicks," he often roared.

A 250-pound fullback was not a gimmick.

A pass was.

I do not think Woody Hayes was a great football coach.

He won a lot, but what does that mean?

And yet having said that I think it is likely he was a great football man. He had many virtues.

He was honest.

He affected people.

He believed in scholarship.

He had no pretenses.

He and his wife, Anne, lived for 36 years in the same house with few possessions.

In classes he taught at Ohio State he told his students how Socrates would walk happily through the marketplace saying, "Look at the things I don't need." Like all great men, he gave us a target.

He was unashamed to do what he felt was right.

When Hayes eventually got around to calling Charlie Bauman on the telephone he did so not to apologize but to find out what defense Clemson was in when Bauman made the interception.

The brass at Ohio State understood the hubris-ridden, unique man for what he was. Six months after firing him as coach, for the Bauman incident, the board of trustees voted him professor emeritus and Hayes kept his small teacher's office at OSU until the end.

It has been reported that Hayes died in his sleep, quietly and at peace.

I hope that is true.

And I hope that somewhere the coach is smiling; it's first and goal at the one, and the big fullback has the ball.

Chapter 20

A JIGSAW PUZZLE

AUTHOR'S NOTE: Back in 1969 I developed a three-part series on Ohio State football for United Press International. The series not only ran in Ohio, but throughout the United States. One of the stories focused on the personality of head coach Woody Hayes. Through the years, I saved some of the clippings. The one that is being reprinted appeared on Friday, November 28, 1969 in the Times-Leader of Martins Ferry and Bellaire, Ohio. The kicker said: "Admired By Close Associates, Players." The eight-column headline said:

Woody Hayes...Coach of Many Personalities.

BY HARVEY SHAPIRO, UPI Sports Writer COLUMBUS, Ohio--Woody Hayes is like a complex jigsaw puzzle. It takes all the pieces neatly fitted together to describe the much-publicized and much-criticized Ohio State University football coach.

Many of the pieces were supplied by Hayes' present and former players, present and former members of the coaching staff, OSU athletic director and an old roommate at Denison University in this exclusive United Press International story.

In all instances, the men who have played for and have known the often gruff, undiplomatic coach held nothing but deep respect and admiration for Wayne Woodrow Hayes.

Bill Hess, a former assistant coach under Hayes and now head coach at Ohio University, has made two post-season trips to Vietnam with Woody.

"Woody worked just as hard during the 18 days we visited servicemen as he did coaching football. We tried to see as many young men as we could. We didn't take time away from our job and families to go over there and loaf around.

"If we weren't showing movies, we were talking about football. He went there (Hayes has made four trips to Vietnam) because he wanted their stay to be a little brighter. They got a tremendous lift. A lot of people told us that we were more like guys from back home than paid entertainers.

"It's always drive, drive, drive with Woody. He does what he thinks and says what he thinks and lets the chips fall where they may. Although I've very seldom seen him in much of a relaxed mood, Woody has a tremendous sense of humor. He enjoyed a good joke," Hess said.

"He's worked so hard and is so completely tied up with his job, and when things don't go well he gets short tempered.

"He's a very intelligent person with tremendous work habits. He'll never take no for an answer as far as solving a problem. He has great persistence."

Bill Mallory, another former aide who is now head coach at Miami of Ohio, calls Hayes "a man's-man."

"You always know where you stand with him. He always says what he believes. He's tough with those kids, but he's also fair with them. He doesn't allow them to get fat or happy. He has the knack of keeping his team on the good edge.

120

"In my three years under Woody the one thing that impressed me most was to work on a few things and do them well."

Dave McClain, a first-year assistant coach at Ohio State, believes Hayes "is just as interested in the last man on the team as he is interested in a Rex Kern or a Jack Tatum.

"Woody always has time to discuss any problems our players may encounter, whether it be in the morning or late at night. He treats every player equal, fair, and shows no favoritism whatsoever."

John Mummey played quarterback under Hayes. He is now Ohio State freshman coach.

"Woody is the first to admit he is not an offensive genius, but his ability to teach basic fundamentals is making Woody what he is today.

"I can remember when I was transformed from a fullback to a quarterback in 1961 and the amount of pressure that he could put on an individual and his team so that when game time rolled around everything became second nature to his squad members.

"No matter how intense the pressure became in actual competition, things always went well. We were definitely prepared for these happenings. Woody made it so."

Richard C. Larkins, OSU athletic director, feels there are several factors that have made Woody Hayes so successful.

"A thorough knowledge of football coaching techniques, dedication and hard work, an ardent belief in strict discipline on the part of coaches and players, an excellent recruiting program, the ability to select excellent assistants and a rigid off-season conditioning program for the players."

Jim Otis, the Buckeyes' All-American fullback in 1969 says, "Woody is the type of man who makes you do things you think you can't do. He has a way of reaching each man as an individual. He knows their potential.

"He varies his techniques. It might be a little gesture in his office, or maybe he'll get mad at you. He wants to see if a kid can get knocked down and get up again.

"I just wish he'd relax a little more. I think Woody is too much football. He might get out of bed at midnight and think why a player made a bad cut."

Otis' father, Dr. James Otis of Celina, Ohio and Hayes were roommates at Denison University from 1933-1935.

"If Woody liked you there wasn't a thing in the world he wouldn't do for his friends. He's very loyal," he said. "Even back when he played at Denison, he was very intense and took defeat very hard. But he's a big enough man to bounce back."

Rex Kern, Ohio State's brilliant junior quarterback, neatly puts the pieces of the jigsaw puzzle together.

"Coach Hayes' success lies within his personality of many phases: kind, considerate, thoughtful, mean, moody, and the determination to succeed."

No doubt W.W. Hayes will continue to offend people, but he will also continue to devote 24 hours a day, 12 months a year to producing a winner at Ohio State. He's produced 125 victories, six Big Ten titles, two national championships and 17 All-Americans. Twice he was selected national Coach of the Year.

Chapter 21

A LIFE OF GIVING

Less than a year before his sudden death, Woody Hayes entered massive St. John Arena in Columbus, Ohio to deliver the commencement speech to the winter graduation class at his beloved Ohio State University. Within a two-year period, the once fiery football coach had suffered two strokes and a heart attack. At age 73, his health was frail, but not his spirit.

The date: March 21, 1986. With assistance, Hayes slowly walked to the podium. The arena erupted in cheers. Deafening cheers.

"Today is the greatest day of my life," he told Ohio State President Edward Jennings in an emotional 30-minute speech. With an inner strength Wayne Woodrow Hayes stood proud and tall during his memorable address.

During the commencement he was awarded an honorary Doctorate of Humanities degree. He offered a blend of suggestions for daily living and reminiscences that had made him a highly sought-after speaker nationally for years.

"There's nothing comes easy that's worth a dime. As a matter of fact, I never saw a football player make a tackle with a smile on his face. Never."

He called on the graduates to "pay forward," returning the help they had received, by helping other people. "So seldom can we pay back because those whom you owe, your parents and those people will be gone."

He displayed humor when discussing his own firing in 1978 after striking Charlie Bauman of Clemson in the waning moments of the Gator Bowl. Thus, his stormy 28-year career at Ohio State was over. A fatal display of temper.

"There's been a lot of great men fired. MacArthur, Richard Nixon, a lot of them." The crowd broke into applause.

In the early morning hours of March 12, 1987, Woody Hayes died quietly in his sleep at home. That should have been the end of this story! But as the years roll by, Wayne Woodrow Hayes takes on the stature of a folk hero. A friend of presidents. A friend of plain folks.

Caring...Cantankerous...Colorful...Controversial.

The public saw only the violent side. His flareups. But only those who knew him best knew of his selfless, unpublicized acts of charity. Woody Hayes wanted it that way.

But ask his players. Ask his coaches. Ask his friends. If anyone needed Woody Hayes, he was there. One moment in time cannot wipe out a lifetime of achievement.

*A 33-year college coaching record of 238-72-10, including 205-61-10 (1951-78) at Ohio State.

*Six unbeaten teams—Denison (9-0 in 1947, 8-0 in 1948); Ohio State (10-0 in 1954, 8-0-1 in 1961, 10-0 in 1968, 10-0-1 in 1973).

*Seven Big Ten Conference championships. Six co-championships.

*Six post-season victories—4 Rose Bowl, 1 Orange Bowl, 1 Salad Bowl. Ohio State appeared in eight Rose Bowls.

*National championships—1954 and 1968.

122

*Woody Hayes was twice named Coach of the Year.

* He produced 58 All-Americans, including two Heisman Trophy winners—running backs Howard (Hopalong) Cassady in 1955 and Archie Griffin in 1974 and 1975. Eleven of those All-Americans played on Ohio State's sophomore domination 1968 national championship team, including nose guard Jim Stillwagon who was twice named winner of the Outland Trophy—emblematic of the top defensive player in the country.

Seven of 'Woody's Boys' would join their coach in the College Football Hall of Fame at South Bend, Indiana. Offensive lineman Jim Parker was inducted in 1974, Cassady in 1979, Griffin in 1986, offensive lineman Orelius Thomas in 1989, Stillwagon two years later, fullback Bob Ferguson in 1997 and linebacker Randy Gradshar in 1998.

Wayne Woodrow Hayes joined 'The Hall' in 1983. At his induction, he said: "The thing it does, it makes you feel pretty small. When you reflect on all of the people who made it possible—your coaches, your players, your family, everybody you work with. It's a team proposition."

Other honors came after his career ended. The massive indoor practice facility at Ohio State was named after Woody Hayes, as was the road running in front of Ohio Stadium: "Woody Hayes Drive." In 1983, Hayes was accorded the honor of dotting the "I" in the band's famed Script Ohio.

From 1936-1940, he served as assistant (three years) and head football coach at New Philadelphia, Ohio, High School. Hopefully, in the Fall of 1999, the renovated high school stadium will be completed and dedicated to him: Quaker-Woody Hayes Memorial Stadium. Price tag for the project: $750,000.

Rex Kern, one of 'Woody's Boys', spearheaded a project to establish the "Woody Hayes Chair" as a scholarship Fund for the National Security Studies at the Mershon Center. The 'Chair' became a reality at Ohio State in 1997 after $1.5 million was raised.

Wayne Woodrow Hayes was born February 14, 1913 in Clinton, Ohio, the son of Wayne Benton and Effie Hayes. The famly moved to Newcomerstown, Ohio, where Mr. Hayes served as superintendent of schools from 1920 until his death in 1939. Woody Hayes credited his father for his love of education.

He graduated from Newcomerstown High School in 1931, and Denison University in 1935, majoring in History and English. At Newcomerstown High, he played varsity football, baseball and basketball. He also loved to box. At Denison, Hayes was on the baseball and football teams.

Hayes recalled: "In 1928 we finally got a radio. We got it in time for the Rose Bowl game. I went down to the mill in town, got a long board and a piece of cardboard. I tacked it on this board and then drew a football field on the board. Then I started to chart the football game, which I did my entire life."

He launched his football career in the Fall of 1935, serving as an assistant at Mingo Junction High School. His salary was a little more than $1,200. He doubled as English teacher. A year later, Hayes moved to New Philadelphia High School as assistant coach to John Brickles. When Brickles left in 1938, Woody Hayes took over as head coach.

In his first season, New Philly won 9 of 10 games. It was even better in '39. New Philadelphia posted a 9-0-1 record.

Class of '68

But even back in those days, his famous temper flared. A disastrous season in 1940 caused Hayes to boil over and he quit after a disagreement with school officials. Losing 23 members of the varsity and reserve squads, the team slipped to 1-9.

While he was coaching at New Philadelphia, Woody Hayes met Anne Gross. They would be married in 1942 after he joined the Navy. That marriage would produce a son, Steve.

By the summer of 1941, Woody Hayes became convinced it was only a matter of time before the United States became embroiled in World War II. He enlisted in the Navy. Military service would mold the man. He learned discipline. Hayes was sent to Officers' Training School and ultimately commanded a destroyer escort in the Pacific. He would be discharged in the Spring of 1946.

At one time in his life he considered a career as a lawyer. While awaiting discharge, he also considered returning to New Philadelphia. But a letter from his former football coach at Denison changed all that. Tom Rogers told Hayes that he was planning to leave and that the head coaching job would be vacant. Would Hayes be interested?

It took that letter a month to catch up with Woody Hayes. His response was much quicker. Hayes sent a telegram to his old coach, telling him he wouldn't be able to be back in Ohio for a few weeks. Much to his delight, when Hayes returned to Granville he discovered the job still hadn't been filled. After an interview with the University president and athletic board, Woody Hayes was hired as head coach.

His first year was a near disaster, but once Hayes' hard regimen had been accepted, the Denison team won 17 straight games.

At the time of Hayes' death in March 1987, Robert Shannon remembered his old coach. Shannon was an 18-year-old freshman end for Denison in 1946.

"Hayes would outwork anybody. He didn't understand anybody who wouldn't work as hard as he would. People (on the team) expressed an opinion and said they weren't going to play. Woody was smart enough to know he had to make some changes."

Woody Hayes met with key players and convinced them to play. So after a 2-6 season, Denison posted back-to-back undefeated seasons.

In 1949, Hayes became head coach at Miami of Ohio, posting a 19-5 record for two seasons. His '50 Redskins amassed a 9-1 record, won the Mid-American Conference and beat Arizona State, 34-21, in the Salad Bowl.

But Woody Hayes had his sights set on bigger game: Ohio State. At that time, Ohio State was known as the 'Graveyard of Coaches.' The title was fitting. Ohio State had five coaches in the previous 11 years. The group included Francis Schmidt, Paul Brown, Carroll Widdoes, Paul Bixler, and Wes Fesler. Since John W. Wilce's 16 years (1913-1928), no OSU coach had lasted longer than Schmidt's seven seasons.

Some of Hayes' closest friends advised him against taking the job. But he relished the challenge and told Ohio State's Board of Trustees just that in a three-hour job interview. It was two-and-a-half months before the announcement came of Woody Hayes' appointment.

At the 30th reunion of Miami of Ohio's Salad Bowl championship team, Hayes told his former players, "Whether you fellows realize it or not, you're the ones who

124

put me into Ohio State. Without that great 28-0 victory in Cincinnati the day of the big snow and the bowl victory, I wouldn't have been hired."

Ohio State's 1951 edition would be in for a shock. Here was a man obsessed with discipline and conditioning. He alienated their affections quickly with something called "gassers"—the running of at least half a dozen laps around the practice field in full gear following a full workout.

The team revolted against this great admirer of General George S. Patton. They locked him out of the dressing room before the Illinois game, then played a scoreless tie with the heavy underdog. The following week against arch-rival Michigan, Ohio State again failed to score and lost 7-0, completing a tumultuous 4-3-2 season.

Banners calling for Hayes' ouster appeared almost immediately in Columbus and there was talk among the more avid booster groups of raising enough money to buy out his contract.

Conditions were only marginally better in the Fall of '52, but players began to tolerate if not accept Hayes' methods. Sputtering through most of the season, the Buckeyes kicked it into high gear in the final two games, pounding Illinois and Michigan by identical 27-7 scores. That closed out a 6-3 season.

The critics were silenced for the moment. Hayes fumed-and-fussed in 1953, but the Buckeyes posted an identical 6-3 record. Well not quite identical.

Woody Hayes never referred to Michigan by name. It was always 'that team up North.' When he arrived in Columbus, Michigan had won 16 of the previous 17 games. In 27 games, Ohio State posted a 15-11-1 record, including four straight victories (1960-1963).

And it made no difference if a former player-turned-pupil was coaching 'that team up North.' That player was Bo Schembechler who played tackle for Woody Hayes at Miami in 1949. Hayes and Schembechler traded insults regularly and once threw chairs at each other. But off-the-field, there was love. Bo Schembechler spoke emotionally, eloquently at a memorial service for his old coach and mentor.

By 1954, all the pieces had fit together for Woody Hayes. For one thing, Lyal Clark returned as defensive line coach after following Wes Fesler to Minnesota. Ohio State's tough defense yielded only 75 points enroute to a perfect 10-0 season, the first Big Ten title since 1942 and a resounding 20-7 Rose Bowl whipping of Southern California.

Ohio State's powerful offense, headed by running back Howard "Hopalong" Cassady, struck for 249 points. Cassady would be named Heisman Trophy winner the next year.

Cassady, who went both ways, finished his fabled collegiate career with 2,466 yards rushing. Oldtimers still talk about his 'play of the year' against Wisconsin in 1954. Ohio State entered that crucial game with victories over Indiana (28-0), California (21-13), Illinois (40-7) and Iowa (20-14).

The Badgers, led by All-American fullback Alan "The Horse" Ameche, were also unbeaten. At halftime, Wisconsin clung to a 7-3 lead and seemed in excellent position of moving in for another score. Wisconsin had marched to the Buckeye 20 in the third quarter.

Wisconsin went to the air. Playing defensive halfback, Cassady intercepted the pass on the Ohio State 12 and galloped 88 yards for the game-breaking TD. Ohio

State then exploded for three touchdowns in the next 12 minutes enroute to a 31-14 conquest.

It set the stage for Hayes' first unbeaten and No.1 rated team. Woody Hayes would have to wait until 1968 for his second undefeated, untied national championship squad.

"Every year since '68," he said, "I expected to be national champion. I didn't make it again."

Hayes' teams won or shared 13 Big Ten championships. They won undisputed titles in 1954, 1955, 1957, 1961, 1968, 1970 and 1975. Starting from 1972, they were champions or co-champions in six consecutive years.

His sophomore-dominated 1968 edition was the last unbeaten, untied and No.1 rated team. His 1973 team went 10-0-1, with only a 10-10 deadlock against Michigan marring an otherwise memorable season.

His 1969 (9-1), 1970 (9-1) and 1975 (11-1) teams all had a golden opportunity to finish unbeaten, but lost in the final game of the season.

Woody Hayes' serious health problems began in 1974 when he suffered a heart attack during the off-season. He returned to coach his Buckeyes in 1975 to an 11-1 record, that one loss to UCLA in the Rose Bowl, 23-10.

In 1981 he underwent gall bladder surgery. Two weeks later Woody Hayes had to be rushed back to the hospital. A sponge was left in his body by mistake.

He suffered a stroke in 1984. The next year, he suffered a second stroke, a heart attack and phlebitis. Hayes began slurring his words slightly and had trouble with his right arm and hand. Woody Hayes was also a diabetic.

Some would say his behavior became more violent the last few years of his coaching career. It would be prelude to 'The Incident.'

For 28 years, Woody Hayes starred on his own show (Channel 10) in Columbus. For the last two years of the run, Lee Vlisides appeared with the volatile, unpredictable coach.

"The temper tantrums were coming often," recalled Vlisides. "He seemed to be a little more taciturn. He seemed to wear down quicker at the end of the day." Less than 24 hours after Woody Hayes struck Clemson's Charlie Bauman in the closing moments of Ohio State's 17-15 loss in the Gator Bowl, OSU athletic director Hugh Hindman fired the living legend.

Woody Hayes remained in brief exile after his dismissal, but once he emerged, he was more popular than ever. A campus street that runs in front of Ohio Stadium was named in his honor. Roasts were held for him in Oxford (Miami of Ohio) and Columbus twice.

Ohio State gave him it's Distinguished Service Award. The University set up the Woody Hayes Athletic Fund to help pay for it's athletic facilities. Hayes was a highly sought-after speaker, traveling all over the country, even to Clemson University. Hollywood was even considering making a movie of his life, with George C. Scott in the starring role.

Hayes raised money for charity. He visited hospitals. His life was busy. His life was full. He continued in his usual high gear.

As a head football coach, Woody Hayes took an occasional day off, but not many. He maintained a seven-day-a-week, work schedule. Despite deteriorating health, Woody Hayes pushed his fragile body.

His last public appearance was Tuesday, March 10, 1987. He was attending an Agonis Club luncheon in Dayton. Bo Schembechler was main speaker.

On Thursday morning at about six, Woody's wife of 44 years, Anne Hayes, couldn't wake her husband. Woody Hayes was dead. He died in his sleep.

Dr. Robert J. Murphy, Ohio State head team physician and Hayes' personal doctor since 1952, marveled at his patient's iron will. "I'm frankly amazed at his ability to keep functioning. He had a fatalistic look at his problems. He wanted to live life to the fullest. The quality was more important to him than the length. That's why he kept going."

Three memorial services were held in as many days in Columbus to honor Woody Hayes. Presidents and plain folk paid their final respect. He was buried in a private ceremony on Saturday, March 14, 1987 at Union Cemetery. Public memorial services would soon follow.

A baseball cap inscribed with the letter "O" lay on a table draped in purple at the altar of the First Community Church. An American flag was neatly folded behind it. They were framed by two white candles.

A crowd estimated at 1,400 squeezed into the church.

Woody Hayes had vehemently defended President Richard M. Nixon during the Watergate scandal which ultimately forced Nixon out of office. Although Nixon hadn't seen his friend for some 13 years, he came to pay his last respects.

Said Nixon, "Woody Hayes is widely known as one of the greatest football coaches of our time. But I know him also to be a man who had a remarkable grasp of history and foreign policy.

"Woody Hayes understood the great forces that move the world. I was privileged to know him as a loyal friend and as an insightful wise counselor.

"He wasn't a Neanderthal, a know-nothing. He was a renaissance man with a sense of history. He was not just a tyrant, but an old softie. The last nine years of his life were probably his greatest. He basked in the warm glow of tributes from those who came to know and respect him and love him.

"His firing would have crushed an ordinary man. But Woody was not an ordinary man. Woody Hayes, in the evening of his life, could look back and see how splendid the day had been."

Said Rev. Barry L. Johnson, senior minister of First Community Church, "Woody Hayes was cursed by the blindness of extremes. The masses did not see the man in the middle, a man doing justice, showing loving kindness and walking humbly with his God."

They slowly filed by Hayes' casket. Former players such as Paul Warfield, Archie Griffin, Art Schlichter, and John Brockington. Michigan head coach Bo Schembechler was there as were Hayes' neighbors, Ohio State alumni and fans. His wife, Anne. His son, Steve. His daughter-in-law and grandson.

Barbara Arend made the solemn trip from San Francisco to Columbus. She was an Ohio State graduate. Her brother, Bob Wise, was a Boy Scout working as an usher when Woody Hayes coached his first game at Ohio State.

She said after the service "My mother is 85 years old and she still sends me clippings. Back in 1981 when she was in the hospital, Woody went to see her and gave her a nice poster. She hung it next to a picture of Ronald Reagan."

Class of '68

The following day some 15,000 attended a memorial service at Ohio Stadium. Flowers were placed on the 50-yard line.

Bob Sawyers, a 1976 Ohio State grad, paid his personal tribute. "You never figured it was going to happen. He was one of those people who you believe is going to live forever."

Ohio State's student newspaper, "The Lantern," devoted most of it's issue to Wayne Woodrow Hayes. "This is similar to what happened with the students when the space shuttle exploded," said faculty adviser Phil Angelo. "But it's different because this is very unique to the university."

He felt time had healed all wounds. Woody Hayes had long been forgiven for his transgression.

"Time sort of softened the memory of Woody Hayes. I think there was a consensus that whatever sins he had committed were absolutely forgiven at this point. Plus, he remained very loyal to the institution. He kept coming back.

"He was just looking out for his guys. He was a fierce competitor. I thought he was very misunderstood."

Tributes came from Schembechler, Woody Hayes' only son, and Earle Bruce who replaced Hayes as Ohio State head coach.

Said Schembechler, "This is a tremendous loss. He was one of the greatest, if not the greatest football coach we've ever had in the Big Ten Conference."

Said Bruce, who would be fired after five very successful seasons. "What sticks out most in my mind right now are all the good things he did for his former players and coaches. He always had a lot of time for them.

"He was a tremendously different person off the field than on. Off the field, he knew everybody's name and always had a word of advice. On the field, he was quite demanding, to say the least."

Steve Hayes, a municipal court judge in Columbus, said he never thought of his father as a celebrity. "To me he was just Dad."

He spoke of those magic moments when his father played with his grandchildren.

Can you picture Woody Hayes sitting on the living room floor, wearing a Darth Vader helmet and wielding a toy laser weapon while playing with his grandson?

Can you picture Woody Hayes playing with his granddaughter's doll?

"I cherish those memories of him," said the only child of Anne and Woody Hayes.

Steve Hayes promised his father wouldn't be far away.

"I submit that come next Fall he will have the best seat in the house," he said looking skyward. "God bless you all. God bless you all."

Who was Woody Hayes?

First and foremost he was an intense competitor.

"Nobody despites to lose more than I do. That's gotten me into trouble over the years, but it also made a man of mediocre ability into a pretty good coach.

"I am not very smart but I recognize that I am not very smart. So I outwork every SOB that comes down the pike." He was a living contradiction. But always he seemed to be in the eye of the storm.

The Big Ten Conference placed Ohio State on probation in 1956. An investigation disclosed that Hayes had personally given small sums of money to individual players. The amount was estimated at $400 annually for five years.

Hayes insisted it was a personal matter. The one year probation was cleared up

128

before the 1956 season. The Conference punishment made the Buckeyes ineligible for the Rose Bowl even though they won the Big Ten title.

Two years later Woody Hayes was on the hot seat again with the Big Ten for his eviction of the Big 10 Skywriters and Big Ten Commissioner Kenneth Wilson from a pre-season practice.

The incident occured when Hayes became angry during a scrimmage between the third and fourth teams. He ordered the practice field cleared. He wanted to chew-out his players without any onlookers on hand.

His battles with the media became legendary.

In 1959 he got into a scuffle with two California sportswriters and was admonished by the American Coaches Association ethics committee.

Twelve years later, in 1971, Woody Hayes exploded in the closing moments of a 10-7 loss at Michigan. He ripped the sideline markers in demanding an interference call on an interception by Michigan's Thom Darden.

In 1973, Los Angeles Times photographer Art Rogers was on the field photographing Woody Hayes during a pre-game warm-up. Hayes was reported to have pushed or hit Rogers, injuring Rogers' eye. Rogers filed an assault charge against Hayes which was later dropped.

Four years later Hayes drew his second Big 10 probation after a fist-throwing incident at Ann Arbor, Michigan. Michigan beat Ohio State, 14-6.

With four minutes to play, Hayes slammed his earphones to the ground, then noticed the ABC sideline camera focused on his reaction. Hayes charged the television cameraman, Mike Freedman, and according to witnesses, pushed him in the stomach.

Asked about the incident in the post-game interview, Hayes said, "Aw, go ahead and write about it. How would you like it if they stuck microphones in your face all the time?" With that he abruptly ended his news conference and left the room.

At the post-season appreciation banquet Woody Hayes elaborated a bit more on his latest outburst.

"I am tired of all the frivolous talk about what I did to the man out there. We were going down the field a sixth time in a great game for a great championship. I've never been so sick in my life. I was tired of having that camera jammed in my face."

While he did not apologize then, he backtracked at the dinner. "I'm sorry for what I did. Do I make mistakes? Sure I do. I make lots of them. Everybody here knows I make mistakes. We all do. Now as far as I'm concerned the thing's over."

A year later he 'lost his cool' during the Gator Bowl and a 28-year-old career at Ohio State was over.

But as his antics became legendary so did his good deeds!

Only then they weren't as publicized as his tantrums.

Here are a few examples of his softer side.

Woody Hayes made four trips to Vietnam to visit U.S. servicemen engaged in that bloody war. A fifth trip was planned, but on-campus disturbances kept the Ohio State coach at home.

He showed football films and talked about home, football, and other sports. Once back in the States, he spent his own money in contacting the families of the men and women he had spoken to.

Class of '68

Certainly not a materialistic man, Hayes' annual salary in 1977 was a modest $43,500. That was after 27 years as Ohio State head coach.

He and his wife, Anne, lived in the same white-frame house with green shutters since he arrived in Columbus back in 1951. It was really Woody Hayes' street. That's how everybody living on Cardiff Road knew it.

One time Hayes stopped to chat with a young man. They shook hands. The young man's handshake needed improvement. Woody Hayes launched into a lecture on the proper way to shake hands. "That's how you shake hands young man," he said, demonstrating a strong, firm handshake.

As age and illness took their toll, Woody Hayes was forced to use a cane. A neighbor commented, "He fought the hardest battle of his life walking with that cane. He was such a proud man. He could have easily hid away, but he liked to walk as far as he possibly could with that cane.

"He was training until the day he died. He taught people in his condition a lot by getting out there."

Woody Hayes was the kind of a man who would receive a $2500 check for a speech, then endorse it over to a friend who really needed it.

A charitable youth group once offered Hayes $1,000 to be speaker at the annual fund-raiser. "I won't come for $1,000, but for such a good cause I'll come for nothing if you send a plane to get me and bring me back so I won't miss spring practice."

In 1975 Woody Hayes met Dave Pavlansky and his wife at an area football banquet. Pavlansky, veteran coach at Poland High School, had been named Class AA area Coach of the Year.

It was discovered before the 1976 season that Pavlansky had a brain tumor. Woody Hayes had just a brief conversation with Pavlansky and his wife, but when he learned of the situation he sprung into action.

Mrs. Pavlansky didn't know it but Hayes had already contacted their family physician. Dave Pavlansky would be admitted to University Hospital in Columbus.

She recalled, "We had just said hello and that was it (referring to her meeting with Woody Hayes). We had no idea where to go. We prayed about it one whole weekend.

"He didn't know us at all. We were admitted to the University Hospital on Tuesday and Woody came over on Wednesday. He was over every night, even after the Missouri game (OSU lost).

"On Thursday, we walked over to the practice field. Woody took us out in the center of that huge stadium and told those kids about us."

After the operation and recuperation period "We stayed down there (in Columbus) during radiation treatments and Woody was just super. He would pick Dave up and take him to practice, and when he'd get tired Woody would have one of his assistant managers take him back.

"If it wasn't for that, I don't know what Dave's spirits would have been. He could not be with his own team, which was his life, but he was with the OSU team and something he loved. It helped so much."

The following winter Woody Hayes was speaker at a community banquet staged for Pavlansky. More than 900 attended, contributing to a fund to defray medical costs.

Dave Pavlansky died November 22, 1978.

130

Said his wife, "Dave and I said so many times that if this had never happened we would never have gotten to know Woody and Anne. We're just grateful. We wouldn't want to go through life without knowing them. If this is what it took, then fine. Things just didn't work out the whole way we would have liked."

Woody Hayes was a fanatic about education. Ask two-time Heisman trophy winner Archie Griffin, now associate athletic director at his alma mater.

"He (Woody) always said that a pro career only lasts a short time, but a quality education lasts a lifetime."

Ohio State was not the first school to employ a 'brain coach', but it was among the first. Jim Jones was the second person to hold that job during Hayes' long tenure.

"He was more education-minded than any coach I've ever known," said Jones. The academic coach kept constant tab on the players' grades, class attendance and set them up with tutors.

Former Ohio State and Cleveland Browns great Dick Schafrath sent a message back to his old coach after a few seasons in the NFL.

That message: "When you get back, tell Woody I've enrolled at Wooster College for this winter. Every time I see him, he gets on me about coming back to get my college degree."

Once upon a time Woody Hayes said, "No alumni and nobody else, not even you members of the press fire the coach. The players fire the coach and as long as I'm on the same wavelength with them, I can coach as long as I want to."

Following his firing in 1978, Woody Hayes 'mellowed' a little.

During a 1984 interview he said he didn't miss it as much as might be expected. "I've coached long enough."

At one of Woody Hayes' memorial services, Bo Schembechler had high praise for Anne Hayes. "What a magnificent woman," he said. "She was as much a part of Woody's success as Woody himself."

Woody Hayes was consumed. Football was his life.

"I count my blessings," Anne Hayes once said. "While he's absorbed in 80 boys and their problems I don't have to worry about one thing, like a blonde in an apartment somewhere. I'm his full-time housekeeper and part-time mistress."

Wayne Woodrow Hayes never wallowed in self pity. It wasn't his style.

"As a football coach you must never, never enjoy the luxury of self pity. You see coaches who do that but they don't last long.

"Going to the bowl games and winning the big games are not what you get paid for. You get paid for the times things are going badly. You have to stay there, stand up to the heat and earn your money."

Woody Hayes stood tall and proud. He earned every penny.

Class of '68

Ohio State University Photo Archives

Woody Hayes made four trips overseas to visit our troops.

Chapter 22

SHE HAD A DREAM

Woody Hayes' countless acts of charity are legendary. And it didn't matter if you were a stranger. That meant you were a friend that Woody hadn't met yet. This little story says it all about this special man.

PHYLLIS SHANNON
Newark, Ohio

I'm a nurse and I work in a hospital here in Newark. My supervisor years ago was a Woody Hayes fan, a terrific Woody Hayes fan.

She went to every Ohio State football game. She liked Woody Hayes. That's why she went to the football games. She had been a nurse in the service, in the Navy and Woody was a Navy veteran.

Well, she developed cancer and was very ill. She was getting some chemotherapy at Ohio State University Hospital. I went to visit her and she said, "You know, Phyllis, I had the strangest dream. I dreamed that Woody Hayes walked into my room.'

I replied, "Oh, isn't that interesting. Probably because you're over here at Ohio State thinking about him." So anyway, I came home and told my husband about it.

He said "You know, Woody likes to visit people in the hospital. I'm gonna call him and tell him about your friend."

My husband, Robert, was one of 'Woody's Boys.' He was a freshman end on the 1946 Denison University football team. It was Woody's first head coaching position in college.

So he called Woody and told him about my friend.

Of course, Woody Hayes didn't know her, had no connection with her at all. But Woody went into her room and visited. She was just overwhelmed and said, "Just like in my dream." They talked for about an hour.

My friend died about six weeks later. She said Woody's visit meant a great deal to her. Woody Hayes just walked into the room, sat down like he was an old friend.

That's the man I prefer to remember.

Courtesy Miami of Ohio

Chapter 23

PERSONAL REFLECTIONS

TOM BACKHUS

I didn't know much about Woody Hayes when I came to Ohio State. When you stop to think about it, he was truly an amazing man. I think about him often. You had to admire him. You had to respect him. Some people think there were two Woodys. I don't know that I ever saw two Woodys. I think he was pretty much 'what you see is what you get.'

I'm just amazed that he constantly shared his philosophies with us, how he constantly bombarded us with various truisms and truths about life and how we should handle other people.

He would say things such as 'Nothing worthwhile in life comes easy'...'For every good thing in life there's something bad; for every bad thing in life there's something good.'...'Don't take things from people because they're going to expect them back from you.'

He was very consistent. I never met anybody who lived his convictions like Woody Hayes. That was the lesson I drew from him. He was constantly teaching. He'd spend as much time during his meetings talking about some issue of the day, a life philosophy, as he did talking football.

Two personal incidents come quickly to mind.

I was a fairly highly-recruited football player when I came to Ohio State. I wasn't gonna be a first round Pro-draft pick. I wasn't gonna be a Jack Tatum, or one of those guys.

Of the starters on our national championship team, if you rated us by true athletic ability, I wouldn't have ranked too high. But I was first team All-Ohio, a Parade Magazine All-American and was used to being on the field and not on the bench.

Freshmen weren't eligible to play varsity football in my days. We had a freshman team. After the season, we went into Spring football.

Going into my sophomore year, I was rated as a second team guard. I'd never been a second teamer before. After Spring practice, I went out, got drunk, and got into trouble.

I was gonna get into more trouble when I went to Woody to tell him exactly what had happened. I was with Woody Hayes for two hours. Within the first 5 or 10 minutes, the whole situation was laid out.

Woody told me what my punishment was going to be and what I was going to have to do. For the next hour and 50 or 55 minutes, we just sat there and talked.

He talked about his Mom and Dad, about his brother and sister. I talked about my parents, my brother and sisters. From that point on, I had a totally different relationship with Woody Hayes.

I got to know him from that point and I think it was one of the turning points in my ability to play and feel comfortable at Ohio State. I got to know him on a totally different level. I got to feel more comfortable with him.

135

I remember this funny situation. When I finished playing, I stayed on at Ohio State as a graduate assistant because I still needed an extra quarter to graduate. That was the year that Rex [Kern] was a senior. I was up in the press box. I used to travel with the team even though I was a graduate assistant.

My first year as graduate assistant, Ohio State lost to Stanford in the Rose Bowl. I left then, bought a one-way ticket to Europe and stayed for seven or eight months.

When I returned, I had long hair which isn't characteristic of me. I bought a motorcycle in Europe and brought it back with me. When I came back to the United States, I flew into New York and visited Dave Foley who was playing with the New York Jets at the time.

Then I came through Columbus on my way home to Cincinnati.

Woody always held closed practices with guards at the gates. Ohio State was already into practice when I came home. Well, I rode that bike right onto the field. Everybody was laughing.

When practice ended, many people including the coaches came over to see me. Woody walked by and was very stern looking. He said 'I want to see you in my office.'

I walked into the facility. Woody was standing in the doorway. I said he was looking very stern. He closed the door behind him as I walked in.

He looked at me with a straight face and said, 'How was it?'

I said, 'It was great.'

So we talked for some 15-20 minutes about my European adventure. Then he actually offered me a job. I went back to Ohio State and coached the next year as John Mummy's assistant on the freshman football team.

Instead of Woody barking, and oh yes, cussing, he was simply as interested in my trip as anybody else was.

That was Woody.

DAVE BRUNGARD

The first time I met Woody Hayes was after the opening game of the season my senior year of high school. I didn't know it at the time. I guess he sat up in the press box.

After the game, he came into the locker room unannounced. He introduced himself, shook hands and that was it.

It was like 'This is who I am...Talk to ya later.'

To say it came as a surprise would be an understatement. Because of who he was, it got a lot of attention. Something like that may not have happened for a long time at Youngstown Cheney High School, or maybe never that a man of his stature walked into our locker room.

Was I impressed? You betcha.

It was the little things that Woody Hayes did I think that made him the better and more effective recruiter. His recruiting was the major reason I went to Ohio State.

His personality in recruiting was very favorable. He would charm the parents. He's very congenial, very nice, very talkative and I think very inquisitive.

He asked all about the family. It wasn't a put-on.

I guess you could say Woody Hayes was the final part of the recruiting process.

Lou McCullough, defensive coordinator at Ohio State, was recruiter in my part of the state. Lou was also a very effective recruiter.

Before any visit or phone contact, you got a letter in the mail. The school expresses some interest in you. You fill out some form giving background, biographical information.

Lou came to see me play and talked to me. A good recruiter calls quite often, keeps in touch, lets you know he's interested. They even find time to come to Youngstown, stop by and visit.

Youngstown was strong Notre Dame territory. It was a long way from Youngstown-to-Columbus.

Back then they didn't have the beat writers, ESPN, and all that kind of stuff you see now. So you didn't get that day-to-day exposure.

Woody Hayes was a widely publicized and highly-respected coach. But you have to see him in action to appreciate the super salesman side of him.

It wasn't a bang-bang sales pitch on the school. He was very relaxed and came across very well. That's a side of him I think was very, very positive and the fact that he did a lot of the recruiting/home visits by himself.

With other schools, you'd see an assistant coach. Or when you went to visit the school you'd get maybe your 15, 20, 30 minute meeting with the head coach. But not with Woody Hayes. That personal touch made the difference. It did to me.

GEORGE CHAUMP

Woody Hayes was very, very complex. He was almost two different people. Woody could be as charming and as nice as anybody you'd ever want to be around. Or he could be explosive, even a man seemingly out of control.
They both were Woody Hayes.

The uniqueness of Woody Hayes was his wide range of personalities.

Sometimes, he was portrayed as this demon and villain and yet the good in this man far outweighed the things he's criticized for.

Woody was a good-hearted guy. He'd rather chew the fat with the janitor in the basement of the school. He wasn't a big timer. He certainly had the right to be. He was the champion of the small man. The coaches loved him. He gave the coaches time. The players loved him because he always had time for them. He always had time. If there was a crisis, Woody would be there. He'd be there when they needed help in a family tragedy.

He was very emotional. He was wound tight game-wise. He'd have a tendency to explode, but as a coach that was with him for 11 years, I took a different approach.

It didn't hit me like it hit everybody else. It wasn't that big a deal. That was just Woody.

He could be mad, literally swinging and fighting one day. The next day, it was as if nothing had happened. He'd say it wasn't personal. 'Dammit, I was just upset.' He'd go on from there.

Woody Hayes was very intelligent, very well read.

He could quote essays at Emerson's alma mater, Harvard, as an Emerson scholar. He could talk at the Naval Academy and have the class on the edge of it's seat as he described a great naval battle. He was a student of military history.

Education was very important to him. His father was superintendent of schools. He got that from him.

He stressed academics at Ohio State. In that respect, I think he was ahead of his time. His biggest thing was you've gotta keep kids in school. He was so right. I know. I tried it as head coach at Navy. If I didn't lose kids because of grades, we would have had winning seasons.

As coaches we had to be on top of our players' grades. We were expected to know all of their subjects, their grade point average, what they made on their last tests.

When I first came to Ohio State I served temporarily as backfield coach. When Rudy Hubbard, one of Woody's very good backs graduated, he became backfield coach. I was also quarterback coach.

Well, I had been warned about Woody. I studied up on my quarterbacks—Rex Kern, Ron Maciejowski, Billy Long—but I spent little time on the backs.

He asked all his assistants about various players. Then it was my turn. Woody looked at me and said 'Tell me about [Larry] Zelina.'

I was startled for the moment. I didn't know much about Larry who was a sophomore wingback in 1968. That was my first year.

My mind almost went totally blank. The only thing I could say was 'Larry Zelina?'

Well, that wasn't what Woody wanted to hear.

He looked at me. 'No, dammit, Bo Bo Zelina.'

I didn't make that mistake again.

MARK DEBEVC

Sure I remember Woody Hayes and his tirades, but I just smile at those. I remember those kind of things.

But I best remember the concern he had and how far he would go to stick up for his players. He was a straight-shooter. He demanded total honesty.

He told us one time; 'I don't mind if you make a mistake. We're all human. If you own up to that mistake then we can get on with the business of getting over it. I can help. But don't you lie to me and cover it up.'

Woody never played games with you. You knew where he was coming from. No one escaped his wrath, me included. I remember playing against Illinois. I don't recall if it was my sophomore or junior year.

Illinois played us real tough, especially in the first half. I'm playing defensive end and lining up most of the time against Doug Deakins. He was a big [about 250], strong and very talented offensive tackle. He went on to play pro ball with the Cleveland Browns.

They ran most of their plays off tackle. He just beat me up real good the first half. He manhandled me, pure-and-simple.

Woody was yelling at halftime, particularly at the defense. Most of it was directed at me. He singled me out. 'And you, get your ass outta your head and get yourself into the game.'

If somebody really gets hurt at the point of attack, they'd take you out or change the defense. Illinois was killing us off tackle. I wasn't doing the job. I had it coming.

Now that I have the privilege of hindsight, I realize that Doug Deakins was just better than me.

Woody stuck with me the second half. We made adjustments and I held my own against Deakins. There are several things you can do to neutralize a bigger, stronger player. Spin moves. Things like that.

I'd line up on his outside shoulder, then shoot to the inside gap and try to disrupt the play. It basically worked the second half.

Woody Hayes wasn't the most innovative coach. He basically believed in good old power football. But to his credit, he opened it up my junior and senior years. We did a lot more passing.

What also sticks out in my mind about the man was his uncanny ability to surround himself with wonderful assistants.

I can never remember feeling ill-prepared in a game. I can never ever remember being tricked in a game. Once in awhile a play or so, but in the course of the game we knew what to expect.

DAVE FOLEY

What do I remember about Woody Hayes?

The straight deal goes like this. During the season you had to hate the guy. You really did.

But away from the football season, you couldn't help but love the guy. I think that's probably been said by other people in other ways.

The guy did everything he could for you as a person. He would do anything he could to make you a better football player, to make us a better team.

I mean, he could belittle you. He could punch you. Any motivational tactic, without regard for personal feeling.

Away from football, Woody Hayes was the most sincere guy you'd ever want to be around.

He had a wonderful memory. Maybe I had said something about my parents, but that was years ago. Here's an example.

I was out of Ohio State for 10 or 15 years. But this day, I'm back in Columbus and here's Woody on the street. Obviously, you're an All-American and you'd like to think somebody will still remember you.

Whenever I introduce myself I say, 'Hey so-and-so, I'm Dave Foley.' You've changed physically over the years and I just want to catch somebody by surprise.

Woody deals with some 100 kids every year. That adds up to a lot of different faces over a 10-15 year period. When I saw Woody I said, 'Hey Coach, Dave Foley. Glad to see you.'

Well, he punches me in the stomach. In that gruff voice of his, he bellows 'I know you, Dave Foley. How's your mother, Virginia? And your Dad, Tom?'

He was clicking these names off and he was mad at me, insulted that I thought he wouldn't know me. That's the kind of guy he was.

He always made the parents feel completely comfortable. He would see my parents at a game four years later and say 'How's the dog doing?'

It was like they were best of friends, even though they'd only met once.

There are some people who have this great talent. Woody used his remarkable memory as a recruiting tool.

Woody always talked about one of the dirtiest four-letter words in the American vocabulary: WORK. He would always be quoted as saying 'somebody might outsmart me, but nobody will outwork me.'

Look what he did for all the guys who coached under him! I mean they kinda had to shake their heads at the experience, but they all speak with nothing but praise for the work ethic and the amount of determination that Woody had.

I'm sure it had a major influence when they became head coaches. I know it definitely influenced Lou Holtz.

Woody was not only a workaholic but as far as I'm concerned he was also an innovator. He's not been given credit for such.

He would use whatever tools he had in order to win, especially if he REALLY wanted to win that particular game. That would always hold true against Michigan. Or he'd put in new wrinkles to avenge a humiliating defeat, such as was the case with Purdue in 1968. He relished that kind of challenge.

I recall two such tactics during our national championship season.

For instance, Woody decided to spring an unbalanced line against Michigan. He had Rufus [Mayes] and I lined up side-by-side, alongside Jan White. We ended up having two All-American offensive tackles and a tight end shoulder-to-shoulder.

It was a surprise tactic. We did it early in the game and gained consistent yardage off of that formation. Michigan didn't know if they should shift, stay in the same formation, or what. Man, that was fun.

We met unbeaten and top-ranked Purdue in the third game of the season. It was our make-or-break game. How do you keep a talented and explosive team like that off balance?

Woody went with a no-huddle offense. We had eight or nine scripted plays that we called 'Red Roof Inn'...'Mustang'...'Cowboy'...or whatever. We would go to the line and call the play. We'd be in a set position. Then we'd snap the ball.

I believe we ran the no-huddle offense the first two series and both times went right down the field. Woody reached the conclusion that Purdue's defense was too big and out-of-shape. So we were gonna be in better shape and we were gonna run this no-huddle offense.

I thought that was quite innovative. Woody Hayes was really way ahead of his time.

LOU HOLTZ

Anybody that played or coached for Woody Hayes loved him, admired him and respected him. He didn't always condone everything that he did or said. He wasn't always fair. He wasn't interested in your point of view necessarily if he felt he was right.

But Coach Hayes didn't worry about being popular. What he did was he believed in people. And after you left him, you really admired and respected him because of the expectations he had of you as an athlete, coach, or whatever the case may be.

Woody Hayes could care less about public relations. He had too much to get done in a short period of time to worry about PR. He was a great human being, a great American. He loved his country. He fought for his country.

He was a historian. He loved military history. He was probably as well read as anyone I've ever been around.

Was he misunderstood by the general public? I think absolutely. I think the next question would be, 'Did he care?' The answer is NO. What he cared about was his players and coaches. He was special.

As far as a man, he was a very caring individual. I don't know if you had a better friend when you needed one than Woody Hayes. But Woody Hayes was not one to cater to you if you really didn't need him.

There were a lot of other people that needed Coach Hayes and so...like after I left Ohio State I would call him. He'd never return my phone call unless I told his secretary, 'Hey, I've gotta talk to Coach Hayes. I've got a problem.' He'd return my phone call within 15 minutes. He'd say 'You don't need someone telling you you're doing a good job.'

It's like I've seen him come back home from Vietnam and call a couple of thousand parents at his own expense to tell them he met their son and relayed the message. He had a whole notebook that he kept with him, jotting down names, phone numbers and messages. Just his generosity towards charitable causes. Just the type of person he was. I mean he had morals. He had values. He had standards. He had beliefs.

Maybe you didn't agree with him, but you talk about a man of conviction. He had it.

As far as a coach, he was a great fundamentalist. He understood people and worked at it tirelessly. I don't know if anybody had more stamina than me, but I promise you this, I did not have more than Woody.

Imagine this. We beat Purdue, 13-0, the No.1 team in the country. That same night, Woody calls in his staff to look at the game films of the Purdue game. It's a wonderful win for us. Everybody's celebrating and we're in the office looking at films of a game that was played only a few hours before.

Today, everybody talks about rights and privileges. In those days, Woody Hayes talked and demanded. He had obligations and responsibilities.

I think whether you're talking about Lou Holtz, Bill Mallory, Earle Bruce, Bo Schembechler or anyone else who's ever coached for Woody Hayes, they all go out and handle it the same way. I'll tell you this. The guy ran as honest a program as I've ever been around.

We all laugh at the way Woody Hayes did things. But doggone it, when we became head coaches we just emulated him the same way.

Coach Hayes and I played it the same way. We put tremendous pressure on players in practice. When they got in the game, there's never any tension. Pressure is when you do something you aren't adequately prepared to do.

141

If you adequately prepare your team, they will have a looseness and wanna play. Coach Hayes certainly had a unique way to do that.

We had great success but sometimes you get stereotyped a certain way no matter what you do. If you go out and look, when Woody Hayes had the least success, it was when he tried something other than what he was, which was just a good hard-nosed teacher.

When he tried to finesse people and threw the ball, and there were some years when he threw a great deal, he did not have success. He had the best success when he had a hard-nosed physical running football team.

Then you had a guy like [sophomore quarterback] Rex Kern who also had leadership qualities. In the opening game against SMU it was fourth-and-long just before halftime. I think we're ahead, 14-7.

Coach Hayes sent the punt team onto the field. Rex waved 'em off, went for it and we ended up scoring right before the half. I mean, that's unheard of for a sophomore quarterback.

Rex could get away with that sort of thing. He had the personality. He also understood Coach Hayes.

We played man-to-man pass defense at times. Coach Hayes had a certain adamancy about putting our strong safety always to the wide field. It goes back to Baron VonSchliffen about keeping the right flank strong.

We did a lot of different things, but nothing novel or unique. We played man-to-man free. We rarely ever played straight man. We went with two safeties, what we referred to as Man Under. Then we did combinations, but mainly we tried to play good hard-nosed football.

Coach Hayes always took pride in the fact that not too many backs rushed for 100 yards against Ohio State. We sorta had that tradition and the players had an obligation to carry that over.

The one thing is, if you had a great back we were gonna find a way to stop him no matter how many people we had to put on the line.

We had real good quickness. We lost some good people during the 1968 season. We lost Dirk Worden who was our linebacker and our captain. A kid by the name of Doug Adams stepped in. We moved Mark Debevc to outside linebacker due to an injury.

You had a guy like Dave Whitfield who played big enough even though he was only 185. We had people like Jim Stillwagon, Jack Tatum, Mike Sensibaugh, Tim Anderson, Ted Provost, Paul Schmidlin. All quality kids.

Everybody cared about one another. They had obligations and responsibilities and they fulfilled 'em.

We had great speed and quickness. The guys loved the game of football and they played it with a reckless enthusiasm.

Woody was the surrogate father to the players. We coaches had our 'big brother.' He was Esco Sarkkinen. 'Sark' was an All-American at Ohio State in 1939. He was Woody's right-hand man. He was our defensive end coach as well as our top scout.

'Sark' had been there for so long. He had an easiness about him. Whenever you got uptight or worried, you just went and talked to him.

RON MACIEJOWSKI

I think I was in awe the first time I met Woody Hayes. He was coming to my home. I was playing basketball. He was already there when I came home. My Mom had given him a piece of cake. He wrote to her that it was the best piece of cake he'd ever had. Of course, Woody probably wrote that to every guy's mother. He was a real charmer. He talked about everything except football.

He watched to see how you treated your parents. He wouldn't recruit you if you were nasty to your parents.

Woody never tried to con you. He said something like 'We'd love to have you play for us. We're building a good program. We have opportunity. We're not going to promise you anything except a good education and the opportunity to play football.'

He was complex. You see a different private person than you would a public person. I mean he would do anything for you.

He was so intense about the game. That's what he cared about. He didn't care about making money. But what he didn't realize was that to some of his assistants it did matter because they had 3, 4, 5 kids. They've gotta be making considerably less than Woody.

He was a great guy. He was a contradiction. He expected you to be so discicplined, so solid, so fundamentally sound. But he wasn't. He was totally different than the discipline he expected out of us. You got to expect that after awhile. That's the way people are. They are what they are.

He was a tough guy during the season. Once football was over, he was great.

When we get together [former OSU players], when we talk to each other, we start laughing. Sometimes we go 'You know that we sound just like the old man did.' We talk like that now.

I guess that's the ultimate compliment because the things he said stayed with us and meant something. Things like 'You win with people.'

You've gotta have quality people to be successful. We know that in our business today. You're either getting better or you're getting worse because you can never stay the same.

You'd better be better than you were yesterday or someone else is gonna whip your ass. Doing things the right way. That's what Woody always preached.

BILL MALLORY

I had the privilege of serving under Woody Hayes at Ohio State for three years. I have wonderful memories of those times, especially our national championship season of 1968.

Woody taught me so many valuable lessons which I carried throughout my long college coaching career. I'll get to that a little later.

What I'll always remember is one crazy moment that happened during my first year [1966]. It's something I can laugh about now but it really wasn't funny at the time it happened.

In this day of video cameras, I wish we had it all recorded on tape. You simply had to be there to believe it.

143

Class of '68

I was defensive line coach in charge of tackles and nose guard. Woody also appointed me in charge of the weather. It was up to me to give him the weather report every day. I mean each-and-every-day. He was quite adamant about that. Woody had a memory like an elephant. He never forgot. He could tell you this-and-this happened when he was coaching at Denison in 1947, or such-and-such happened during a game with so-and-so. He simply had an uncanny memory.

Well, it seems one of his backs at Ohio State had suffered a badly sprained ankle on a wet and slippery field during practice and was lost for the rest of the season.

To avoid that ever happening again he wanted to know what the weather forecast was going to be. I'd call the weather bureau. I'd check the airport.

If the weather was going to be bad, I was to get a hold of our groundskeeper and make sure the field was covered.

To make a long, long story very short, we were getting ready to go to Minnesota. I got the weather report. It was gonna rain. I contacted the groundskeeper and said, 'Let's just cover the field.'

That didn't make him happy. 'Don't like it. It will kill the grass if we cover that turf.'

I pleaded with him to cover the practice field. By then it was time to go into our coaches meeting. We'd start those meetings at eight in the morning and they'd go until midnight and even beyond.

At midnight, Woody was still at it with his offensive coaches.

The defensive coaching staff, including me, was leaving for the day. The other coaches beat me out the door. They'd already left by the time I was heading for my car in the parking lot.

It's raining cats-and-dogs. I ran out to the practice field and it's not covered. I had to go back in and tell Woody.

I knocked on the door. Woody yelled 'Yeah.'

I told him who I was and walked in. 'We've got a problem.'

'What is it?'

'The field isn't covered.'

'You're damn right we've got a problem. Are the defensive coaches still here?'

'They all left awhile ago.'

'Well, call 'em and tell 'em all to get right back here.'

I called each and every one of them. Lou McCullough, our defensive coordinator, was already in bed. Earle Bruce, our backfield coach, had about an hour's drive home. He wasn't there, so I left a message.

We all got there, including Woody. It's like one in the morning.

It's not only raining hard but the wind's really blowing. You couldn't have picked a worst possible scenario to put down the tarps. They were scattered all over the place. Heck, we didn't know what we were doing.

We must have been there for 90 minutes. We'd get ahold of a tarp and the wind would pick it up like a helium balloon. We're getting drenched and not making much progress.

Finally, the rain stopped and the wind calmed. We were finally able to get the practice field covered.

I'll never forget that one.

There were a lot of things I admired about Woody Hayes. First and foremost, his work ethic. Nobody was more dedicated. There couldn't have been. Football was his life. I marveled at his energy. It was always GO, GO, GO. A real workaholic. He really loved what he was doing.

You never could outwork him. Nobody could ever outwork Woody Hayes. There just aren't any more hours in the day. It was football round-the-clock.

He knew what he wanted to do and how to do it. Nothing was gonna hold him back. He was consistent. He lived in a fishbowl that is major college football.

The general public really doesn't know the pressure put upon a head football coach. Yet Woody thrived on pressure. It was just another challenge to him.

Just when you thought he was down, Woody Hayes bounced back. He went 4-5 my first year and he really didn't know what the future held for him.

He coached at a state university. He worked on a one-year contract which was renewed after each season. After the '66 season, he gave each of us permission to look for another job. He wouldn't hold us back.

That super sophomore group surfaced in '68 and the rest is history. He went unbeaten, untied and won the national championship. Woody was named Coach of the Year.

He did such a great job in game preparation. His players were mentally and physically prepared. We did an awful lot of repetitions that became second nature.

When you coach for Woody you could virtually forget about your home life. You didn't have any. You weren't around home too much. You had to have a special kind of wife to endure. You either made that commitment or you go find another job. You had to make the sacrifice. That's the way it was.

There wasn't a whole lot you could do about it. Woody would never back off. We'd play a game on a Saturday afternoon, go home for a little while, then return to school to grade films. You'd be back the next morning at eight.

All of us had to travel. I know I had to go 40-45 minutes to work. Columbus is a big city. If you live out in the suburbs, you had to get up early to beat the traffic.

Woody always started his meeting with his entire staff. Woody was a great reader. He loved to read. That was really his pastime.

The man never took a whole lot of rest. He would stay at school many a time at night. He'd sleep on the couch in his office. Anne [his wife] would bring him his clothes.

He was an interesting guy to be around. He was a real history buff, especially World War II history. He was a strong advocate for education.

When I came to Columbus for my interview, I thought we were going to talk about X's and O's. Not once did he mention X's and O's. He emphasized education. That was his No.1 priority.

Certainly, he was in the business of winning football games. But he was also in the business of preparing a young man for life-after-football.

He fully expected his coaches to be involved in their players' academics. He wanted his young men to leave Ohio State with a diploma. It was virtually a 12-month-a-year job for Woody and his coaching staff. Not just the actual Spring and Summer practice, the season, but the recruiting as well. I've always enjoyed the recruiting end of it.

You only get out of something what you put into it.
It's that way in coaching. It's that way in life.

LOU McCULLOUGH

Woody Hayes was tough, but he wasn't that tough. I mean as far as working his offense, our defense worked a lot harder than that.

Woody didn't like to scrimmage us much because that was the toughest thing they had to do. They didn't play anybody as good as we were on defense. We chewed 'em up and he didn't like that at all.

I think Coach Hayes' greatest asset was his work ethic. He outworked everybody. He worked all the time.

Typically on Sunday you went to work at 8 in the morning and you got home at 11 that night.

You went to work at 8 Monday morning. You got off at 11 at night.

You went to work Tuesday morning at 8. You got off at 11 at night.

Wednesday was the same thing.

Thursday you're supposed to have off. You didn't have off because you worked on recruiting. You called all your players. You worked until 11 o'clock that night.

You spent Friday night with the players.

We're the only team in America that on Saturday night, right after a ball game, we ran home and ate something, then returned to work until 11 o'clock. We had our game film. We got everything charted and ready for Sunday.

Tuesday was our biggest practice day of the week. By then, we had all of our defenses set. We very seldom changed after Tuesday night.

We did that for years. The Fourth of July was no different.

After I became defensive coordinator in 1965 I made a rule for my staff. We were gonna stop at 10 o'clock at night. But the offensive coaching staff was there with Woody for at least another hour.

I felt anything after 10 we were just spinning our wheels. From my standpoint, it worked out great. When we walked down the hall the offense was still going strong. They always used to tell us, 'make a lot of noise so he'll [Woody Hayes] know you're leaving.'

If there was one thing Coach Hayes couldn't tolerate it was fumbling the ball. I could tell you a story of three players, but I'll limit it to just one.

We had a fullback that should have made All-American. But he fumbled, so he was moved to the offensive line. He was just an average guard or tackle. He's in Columbus now, giving Ohio State a lot of money.

Coach Hayes had some great qualities. One thing about him, he didn't give lip service to you being a student. He made sure that you were a student. You'd better go to class or you're off the team.

We had a good study hall. He had a class himself that started at eight o'clock. He had 82 in the class. He'd shut the door. If you were a minute late, you didn't get in. If you missed three classes, you flunked.

JIM OTIS

I knew Woody Hayes from a different perspective when I was growing up in Celina, Ohio. I knew him away from his office. I knew him when he was with his family. He'd bring Anne [his wife] and Steve [his son] to visit and maybe spend a couple of days.

My Dad and Woody went to college together. They were classmates at Denison. I always felt like he was Uncle Woody.

When I was a youngster, we'd sometimes go up to his house. We'd go there for games and stuff. I remember one time Woody took Steve and me down to Ohio Stadium and we played a two-man football game. Just the three of us in an empty 80,000 seat stadium.

Dad never talked too much about some of the stuff they did in college. Although, as a kid, I remember he would kid Woody about certain things they did in the old days. He was the announcer who introduced Woody in the ring when Woody was a boxer in college.

My Dad was an avid golfer. Sometimes when my Grandma came to Denison to visit, my Dad would be out playing golf. Of course you know who would be driving Grandma around? It would be Woody. Grandma loved Woody and always felt he was a great influence on Dad.

Dad and Woody were very good, very close friends. They were roommates together for two years at Sigma Chi House. I know my Dad loved Woody. I know they had a very close friendship, almost like brothers.

Woody spoke at my high school banquet when I was a senior. Then he'd come back to our house. He excused everybody except me. We're in the kitchen and he said, 'I need to talk to Jim privately.'

He started talking. 'You know I'm recruiting another fullback who's a little bigger than you are. I'm not sure, but he might be better than you.'

I looked at him and said, 'Coach, are you offering me a scholarship to come to Ohio State?'

He looked at me and smiled. 'Yes, I am. But I'm telling you right now, we might be getting a fullback who might be better than you.'

You know what I told him? 'If you're offering me a scholarship, then we'll have to see just how good he really is.'

Once I reported to practice at Ohio State, our relationship changed. It had to. I think Woody was awfully tough on me...and that's okay. He made me a better football player.

There's no question that he demanded a great deal from his players. I think he was tough on me because he wasn't gonna ever allow my teammates to say 'He's playing because his old man and Woody are friends.' He just would never allow that to happen.

The first time I ever saw Woody in action as a coach, tears came to my eyes. It really did. I'd never seen him like that before.

While Woody was awfully tough and demanding, he was also very, very fair. I know when Woody benched me as a sophomore, that had to have caused a

147

strain on the relationship between my Dad and Woody. Dad and I never spoke about it. Not to this day.

Woody got on everybody, not just me. I'll tell you. Nobody was left out of that part of it. If you were left out, it means you probably weren't playing.

I played for a lot of great coaches. I played for Bud Wilkinson, Don Coryell, and Hank Stram in the pros. I played for Woody Hayes. He was the best. He was the greatest. I mean he made me do things on Saturday that I could never do on Wednesday.

He was a great motivator. He was a great coach. He cared so much about his players. He invented tough love. That's the hardest part of being a parent. You love your kids so much it's hard sometimes to discipline 'em when you know you should. Well, Woody knew. Woody would have felt like he was cheating the player if he let the player get along on less than his best effort.

I'll tell you something. When all these people in Columbus and around Ohio saw these great, great players with all that success and popularity, there was one man who could snap his fingers and each player would come to attention. Woody was the man who could do it.

The greatest compliment you could pay Woody was wanting your son to be coached by him—taught by him.

Sometimes I noticed that the younger coaches at that time like Lou Holtz and George Chaump had their thoughts on how it should be done. They were serious scholars of football. But each one of those would tell you today that their respect of Woody as a coach grew as they became older and more knowledgeable about coaching.

They would tell you there's no question how great Woody was. We discovered, to our surprise, that as we got older he got smarter. He did things one way. His way. He did them the right way.

Woody NEVER humiliated anyone. He was tough on 'em. He made 'em do things they didn't want to do, or thought they couldn't do. He made people do the things he expected them to do. He made people do a lot of things, but he never, never humiliated them. That's why he was such a great coach and leader. He made his players much better than they ever expected to be.

Some people think Woody Hayes went out in a bad way. But you know, that was just one moment in time. That's not the memory I have of him.

He was truly one-of-a-kind.

MIKE POLASKI

The thing I remember more than anything about Woody Hayes. He was two completely different people.

He was Woody Hayes the football coach. He was very single-minded. If there was something that he wanted to see on the football field, he was bound-and-determined that it was gonna happen.

When it didn't, he'd go into temper tantrums. It was absolutely unbelieveable. He'd tear the hats, the T-shirts, break his glasses, stomp on his watch, punch himself in the head.

148

He'd swear like a sailor. Here's a man that has a very good vocabulary, but when he'd lose his temper the vocabulary would be reduced to four letter words. The stream of 'em would go on almost continuously.

That was what we saw in private, on the football field.

In public you would take him anywhere in any setting. He was well-read. He was intelligent. He was opinionated.

He had things that truly interested him such as military history and to some extent political science. He would sit there and discuss social studies, just about any topic you wanted to talk about, and he'd do it very well.

It got to the point in the conversation where you disagreed about something, Woody was gonna have his opinion on the matter. He would listen to your opinion. He would honor your opinion, but for you to be able to change his mind your argument had better be damned good.

Did I ever see anyone change Woody's mind? I can't say that I ever saw anybody change his mind about how he felt. If you were blowin' smoke, Woody didn't even want to hear you.

As a defensive player, I really didn't spend much time with him. Woody was responsible for the offense. They actually practiced on a different field. We had two fields at the training facility.

The offense was on one field with their scout team. The defense was on the other with our scout team. We'd work on what we had to do. They'd work on their particular needs.

We even joked in the locker room. We'd introduce ourselves to each other. 'Rex, my name is Mike Polaski. I play defensive halfback. I hear you're our starting quarterback.'

We saw Woody in the halls, at the facility, over in his office, and on game day. He was never in our defensive huddle. We always had Lou Holtz, Bill Mallory and Esco [Sarkkinen]. They were the ones on our field.

During my career at Ohio State, Woody never really got on my case. That didn't happen until after I was gone. Mike Bordner was the team trainer. He was also a friend of mine. One time I'm back at Ohio State, going to see Mike to set up a golf date.

I stop at the practice field where Woody is running his offense. He's working on the passing game and things aren't going well.

I happen to see several of the local sportswriters who are standing on the sidelines. I start to talk with them. There's Kay Kessler and Tom Pastorius [Citizen-Journal] and Paul Hornung [Dispatch] as well as Ted Mullins who used to do Woody's television show.

Ted starts telling me a joke. When he gets to the punchline I come unglued. I'm laughing. It's a funny story. As I said, on the field the passing offense has not gone well. Their quarterback is throwing the ball up for grabs and Woody's really ticked.

He's in the huddle. He's screaming and carrying on with the quarterback. All of a sudden he looks to the sidelines and sees me laughing. I don't know whether he thinks I'm laughing at him, at the pass offense or what.

Like a wild bull elephant he charges the sidelines, gets to about four yards from where I'm standing. He looks at me for a few seconds. Then he explodes. I'll try to clean it up.

'Damn it, Polaski. We don't need you. We don't want you. Take it on in.'
He's sending me to the showers. He's kicking me out of practice like I'm still playing for him. I just stand there and look at him.

We look at each other for about 30 seconds. Then I think he realizes I don't play for him anymore. I'd been gone for about four years. He just turns and goes back to the huddle.

I just looked at Pastorius, Mullins, those guys.

Ted said, 'I'm sorry. I didn't mean to get you into trouble like that.'

I said 'It's not your fault. You know how the old man is. I should have been over on the defensive field anyway.' I went on to see Mike. We played golf that weekend.

All the time I played at Ohio State, he never threw me out of a meeting. Never threw me out of practice. Once I'm gone, that's when I get the heave-ho.

I have to tell this story. It's the other side of the coin. The other side of the man.

After I was done in school with my eligibility, I hadn't graduated. I hadn't gotten my degree. Every time I'd see Woody, the first thing he'd ask was, 'Mike, did you graduate yet?'

I always had to tell him, 'No, Coach, I haven't.'

'Well, goddammit, are you working towards it?'

Sometimes I had to tell him 'No.' Sometimes I'd tell him 'Yes, Coach. I'm working on it. I'm getting money. I'll be back next quarter.'

Well, we went through this same dialogue for about five years after I'd left.

I saw him at Marty Karow's retirement dinner. He was retiring as Ohio State's baseball coach. Woody was there.

We went through the same scenario.

'Hi, Coach. How are you doing?'

'Well, Mike, have you graduated yet?'

'No, Coach, I haven't.'

Then he starts in on me. But before Woody can get too far, I interrupt him.

'Coach, time out. That's going to happen tomorrow morning. I'm going to commencement exercises tomorrow. I'm getting my degree.'

You'd have thought I was his own son. Woody grabbed me, hugged me and shook my hand.

"You can't believe how happy that makes me. It took you a long time to do it. You stuck with it. We brought you here to get an education. Goddammit, it will serve you well."

You can't fake that kind of sincerity. That kind of caring.

TED PROVOST

I really didn't have that much contact with Woody Hayes as a player. He ran the offense. I was on defense. We'd have a team meeting with him, then go to our individual coaches. Then you went to practice and you never saw Woody.

Only time I had much to do with him was my freshman year when we were scrimmaging with the varsity all the time.

Certainly I heard of Woody Hayes before I first met him. But I never heard all the stories, the stuff he did at practice.

I knew he was supposed to be a tough coach, but that didn't bother me. My high school coaches were as tough as he was, maybe even a little tougher. He was definitely a no-nonsense coach. But he was a true scholar and a gentleman to me.

There were a couple of moments when you kinda wondered. Like when I was a freshman and the varsity lost at Minnesota. I went to practice the following Monday. Woody had two black eyes.

I asked the varsity guys, 'What the hell happened? Did he get into a fight with somebody?'

'No', they said. 'He was so mad after the game he started punching himself.'

I saw the antics when he ripped his cap. You saw plays where Rufus Mayes [offensive tackle] missed a block and he'd go over and slug Rufus on the side of the head. Woody treated everybody fair, but he treated us tough.

I returned to Ohio State as a graduate assistant under Woody Hayes. After my career at Ohio State, I was drafted in the seventh round by the NFL Los Angeles Rams. I was drafted as a safety.

George Allen was head coach. He didn't like to play rookies. In fact, he pulled Eddie Meador out of retirement. I was third string.

I was in training camp about six weeks and was traded to Minnesota. I played one year with them. The next year I made it through training camp but then I was cut.

So, I contacted Woody and he let me be an assistant graduate coach. School started two weeks later. Woody took care of everything.

He took care of anything you needed. If you needed money or if you needed some help with your classes, Woody Hayes was there for you.

It was then that I began to really appreciate the man. The dedication he gave to his job. He was there early in the morning and stayed until late at night. Sometimes, he slept in his office.

Then you start learning about his charity. The hitchhikers he'd pick up, the people he'd visit in the hospital, the fees he would donate after a speaking engagement.

The guy didn't care about money. Money was not his motivation.

I stayed with Woody and the team for most of the season. With four games left in the NFL season, I got a call from the St. Louis Cardinals. Woody wished me the best of luck.

JIM ROMAN

I knew I was going to coach after my college football days were over. For whatever reason, I needed a few more hours to finish my student teaching.

I wanted to go and coach in high school and I figured a year under Woody Hayes would look real good on my resume. So, I became his graduate assistant.

I learned a hell of a lot of football that year. I ended up being the guy who follows him around with a clipboard. When he called a play during the game, I was the guy who wrote it down.

Then on Sundays, I was the only student that ever had a key to St. John Arena. I had to go over and pick up the game film at the photo lab, go back to St. John, call Woody and wake him up at about 5:30 in the morning.

I'd say, 'Coach, what do you want on your TV show?'

Then I'd edit out those plays and write a script. When he came in later, I'd go over it with him. Then we'd have a meeting at the TV station. I'd wait for him.

If he'd forget the film, which he'd do, I'd have to drive back downtown and put it back together.

Woody became like a surrogate father. In fact, he and my Dad resembled each other. The same kind of build, the same kind of attitude, the same kind of mouth, the same kind of work ethic.

My Dad worked in a steel mill for 42 years. In high school one time I got mouthy at some blue-haired old English teacher when I was a freshman. She sent me to the office.

The assistant principal beat the hell out of me with a board, then made me sit there while he called my Dad at the steel mill.

When I got home, he was standing at the top of the steps with a razor strop. I got it all over again. So for the next three-and-a-half years they didn't even know I was in that school, had it not been for athletics. I'm not a slow learner.

Woody was the same type. When you screwed up it wouldn't be above him to let your parents know about it.

I don't think there was a player on our team who didn't hate Woody Hayes at one time or another. It didn't last. There were times when he'd cuss and scream at you, but I tell you he was always right.

If he was sure you were doing your best you were safe. He wasn't going to ask you to do something you couldn't do. But if he thought you were doggin' it, he'd get after you.

The first time I ever went on the field was during my sophomore year. We were playing at Minnesota. The game was on national TV. I was backup to our All-American center, Ray Pryor.

Pryor got hurt early in the second period. There I am in my first varsity game and I'm lining up against a big, big man, a monster named Aaron Brown.

I mean he was 6-7 and weighed about 260-270 which was huge at that time. He's playing nose guard. I'm not going to take him down, not at 215 pounds. All I could possibly do was to occupy him, keep him as busy as I could. I was like a fly on the back of an elephant.

I played a pretty good game. They ended up beating us. I remember Woody just ravaging a couple of lockers after the game. He was fuming because he thought we should have won.

The next day we're back in Columbus. Woody saw me and started to say 'Goddam you', but I interrupted him.

'What's the matter, Coach?'

He said, 'Why don't you practice like you play? You had a hell of a ballgame yesterday. You took that big All-American and made him crazy. You had a hell of a game against a great football player.'

I said 'Thanks.'

'Thanks my ass. You'd better start practicing like that or I'm gonna run you outta here.'

That was Woody Hayes.

I wasn't a great practice player. I'm playing behind an All-American. I don't expect to see much action so I'm not gonna kill myself at practice just to sit on the bench. But after that I started to practice a little harder. As I said, he couldn't tolerate laziness.

I missed an extra point kick against Michigan State my senior year. I came off the field and then he let me have it.

Not with his mouth but with his fist. He punched me in the chest so hard I thought my heart had been rammed back to my backbone. He yelled, 'Now you SOB, we're gonna have to throw the thing the next time.'

I knew what that meant and I said, 'Why don't you hit me again?'

It meant that after we'd score a touchdown, we'd go after the two-point conversion with me throwing the pass.

It was a fake kick. They snapped the ball straight to me. I was supposed to run to my right and throw it back to our holder, Billy Long.

They snapped it to me. I only took about three steps. All I could see was green and I got slaughtered.

If Woody was hard on you at practice or during a game, he'd make sure he set it right. It was up at Wisconsin. We were playing on artificial turf. It was the first time any of us had played on a carpet.

I missed an extra point and Woody ripped me for it.

We're flying back home after the game. I'm 22 years old and just about to cry. I was distraught. Woody sat with me for most of the flight.

I was so upset with myself. It's really harder to miss an extra point than it is to make one. If you don't see your foot hit the ball you can slice it or shank it. That's what I was doing.

He was very calm, very conciliatory. All he said was, 'You're not gonna miss any more, are you?'

I said, 'No I'm not, Coach. It's a matter of concentration.'

When I was a high school coach I followed Woody's example. If I was tough on a kid, I made sure I saw him before he went home. Coach was right.

My relationship with Woody Hayes didn't end after my graduation. I kept in touch. I'd see him once or twice a year even after he was out of coaching.

In 1979 my New Philadelphia High School team finished 7-3 with 13 sophomores in the starting lineup. We were expected to be real tough for the next two years.

One of those kids broke his neck in a practice scrimmage in 1980. He was a quadraplegic. The doctor said I could have dragged him to the hospital by his face mask and it wouldn't have hurt him any worse than the damage that had been done when he hit the ground.

We had to announce that to the kids the next day. It was devastating. I called Woody. I also called another guy I knew real well. Ron Apperson coached in Zanesville. 'AP' had a kid struck by lightning during practice. He was killed.

I called Woody's home and his wife, Annie, answered.

I said, 'Annie, is Coach around?'

She said 'No.'

'I've really got to talk to him.'

She said 'What's up?'

I told her. She said 'You stay close to your phone and I'll call him.'

Woody called back in 20 minutes.

He said 'What do you need?'

'I don't know what the hell to do with these 65 kids. Everybody's walking around staring into space, wondering if this is the right thing to do [playing football].'

Woody listened and responded.

'Just get back to work. Keep 'em busy. You don't have to get 'em out there and kill 'em. Go helmets and shorts for a day or two. Just get back in your groove. Don't give 'em time to sit around and think about it and mope. Get back to work.'

That's what we did. It turned out pretty well. Coach called a couple of times after that to see how we were doing. Later in the year, he came back and spoke at our banquet.

About the same time my kid was hurt, a hell of a player at Dover High School found out he had cancer. We ended up having a benefit, a dinner and auction at the end of the year to raise funds for those two families.

I called Woody and asked if if he could come and speak, that we were trying to raise funds for my kid who broke his neck and for the other kid who had cancer.

Without any hesitation he said, 'Just tell me when. I don't care what's going on. I'll rearrange my schedule and be there.' Woody Hayes was there. He even wrote a personal check of $500 for the fund.

He'd come to New Philadelphia a couple of other times over the years. His wife was from New Philly.

A lot of his players, me included, attended his funeral and memorial service when he died [March 1987]. Former President Nixon spoke at one of the services. I was very impressed.

We [the former players] reserved a ballroom at a local hotel. It was sorta like a reunion, but most of the stuff centered around Woody.

Woody began his coaching career as an assistant at Mingo Junction, down by Steubenville. Then he came up here as an assistant coach. He took over the head job at New Philadelphia in 1938 and remained until he went into the U.S. Navy.

Our football stadium was built in the 1930s. It was getting run down. We put together a committee to raise funds to renovate the stadium and to rename it Quaker Woody Hayes Stadium. It was called Quaker Stadium.

Hopefully, the stadium will be dedicated in 1999. I'm thrilled that the stadium will be named for Woody Hayes and tickled to death that I was asked to be involved in the project.

It's the least I could do for a man who gave me so much.

PAUL SCHMIDLIN

I was a very sheltered youngster, a shy kid of 17 my senior year in high school. We lived a basic nuts-and-bolts kind of life. I was a highly-recruited defensive lineman. Those were exciting days.

I visited seven campuses. Eight of the Big Ten schools were very interested in me, as was the Mid-American Conference. I guess it boiled down to Indiana or Ohio State.

I was very impressed with Indiana head coach John Pont. He was a quality individual. Hugh Hindman had the Northwest Ohio area as an Ohio State recruiter. I think every assistant coach did recruiting.

Harvey Shapiro

I made a visit down to the Ohio State campus for a weekend and then a little later, I made arrangements to take my parents down to Columbus to meet Coach Hayes. I stayed with Vic Stottlemyer that weekend. He was a freshman and a middle guard.

The final sale was made when Woody made arrangements for my mother and I to go visit with Dean Bonner who was dean of the Arts and Sciences.

My Dad had suffered a heart attack a few weeks earlier. He needed to take a nap after every lunch. We had a nice lunch down at The Union. Afterwards, Woody and my Dad went back to Woody's office to take a nap. My Mom and I went over to visit with Dean Bonner. From that point on my parents were completely sold.

Woody Hayes was definitely the deciding factor. I wouldn't say that I was in awe of him. I was meeting a lot of head coaches. He just had a good personality, good personal skills.

My parents warmed up to him immediately. As a result, I felt very comfortable making the decision to go to Ohio State. Generally, I felt more comfortable with the people I met there. I was comfortable with the situation even though it was a huge campus.

He preached and lived fundamental conservative values. He had a good work ethic, "Know that you've got to put in the time and effort in order to succeed, in football or in life."

He affected my life in a lot of ways. He was a quality man. Of course, being young and impressionable, I always enjoyed his stories even though Woody told them so many times.

If he said it once, he said it a thousand times."There's a lot of coaches out there smarter than I am, but I'll tell you this. Nobody could work any harder than I do."

The one thing I will always remember took place when I was about 18. I wanted to move out of the dormitory and into the fraternity house. But in order to do that you had to get Woody's permission.

I went to see him with fear and trepidation.

He invited me into his office. I went in and closed the door. For the next hour he proceeded to just talk about things. Asked me how I was doing, talked about who I might be dating. Just anything and everything, sharing thoughts and ideas about life. It was just one of those very inspiring moments.

It wasn't until the end that Woody got down to business. In all honesty, I think it was his way of evaluating whether or not he thought I was mature enough to be able to handle life in the fraternity house.

He really made a difference in my thought process, my approach to life. Woody's death didn't come as a shock.

He'd been ill for some time. Each time that I'd see him, he looked a little weaker, a little less able to function, to maneuver. It wasn't a shock to me when he died. He was struggling.

MARK STIER

I don't think I'm saying anything startling about Woody Hayes. You either loved him or you hated him. Nothing in between. I loved the man.

Lou McCullough was our defensive coordinator. Woody didn't coach a lot of

155

the defense. He was the offensive guy, but he had general oversight of the defense.

Woody was a great motivator. It was all the stuff all week long. It was the intensity. There were no days off for Woody and his coaching staff. There were times when he even slept in his office.

It was doing things right. There were so many things. As you look back at your life and you say 'Gee, I got this from him, I learned this from Woody.'

He was a great educator. People forget he was extremely intelligent, extremely well-read. If you had to rate professors he would certainly be considered one of the best.

Woody got an "A" for his college coaching which is as much a teaching experience as chemistry, math or history. College coaches should be looked upon as professors because, in essence, they're teaching football.

He loved young men. He loved the University setting. He obviously loved Ohio State. He loved the academic setting. His father was head of schools in New Philadelphia. He was raised in that environment. Education was an important factor in his life. He was raised in that culture, so why not bring it to Ohio State?

I looked at him as a father figure. He was the kind of individual who would guide you. His counsel was pretty much right on target even if you sometimes didn't like it.

After my last season I had a couple of offers from the pros, but nothing heavy. Nothing really solid. I had a teaching job waiting for me in the Fall of 1968. All I had to do was complete my summer of student teaching. I was an Education major.

Believe me, I wanted to play football. I can remember talking to Woody. He said, 'Look, Mark, you can try out for the pros if you want to. I'm not trying to make you feel bad, but I don't think you're good enough.

'You might hang on for a year or so. You've already got a job lined up in the Fall. If I were you, I'd go to school this Summer, finish your degree and get on with your life.'

I could see it myself. I wasn't fast enough. I wasn't big enough. If I had four or five teams that were interested, that would have been something else. The only kind of interest I got was, 'If you want to pop in.'

Woody gave me pretty good counsel.

JAN WHITE

I knew two different people in Woody Hayes. The one off the field. The one on the field.

Off the field he was always charming and soft spoken. He had a mind like an elephant. He'd tell story-after-story. He was always very much at ease.

But on the field he was different. He was pretty fiery. There were times you just stepped out of his way.

He was short tempered, but I believe some of it was by design. He'd wear a baseball-type cap at practice. If he started barking at me, for instance, saying I was lazy and not putting out 100 percent, he'd grab that cap and start ripping it.

Then he throw it on the ground, stomp on it, and jump up-and-down. He'd be jumping and yelling and we'd just sit there and laugh.

We found out that Woody actually cut a slit in the cap. Pretty sly old fox.

It was definitely staged, but you still wanted to stay out of the way when he'd get fired up. He just wouldn't pick on me. He'd pick on everybody. You could say he was quite a character. We all loved him. You wanted to play for Woody Hayes. He worked just as hard as we did, maybe even harder.

He cared about us, not just as football players but as students. As people.

Earle Bruce was the one who initially recruited me for Ohio State. He softened me up, but it was Woody Hayes who delivered the knockout punch.

I remember one day Woody Hayes came to my high school to address the entire student body. I don't remember what the discussion was about. But during the discussion, he made several comments about me. That made me feel 10 feet tall.

Later, he came to my house for a visit. By the time he left, both my parents were sold on me going to Ohio State. He was a very charismatic guy.

Charisma. That's the word right there.

DIRK WORDEN

I was an Ohio State fan for as long as I can remember. And for as long as I can remember, Woody Hayes was head coach.

So by the time Ohio State showed interest in me, I pretty much knew about him. He was a tough guy, a disciplinarian, a great football coach. He had a pretty violent temper at times.

I heard there was nothing he wouldn't do for his kids. If you put a lot into the program, there was nothing that Woody wouldn't at least try to do for you.

I knew it would be an honor to play for him. That's how I felt.

When Woody invited me to campus, I took a bus to Charlestown, West Virginia and then a plane to Columbus. My recruiter, Max Urich, picked me up at the airport.

As we drove to Woody's favorite restaurant, he tried to prepare me for the meeting. 'First he's gonna ask how your family is, then if you like school. Would you like to go to school here? Are you interested in the academics first?

'He's gonna ask you all that. Certainly he's gonna look you right in the eye and say 'Son, do you think you can play football for Ohio State?'

'When he does that, and if you have any intention of getting recruited, you'd better tell him 'Yes.'

That's pretty much the way it went.

When the assistant coach told me that I remember asking him, 'I don't care who asks me can I play here or can I play anywhere. I'm gonna tell him YES. Not because you're telling me what to do, but because that's how I truly feel or else I wouldn't be here now.' I remember telling him that.

Woody was already there, as well as several other recruits and their recruiters. He was working the room pretty good.

I remember meeting Dave Foley on that recruiting trip. They took me over to the athletic offices at St. John Arena. Dave Foley was coming up the steps and I was on the way down. I remember specifically shaking hands with big Dave.

Sometime during that trip they told me they were prepared to offer a scholarship. I had already taken one trip and had a trip scheduled to Kent State.

When I got back to prep school, I told the recruiter at Kent State not to waste his time. I was going to Ohio State. I told Virginia the same thing.

I was the first kid from my area to go to that big a school.

The natural concern would be to wonder whether or not you were good enough to play at Ohio State. It seemed to me you had to be Superman to play there. Right?

Funny thing is that I've never been an overconfident, arrogant kind of person in my personal life, but I've always had a lot of confidence in my football ability. I just knew I was destined to play there.

I had a solid background of football. I had full understanding of the game. I was a decent athlete with big-time hitting ability. I felt whatever situation I got into I'd be a major contributor.

I probably had more contact with Woody my freshman year than I did my next three years. Freshmen couldn't play on the varsity. We practiced against the varsity.

They ran a pretty strict split schedule. They'd run an offensive and a defensive practice. From my sophomore year on I was over on the defensive end of the football field.

I had it in my mind I had to bulk up a lot the summer before my freshman year, so I gained about 20 pounds. I was eating like crazy. I had to get up to about 215 to play at Ohio State. I couldn't possibly play at 195.

I was really 15 pounds overweight, but so many people were telling me I needed the extra weight. When I first reported to practice, Woody got on my case. Of course, when you're one of about 130 kids and you're a freshman he didn't really pay too much attention to me.

Eventually, I started practicing quite a bit against the varsity. I can remember one day specifically. I was having a pretty good day. They had a tough time blocking me. I was in their backfield quite a bit. Then all of a sudden he exploded.

'You damn butterball. Lemme tell you something. You get yourself in shape and you can play football for me next year.'

Later that week he visited me in the dorm room. He asked me 'Why did you let yourself get so heavy?'

I said, 'Well, I just had it in my mind I had to gain some weight.'

'What you gotta do is get in shape. That's what you gotta do. Your ideal weight is 195 pounds. That's big enough. You can play at 195 in this league.'

Woody had his faults. After all these years I'm not willing to look back and forgive that vicious temper that he had, that he never really got full control over.

I think he was so successful basically because he was so intense and put so much into his job. I really feel like he just threw himself into his job so completely and concentrated so hard on that job. That's why.

He always said 'There's a lot of coaches, a lot of people that are a lot more talented than I am. There are people more talented than you, but one thing about it. The great equalizer is hard work. Nobody's ever gonna outwork me. I've found that pays dividends.'

Ultimately, that was his real key to success. I think that's it in a nutshell.

When we met after the Rose Bowl game, Woody called a team meeting. He was always calling team meetings. First you get in there and he starts with the small talk. He looks up at everybody and says,'I'm sure you're wondering why I called this meeting.'

One day he called the team meeting in the morning. He said, 'This is the last day we're going to meet as a football team. We'll have a little get-together when we get back to Columbus.'

He basically said, When you look back at this season, look back at the last 2-3 years of your career, it's been work, sticking together, pulling for one another, growing as individuals that has paid off.

That ultimately is the real reward. That you can set your goals as a team and that if individuals pull together and work hard they can accomplish great things. That's what Woody left with me.

Ever since then whatever it is in life that I've accomplished, that I've been proud of, it's because of hard work. We had a saying when we were facing Purdue, when we were facing the Southern Cals. He'd always say, 'Can we win this game? Damn right we can.'

He knew that 'nothing in life that's worth a damn ever comes easy.'

Woody Hayes was a complex guy, largely misunderstood. If they want to portray him as just a bull in a china shop, he was much more than that.

There was a human side to him that a lot of people were never able to see. We'd beaten Michigan my senior year for the Big Ten championship. Southern Cal got tied by Notre Dame, so that made us No.1 in the nation.

The New York City Touchdown Club, or the Downtown Athletic Club, I don't know which, gave out a trophy that was emblematic of the national championship. It was called the MacArthur Bowl. They awarded that before the Ohio State-Southern Cal Rose Bowl clash. It went to Ohio State.

Woody calls me up in my dorm room. 'Dirk, you're gonna have to accompany me to New York. Now go down to such-and-such-a-place and get measured for a tuxedo and get your bags packed.

'This is gonna be a quick trip. I'll pick you up. I've got plane tickets. We'll meet Dave Foley. He's in New York for the Kodak All-American team. They're gonna give us the MacArthur Bowl.'

I did that. He picked me up. We're on our way to New York, just Woody and me. I mean he's talking non-stop the whole time. When Woody's talking I don't care if you're Lou Holtz, or George Chaump, or Billy Mallory, or Richard Nixon. I mean when Woody's talking, you just sit there and you listen.

He's on a complete roll. He's talking about a lot of things. The full scope of the season. Then he starts talking about me personally. It just amazed me how much he knew about my father and my family.

He just rambled on-and-on like that. In those days I forget how long it took to fly to New York. He had a newspaper in front of him. He'd close it and keep on talking.

Finally, he shut up. He just paused for about 10 seconds. That was my chance. I was gonna tell him, 'Coach, I really appreciate how much you meant to the team, how much you meant to me personally, thank the Lord I've had the opportunity to come to Ohio State and play for you...and so forth.'

I'm getting ready to say all that. I lean over to talk to him and there he is sound asleep. I'm thinking to myself 'My God, he is human after all.' You could never conceive of Woody Hayes sleeping.

We went to accept the trophy. I remember doing that and meeting a lot of great names such as Lindsay Nelson, Bobby Layne- just a tremendous amount of people that night. It was just a great thrill. That was a great trip.

On the way back he picks up two Ohio State students right outside of Columbus Airport. They had a sign up 'Ohio State University', so he picks them up. He takes us all over to campus. He drops us all off at the same street, near High Street and 11th Avenue.

We get out and I say 'Coach, I'll see you tonight.'

Those two kids look at me and ask 'Who was that?'

I said 'That was Coach Woody Hayes.' They never realized who had picked them up. There's a look on them that says 'Oh, my God!'

That's how much in awe they were of him.

And the older I get, the more I appreciate 'The Man.'

LARRY ZELINA

Everyone knows that Woody Hayes was the most successful coach in Ohio State football history. My teams went 27-2, won the national championship in 1968 and beat O.J. and Southern Cal in the Rose Bowl.

But to me the measure of the man is not his won-and-lost record. That to me is secondary. To me the way you measure a man is how he lives his life and how he affects the people that are around him.

Woody Hayes was one of the finest humanitarians I've ever met. He had a temper, but what a great man, an educator, a guy who didn't want the public to know that there was a special, soft side of him.

That to me is what made Woody Hayes great. He has my respect because he was a great human being.

I don't know too many coaches that had that kind of a record who weren't great people. Anybody who had that many wins and that winning percentage like Woody, like Bear Bryant (Alabama), like Joe Paterno (Penn State), like Tom Osborne (Nebraska), is a special person.

I don't really remember the first time I met Woody. The time I remember was when he made a visit to our home. He spent more time talking to my Mother and Dad.

Dad was a World War II veteran. He was an infantry Sergeant who won two Purple Hearts. He and Woody talked for hours.

I liked the way Woody treated me. He was sincere. He cared about you, and I think that influenced me the most. You can hear all the horror stories you want about Woody.

In my opinion, he truly cared about us as human beings more than he did as football players. That's what impressed me the most about Coach.

I'm not the greatest story teller in the world. One time Woody came out and showed us a brand new watch that his wife, Anne, had brought him. He stopped practice to show us this watch.

A week later he took this expensive watch off his wrist, threw it onto the ground, jumped on it, and it broke into a million pieces.

We didn't find out until later that he had sent one of the equipment managers out with his expensive watch to find a look-alike cheap watch. It was the cheap watch he stomped on.

I don't remember why he threw that temper tantrum. That was Woody. Maybe it was his way to motivate us. Woody was tough on us but Woody was tougher on himself.

That's another reason why I respected him so much.

He was tough on us. He was a disciplinarian, but he was doing it for our own good. Believe me, he worked himself harder and demanded more of himself than he did of anyone else. You've gotta admire a guy that does that.

He was a great humanitarian, a wonderful human being. After I was out of Ohio State for seven or eight years, my Dad was dying of cancer. My parents still lived in Cleveland.

Woody heard about it. I used to go in and see him once a year. I wasn't the kind of person who hung around for the sake of hanging around.

As I said, Woody had heard through the grapevine that my Dad was real sick. He called me. I hadn't talked to Coach in probably a year. He called me and I went down to his office to see him.

He asked me what was going on. I told him. He got on the phone and called the chief of the cancer research department at the University Hospital, and had my father's medical records transferred from Cleveland to Columbus for a second opinion.

Woody did everything he could to help my Father.

He loved you forever or he hated you forever, but he never forgot you.

He met my uncle one time after a football game. My Father's brother came down to Columbus to watch a game. Afterwards, I introduced him to Woody. Woody talked to him for a couple of minutes.

Four years later, my uncle went to listen to Woody speak at a banquet in Cleveland. Afterwards, he was standing in line to shake Woody's hand and say hello.

My uncle got in front of Woody, and before he could say a word Woody said, 'You're Larry Zelina's uncle Paul, aren't you?' He was incredible. He was just uncanny.

Woody was the offensive coordinator. He had a sheet of paper with all his notes. He gave Rex (Kern) and Mace (Ron Maciejowski) the freedom to change the play at the line of scrimmage. I'm not sure about Billy (Long).

The old man would say 'If you make the call you'd better make sure it works.' If the guys weren't calling the right plays, or switching into something and not making the right reads, they wouldn't have had the freedom. They wouldn't have gained the old man's confidence.

Thank God we never had to practice on a Monday after losing a ball game. We lost our last game my junior year and our last game my senior year. So we never had a week of practice the next week with Woody after a loss.

We saw what happened when we were freshmen. He was a maniac. He pulled his stunts, but we never saw the worst of Woody because we were lucky enough to be 27-2 and didn't experience a lot of real crazy stuff he used to do with other teams.

The older we get the more we realize how fortunate we were to play for THE MAN. He taught us so much more than just football. He taught us about life. The older we get the more we realize how much of an affect Woody Hayes had on our lives, even to this day.

Class of '68

As a 19-year-old sophomore you don't really realize what you accomplished until you're away from it for a few years, until you've had a chance to reflect.

You're busting your fanny for yourself and your teammates. You do it as well as you can. You expect that from yourself and you expect that from your teammates.

When you're a little older you realize how truly lucky you all were to be at the same place at the same time.

Just think of it. Of the 22 starting players on offense and defense, 17 got drafted by a professional football team, and of those 17, I think 13 actually played pro ball.

I don't think any other school could say that.

If there's any regrets during this magical time it's that we had a chance to win three straight national championships. We won it in '68 and should have done it in '69 and '70. But we blew the last regular season game to Michigan and the Rose Bowl to Stanford.

Sophomore quarterback Rex Kern confers with Woody.

Chapter 24

STORY OF A STATUE

In May of 1997, Urbana artist/sculptor Mike Major became part of college football history. His life-like bronze bust of Woody Hayes became part of the permanent display at the College Football Hall of Fame. Hayes had been inducted into The Hall in 1983. The statue stands 17 inches tall from the base to the top of Woody's famous baseball cap. It weighs 45 pounds. Since that project, Major has completed a bust of baseball great Jackie Robinson. Other projects in the works include busts of actor James Dean, and Civil War General William Tecumseh Sherman.

But without the help of long-time friend Jan Ebert, a retired music teacher/composer who also lives in Urbana, the Woody Hayes bust would have remained in clay. An old friend of Anne and Woody Hayes, Jan Ebert set up a meeting with Hayes' widow. The result: Anne Hayes ordered two statues which she then donated to the Varsity 'O' Club and the Mershon Center. The Center sponsors research, organizes conferences and is host to visitors in the field of international security. Money raised in part from the sale of the statues helped to raise $1.5 million to fund the Woody Hayes Chair in National Security Studies. OSU All-American quarterback Rex Kern spearheaded the drive.

MIKE MAJOR
Urbana, Ohio

John Quincy Adams Ward was the dean of American sculpture. He once said the best preparation for becoming a sculptor is doing drawings.

I had plenty of practice, some 30 years. What happens when you do drawings is that eventually you begin to sense the third-dimension.

I'd done some sculpting over the years, but nothing I'd done held my fascination. Nothing to lure me away from the sketch pad and canvas.

That was until September of 1996. I had been a member of a committee in Urbana, the Simon Kenton Historic Corridor, which was originally set up to draw attention to the history of this area.

Simon Kenton was the first trailblazer through the area. He founded the city of Urbana. His life span went from 1790-1834.

Ward had actually done a small mockup of a Kenton statue, but nothing happened. There wasn't enough money to fund completion of the project because of the Civil War.

163

Kenton's widow had donated the statue to the Urbana library. A four-foot-high pedestal had been built at the cemetery, but there was no statue atop the base.

The committee began looking for an artist to do the bronze statue, but without much success. I thought I could do better, so I asked the committee if I could take a crack at it.

I began work on the six-foot-high statue in September. The completed piece came back from the foundry in January of 1997.

It was a work with a lot of passion. It was a work with a lot of momentum because it was so exciting to see it evolve and come to life.

My full-sized statue was based on the Ward mockuette. It was dedicated on the Fourth of July.

It felt natural to know where to press, where to pull, where to dig away and where to add on. I was very much at ease, excited about how well it turned out.

Doing a piece that size really draws a lot of energy out of you. But at the same time, it puts a lot of energy into you. A bronze statue is so permanent, so classic. I guess that's kinda selfish, to know your work is going to be around for many generations beyond one's own lifespan.

You could say I was hooked. What would I do next?

It really didn't take much pondering. I would do a bust of Woody Hayes.

It seemed to me that a Woody Hayes statue would be in keeping to a theme of significant Ohio figures. But it was much more than that.

As a kid growing up on a farm in west central Ohio, I became an Ohio State football fan, a Woody Hayes fan. He was an important factor in Ohio pride and Ohio football. Ohio is football.

Certainly he was an important everyday name in Ohio.

There are just a few rare football coaches who seem to spill over with the game. There seems to be something above the ordinary.

It is their passion for the game. Woody Hayes had that passion. So did Vince Lombardi. I felt their passion, their enthusiasm. It's infectious.

Woody Hayes had become larger than football because of his interactions with people in the community. He was always there to help people. Strangers, players or friends.

He was a multi-faceted individual, and to judge the man for one act of insanity would be ridiculous. I already had seen so many other facets. Actually, the incident at the Gator Bowl is part of his human quality.

It seemed to me that Woody Hayes was a neglected person, as far as sculpture was concerned. I felt that a solid, good quality needed to be there.

This was a way to keep that candle lit, keeping a sense of the life of an individual burning in the minds of the public, to keep people asking this question: Who was this man? I felt it was a fitting thing to do.

So, I began my project. I wanted to know as much about Woody as I could. I bought several books. I went to the archives at Ohio State University, which is an excellent resource.

I told them what I was up to. They were very helpful and gave me all their proofs on Woody Hayes. I probably brought home 20 different photographs of Woody.

The photos showed every conceivable angle. The right side of his head, the left side, the front, the back. I had several different expressions, some smiling, some focused. Whenever I do a bust, I do a lot of different photos and mixed expressions.

That's how I was able to come up with a Woody Hayes who's concentrating. He's himself, not putting on a facade. He's not smiling, but he's not frowning either. He's just won a game. He's felt a surge of success, or a fulfillment. There's a subtleness on his face.

In subsequent projects, I've sketched the subject first, then began working in clay. With Woody, I went right to the clay.

I think there are three phases to a bust. The first phase is a cartoon, or caricature. The second phase is a refinement to the point where I think 'Okay, this is Woody.' The third stage is a critique.

In this case, Mrs. Hayes saw the photograph of the clay and said it needed more weight in the jowls. This stage was added on as a response to her comments and 'Bingo', it was him.

I had photographs taken of the clay bust when I was finished. It's not like seeing the piece in person, but it's a useful tool.

A long-time friend named Jan Ebert is the one who made it work. She was a long-time friend of Anne and Woody Hayes. Jan and I served on several committees together.

Once Jan saw my finished Woody she said, 'Oh, you need to meet Mrs. Hayes.'

'Do you know Mrs. Hayes?' I asked.

'Do you know Anne Hayes?'

'Yes, I've known her for years. She used to come over to my house with Woody. We're good friends.'

That's how it began.

Anne Hayes was sent the photograph. A short time later, the three of us met at Anne's retirement complex. We had lunch at a very nice restaurant right at the site.

We had a wonderful talk, and then it got time to talk about the statue. Anne said 'Look, frankly I'm not interested in a bust of Woody.'

She told me she'd had a bad experience with an artist who had approached her about a Woody Hayes statue. 'We don't really need this. It's not important.'

It had taken about four weeks to complete the bust, from the time Anne Hayes said the jowls needed more work until the time we had lunch.

I looked at Anne and said 'Well, fine, that's your decision.'

At that point, Jan interrupted and said 'Wait a minute, Anne. I think you need to look at this bust.'

Anne said 'Well, okay then. I will if you want me to.'

Anne Hayes trusted her old friend.

Then she added, 'Let's go back to the apartment.'

I said, 'Fine, I'll go to the car.' I had the clay bust in a box in the car. They went to Anne's apartment and I went to my car.

I returned and put the box in the kitchen, took out the bust, went into the dining room and placed it on a table.

Anne Hayes looked at it and said, 'Oh, this looks like him.' She lowered herself a little bit to the table level and looked at it again.

She said 'This is good, this is really, really good. I like it.' It wasn't long before she was shedding tears.

Naturally, I was on Cloud Nine. I thought to myself, 'Gee, she likes the piece.'

Class of '68

That was on a Thursday. At 7:30 in the morning on Saturday, Anne Hayes called Jan Ebert, and told her what she thought of the sculpture.

At that point she really wanted to buy a statue. But in fact, she bought two and wanted to pay the full price, which is a lot of money. I mean $5,000 apiece.

She doesn't care about material things. She doesn't care about money. She's not a wealthy woman. She likes to have enough. She said she was always the money manager when Woody was alive.

As long as Woody had a few bucks in his pocket, he'd just as soon not deal with the money issue. He wanted to be able to write checks and know they wouldn't bounce. Beyond that, Anne Hayes dealt with all the money matters.

She wanted to donate one statue to Varsity 'O', and one to Mershon, to the chair that was endowed in Woody's name. Varsity 'O' had been an organization that had given her and Woody a lot of support over the years. She had many friends there. Of course, the Mershon chair, because it was a scholarship fund endowed in Woody's name.

According to Jan, she and Anne talked for 90 minutes. What made me feel so good is that Anne Hayes is the kind of person who says exactly what she feels. If she doesn't like something, you know it in no uncertain terms.

She provided the capital when it was necessary for us to go to the bronze foundry. She paid the full amount, wouldn't take a discount, and gave the project her blessing.

Once she commissioned the two pieces, the project moved quickly. I went to the foundry within a week.

When I get started on a piece, especially a smaller piece such as a bust, I burn the candle at both ends. I can listen to a book on tape or good music and work for hours.

There is a level of concentration or focus where things are just emerging. With the Woody Hayes bust, for example, I would have a stage for the right ear, work on another setting on the left ear. The entire nose, eyes, lips, chin area was pretty much worked on in another setting.

There's no part separate from the other. Everything has to work in concert. I can't isolate any particular problem.

The cap had to be his. It had to be at the right angle. I wanted details in the ears. I wanted not just typical ears. I wanted Woody's ears.

I would suppose the most surprising part of Woody would be the chin and the jowls. I have a certain proportion in mind, what I call normal, but I had to put a lot more clay in his chin and a lot more clay on his jowls. And yet, that's what made Woody.

He was beefy around those areas.

I put creases, smile lines, at the corner of his eyes. That came naturally. That's what I wanted. That's part of the sincere look that he had.

I pulled sincerity out of three different poses. One was the mouth, one the eyes. The other was the angle of his head. I combined all three into a pose that wasn't in any photograph.

There's a spirit within that piece. That's what's electrifying. Others have described it this way. They say 'Woody Hayes is alive.'

We decided I was going to make the Hayes bust a limited edition. I decided on 99

166

pieces because in my way of thinking a limited edition is not 500, 200 or even 100. For each piece sold, $1,000 is donated to the Mershon chair.

It's been a wonderful experience for me. When a door opens and the wind is blowing quickly and pretty hard, you'd better grab it and hold on.

The Simon Kenton and Woody Hayes pieces have led to the commission of almost a dozen other pieces so far, and for an artist who must live on his art, that's just fine.

Two experiences with the Woody Hayes piece will always stand out in my mind, and remain in my heart.

In May of 1997, I thought I was going to the College Football Hall of Fame just to deliver the bust. I thought it would be a quick trip from Urbana to South Bend, Indiana.

I was wrong!

Woody had been inducted into the Hall of Fame back in 1983. It's an impressive exhibit.

I didn't realize there was going to be a reception, a formal presentation. They received it very graciously, and said some very nice things about Woody Hayes and Ohio State. I may be wrong, but I think it's the first bust of a coach.

Certainly I'm human. I take great joy in compliments. But what gets me in the gut is watching and seeing some tears start falling.

There was one person, I can't tell you his name, but he was the former chairman of the Rose Bowl Parade in Pasadena. He just happened to be at the Hall of Fame the day I presented the bust.

The man didn't know I was watching. There was a very emotional response, an electric connection between the bust and the man's memories. If the work is good enough to trigger that kind of reaction, that's a good feeling. No, that's a great feeling.

Woody Hayes was head football coach at New Philadelphia (Ohio) High School in the late 1930s-early 1940s. Funds are being raised to renovate and rename the football stadium in his honor. Fundraisers, such as a golf outing and an auction, are helping to raise those funds.

I was invited to bring one of the Woody Hayes busts to a May 1997 auction. The bust was provided for the $5,000 level originally. Once we got involved in the event I thought I'd reduce the cost of the bust to $4,500 and still make my donation to the Woody chair as promised, thus allowing more money to be raised for the stadium renovation in Woody's name.

The bust brought $8,500 at auction, so they raised $4,500 which is the most money they've made from any single item from any single auction. I feel good about that.

I have a secret. I actually have a full-figure Woody sitting down in my studio that no one's ever seen.

At the same time I did the bust, I did a full-standing piece. It's approximately 30 inches tall. I think the face is as successful as the large bust. It's just a miniature scale.

He has his hands on his hips as if he's waiting for a play to unfold. It's very much Woody, but it's in clay.

Someday I'll finish it. It's still at that second stage.

I've never showed it to anyone, never mentioned it to Anne Hayes because I didn't want to distract from the limited edition bust project.

JAN EBERT
Urbana, Ohio

I came to Champaign County to teach. That was back in 1958 and I've stayed ever since. I've lived in Urbana for almost 30 years.

When Mike Major came to the community, he came to Urbana University where I had taught. We met through university contacts. He and his family attend the same church that I do.

We just came to know each other over the years. We wound up working together on a great number of artistic, community and church endeavors. We've become well acquainted over the years.

He's a fine, fine artist. He's done so many different things. He's done contemporary kinds of pieces. He also does marvelous sketchwork.

I was a member of the Simon Kenton Historic Corridor, as was Mike at the time. We had been looking for someone to do a statue of the famed Ohio frontiersman.

More than 100 years ago, John Quincy Adams Ward had done a small statuette of Kenton, proposing a full-size statue. But nothing came of it. Eventually, Ward's widow gave it to the library.

It all began when I went to a meeting where we had the leading expert on Ward, who grew up in Urbana. I said, 'we've got this momument out in the cemetery. Every other monument has a statue on it. Was this one supposed to?'

He said, 'Why yes it was,' and then we got into what it was supposed to look like. It was supposed to be like the statuette of Simon Kenton. I went back to the group which promotes tourism and said, 'Look what we could do. We could put that statue up there.'

Everyone got excited about it and pretty soon we had some seed money.

By then Mike Major wanted to do it. We agreed.

First, Mike brought us a mockup, a full-sized drawing of what it was going to be. Kenton was a tall man. He was 6-2. Mike did a full-sized statue of Kenton standing. He was holding a long gun. He was standing next to his dog.

When he brought back the statue in bronze, I stood there and burst into tears. I was so thrilled. All of a sudden we're making something that's 131 years overdue into a beautiful momument that's going to last for centuries.

Mike Major just has that special talent. That magic translates through his fingers.

Since then he's done some wonderful sculptures, including Woody Hayes. I'm honored to have played a small part in that story.

Mike had probably started the bust when he called me and talked about it. I thought, 'Why are you doing that?' Then I thought, 'Well, that's a neat idea.'

To this day I don't know what it was that made him think about doing it. I have no idea whether he was fascinated with the person or what it was that came into his head.

He was talking about a full-sized statue. Instead, he would do a bust. I was able to come up with an awful lot of pictures of Woody. I had a bunch of different pictures of Woody Hayes on the field. From the front, the side, the back. If you can walk all the way around that baby and it looks good, it looks life-like, then you've got a quality product.

When he finished with the clay bust, Mike brought it over. I wanted to take a picture, but my camera malfunctioned.

For some reason he placed it down, and the sun played across Woody's face. It was magnificent. I said, 'Anne's got to see this thing.'

When Mike brought the finished bust over, I nearly fainted. I looked at him and said, 'I don't know where you got his twinkle. I don't know how you translated that into this bust.'

Putting glasses on a bust in the first place is extremely difficult. And then to somehow have that twinkle that Woody had in his eye...I just couldn't believe it.

I wasn't that close to Woody Hayes. Whenever I was with him and Anne, he was that wonderful, gentle educator with that tremendous vitality of intellectualism.

So many people just paint his picture, but they miss the vast humanity of the man. I don't know how Mike got that in the clay, but it sure is there. And it's beautiful.

I called Anne and told her about the bust. She had had a bad experience with a sculptor who'd pushed himself off on her. She absolutely refused to let him do anything.

Then we sent pictures to Anne. I talked to her a bit. She felt it didn't look right straight-on. So Mike fixed it.

I arranged for the three of us to meet at Anne's apartment. Mike sat the bust down on her dining room table. Anne Hayes walked over to it. She started putting her hand on the bust. It was such an electric moment, I was incapable of watching it. I had to turn my back and walk out.

She said, 'This is wonderful.'

Anne felt that Mike had really captured the essence of what is Woody Hayes. I thought he'd done a wonderful job. But nothing happened until the next day.

It must have been around 6:30 in the morning, I was working in my attic when the phone rang. It was Anne. She said, 'I want two of these' (to give to the University).

I didn't care how early it was, I was going to call Mike. If I got him out of bed, too bad. It was really neat. I just always loved the idea of bringing artists into prominence.

Not that Mike Major needed anybody to bring him into prominence. The fact that I could assist in some way just gave me a big thrill.

I went to Ohio State for both undergraduate and graduate work. I graduated in 1958 with a BS degree in Education, a Master of Arts (1962) and a Ph.D in 1973.

Class of '68

Woody Hayes was the coach when I arrived. He was the kind of man you could see on campus, walk up to and ask, 'Coach, how is the team?'

He would take the time to talk to you for a few minutes, even if he didn't know you.

Over the years our paths crossed, but it wasn't until I was invited to join the Ohio State alumni marching band that we came more-and-more in contact.

I was secretary of the alumni band for some 22 years. I was the first woman in the band. They asked me to march with them. I think because I was not only a musician and had taught band for many years, but I knew my left foot from my right. It was a great honor.

The alumni band is very, very active. We march at the first football game every year. I can't march anymore since I had a blood clot in my leg, but I still do concerts.

We have a year-round band that plays concerts and parades. That's called the 'active' band. We also have what we call the 'hyperactive' band that does funny little gigs like parties and stuff.

I guess the most exciting thing that's happened to me is that in 1983 I conducted the Star Spangled Banner for the Oregon game. I'm still the only woman to have ever conducted on that field (Ohio Stadium).

As secretary of the alumni band, I was in touch with anybody if they were our invited guests for reunions, banquets and other events. I always wrote to Anne and Woody Hayes.

Anne Hayes was a very active woman. She worked as hard as Woody. She went out and made a lot of speeches to alumni and other groups. She was a very electrifying and wonderful speaker. They both had this commitment to kids and to education. They were a wonderful pair.

This is a very gifted woman, a very humble woman. She had a presence about her. Everyone knew Anne Hayes was there. She was much adored.

She was a very attractive woman. She wore her hair back in a tight bun. I'd say she's slightly built. A very strong personality.

Anne said everybody always asked her if she ever thought of divorcing Woody. She'd say 'Divorce, Never. Murder, Yes.' She traded on that line and it always got a laugh.

I had gotten to know her, but I'm sure I was in the periphery of her vision. In later years we got together for a number of occasions.

She'd been up here at our home, and I've been to her home. We had meals and chats together. I just can't say enough about Anne Hayes.

I'll always remember our first get-together. It was at one of our alumni band reunions. My children were there too. They were very, very young at the time.

Anne called me aside and said, 'Woody and the team want Jan to have her varsity letter.' She brought me an "O" that was stained glass. I was just thrilled beyond words.

I have no idea whether or not Woody and the team knew they were giving it to me. Whatever it was, it was a lovely gesture.

Then, of course, in her usual generalissimo manner she turned to the band, shook her finger at them and said, 'You people just don't appreciate what this woman does.' She gave them quite a lecture.

In many respects Anne and Woody Hayes were the folks next door. They never had an unlisted number. They lived right in the middle of everything. They went grocery shopping like everybody else.

What stood them way above the crowd were the tremendous kind things they did. Woody's trips to the hospital are just legendary. He would go and call on sick people. That was part of what he viewed as his mission in life.

Woody Hayes was an intellectual. I don't think people ever saw this side of him. He was an expert on military history. I think he memorized everything that Emerson ever wrote. His father was a school superintendent.

He was also a humanitarian!

Woody was a student. He was that first. Everything came after that. I would say he was a student first, a teacher second, and out of those things came his coaching skills. With teaching comes that dedication to knowledge and to kids. I never saw anything else in the man.

One time the NCAA looked into Woody and the school when he was football coach. What happened was Aurelius Thomas was a black kid. Back in the 1950s there wasn't much scholarship money for black kids.

Aurelius had gotten a scholarship to Ohio State, based on his football-playing ability. I don't know whether it was an injury or what but he couldn't play football his senior year. That meant he wasn't going to finish school.

Woody said, 'You have to have your education.' And there wasn't anything that anybody could do, so Anne and Woody took care of him and saw to it that he finished his education.

There was no way he was going to do Woody or the University any good as far as his football scholarship went. They took that away because he couldn't play.

Woody was insisting that the young man needed to finish school. I don't know what he needed, a quarter or two. I don't know what he needed to complete.

He stayed with Woody and Anne. I wouldn't be a bit surprised if they didn't pay his tuition as well. They were that kind of people, and Woody was that strong on education.

He said a young black person, in that day-and-age especially, had to have an education to get anywhere in life. They were very quiet about their charities and the things they did. They never looked for any kind of spotlight.

I think in that case, the NCAA backed off. That was the end of it. The young man graduated. That was the important thing.

The first time I ever spoke to Woody, I walked up to him. He was sitting. I don't know if he was waiting for an appointment or what.

I happened on him at a lounge on campus. I was an undergraduate. I walked up and asked, 'How's it look for this year?'

He said, 'I think things look pretty good.' We talked football for awhile. He had no idea who I was. He didn't turn me away. I was a kid asking him about his team. I always thought that was typical of him.

Before that terrible incident [1978] at the Gator Bowl, I felt Woody was going to get fired. He'd lost to Michigan three straight times, or something, and he wasn't going to be back. I had that feeling before they ever played Clemson. I thought he was gone. I thought it was wrong [his firing] and so did a lot of other people.

Class of '68

I don't know how Woody thought, but I can tell you one incident that could provide the answer. Woody had some very serious surgery. I don't know what it was for at the time.

He had to go back to the hospital two weeks later. They'd left a sponge in him. By then he was pretty seriously ill. I went by the home and said, 'Woody, I just feel terrible what's happened. Weren't you angry with the guy for leaving a sponge in you?'

He looked at me square in the eye, which was the only way he looked at you, and he said, "Janet, everybody makes mistakes." That was THE ONLY THING he ever said about the incident.

Some time after the Gator Bowl incident, a friend of mine called me. He was Athletic Director at a small county school. He needed help. He said, 'Jan, we're trying to raise money to finish the track out here. We really need to get Woody to come up.'

The track was going to be named in honor of the man's father who did so many things for the school, including driving the bus.

I couldn't get anywhere through the University, so I called Anne Hayes and told her what the situation was all about. Finally, Anne called me back. She said Woody said to have him call at a certain time. My friend called Woody and made the arrangements.

They also asked me to come up as an invited guest. Then they asked me to introduce Woody. I was so pleased to have that opportunity.

It was an icy night. Woody showed up with that big old truck of his. I was so pleased with my introduction. I thought it captured the essence of the man.

'Everybody says that Woody's blood runs scarlet-and-gray. That may be, but I'm here to tell you it runs through a heart of gold.' I'm so proud of that.

Woody came in bad weather. He gave his speech. The crowd overflowed out the front door. It raised enough money to finish the track. Woody Hayes would not take a fee. He said, 'Whatever my fee would be, for Pete Sake, put it into that track.'

You hear of these folks going out and getting exorbitant fees for speaking and here's Woody. This little county school needs a track and Woody rides to the rescue.

People don't know these things about him.

The athletic director found these really fine old books on military history. He gave them to Woody and Woody's face just lit up. You'd have thought someone gave him the crown jewels.

Sometime after the infamous Gator Bowl incident, I can't remember when, the alumni marching band was having its annual reunion. The "Skull Session" was at St. John Arena. We had decided to give Woody an honorary membership into the band.

Woody hadn't officially been back on campus although we knew he had been in the press box, been here-and-there. But he had not made an official appearance.

He agreed to come. I went to get him. Until he walked out onto that arena floor, Woody Hayes was shaking. He was a little nervous. But the moment he was sighted, the place went crazy.

There were 5,000 people standing, cheering, screaming. The band went nuts. At that moment, he dropped my hand. He wasn't the same man I was escorting to the floor.

He was Woody Hayes.

It was just incredible watching that man. It was an electric moment. The person that I took down there was not the same person that walked out on that floor.

There was no question how much love was coming out of the stands, off the floor, every place it could come from. And Woody felt that love.

It was funny because he gave me a big kiss out on the floor. Then, that night at the banquet, Anne stood up to speak.

'I want to say something. If my husband can stand out there in front of everybody and kiss Jan Ebert, then I can certainly kiss Harry [Jan's husband] right now.'

She ran back and kissed my husband. He just loved it.

It was so neat. Just a really lovely moment. That's the kind of people they were.

Very few people knew that Woody was a diabetic. My late husband was a severe diabetic. Maybe that's how I knew. I've always attributed a lot of Woody's problems to his diabetes. I am convinced that was the source of a lot of it.

I have so many memories of Woody Hayes, but none more vivid than when I was in graduate school at Ohio State. It was the time of the Vietnam War. It was the time of protests on college campuses.

Demonstrations seemed to be a daily occurence at Ohio State for awhile. The incident I'm thinking about took place either just before or after the tragic killing of students at Kent State.

The faculty wore green armbands and went around trying to be peacekeepers, Woody Hayes included. My particular adviser got hit in the head with a rock. Believe me, it was a good-sized rock.

Woody went down, bless his heart, stood there and tried to talk to those kids. He did that time-after-time. They weren't listening. They were booing and carrying on.

I always admired him that his convictions took him to the center of whatever it was, no matter the personal danger. And there was personal danger to those faculty members who tried to help.

Most of the great old coaches are gone. Bear Bryant's gone. Woody's gone. Bo [Schembechler] is retired. That era of coaches came out of what I call 'a gentleman's game'...but it's something beyond that now.

Football was still part-and-parcel of an educational institution. I don't think we're going to see that kind of coach again, except maybe in Division 2 or Division 3. The smaller schools.

I grew up attending Capital University's games [in Columbus, Ohio]. My Dad taught there. The coach, Bill Bernlohr, was a gentleman first. He was a Christian. He was a good person and it was that kind of a game.

Now we see the coaches with their extra contracts with Nike and whatever it is they want to sell. That's the accepted norm. I don't see the chemistry professor getting contracts to sell for supermarkets.

The great coaches from that era aren't with us anymore and I think there's a realization of what we've lost.

Chapter 25

TWO HOMETOWN HEROES

The distance between Newcomerstown and New Philadelphia, Ohio is only some 20 miles. Two towns in Tuscarawas County. Woody Hayes traveled that road on his way to become a giant, both on and off the football field. The character of the man was formed during his early days in Newcomerstown. That's where he grew up, went to high school, and then ventured forth to find his place in the world.

Some five years later, he returned to his roots. Twenty miles down the road, to New Philadelphia where the legend would really begin. His first head coaching job. His first undefeated team.

He was not a man who simply 'passed this way', never to be remembered. Villagers in Newcomerstown have named a street after one of their favorite sons. A high school football stadium will be re-dedicated in Woody Hayes' name in New Philadelphia. Generations to come will learn his story. His triumphs. His tragedy. Just a small town boy who never forgot his roots.

Travel on Interstate 77 in Ohio and you'll bump into a small town called Newcomerstown. Population about 4,500.

The sign entering the town proudly proclaims "The Home of Cy Young and Woody Hayes."

Those folks have good reason to bang their collective chests and honor two of their illustrious sons. Two men who became winners in the games they pursued. Fierce competitors. Men to be admired.

Cy Young was a major league pitcher. During his long career in the early 1900s, the righthanded pitcher won 511 games. A feat that will never come close to being duplicated.

His bust adorns the baseball Hall of Fame in Cooperstown, New York. Each year the top pitchers in both the National and American Leagues are selected as Cy Young Award winners. It doesn't get much better than that.

Woody Hayes was the winningest head football coach in Ohio State University history, posting a brilliant 205-60-10 record in an unprecedented 28 seasons.

Twice (1954 and 1968) his Buckeyes were named national champions. Hayes was named Coach of the Year not once, but twice.

His bust adorns the College Football Hall of Fame at South Bend, Indiana. Hayes was elected in 1983, four years before his death.

Woody Hayes was 74, Cy Young 88 when they died.

Young, whose career spanned from 1890-1911, is remembered every year at a weekend festival. He died in 1955.

Woody Hayes often bragged about his friendship with the famed pitcher.

"He and I were damn good friends," he said. "He used to call me 'Wood-row.' I respected that man. He bragged up Walter Johnson, who won the World Series in 1924 (for the Washington Senators).

"Young would talk about Walter Johnson as the greatest pitcher of all time. And doggone it, when Walter Johnson got beat in the seventh game of the World Series in '25, I couldn't eat for a week. I was always a bad loser.

"Then Walter went up to Cleveland to manage, but he was too nice a guy. I learned something from him there. You can't be a nice guy if you want to be a coach. You've got to bear down on them a little."

Young pitched for the Cleveland Spiders, St. Louis Cardinals, Boston Red Sox, Cleveland Americans and Boston Braves.

His given name was Denton, but his fastball earned him the nickname 'Cyclone,' which was shortened to Cy.

In Newcomerstown, there's a monument in Cy Young Park, a two-acre park with a baseball diamond, swimming pool, picnic tables, tennis and volleyball courts.

Dozens of items are on display at The Temperance Tavern Museum on East Canal Street. The museum is open from Memorial Day to Labor Day.

Items include Young's Boston Red Sox uniform (worn in 1906), his rocking chair, his last pair of street shoes (shiny black high tops with thick soles), his father's Civil War medical bag.

Young's father, McKenzie, was a medic during the Civil War. After the war, he raised corn, soybeans, hogs and cattle on a farm near Peoli, Ohio.

When Peoli's post office was closed, Young's hometown became the next closest town, Newcomerstown.

"His farm was out in the middle of nowhere," says Vane Scott, age 73, who knew both Cy Young and Woody Hayes. He and his wife, Barbara, run the local historic society.

"I don't think he had a tractor. They didn't even have electricity out there until the 1950s. Cy was a big-boned, tall guy who loved kids.

"Woody Hayes came to Newcomerstown as a youngster when his father, Wayne, was named Superintendent of Schools. I knew Woody most of my life. He was a family friend.

"He used to come back here all the time. He bragged that this was his real hometown. He graduated from high school here. His older brother, Ike, was an All-American football player. They used to do a lot of boxing around here, put on shows when they were younger.

"Their older sister, Mary, struck out on her own first. The town just forgot about her after he came along. She went to New York and starred on Broadway. She worked with Bob Hope and George Jessel. She was also a pioneer with soap

175

operas on radio, then right into television. She's the gal that used to write 'em all. "We're building a dinner theater here and naming it after Mary Hayes. She's still living. She's in New Jersey. She's pretty old now, about 93, and legally blind.

"It wasn't unusual to see Woody here on a Sunday for a wedding across the street, at the church, or over at the Elks Lodge. He had a lot of friends there.

"Every once in awhile you'd pick up the paper and he's the speaker at the Chamber banquet. He's the speaker at the high school. He was just here a lot. He'd even come unannounced, just to say hello and spend a little time with us.

"The last time I saw him was about two years before he died. I was out front, working on a boat. All of a sudden there comes all these people across the street, at the church.

"I hear somebody yelling at me. 'Hey, Great Scott. You aren't supposed to work on Sunday.' I looked up. It was Woody. He was here to attend a distant relative's wedding.

"He had all that success, all that fame, and yet he never forgot his roots. He was always glad, and proud, that he grew up here."

Several of Woody Hayes' personal items are also on display at The Temperance Tavern Museum. Barbara Scott serves as president.

Says Vane Scott:

"I wish we had more Woody memorabilia. Let's just say that Ohio State is unbending about the Woody Hayes name and materials. For instance, we wanted to put some of his stuff in his museum, but Ohio State scooped it up.

"They don't want to even talk about it. They own Woody Hayes lock-stock-and-barrel. We're rather unhappy about that because we get a lot of tourists who want to see that stuff.

"Fortunately, we're able to display some items that Woody gave us. We have several autographed books, photographs, as well as three items in a case. It's called 'A Coach's Tools', and contains a bronze cap, a pair of shoes and a whistle. Woody gave it to us about 15 years ago."

In 1983, the town folks in Newcomerstown renamed a portion of High Street, calling it Woody Hayes Drive. It's a small street on the east side of the high school.

Following the ribbon-cutting ceremony, Woody Hayes said a few words at Lee Stadium, the high school football field where he once played.

He said, "You play together. You all run the right play and you block together. When you do get beat, you get up and go again. When you learn that and get out of high school, then you are going to be a success in anything you get into.

"Winning doesn't come easy. Nothing comes easy. Nothing in this world that comes easy is worth a dime."

Telling the students that "a small town is the greatest single advantage of your life," he urged them to study computer science, take a foreign language and go on to college.

"The brain is a terrible thing to waste."

In his closing remarks, Wayne Woodrow Hayes noted:

"Integrity is more important than anything else. The pressure is seldom on the intellect, but is always on the character."

Vane Scott, whose ancestors were the first to settle in Newcomerstown in 1801, wishes the village had done more. "It's just a short street that runs into the high school. I would have named the main drag after him."

Woody Hayes was born on St. Valentine's Day in 1913 in Clinton, Ohio, the son of Wayne Benton and Effie Jane Hayes. He grew up in Newcomerstown where his father was appointed Superintendent of Schools.

He was always proud of his small town upbringing.

"Small towns help people learn about life. You never outgrow what you learn in a small town," Woody would say. "People are always helping each other in times of need. You don't see that in the big cities. That strength stays with a person forever."

His parents played a major role in shaping their son.

"Dad, a fine teacher and scholar, was a great influence on me. Mother was the balance wheel. Honest, confident and unyielding in her opinions.

"When I was growing up, our family gathered around the dining table right after church on Sunday, and discussed anything and everything of interest.

"We wore our Sunday best. Mom set the table with the best linens, best china and candles. Sometimes our talks would last three hours.

"Everyone had to participate although I, the youngest child and not outstanding in any way, didn't talk as much as my brother, Ike, who loved sports and music.

"My sister, Mary, was a pianist and as an adult, an actress and the first female radio announcer. It was a wonderful time because of our love for one another and the excellent communication between us.

"The habit of discussion around a table followed me throughout life. I used the technique in meetings and at the study hall when I tutored the football players."

Woody Hayes enjoyed recalling the many good times at Newcomerstown High School, playing on the baseball team, captaining the football team.

He was a member of the 1929 Class A state championship baseball team.

Despite his size, Woody Hayes was center on the varsity football team. He weighed less than 145 pounds. He was also an outstanding boxer.

He also liked to tell one story about his father, just before his father's death.

"My father told me he wasn't feeling good and was concerned because he had bought a pair of shoes from Russell Bean on credit.

"He told me to go down to Baltimore and pay the bill because if anything would happen to him, he knew Russell would never send the bill. I paid it and a week later my father died.

"That taught me a lesson. My father left this world without owing anyone a dime. And any job I've left, I've tried leaving without owing anybody anything."

Some of his teammates fondly remembered Woody Hayes following his death in March of 1987.

"Woody was the poorest runner I ever saw," recalled Junior Swigert who played high school football with Hayes. "He couldn't run worth a hoot," agreed his cousin, Alfred Swigert who played right guard as a sophomore.

"He was rough. Tough. But a damn nice sportsman. We were playing schools way out of our class and we played rough in those days. One of our players, Homer Dennis (left end) had his right eye almost knocked out of the socket in New Philadelphia.

Class of '68

"They just taped it up and he kept on playing. I don't recall Woody ever getting injured." His cousin agreed. "He always took care of himself," said Junior Swigert. "I don't recall him ever drinking or smoking."

Eugene Parks, a sophomore halfback, was two years behind Woody Hayes. "Woody always wanted to catch a pass. He devised a play where he'd be eligible as an end.

"In those days you didn't move the ball from the sidelines like now. You just played it where it was. So, if you were right along the sideline, everyone lined up on the other side of Woody, making him eligible for the pass. But I can't recall if we ever used it."

Hayes caught at least one ball, but that was on defense. He intercepted a Denison pass in the fourth quarter to salvage a 12-12 tie his senior year.

In a class prophecy, it was predicted Woody Hayes would win the heavyweight boxing championship of the world. But he met his match long before that.

Recalled James Tish, another teammate:

"Woody was cocky about his boxing ability. He and his brother Ike, who got honorable mention at Iowa for All-American, were always boxing each other.

"Anyway, Woody kept challenging our coach Ray Coleman to put on the gloves with him. After so much pestering the coach put them on and proceeded to put the cleaners on Woody on the gym floor one evening.

"That little episode ended Woody's aspirations on boxing the coach. We found out later that Coach Coleman had been the champion boxer at college for his class."

Mrs. Margaretta Brenneman was a cheerleader and a classmate of Woody Hayes at Newcomerstown High. "His father was a strict disciplinarian, but was well-liked and respected. I recall once we cheerleaders wanted to go to a baseball game and Professor Hayes said 'No'. We went anyway and got two weeks detention.

"Once he caught Woody and another boy fighting and he gave equal punishment to both boys."

Woody Hayes called Clyde Barthalow one of his favorite teachers. "Clyde made you learn. I never saw a better teacher. He was tough, but he was fair. He was a person I really looked up to. And he told stories that sure made history interesting."

Barthalow, who taught History and English, died in 1991 at the age of 87. He said of his famous student:

"I well recall Woody when the Hayes family came to Newcomerstown. Mr. W.B. Hayes was Superintendent of Schools. Woody was in the second grade at the old East School.

"I taught Woody three years in the sixth, seventh and eighth grades. He was an outstanding student, a voracious reader, and like his father, was especially interested in history dealing with wars, and great leaders of past times.

"He was extremely interested in English grammar and the correct usage in expression, in both his speaking and writing. His papers had to meet his exacting standards of perfection or he simply wouldn't hand them in.

"In those days classes had a recess period. There was always great activity in the playground, and one was always certain Woody was a vital part of any 'horseplay' that took place.

178

"His successes as a coach, his leadership, the esteem accorded him for his influences to countless numbers is no surprise to me.

"He is interested in people as individuals. A tremendous book with many chapters could be written about all those whom he has aided through advice, and helped find security in good jobs and plain good citizenship in everyday living."

Less than two weeks after Hayes' death in March 1987, some 150 of his friends gathered in Newcomerstown to honor one of their own.

On hand was Woody's sister, Mary Hayes North, who thanked the community for it's tribute. "Whatever substance of goodness there may have been in our family, we owe much of that substance of goodness to this town, which we loved."

George Brode, whose father (Gordon Brode) was a good friend of Woody Hayes, said those friends who remembered Hayes as a young man must have "had an inkling that he was an uncommon man.

"As he grew and his life progressed and successes mounted, it became obvious to all that there was a greatness about him."

Despite his success and fame, Woody Hayes refused to change.

"He was the same old Woody. He'd call you by your first name and ask about your mother, father, sister, brother, and generally knew them by their first names, too."

Brode told a joke, saying he was sure Woody wouldn't mind a little humor. The joke was about three football coaches in heaven. Each was given a wish.

"The first two coaches asked for victory in the big game, but when God turned to Woody to ask him what his request was, he was gone."

"When God asked where Woody was, someone answered. 'He's over there talking to your son about playing at Ohio State."

George Brode concluded, "I doubt there is much recruiting going on up there, but we can be certain Woody is walking with his God."

Chapter 26

ANNIE AND 'THE BOYS'

It would be the last public appearance for Anne Hayes.

Less than three months later, the widow of legendary Ohio State football coach Woody Hayes would succumb to congestive heart failure. Anne Gross Hayes died in a Columbus, Ohio hospital in January of 1998. She was 84.

Despite her failing health, it was important that she keep a date with 'Woody's Boys.' Her boys as well.

It was a special weekend, October 24-25, 1997, at Denison University, Granville, Ohio.

A time for old warriors to recall those wonderful days of yesteryear.

A time to spin tall tales about their fiery leader, Woody Hayes.

A time for Anne Hayes to lend her personal touch, a half century after back-to-back undefeated seasons in the years that followed World War II.

That weekend was a real happening. On Friday night, some would be inducted into the school's sports Hall of Fame.

It was Homecoming Day on Saturday, with Denison meeting old rival Wittenberg. A perfect setting to bring back as many as possible who played under Hayes from 1946-48. After a 2-6 record in his first season as a head football coach, Hayes directed back-to-back undefeated teams in 1947 and 1948.

Bob Shannon, an 18-year-old freshman receiver on Hayes' '46 edition, orchestrated the reunion. "I wish I could say the idea was mine, but it wasn't. Give Ken Meyer the credit. He played at Denison in 1947-48-49. Ken's the one who first suggested the idea to me.

"I sent out about 95 invitations to anyone connected with those teams, including Bob Willis who was team manager, and the Geiger Brothers who were our twin drum majors.

"I didn't know the Geigers were letter winners until I went back through the old yearbooks. Woody was so impressed with them that he awarded varsity letters. One of them, Don, came back. The other couldn't make it.

"I received some 55 replies, and of those 55, 29 made it back for the reunion, including Jerry Gaynor who was right halfback on our unbeaten team of 1947.

"Gaynor is the only player in Denison football history to play in a major college all-star game. He started in the Blue-Gray game at Montgomery, Alabama.

"I was extremely proud that we had such a good turnout, and that so many of us were still above the ground. Really! It was great.

"On Friday night we had our socializer. On Saturday morning, we had our breakfast. So many wonderful things took place that weekend.

"Jerry Gaynor was named to our Hall of Fame. The football stadium was re-named after Keith Piper who coached for some 30 years after Woody Hayes left.

"Anne Hayes highlighted our breakfast with her presence. That meant an awful lot to us. When I began my queries in April of 1997, Anne Hayes said she'd be happy to come.

"In the interim, she had a flareup of health problems, and at best I thought she'd be a question mark. As it turned out, the same weekend we were having our reunion, Ohio State held a private breakfast to announce that the $1.5 million had been raised to name a chair for Woody (at Ohio State).

"Anne said, 'I can't go to that. I'm going to Granville, Ohio to be with my boys.'

"Mind you, the breakfast wasn't an official college affair. There was just one little line in the alumni bulletin that she was going to be there. From then on, the phone never stopped ringing.

"The Anne Hayes I first knew at Denison was the typical wife of a football coach. She'd come to the games, but the rest of the time she was home taking care of their young son, Steve. When Woody went to Ohio State, Anne became very active. She was an eloquent public speaker who attracted a lot of people.

"At our breakfast, her mind was keen. She was sharp. She gave us all the praise. She could recall everybody that was there and had a story to tell about everyone, including the manager. She didn't miss a trick.

"I'd seen her in the spring of 1993 when I retired from coaching after 40 years at Denison. They had a great get together for me down at the local Elks.

"Anne Hayes made the trip to Newark so she could be a part of my party. That's what she talked about."

In part, she said:

"The success Woody had always depended on the players. Woody never would have been successful without you guys. You don't ever want to forget the people who helped you.

"Thank you for not only playing for Woody and doing a good job, but for being good human beings."

Anne Hayes left a son, Steve, a Municipal Court Judge in Columbus, a daughter-in-law (Kathleen), two grandchildren (Philip Woodrow and Laura Louise), a brother (R. Trevor Gross), and a sister-in-law (Mary Hayes North).

She was a member and honorary member of many organizations and clubs of The Ohio State University as well as an 'adopted mother' to thousands of OSU football players.

She was born February 11, 1913 in New Philadelphia, Ohio. She graduated from New Philadelphia High School (1931) and Ohio Wesleyan College, Delaware, Ohio (1935) with a major in Sociology and Psychology.

She married Woody Hayes in 1942 while he was in the U.S. Navy. Their son was born in 1945. Steve Hayes graduated from Ohio State University with a B.S. in International Studies and from Ohio State's Law College.

Current Ohio State head football coach John Cooper made a point to get to know Anne Hayes when he and his wife, Helen, arrived in Columbus in 1988.

"She has been a dear friend ever since," he said. "More than anything, she always had an encouraging word for Helen. She was always so uplifting."

Said Helen Cooper:

"She was one of my dearest friends in this town. She always had time for me. If I had a problem, all I had to do was pick up the phone. She was just a great lady, and so intelligent. I wish I could be half the lady she was. I just marvel at her and the way she was."

Class of '68

All-Americans Jim Stillwagon (nose guard) and Rex Kern (quarterback) played major roles in Ohio State's last national championship team of 1968. Said Stillwagon:

"She was always up. Even when she was really sick, she was up on things she wanted to know, how everyone was doing. She was just a wonderful lady.

"She had real strong character. I think she was a lot of strength for Woody Hayes because of the way she was."

Kern marveled at her ability "to diffuse any situation. She was just a marvelous, marvelous lady.

"She and Woody always had their telephone number in the book. After a bad game, she would get some bad calls. One of the funniest she told me about was a person calling one time and saying, 'I don't know why that crazy coach called that play when he did.'

"And she told the caller, 'I don't know why he did it either.' The next thing you know, she's in a conversation with the person. And those conversations might lead to her inviting him over for coffee."

Then Kern added:

"It's the passing of a great lady and a great legend. She was a wonderful complement to Woody. She was the antithesis of a spouse who supported her husband.

"She did so many things for the University and for people. She did just as many things as Woody did, but in her own quiet way. But she was parallel with what he did. She was always involved in so many ways. She was just a wonderful woman."

After Woody Hayes' death in March of 1987, Anne Hayes talked about life with a 24-hour-a-day, 12-month-a-year coach.

"I felt he should live life the way he wanted. I tried very hard to give him time to do his job. It was sometimes difficult, but he was a man of the world. You do what you have to do. I was part of his life, and fortunately, I loved the game of football."

At his memorial service, the late Richard Nixon read a letter that Woody had written to the former two-term President after Pat Nixon had suffered a stroke. In part, the letter said: "Neither of us deserved to do so well."

Bo Schembechler, who played under Woody Hayes at Miami of Ohio, coached under him at Ohio, and later became Hayes' arch-rival at Michigan, remembered Woody's love for Anne Hayes.

"He worshipped her, worshipped the ground she walked on."

In 1990, Anne Gross Hayes donated her husband's memorabilia to Ohio State University. "It's amazing," she said during a brief ceremony. "I didn't know a man could accumulate that much."

In 1996, she was honored during the Ohio State graduation ceremony, receiving a distinguished service award. That same year, she received the Ohio Gold Award.

Above: Denison football manager Bob Willis recalls the 'Good Old Days' with Anne Hayes. Below: Annie Hayes and her boys at the October 1997 Reunion at Granville, Ohio.

Photos courtesy Bob Shannon.

Chapter 27

ON THE GRIDDLE

Treading 'hot water' was almost a way of life for Wayne Woodrow Hayes. Call it his 'stylin-and-profilin.' Call it his bulldog approach to life. Add to that his salty language.

He was strictly 'his own man.'

Doing things his own way. Toes get outta his way 'cause Woody's walkin' tall-and-proud'. Damn the torpedoes, full speed ahead.

His career began in the depths of the Great Depression and abruptly ended almost 10 years after man had taken his first giant step on the Moon.

Born in Clinton, Ohio on February 14, 1913, Hayes attended Newcomerstown High School, then Denison University at Granville. He graduated in 1935, majoring in History and English.

A star lineman at Denison, Woody Hayes almost began his legendary career at Dundee High School. Only problem was Dundee didn't have a football team. He wanted to coach football. But Mingo High had a football team, so he packed his bags and the love of the game and stayed on for one year.

On July 1, 1936, he became assistant coach under John Brickles at New Philadelphia [Ohio] High School. It was certainly a step up for Hayes. In 1934, New Philly had registered the first unbeaten season in school history. Football began there before the turn of the 20th Century.

Brickles moved on in 1938. Woody Hayes took over as head coach and guided the Quakers until July 6, 1941 when he joined the U.S. Navy.

In his first season as head coach (1938), New Philadelphia went 9-1. That was exceeded by a 9-0-1 effort in 1939, the only blemish a 7-7 standoff against Lorain. The Quakers' lack of experience proved too much to overcome in 1940, as they lost nine of 10 games.

No sooner had the season ended than Woody Hayes was on the griddle, his job in jeopardy.

On the sports pages of the November 5, 1940 edition of the hometown New Philadelphia Daily Times, a short story described how members of the Board of Education "heard complaints against football coach Woody Hayes to the effect that he had abused members of the football squad during recent games."

The story emphasized, however, that no formal complaint was made.

Twenty-one days later, the lead story in the sports section followed this blaring headline: 'Quaker grid coach may lose position.' School Superintendent H.S. Carroll was opposed to rehiring Woody Hayes.

He said Hayes had used profane language on the practice field and added Hayes had been "admonished" for three years. The story said the Board had informally approved the dismissal but it wasn't by a unanimous vote. Two members admitted they had not been in total agreement.

The newspaper reported the next day that Hayes had quelled a student strike after disgruntled students made plans to skip classes. Hayes had spoken to "the ringleaders." No one missed classes.

184

Hayes said he had been promised a full hearing before the School Board. Board President Walter Ritter said the embattled coach was indeed entitled to a hearing.

Hayes then issued a statement:

"Superintendent Carroll has made no attempt to definitely establish authenticity of rumors and refuses to listen to any argument I want to give, so I have appealed to the Board.

"Several times during the year I have invited Carroll to practice so that he would know I was complying with his request, but he declined.

"I regard the attack on team members as unfair and unwarranted and I feel I have the full cooperation of my squad at all times.

"I am deeply sorry such a situation has arisen, but since charges are of such a personal nature, the only satisfactory means of vindication is a full hearing before the Board."

On November 30, 1940, the Times reported that the New Philadelphia Booster Club, boasting a membership of 400, met in City Council chambers.

A resolution was passed asking the Board to return Woody Hayes to "his present capacity" for the 1941-1942 school year.

Carroll announced on December 3 that he would approve the re-hiring of Woody Hayes. 'Since I talked with Hayes, you people have apparently been more upset than I was," he said at the Board meeting.

The Times reported that all differences had been ironed out.

Hayes agreed not to use profanity, to discourage profanity among his players, to attend exclusively to his duties as football coach and leave the administrative duties in the hands of the principal.

Carroll said there was never a question as to Hayes' coaching ability. "He is one of the best in the state and he has every right to discipline his boys for impudence."

He and Woody Hayes then shook hands. Carroll said "bygones are bygones." The crowd applauded.

In March of 1941, Hayes announced that he had been drafted for military service. He said he would not seek a deferment. He coached the Quakers during Spring practice of 1941 and then entered the Navy.

Even with fame, Wayne Woodrow Hayes never forgot his roots. He would return to New Philadelphia, to Granville, where he kicked off his college head football coaching career at Denison University, and to Newcomerstown where he and his family moved when his father became Superintendent of Schools.

For instance, after his forced 'retirement' after 28 years at Ohio State, Woody Hayes returned to New Philly for a fundraiser to help the O.S.U. Tuscarawas County Scholarship Fund. He even donated $500.

Dr. T.W. Hoernemann, who performed the 1942 wedding ceremony for Woody Hayes and Anne Gross, gave the invocation. He was 90 years old.

Hayes touched all the bases in a rambling, heartwarming speech. The crowd, naturally, most enjoyed his recollections of players and seasons at New Philadelphia High School.

New Philadelphia, he said, was the only Ohio school ever to field undefeated football and basketball teams in the same season (1939-40).

Hayes coached the unbeaten football team, which had one tie, and Paul Hoernemann coached the basketball team which won the state championship.

He singled out three players from his team—Leo Benjamin, Lloyd "Bronco" Reese, and Herb Hines—and called the late Diz Simonetti "one of the greatest athletes I've ever seen."

Despite deteriorating health, news of his death hit the New Philadelphia community hard.

Dr. William Belknap graduated from New Philadelphia High (1931), with Woody's wife. He knew Hayes in the late 1920s.

"A great man has fallen—that is all there is to it. He was a true friend, not only to me, but to Tuscarawas County. This county was almost like family. He was always here in the county whenever we needed him and wanted him. If it was a fundraiser, he always left a check behind, but never took one.

"We have always kept close contact. In fact, we were going down to visit him next week. We saw him about a month ago. He was alert, enjoying life and told us that he and Anne were taking daily walks whenever the weather permitted. It is just a terrible shock. He will be missed."

The same All-Ohio player, Leo Benjamin, was New Philly mayor when his old coach died.

"There are a lot of memories, too many to talk about and certainly one can't rank one above the other.

"I never played for him in college, but he was always after me whenever he felt a good coaching job was opening up. I always remember every time I went into the hospital for anything, he would always know about it and there he would be, cheering me up. He was probably the greatest guy I ever knew."

Brenton Kirk Jr., suffered through New Philadelphia's 1-9 season of 1940.

"He certainly could communicate," Kirk said.

"People talk about his behavior at Ohio State, but as a young coach he was a lot more volatile. He wore a regular fedora in those days and would tear it apart."

Kirk also saw another side of Woody Hayes.

"He was probably the greatest history teacher New Philadelphia ever had. He really made it interesting."

Dick Klar of Dover knew Woody Hayes as an opponent. He recalled a little-known fact that Hayes was an excellent boxer, participating in several fights in the area and once scoring a knockout during a bout at Tuscora Park.

During a 1978 interview with the New Philadelphia Times, Woody Hayes said, "I cared a lot about boxing then, but I don't give a damn for it now."

Klar called Hayes "a great man in so many ways. I have only the best memories of him."

Chapter 28

EMERSON WOULD BE PROUD

Every high school should have a Quaker Club. A group of tireless, dedicated people who make the impossible possible. Countless fund-raisers to improve the life of their high school athletes, girls as well as boys. By the Fall of 1999, the $750,000 major renovation and re-dedication of Quaker Stadium is scheduled to take place. It will be re-named Woody Hayes Quaker Stadium for the man, the legend, who coached for five years at New Philadelphia High School, his last three as head coach. It was Hayes' first head coaching assignment in a career that would span five decades. This is the story behind the story.

Tom Farbizo graduated from Ohio State University in September of 1967. He's been involved with the Quaker Club ever since. In 1990, the New Philadelphia native was elected club president.

"We're an adult male booster club," he says. "We support both male and female athletes in the New Philadelphia School District.

"We are a legal 501-3C non-profit organization.

"Actually, the renovation is the third phase of what we've been doing over the years. It's been an on-going project since the early 1980s."

Funds were raised [1981] for a new 9,200 square foot locker room and weight training center, including two concession stands. A new-and-improved lighting system was installed in 1988. Two years later, a new seven lane polyurethane all-weather track was laid down.

Not one penny is passed on to the taxpayer.

"Our membership is up to about 100," says Farbizo. "We meet twice a month. Actually, we get from 25-40 guys a month for the meetings."

New Philadelphia, a town of about 14,000, was founded in 1804 by John Knisely. He and 33 pioneers founded the new town. In 1804, Ohio was almost a complete wilderness. Largely through his efforts, New Philadelphia was named the county seat for Tuscarawas County in 1807. It has remained the county seat.

Football at New Philadelphia High School celebrates its 100th anniversary in the Fall of 1998.

"New Philadelphia is called 'Quaker City'," says Farbizo. "The high school football stadium is Quaker Stadium." Seating capacity: 6,000.

Construction on the football stadium actually began in 1927 with support from local service clubs, the Chamber of Commerce, Stadium Association and the New Philadelphia City Board of Education.

Then came The Great Depression.

Under President Franklin Roosevelt, the WPA [Works Progress Administration] was founded. The WPA provided government funds and local labor for the project. Construction was completed in 1937. Government costs: $45,000.

187

"Our stadium is different, unique in one respect. It's actually owned by the City of New Philadelphia which leases it to the school district at $1 a year for 99 years. During the course of time, the stadium had deteriorated. Something had to be done.

"The concrete was falling out. Big pieces of the original concrete were falling out. There were holes in it where you could see through from the inside to the outside. Bricks were chipping and cracking. Sections had to be roped off. They were unsafe. The place was in bad shape."

A battle plan was carefully drawn. Tom Farbizo and the Quaker Club would leave nothing to chance.

Farbizo had played under Woody Hayes at Ohio State for three years [1964-66]. Hayes had been a major influence in his life.

"Woody was an Emerson scholar. He used to quote him all the time. He talked about paying forward because we cannot pay back."

Tom Farbizo not only wanted to say 'Thank You' to his old coach, but to "pay forward" future generations of New Philadelphia athletes.

"Woody was at New Philadelphia High School for five years, two as an assistant to John Brickles and three as head coach. When he left Denison University to become head coach at Miami of Ohio, he wanted to bring one assistant.

"At first they said he could. After he was hired, the school president said they didn't have any room for another coach. Woody Hayes basically said 'I don't want the job.'

"Well, suddenly a spot opened up. That assistant happened to be the same John Brickles. I got that story right from Mrs. Hayes."

He continued:

"We started by doing our homework. We had one of the Club members go back to the old Board minutes of New Philadelphia High School and look up all the records, just to make sure we were accurate that Woody indeed was here. What his roles were. The whole nine yards.

"While we were doing that, I got a bunch of old yearbooks and made copies. We fully documented that Woody Hayes was at New Philly for five years."

With the blessing of the Quaker Club, he contacted Anne Hayes, widow of the fiery, colorful, controversial, Buckeyes' head football coach.

"She was in New Philadelphia on Thanksgiving morning about six years ago," recalls Farbizo.

"I met with her and Mrs. Benjamin who was a real good friend. We sat in a restaurant for four hours.

"I asked her permission to use Woody's name. She gave me her permission and her blessing."

Anne Hayes, the former Anne Gross, was born-and-raised in New Philadelphia. A 1931 graduate of New Philadelphia High School, she returned to her home town after graduating from Ohio Wesleyan.

It was there that she met Woody Hayes. She was at the Brickles' home the night he interviewed for the job as assistant football coach.

Concerning the re-naming of the stadium in honor of her late husband:

"Oh, how proud we were of that stadium. And I can't tell you how nice I think it is that it will be named the Woody Hayes Quaker Stadium. The Quaker has always been their signature and it should always be."

The stadium, located in Tuscora Park, is a glorious old structure built of red brick. A center of community pride, the stadium is used throughout the year for community events such as Special Olympics, First Town Days activities, band shows, graduations, etc.

The next step was to determine just how much it would cost for the major stadium renovation.

"I had everything professionally done. We called in a contractor, an engineering firm." Price tag: $750,000.

Renovation would take place in phases, pending approval of the mayor, city council and school board.

"I went to them saying, 'Look, I've documented this, this and this. I have Mrs. Hayes' blessing. Will you allow us to undertake this project?'

'At the culmination of this project, we're gonna add the name of Woody Hayes. We're not taking the Quaker off. We're going to call it Woody Hayes Quaker Stadium. It's the same thing they did at Massillon by renaming the stadium Paul Brown Tiger Stadium.'

And as the old saying goes, 'The Rest Is History.'

New Philadelphia mayor Tim Hurst was impressed.

"Even though we can't appropriate tax dollars, this city is making a commitment to this project from the standpoint of services, or whatever we can do."

Added school superintendent Hank Smith:

"Whenever the students are in need in this community, volunteerism grows strong and helps unite the community."

After years of preliminary work, details of the project were formally announced during a February 6, 1995 press conference at the high school.

Tom Farbizo called it the first step on a journey of a thousand miles. In borrowing that old proverb, he announced a three-phase renovation project.

He said: "This was coach Hayes' first and only head coaching job in the State of Ohio at the high school level. Ohio is a great football state and we in Tuscarawas County are right in the heart of this.

"When this project is completed, we hope to be able to proudly say that New Philadelphia has Woody Hayes Quaker Stadium right in the heart of football country.

"Coach Hayes was a great football coach, but more than that. He was a great educator and a great American patriot."

The first two phases included installation of new aluminum bleachers and repairs to the wall that would remain behind the bleachers on both sides.

Seats on the visitors' side were scheduled to be replaced. Also scheduled in the initial phase were repairs to the press box and ticket boxes on the home side of the field, a new scoreboard and commemorative plaque for Woody Hayes and some former players.

Cost of Phase I was estimated at $315,000.

This project would be strictly pay-as-you-go. Phase Two wouldn't begin until funding was available.

The final phase of the ambitious plan included construction of a new press box on the home side of the field, band shelter restoration, a new toilet facility and the addition of an eighth lane to the all-weather track.

The visitors' side was targeted first because most repairs were needed on that side of the field.

The Stadium Fund began empty, but not for long. The Quaker Club committed $10,000 to pay off the preliminary work.

A New Philadelphia High School alumnus gave the project a huge boost with a $51,000 contribution in May of 1995. Orley R. Herron was a 1951 New Philly graduate. He played football under the legendary Bill Kidd.

"His parents still live in New Philadelphia," says Farbizo. "He still has ties to the community. He found out, through one of his high school friends who's an attorney here in town, what we were doing.

"On one of his trips back East, Dr. Herron asked to meet me. He told me he donated the money for two reasons. He said the plan was superbly done.

"To paraphrase him, 'You've laid out a plan and you're working your plan. You're just not talking about it, you're doing something. I think this is phenomenal.'

Dr. Herron is president of National-Louis University in Wheaton, Illinois.

Tom Farbizo also played his high school football under Bill Kidd. "Kidd coached for fourteen years. He was highly successful. He's one of four New Philadelphia High School coaches to be inducted into the Ohio High School Coaches 'Hall of Fame'."

It's an interesting chronology.

John Brickles hired Woody Hayes as his assistant. Paul Hoernemann followed Hayes. Kidd followed Hoernemann.

Brickles was named to the Hall of Fame in 1970, followed by Hayes [1971], Kidd [1972] and finally Paul Hoernemann in 1994.

"Kidd was in the twilight of his career when I played for him. We just renamed a road in his honor, commissioned a $5,000 plaque and recessed it into cement.

"Today's students and the generations to follow don't know Bill Kidd and Woody Hayes. We're trying to capture history and put it in its proper place. Very few places have a chance to do some of these things."

The project was off to a good start when Dr. Herron presented the check to Tom Farbizo on behalf of the 1950 undefeated football team. He challenged other outstanding New Philly teams to match that kind of gift.

He and Dave Leggett served as co-captains in 1950. Leggett went on to play at Ohio State for Woody Hayes.

Richard Stephenson, legal adviser for the Quaker Foundation, called it "an outstanding kickoff for the stadium renovation project.

"He [Dr. Herron] presented it as a challenge of what can be done. When he spoke to the high school students today, he told of his belief that you should pay back while you're living what you've received."

In the Fall of 1995, Farbizo and the Quaker Club announced it would stage a Kick-Off Banquet with Michigan head football coach Bo Schembechler as main speaker. Columbus TV personality Jimmy Crum would serve as emcee.

Two days before the banquet—October 25th—it was announced that 275 tickets had been sold at $100 a ticket.

The event raised $35,000 for the stadium renovation fund.

190

Farbizo recalls, "I went to Ann Arbor, sat down and talked with Coach Schembechler. I showed him a 23-minute video put together for the project. "He saw Mrs. Hayes and said 'I love Annie.' When he saw the clip about Woody making the 1986 commencement speech about paying forward, and Woody was in poor health then, Bo Schembechler got a tear in his eye. 'You know,' he said. 'Damn it. I miss the old man.'

"Why did Bo Schembechler come to our banquet?

"He told me, 'You're tackling this project in the name of Woody Hayes. I think it's the right thing to do. It's legit. It's not lining someone's pockets with money.'

It certainly didn't line his pockets.

"A man of his stature commands a huge speaking fee but Bo Schembechler wouldn't take a dime. He played for Woody at Miami. He was his disciple. He loved the man."

Then, according to Tom Farbizo, he told the capacity crowd, 'When I took that job at Michigan, I had one job to do and that was to beat Ohio State and Woody Hayes.

'Let me tell you. He was at the top of football. Everybody laughed at him. He taught me everything that I know about this game. It was all basic stuff. You don't have to be fancy. You line up. You block and tackle. Woody Hayes did it to a science.'

That same Dave Leggett couldn't make the banquet. Instead, he sent his regrets.

Tom Farbizo read the letter addressed "To All New Philadelphia Quaker Fans And Athletes."

It said:

"I'm sorry I can't be with you tonight for the Woody Hayes Stadium Kickoff Celebration, but I would like to wish you all success and a special hello to Bo Schembechler who I haven't seen in almost 40 years.

"Now, a little bit about Woody Hayes. He was the ultimate fighter and winner—just like all the New Philadelphia athletic teams of the past, present and future.

"I was very fortunate to have played for Woody during his first four years at Ohio State, which included his first Rose Bowl team.

"If we would all have followed the examples set by Woody—his determination to succeed, his preparation for each and every game, his detailed plan of attack for both the offensive and defensive teams—we would all be successful, honest, law-abiding citizens today.

"The thing I remember most about Woody was his intense desire to have all of his players get an education while they were playing football for the Buckeyes. Many times he said that if you had a class or lab that interfered with football practice, he wanted you to miss practice instead of missing an educational opportunity.

"Woody was the best thing that ever happened to Ohio State football and quite possibly to the Ohio State University itself. He loved Ohio State the way I love the town and people of New Philadelphia, Ohio.

"Working together we can get the stadium renamed, and all of us will be proud to have had a part in this undertaking.

"As a former Quaker athlete and a quarterback for the best coach in Ohio history, I say to all of you—Woody Hayes Quaker Stadium has a nice ring to it."

While Leggett lived in Colorado Springs, Colorado, his heart remained in Ohio.

Dick Vermeil, now head coach of the NFL St. Louis Rams, was the banquet's guest speaker in 1996. A year later, retired Yale University coach Carmen Cozza headlined the event. Cozza was one of 'Woody's Boys.' He played for him at Miami of Ohio.

Golf outings generated some $50,000 plus in 1996-97-98, including $21,000 in 1996. That event also included an auction. Items included a bronze bust of Woody Hayes, created by Urbana, Ohio artist/sculptor Mike Major.

The task of raising three-quarters-of-a-million dollars is an ongoing exercise. Actual renovation of Quaker Stadium began in the Winter of 1996.

"We're small town, but the people here have big hearts," says Tom Farbizo.

"Nothing you want to do is impossible. Someone said it just takes a little longer. We hope to have the project completed and the stadium dedicated for the 1999 season.

"If not...The Quaker Club will just keep on plugging away, one dollar at a time."

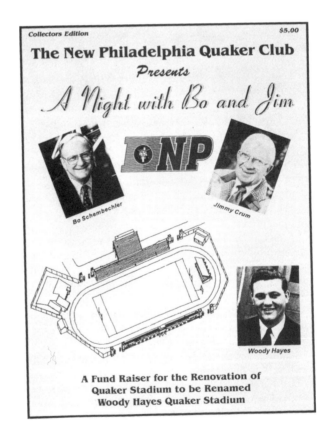

Collectors Edition $5.00

The New Philadelphia Quaker Club

Presents

A Night with Bo and Jim

Bo Schembechler

Jimmy Crum

Woody Hayes

**A Fund Raiser for the Renovation of
Quaker Stadium to be Renamed
Woody Hayes Quaker Stadium**

Chapter 29

HIS MOMENT OF GLORY

Tom Farbizo was born-and-raised in New Philadelphia, Ohio. A six-time letterman in football, track and baseball at New Philadelphia High School, he attended Ohio State University and went out for the football team as a walk-on. In three varsity seasons, he was on the field for only a handful of plays.

A 1967 graduate, he believes in giving back. A man constantly 'on the move,' Farbizo wears many hats. He is special adviser to the mayor for economic development and planning, as well as a teacher at Belmont Technical College. He lives in New Philadelphia.

In his own words:

Two men have had a major influence in my life, my Dad and Woody Hayes. Two tough men. Two men of honor.

I'm of Italian heritage. My Dad, who died about 14 years ago, was a first-generation American who made it to the eighth grade. But you don't have to have a college degree to be smart.

He had smarts and a grip of steel.

He wasn't a big man. When we used to talk, a lot of times he'd grab me by the right arm. Right at your biceps. The more he talked, the tighter his grip.

Woody was Woody. Larger than life. Volatile. Loyal to his kids. But most of all fair.

I played football, basketball, track and a little bit of baseball at New Philadelphia High School. I played offensive guard and any place they needed me on defense. Linebacker, tackle, end.

I was tri-captain my senior year. I was 6-foot and weighed 175.

In track, I threw the shotput and was on the state qualifying 880-yard relay team. We held the school record for about 10 years.

My guidance counselor, who was my track coach, encouraged me to take the exams for the Air Force Academy. To be honest, I really wasn't planning to go to school.

My Dad made it to the eighth grade. He had his own business and I figured I'd work for him after high school. I knew I wasn't going to qualify for the Air Force Academy, but I took the exam anyway.

I was encouraged to go to a Division 3 school, but as I said, I really wasn't interested.

I had a rough senior year in high school. My Dad was ill and was forced to stay in bed most of my senior year. He was that sick. The doctor used to come and visit 2-3 times a week. I figured my place was at home. After all, I'd be a high school graduate. Well, my Dad had other ideas.

In the Spring of my senior year he finally got out of bed. He was able to sit up in a chair. Sometime that June he asked me, 'Where are you going to school?'

I said, 'I'm not planning on going to school.'

Class of '68

My Dad was a strict disciplinarian. If the wall I was looking at was white and he said it was black, I just said 'Yes Sir.' There was no debate. He sternly said 'You're going. You don't understand. You have an opportunity to do something I couldn't do...and you're gonna do it.'

So I responded, 'Well, if that's the case, I might as well enroll at Ohio State.' One of my sisters had graduated from there. Another sister was going into her junior year at OSU.

I figured a state school had to accept me. It was late in June of 1963 when we had that conversation. I enrolled and was accepted.

I figured if I'm going to college, then naturally I would go out for the football team. I became a walk-on. If I remember correctly, there were some 20 guys who walked-on. About three of us lasted.

The rest of 'em quit the first or second day. I mean they just packed it in. I simply loved football. All we were was cannon fodder for the varsity during the week.

Back in those days freshmen weren't eligible to play varsity ball. We didn't even have a freshman schedule, so we were either scrimmaging against the varsity or scrimmaging against ourselves.

Glenn 'Tiger' Ellison was our freshman coach. He came from Middletown where he was highly successful. Woody recruited him. Tiger was a great guy.

We had a series of graduate assistants who helped the team. Guys like John Mummy and Bill Murkowski.

All of my friends would ask me, 'What in the hell are you doing?' I replied, 'If I'm gonna go to college, I might as well play some football.'

They all thought I was crazy.

Back in the 60s, you had to learn both sides of the ball. They put me at fullback on offense and outside linebacker on defense. We used the T formation.

By my sophomore year I was up to 191. My playing weight ranged from 191 to 195 pounds, maximum.

I had a tough freshman year. I wasn't too crazy about the books and because we had no games, there was nothing to look forward to, just the same recurring nightmare. Strap it on and get the hell kicked out of you. I mean it was an acid test. Believe me.

I can't tell you how many times I thought about quitting school, but I gave a handshake to my Dad. Anyone who knows me knows that my handshake is my bond. If I've made a commitment, I'm gonna keep my word.

When I was a freshman, guys like Paul Warfield and Matt Snell were seniors. You face off against those guys. They're phenomenal and you wonder if you belong on the same field.

I basically ended up on the defensive end of the ball against Woody's guys. That was your test. To see if you're the kind of guy they want the next three years.

You won't see my name on any All-Big Ten or All-American list. In fact, you'd need a microscope to find my name at all. I was involved in only two or three total plays at Ohio State. I wore jersey Number 34.

I carried the ball once and gained three-and-a-half yards against Iowa. What a thrill.

I knew early on that my chances of playing were slim or none. It was the comraderie. It was being part of something. We called ourselves 'Woody's AYO.' Meaning All You Others.

We were important members of the team. We knew it and that was good enough. As I said, I came to Ohio State as a walk-on. No scholarship. You had to pay your own way. But all that changed in December of 1963 when Woody Hayes called me into his office.

'When you come back to school in January, there will be a grant-in-aid for $1,000 waiting for you.'

I was stunned.

'Thank you. I really appreciate this.'

Woody Hayes slammed his fist down on the table.

'Hell no, you don't thank me. Damn it, you earned it. That's the bottom line.'

It was three-quarters of a full-scholarship. That took care of my tuition, books, room. I was responsible for my own meals. That's how it went.

I got a part-time job in the off-season. I basically came out of Ohio State in 13 quarters debt free. That scholarship was a lot of money in those days.

There was nothing that said Woody Hayes had to give me that scholarship. That was just the man.

I can recall two incidents that took place during my sophomore year.

We were on the practice field. I was hitting a gurney which is a big overstuffed bag on a spring. You're supposed to go up, give a hand-shiver like you're getting somebody away from your body so they couldn't block you. It was a defensive drill.

The next thing I know I heard a whistle blow and somebody hit me on the helmet and said, 'Damn it, who is this?'

I turned around.

Woody looked at me. 'That's the way you're supposed to do that. Get in there again and show these guys how to do it right.'

I was stunned. I was absolutely stunned.

That same sophomore year, my Dad got sick again. My mind wasn't on school. My mind wasn't on football. I thought 'I'm gonna go home.'

I went to Coach Hayes' office and asked to see him. I requested that he red-shirt me. I told him my Dad was sick and that I needed to go home. He let me speak for 15-20 minutes. It seemed like an hour. When I finished, he pounded his fist down on the desk.

'I'm not going to red-shirt you. Football is a short period of your life. You need this education.

'If I let you go home, you'll never come back here.

'No, I'm not going to red-shirt you. What I'm going to do is give you a week. You go home for a week, get your mind in order, take care of what you have to take care of.

'But if you're not back here in a week, I'll come to New Philadelphia and bring you back.'

I sat there frozen.

Then he said, 'What the hell are you waiting for? Get the hell outta here. Get going.'

So I went home.

When I arrived home, I opened the door, brought in my suitcases and set 'em down.

My Dad watched the whole thing. He sounded just like Woody Hayes. 'What the hell are you doing here?'

I started to answer 'Well, Dad', but he never let me finish my sentence.

'What did Coach Hayes say?'

He told me he'd give me a week and I'd better be back there.

'I'll give you less than that. Don't unpack your bags.'

During my junior year, I got in some trouble. I was out late one night, along with two of my friends. They were guys who had full scholarships but quit the football team.

One of 'em just said, 'I hate football. I don't want to be here anymore.' So he gave up his full scholarship. The other guy got into an argument with Woody and quit.

Anyway, I was out late with these two guys. We're coming across campus. We stopped. Back then they had barricades instead of the orange barrels.

We moved the barricades. We're having a good time, laughing. Next thing you know a University cop popped up from behind these bushes and took us down to the University police station.

Here, we didn't realize there had been a bomb scare called in at the Chemical Abstracts Building. Guess who they were looking at? The three of us.

They interrogated us all night. The next day when I went to practice a team manager was waiting for me. He said, 'Woody told me to get my ass down in front of your locker and when you get here to go immediately to his office.'

I said 'Okay.'

I went to his office, knocked on the door and went in. Woody Hayes had his glasses about half down. He did that lots of times. He peered over the top of 'em. He told me to sit down, and typical Woody, he'd ask you questions and before you could say anything he already knew the answer.

He asked me, 'Number One. Where were you last night?'

But before I could get it out, he said, 'Dammit, never mind where you were. You were not where you were supposed to be.' Then he said, 'Who was with you?' I really thought 'Oh shit.' I started to say that and he said, 'never mind that either.'

He then asked me 'Did you or didn't you do it?'

I said 'Yes sir. I moved those barricades.'

He said, 'Nah, I'm not talking about that. I'm talking about the bomb scare in the Chemical Abstracts Building.'

'No sir. I didn't have anything to do with that.'

'Dammit, I knew I could believe one of my boys before I'd believe those cops.'

Man, I breathed a lot easier.

I thought the ordeal was over, but it wasn't.

Woody said. 'Wait a minute. I'm giving you one more chance. Did you or didn't you do it, or know who did it?'

And I said, 'No sir.'

He said 'That's fine.'

Then he looked at me.

'Number One, you've been working your tail off. You deserve to eat at the

Training Table. This incident blew it.

'Number Two. I'm not letting you dress this Saturday for the home game.' But then he hit me with the real test.

'You're gonna run quarter miles before-and-after practice in full uniform. There will be somebody timing you, just to make sure you run it.'

Woody made me do that for the rest of the season. He never put me back on Training Table, but he let me dress from then on.

Was I mad at Woody? No way. I was mad at myself for doing a stupid thing. The man was fair. He taught us an aspect that I think is lacking today. We were loyal. He was loyal to us. We didn't win some games, but we were loyal.

I earned a Bachelor of Science degree in September of 1967, with a major in Public Recreation. I owe it all to my Dad and Woody Hayes.

Chapter 30

IN THE BEGINNING

Memories of Woody Hayes date back more than 50 years for Rix Yard, Robert Shannon and Richard Mahard. Back to the 1940s.

Rix Yard met Woody Hayes in 1941 when both served in the Navy. Yard joined him as line coach at Denision University in 1946 and remained for three years. He left Denison to pursue his own career. Stops along the way included the University of Pennsylvania—his alma mater—return to Denison as athletic director, a move to Tulane University in the same capacity.

Robert Shannon was a freshman end at Denison when Woody Hayes launched his college head coaching career in 1946. A three-year letterman, Shannon remained at his alma mater for some 40 years as a well-respected track and football coach.

Richard Mahard, a Ph.D in Geology, taught at Denison from 1941 until his retirement almost 40 years later. A sports enthusiast, Mahard was on campus when 'The Woody Hayes Saga' began. He followed Woody's career until the end came in 1987. All three are now enjoying retirement. These are their stories.

RIX YARD, Poquoson, Virginia

I met Woody Hayes in 1941 when we were in the Navy. I went into service in May of 1941. That was seven months before the start of World War II.

Woody and I were both in the Gene Tunney program, in the same group. For those youngsters who don't know anything about Gene Tunney, he was the undefeated heavyweight boxing champion of the world who beat Jack Dempsey in the controversial 'long count' fight in the 1920s.

Gene Tunney had been a Marine. He'd been recruited by the Navy at the rank of Lieutenant Commander, I believe, to develop a physical fitness program for recruits.

He recruited, I suppose, 200-400 for the program. Woody and I were in the initial group of 115 men. We all went into the Navy with the rank of Chief Boatswain's Mate.

It was a very select group. Woody and I had been college football players. We had a couple of boxers, even a major league baseball player named Sam Chapman who had been an All-American in football.

Basically, we had to be introduced to the Navy because we were all civilians. We were given a very basic recruit training program so that we could give the physical training to the recruits. We became drill instructors at the Norfolk [Va.] Naval Base.

As I recall, the program lasted 4-6 weeks. We all lived in the same barracks.

Woody and I were together for about six months. We became instant friends. We talked football right from the start.

Harvey Shapiro

Woody had been a Single Wing high school coach before he went into service. I had played Single Wing at Penn. We talked basically about the Single Wing. Things like the guard-buck lateral series. How you read it, how to time it. That type of thing. Woody Hayes was a terrific person, a very good friend. He had a horrible temper, but once he cooled off he was fine. His temper would flare up at different times, with different situations.

For instance, if someone would disagree with him on what was right and what was wrong, he heated up real quick. Woody was ready to fight for his point of view. Very often he would want to settle a discussion with his fists. He'd say 'Let's go outside.' But in the six months we were together, I never saw him get into a fight.

We were such good friends that when I got married, Woody loaned me his car to go on my honeymoon.

After our initial program, most of us were kept at Norfolk to train recruits. After six months, I stayed on and Woody was assigned elsewhere.

I can't recall Woody talking about wanting combat duty, but I think he was eager to do something else other than train recruits.

I'm not sure how it worked out for Woody. Eventually, he went through some sort of officer's training, probably OCS [Officer's Candidate School].

He was a shipboard officer. At the end of the war, he was in command of a Destroyer Escort.

Was I anxious for combat duty? Yes and no. I was one of the first of that group that married. The drill officer, who was third in command, wanted me to remain at Norfolk.

I got my commission in 1942. I was supposed to go to the Armed Guard School, but he pulled some strings, got my orders cancelled and kept me there at Norfolk.

I stayed at Norfolk for three years. I switched from the recruit training program to anti-submarine warfare. To be honest, Woody and I kinda lost track of each other during the war.

I went all around. I was at Notre Dame for awhile, went on a Destroyer Escort for a shakedown cruise in Bermuda, then was shipped to Guam and assigned to recreation. I was discharged with the rank of Lieutenant.

When I got out of service, I went to teach and coach at Swissvale High School, outside of Pittsburgh, Pennsylvania. I had been there only four or five months when I got a phone call from Woody. He told me he had the Denison job and wanted me to come out as his line coach.

Woody's call came strictly out of left field. I don't know how he found me. It took me about 10 seconds to tell him I'd accept the job.

I did so even though Woody really threw me a zinger. I also had to coach basketball.

I didn't know anything about Denison football, but I knew something about the university. The chairman of my department at Penn was a Denison graduate.

I don't think I got a $200 raise when I went to Denison. I believe my salary was $3,600. Woody must have been making $4,000. I was married and had a child in 1946. We rented an apartment on Pearl Street in Granville.

I think Woody and I walked into that situation kinda blind, not knowing what sort of material we'd have, equipment, or anything else.

Class of '68

He was the backfield coach. I was the line coach. Just the two of us. I was responsible for line play, both offensively and defensively. Woody handled the overall teamwork as well as the backfield.

The second and third year we were there, we had a couple of student assistants- George Strickland and Dick Marquart. We didn't have any our first season.

While we were both Single Wing men, Woody switched to the T formation almost immediately. I think that Woody was somewhat influenced by Don Faurot who'd been very successful with the T. As I recall, during the war Faurot was coaching at North Carolina Pre-Flight.

I don't know if Woody had been in contact with Faurot or just followed his success. It was basically a power T. Woody often said three things can happen when you throw a pass and two of 'em are bad.

We had to quick-study to learn and then teach a new concept. There's quite a bit of difference in the offensive line play.

In the T back in those days, you didn't trap very much. It was more of what I call shield blocking. You're trying to screen a man, rather than knock him down.

In the Single Wing, you trapped an awful lot. You double-teamed on one side of the hole and trapped on the other side.

Defensively, I was in much more familiar territory. I had been brought up on a six-man front. I had been taught by Rae Crowther, who I think was the greatest line coach who ever lived. That's what we used at Penn.

And that's what we used at Denison. We were doing an awful lot of looping and slanting when I played in college. We took that into Denison and it worked very well.

Behind the six-man front, we had two linebackers, two halfbacks and a safety. Most other teams after the war, as I recall, used a five-man front.

Offensively, most teams ran from the T, although from time-to-time, we'd still run up against the old Single Wing.

Basically, we were a small team. We had one guard, "Snowball" Miller at about 165. The other guard wasn't much heavier. One of the tackles might have gone 200, the other about 210. That's the weight I played at Penn.

We didn't do very well our first year, but we really turned it around the next two seasons, basically with the same players.

We won 17 in a row in 1947 [9-0] and 1948 [8-0]. We just had a whole bunch of doggone good athletes who were dedicated to football.

I think the difference between being a loser and being a winner was breaking a lot of old, bad habits. Most of our players had been in the service and hadn't played for 2-3 years.

We had to break 'em in. I don't want to sound puffed up about this, but I think we were both pretty good coaches.

Woody and I had entirely different approaches to coaching. My coach in college, Rae Crowther, was a very calm person and a teacher, more than a hollerer and a screamer.

In other words, he'd take you aside and say, 'You do it this way for this reason.' He'd always have a reason for why you did things. I think I adapted that to my style of coaching. Woody was usually very short on explanations.

In those days, the players went both ways. No offensive unit. No defensive unit. Both ways.

Country Wehr was our center. He was a good one. He was a Navy pilot who came to Denison.

Bernie Wentis was fullback. He was a Marine Corps captain.

Billy Fleitz and Bob Shannon both came from Newark High School. Both were excellent football players. They were freshmen in 1946.

Eddie Rupp was halfback for us. As I said, we didn't throw the ball much. Only when absolutely necessary. Our 'trick play' was a halfback pass. Eddie Rupp was the passer.

Back in those days, you didn't have the weight room and all of that off-season training. I thought our teams were pretty well prepared physically.

With a two-man coaching staff, you didn't have the luxury of scouting an opponent. We relied a lot on alumni in the area who were former Denison football players.

But those reports weren't always that accurate. For instance, we would get a report that our opponent was using the Single Wing. We'd walk into the stadium only to find out it was the T.

Those were very long days. I can remember sitting home one evening after dinner, reading a magazine. Woody came in. We were gonna work that night. He said, 'What are you doing reading that magazine? You oughta be working on football.'

Woody Hayes was very intense, an excellent coach. There's no doubt he demanded a lot, from his players, his coaches, from himself. I really wouldn't have wanted it any other way.

He was the type of person who would be tough on the field, but once he left the field he was the player's best friend. No matter whether the person was a first stringer or a tail ender.

He was great to work with. I enjoyed all the time with Woody. We would get into arguments about what we should do, but he was the boss.

Like I remember one time. As you know, if you're a pulling lineman there are two or three ways you can take an end down. But to Woody, there was only one way. You had to hook him. He wouldn't think of anything else.

To me, Woody Hayes must be considered one of the greatest all-time college coaches. His total dedication to the game of football is legendary. Woody always thought about football. Everything was in relation to football.

He was a bread-and-butter coach. All of his teams were fundamentally sound. Not much razzle-dazzle. Just plain knock-'em-down, basic football.

I have to say something about Anne Hayes.

She was a perfect wife for Woody. When Ohio State wasn't doing too well, irate fans would call him at home and complain.

He usually wasn't home. He'd sleep at the stadium. When they'd bitch, Anne would say 'Well, you oughta have to live with him.' Anne was a great person.

I'd already left Denison to go back to Penn when Woody left to take the head coaching job at Miami. He called and asked me if I'd come to Miami, but I had to turn him down. I was back at my alma mater and working on my doctorate. I thought I'd stay.

Three years later he went to Ohio State. Once again Woody Hayes contacted me and asked if I'd come to Columbus as his line coach. Certainly, I was very flattered, but I was very leery about that situation. Head coaches didn't last long at Ohio State. I considered the situation too unstable for me.

As I recall, I think his ultimate goal was to coach at Ohio State. We didn't discuss it very much, but he would mention it every once in awhile.

Over the years, I'd see him at least once a year. We always went to the football coaches convention. We were always together for at least an evening, or an afternoon. We always talked football.

When I was coaching at Penn as line coach, we had played Navy. They had a short trap and just crucified us. So we put it into our playbook and loved it.

I talked to Woody about that play at the next convention the following December or January. He said 'Oh, we tried that. It's no good.'

The following year Ohio State played a team that used the short trap and cut up Ohio State pretty good. I happened to have seen that game.

When I saw Woody the following year I said, gloating a bit, 'Well, that's the play I told you about.'

Woody Hayes cracked a smile and replied, 'Yeah, we've got it in our system now.'

ROBERT SHANNON, Newark, Ohio

I was born-and-raised in Newark, Ohio. I lettered in football, basketball and track at Newark High School. As a senior I used to like to think I was 6-feet tall. But I never quite got there. I was 5-11 and weighed about 160.

I played offensive and defensive end. We had an undefeated team my senior year [1945]. We had one of the better teams in the state. The Dunkel Ratings were used for the first time in Ohio and we were ranked No.1 until our last game. We won by something like 20-6, but slipped to second or third.

I was one of three players from Newark High School to be selected to play in the first Ohio high school all-star game. I was just a player who happened to play on an undefeated team. The best player in Ohio was a teammate of mine, Bill Fleitz.

Everybody wanted Billy. He was recruited by Bear Bryant of Kentucky, Rip Engel at Penn State, as well as by Ohio State and Miami of Ohio. Sid Gillman was coaching at Miami. I honestly thought Billy was gonna go to Miami.

I got a few questionnaires. For example, I got one from Miami but they didn't pursue me. I had good grades but my plan wasn't to go to college right away.

My Dad was a mailman and he had a reasonable income. We lived comfortably but I didn't have any money to go to college. My plan was to go into the service, have the government take care of my college education.

But then along came Wayne Woodrow Hayes.

After he got out of the Navy, he was given the head football coaching job at Denison. How Woody heard about me, I don't know.

I suppose he'd go to high school coaches, find out about you and where you lived. Newark was only seven miles away from Granville and Denison University. I had good grades and I suppose he was looking for that kind of student-athlete.

Woody was the kind of guy who would go door-to-door, ringing doorbells, if that's what it took to recruit players.

I didn't know Woody Hayes at the time. To me, he was a New Philadelphia High School coach who was head coach at Denison. That didn't mean anything to me. I was working at the time with no intention of going to school.

I came home from camp for the weekend and my mother said to me, 'Do you know who's here?'

It was Wayne Woodrow Hayes.

He was the kind of guy who kinda dropped in unannounced. It wasn't like he made an appointment. There'd be my mother cooking over the stove and he'd just pop in.

She'd be embarassed because she wasn't dressed up, but that didn't make any difference to Woody. We'd be about to eat and Mom would say, 'Would you like to eat supper with us.'

And, of course, he would.

The family was very important to him. He just had the gift of being able to talk to families, especially the mother. He just kept on talking. You know that if you can convince the mother that you're honest and you know what you're saying, it's gonna have an effect on a boy. It did.

Not that my mother told me what to do. I don't mean that. I could just tell that she thought Woody was alright. That made it alright with me.

Woody and my mother became great friends. She thought he was the greatest person that ever lived. She lived to be 93.

Woody ate at her table. He treated her son honestly and fairly. So when Woody hit that Clemson player, she insisted he was innocent. 'He didn't do it. He didn't do it.' Nobody like the man she knew and loved could possibly do such a thing.

The businessmen of Newark were great sports fans. We'd had a couple of state championship high school basketball teams. We had some pretty fair athletes, like Freddie Schaus who later played with the Lakers.

What happened was Woody Hayes not only offered me a financial aid package, but my teammate Billy Fleitz as well. He was able to do that through a guy named Mike Gregory who owned the local hardware store and was a Denison graduate.

Gregory got several local businessmen to make contributions to pay our tuition. Among them were the owner of the local newspaper and a fellow who owned a restaurant. That wasn't illegal 50 years ago.

Woody took me to Granville and showed me the campus. In those days, Denison recruited nothing but girls whose parents could pay their way. All the girls lived in dorms on one hill and the boys lived in dorms on the other hill. The college was in between.

Woody would say 'Now look, if you know what you're doing, you can date one of our coeds. Then you're gonna have a car available and when you graduate from college you can marry your college sweetheart. You're gonna have a built-in job because you could work for the old man.'

That was part of his sales pitch. Now, he may have been joking a little bit, but there's a lot of truth in what he said. I didn't follow his advice. I married a lovely girl from Newark who was a cheerleader.

When World War II was over, we still registered for the draft. I wasn't drafted and I went to Denison. I had osteomyelitis, which is a bone disease. I would miss a year of football because of it.

I'd say we had 40-45 players on the roster in 1946. This wasn't a typical freshman class made up of 18-year-olds straight out of high school. Many of the guys had served in the war. They were men and not boys.

Our fullback was a guy named Bernie Wentis who was a super athlete. He had served in the Marines and had a comparable military rank to Woody. He was also a Sigma Chi, so he was a fraternity brother of Woody Hayes.

Woody had that military background. He was the commander and he barked the orders. That held true throughout his life.

I had a high school coach who was probably tougher than Wayne Woodrow Hayes. That was what you did in those days. You intimidated people.

Back then, we didn't run 40 yard dashes. We'd run a series of 100s, as many as 10 in a row. I was 18 years old and in pretty darned good shape.

But if you were a veteran who had been away for a few years and came back with rubbery legs, it wouldn't take you too long to get real ticked off.

Mind you, these guys were good athletes. They just weren't really in good shape. It was one of those long, hard practices where Woody ran the same play over-and-over again. You'd think we would get it right. But something went wrong every time.

Woody would just scream louder and louder until it finally came to these two guys. Woody Hayes and Bernie Wentis. They went head-to-head, nose-to-nose.

Bernie yelled 'F-U' and walked off the field.

That old boy wasn't gonna do that to him anymore. He had all that in the service. That kinda stunned me, I'll tell you that.

Bernie cooled off. Woody cooled off. Had Bernie stayed away from the team, I'm sure it would have had a great influence on the rest of the players. As it turned out, they became great, great friends.

We lost six of eight games in 1946. Only one I can recall was a blowout. Ohio Wesleyan beat the heck out of us.

We opened our season at Otterbein and lost 18-13. Otterbein went on to win the Ohio Conference championship, losing only to West Virginia by a touchdown that season.

In that first game, Billy Fleitz got a severe charley horse. He had a lot of blood in the leg and was never quite the same. He didn't have his old speed.

We lost to "Deacon" Dan Towler and Washington and Jefferson by five points, 12-7. Towler went on to become a great pro fullback with the Los Angeles Rams.

If you don't win and you're close, pretty soon you believe you can't win. That's what I think happened in 1946.

We weren't winning, so there was carousing and drinking. The guys who had been in the service were acting like they were still in the service.

The training wasn't what you'd call the greatest. There had to be a coming of the minds which there was over the winter.

Woody may have been tough but he sure wasn't stupid. He knew we couldn't continue on the same collision course.

Fraternities were strong at Denison. So he'd go to Beta House, for instance, get the two Betas he thought he could talk to and say 'Now look, I know I made some mistakes. I was bullheaded. All we want to do is to have a good football team.'

He'd do the same thing at Sigma Chi, etcetera. Through this kind of arrangement, the same team came back in 1947, followed training rules and turned the whole thing around.

We went undefeated in both 1947 [9-0] and 1948 [8-0] with virtually the same personnel.

I got a pain in my leg before Christmas in 1946. I started getting pain in my left leg. It was constant, like a toothache.

Woody thought I was losing my mind. I go to a doctor and he begins to think I'm whacky too. One time I got a shot that must have been in that particular area, so I didn't have pain for a few days. I thought it was over with. It wasn't.

Finally, my brother-in-law takes me to see Dr. Judson Wilson in Columbus. He was the best orthopedic man in the Midwest. X-rays showed I had osteomyelitis. The infection was down in my shin and was shooting pain up to my knee.

They scraped the infection out of my leg. That was in the Summer of 1947. I limped my way through the year. Because of my treatment, Dr. Wilson became Woody's orthopedic surgeon at Ohio State during his career there.

I coached the freshman team in 1947 and did some radio.

Every week during the Summer, Woody would write a letter to the returning players. It was in terms of what he was doing, who we expected back, something about the schedule.

He would always say something like 'When you were doing your sprints today, you had better wonder how many sprints "Deacon" Dan Towler is doing today.' In other words, he was trying to motivate our people.

Every week we got one of these letters.

The game against Washington and Jefferson was a dandy. I worked for a radio station. I got to see the game. It was played at Washington, Pennsylvania. Fortunately for us, they thought their speed could outrun our outside defense. Their slowest man in the backfield ran a 10-second flat 100.

They ran the tailback one way and the little wingback another way. They couldn't get it done because the Denison defense would play 'wide tackle 6' and the ends played loose. The halfbacks came up on the outside of the ends.

When Washington and Jeff gave Towler the ball—he played fullback—he would make some yardage. Fortunately for us, they didn't do that enough. When they did, somebody on our side would make a great play.

Willie Hart was our defensive left end. He made Little All-American in 1947. He played a tremendous game. When those kids from Denison came off the field, they were wilted. There wasn't one ounce of strength left in 'em.

Washington and Jefferson played the old Single Wing. Denison played the straight T, the same formation that Frank Leahy used at Notre Dame.

Guess who my high school All-Star coach was? The same Frank Leahy.

I was a Single Wing end in high school, but by the time I came to Denison I had a head start on everybody because I knew the straight T. That's what Woody used.

Our center, Bill Wehr, had played a little bit at Ohio State. He tried out for the NFL Detroit Lions, got to the last cut but racked up his knee in a pre-season game.

Woody still ranted-and-raved in 1947. But he didn't make it personal to the point where he was picking on somebody. Woody never mellowed that I know of.

Class of '68

By 1948, I was ready to play football again. When doctors say you won't ever run as fast as you did, you use that as motivation. If anything, I was a little faster. I worked my fanny off to do it. I ran 10 flat which was pretty good back then.

To be honest, I don't think our schedule in 1948 was quite as tough as it was in '47. We ended our second straight unbeaten season with an easy win over Case. We had a great game against Case. It was played on our field.

We had a halfback pass that we ran to death early in the season. The quarterback gets the ball, pitches to the left halfback who sweeps around right end.

I played right end. I'd release out flat to the right, as if I'm going to get an outside position on the defensive halfback. Then I'd spring straight down the sideline. The halfback would stop the sweep, set up and heave the ball. That play was quite successful for us. I'd say we scored on it four or five times.

Woody figured Case would never fall for that play. He didn't think it would fool anyone, so he added a wrinkle to it. When the pitch was made from the quarterback to the left half, he goes to his right. I'm blocking down on the tackle, crawling on my hands and knees across the field to my left.

Now I release and I'm on the opposite side of the field. I'm so wide open. That's the only time in my life I ever worried about dropping the ball.

I'm saying to myself, 'My God, don't drop it.'

Fortunately I didn't. There wasn't anybody even close to me. The play covered 40, maybe 50 yards. I don't know. I can't remember.

I really wasn't a star on the team. I got a lot of recognition because we threw the ball. Isn't that strange for Woody? We threw a lot in 1948.

We had only two coaches. Woody and Rix Yard. Woody coached the backs, Rix the line. He was an excellent coach. Before the 1949 season, Rix had already decided to go back to the University of Pennsylvania to get his doctorate degree.

Sometime after Rix left, Woody called a team meeting and told us what he was going to do. He was going to Miami of Ohio as head football coach.

He wished us all well. After the meeting he told me, 'Bob, you are going to finish your education. The arrangement that you had for three years will continue through the next year.'

That was one of the things my mother was most concerned about. Wayne Woodrow Hayes wasn't going to leave you hanging. He was a very honorable man.

We were in a rebuilding year under Jack Carl in 1949. We finished 5-3-1. I graduated from Denison in 1950.

None of us were immune from Woody's wrath. Whenever I got it, or most of the time, I deserved it. You weren't gonna put anything over on him. He would play his little games.

We had three ends on the team, including me. We'd have pass pattern practice before regular practice began. I'm running 25, 35 yards, then I'm running back. Then we run a play to the other side and you're resting.

Maybe he thought I wasn't in the best of shape. He would run you silly, trying to make you say 'Uncle.' I would continue to run those patterns because I wasn't going to quit. He would stand there and stare at you.

He wants you to say 'Uncle' and you're not giving in. It was rough, but that made you awful tough on Saturday.

Wayne Woodrow Hayes wasn't an innovator. We had a counter play that was just beautiful, but it was the Army counter. We had Notre Dame's halfback pitch-pass. The only thing he did run through the years was the off-tackle play to the right, the off-tackle play to the left.

I remember Woody talking about the Tennessee coach, General Robert Neyland. It was something about, 'If you didn't run a play a thousand times in practice you weren't gonna run it in a game.' And by golly, we ran a thousand off-tackle plays in practice.

As an end that played for him, there was never a time I couldn't talk to Woody Hayes. If I had a personal problem or needed to talk to him, the world would stop and Wayne Woodrow Hayes would find the time to meet with me, talk to me for as long as I wanted.

I can't say enough good things about him. Even up until he died, Woody still had a fondness for the people at Denison. He remembered his beginnings, where he started.

He would come back and speak at banquets. He would come to football games after he got out of coaching. He'd just come over unannounced, take a seat in the stands. Or he'd just pop in and talk to our kids. He just had a love of where he came from. That NEVER left him.

It wasn't until I got older that I really began to realize how lucky I was to have played even a small role in his story. When you're a kid you're just playing the game, doing what you've been taught all your life. Win. Give it your best effort.

It's still hard for me to believe that the same person who touched me could be the same person who touched so many others.

DR. RICHARD MAHARD, Granville, Ohio

I came to teach at Denison University as a geology/geography instructor in 1941. Although I had registered for the draft, I was exempt from military service because I was teaching 600 men who were in the military.

I was teaching military map reading to 200 Marines. The other group consisted of 400 Air Corps men. I was teaching a world geography course.

In late 1944, I lost my exemption for service because the Marine contingent program had been pulled out of Denison. I was finally drafted into the Army in April of 1945 and served for 14 months.

I ended up in Tokyo, Japan for the first five months of 1946. We arrived in Tokyo on New Year's Day. It was a wonderful assignment. We billeted right in downtown Tokyo and saw that city literally rise from the ashes.

I was back on campus at Denison in time for the Fall semester and remained at that wonderful institution until my retirement 39 years later.

I've always enjoyed college athletics. We actually had some exciting athletics during the war. We had the finest basketball team we ever had in the history of Denison during the war because of the V-12 program.

We had a man that played for Denison named Knorek. He later played professional basketball for the New York Knicks.

All of the rules were off during the war as far as eligibility was concerned.

That pertained to all sports, including football. For instance, the great "Crazy Legs" Hirsch played at several different schools during the war.

But getting back to Denison, in the Fall of 1946 Woody Hayes arrived as head football coach. Rix Yard was his assistant.

Woody had graduated from Denison six years before I arrived. I really knew nothing about the man but in 1946 stories began to surface.

As I recall, I think the chief emphasis related back to his undergraduate days. He was short-tempered. He was almost violent if he lost his temper. He was hard-boiled, a fighter, a winner.

There was one story about the time he participated in an intra-mural boxing match. In those days many colleges, including Denison, had intra-mural boxing.

The story goes that Woody was facing an opponent who belonged to another fraternity. Woody was a Sigma Chi. Well, this guy landed a pretty good punch that surprised Woody.

The punch made him angry. Woody lost control of himself and began to beat the devil out of the other guy. The inexperienced referee didn't get to him before Woody had pretty badly hurt his opponent.

In other words, Woody Hayes just lost control, somewhat the way he did later in some of those unfortunate incidents. The break-the-stick [yardline marker] at Michigan in 1971 tarnished his reputation.

I have a friend on the Denison faculty who was working for the Michigan student newspaper at the time it happened. Ask him about Woody Hayes. He has a totally different version than most people because he actually witnessed that outburst, that totally unacceptable behavior.

Woody sealed his own fate, so to speak, by hitting that Clemson player at the Gator Bowl [1978].

The whole matter of his character became a controversial issue, not once but three times at Denison. The big question was should Woody be granted an honorary degree from his alma mater.

The faculty is very, very powerful in such matters. Three times he was nominated for such an honor and three times that proposal was defeated.

On all three occasions, I voted the other way. I was angry at some of the opposition, very angry, because I think they were being very narrow-minded and homing in on those two temper tantrums, not paying attention to all of the positive things that were involved in his lifetime.

Isn't it almost unprecedented as far as an outstanding coach is concerned? They simply felt that this was not a man that was worthy of such an honorary degree in spite of the fact it was his alma mater.

The college lost a lot of support as a result of this because there were alumni who were absolutely outraged by it. They are still outraged by it.

There is one group that was so outraged they were instrumental in raising money to have a memorial stone arranged on campus with a bronze plaque.

It is in a prominent place just outside the gate of the beautifully remodeled football stadium. It was shortly after the stadium was remodeled in 1987 that this group raised this money.

There happened to be a big glacial boulder on campus. They moved that boulder to a more prominent position. A beautiful plaque was done by a sculptor. And there it is in all it's glory.

By doing this the college has honored this man, but not with an honorary academic degree.

Woody Hayes was a bright guy academically. That's one of the things that angered me so with regard to turning him down for the honorary degree.

They never accepted the fact that the man could have probably been an outstanding teacher of history had his career taken him in that direction.

It brings up all of the philosophical considerations with regard to the emphasis of athletics in the United States. The following incident took place when Woody was so prominent at Ohio State.

Denison University is only 25 miles from the Ohio State campus. I drove over one day to attend a geology lecture. I parked my car and started walking to the geology building which was located adjacent to the Ohio State Faculty Club.

As I was walking, here comes Woody Hayes. We came face-to-face. I recognized him and he recognized me. He seemed very pleased to see me. I was delighted to see him and we had a nice little chat.

. Then, I had to hurry along to my lecture. As I was heading to the classroom where the lecture was to take place, I met a prominent geology professor named Robert Bates. He was a full professor who had been at Ohio State for some 20 years.

Bob Bates was a man with a wonderful sense of humor. He was a close friend of mine. As he was coming towards me, I said, 'Bob, would you like to shake the hand of a man who just shook the hand of Woody Hayes?'

Without a moment's hesitation, Bob Bates said to me, 'There's a washroom just down the corridor.'

I think that's an excellent story in terms of the attitude of a substantial number of faculty people at Ohio State during the time of Woody's prominence.

Why would that be the case?

My friend and his colleagues had every right to have it be known that their department was one of the outstanding geology departments in the country. But nobody knew this about Ohio State.

I first met Woody Hayes in 1946. I used to go down once in awhile to watch the football team practice. I didn't do it quite as much in those days because my boss at the time didn't approve of it.

Woody was a very personable guy who was interested in having his kids do well in geology. He would ask about them.

Woody didn't have a good first year [2-6], but there was no 'Bye, Bye Woody' kind of thing that they had at Ohio State. I'd like to believe Denison was above that won-lost mentality.

The story goes that during the Spring or Summer of 1947, Woody's assistant, Rix Yard, talked turkey to Woody Hayes. Many of Woody's players were World War II veterans. They were mature men, some who had been officers, and they weren't happy about taking some of Woody's guff.

Yard urged Woody Hayes to change. While it was difficult for Woody to deal with that kind of criticism, he did deal with it. So when the men showed up in the

Class of '68

Fall, ready for the season, Woody was a different person.

Denison had consecutive undefeated seasons. The president of the university cancelled classes for a whole day. We had a celebration. I think it was repeated the following year.

I think there was sorrow when Woody left Denison and went to Miami.

I know I was sorry to see him leave. He will always be part of Denison University. I'm glad I had a seat on the 50-yard line.

Chapter 31

THE BEST OF FRIENDS

Dr. James Otis of Celina, Ohio has been practicing medicine for almost 60 years. He became a doctor in 1940 and for many years worked alongside his father. Back when he was an undergraduate at Denison University, he struck up a friendship that would last a lifetime. He and Woody Hayes were juniors when they became roomies in the 1930s. They became best of friends and that friendship endured until Woody Hayes' death in March of 1987.

It seems that ever since I can remember I wanted to be a doctor. My father was a doctor and surgeon. His name was Lloyd M. Otis.

Dad was one of the great pioneer doctors in our area. He founded the first private local hospital in our area back in 1915. It was called Otis Hospital.

That was in the days when he had to operate on tables. There was no hospital in our whole area except maybe at Fort Wayne, Lima or Dayton. He built this hospital and made it into a modern hospital in those days. That's how it was.

We were building a modern courthouse in those days. There was a lot of mishaps. I remember Dad fixing up people, splinting their bones. One thing and another. They'd come to our hospital.

From infancy on up, medicine was the only thing I ever thought of. I knew when I was in high school I was supposed to study pre-medicine.

Since my Dad went to Michigan, he wanted me to go there too. I went there my freshman year and averaged between a C and a B. I passed everything. I got all my credits.

But they thought it was too damn tough for me coming from Celina. They studied about Denison University and thought I'd have much more of an excellent education there. So I went to Denison my sophomore year. That's when I met Woody Hayes.

I graduated from Denison in 1935, then went to the University of Cincinnati Medical School and graduated from there in 1939. In those days you didn't get an MD degree until you completed 12 months of internship. I interned at Christ Hospital in Cincinnati [1940] and passed the State Boards.

After that I took a short residency in obstetrics and gynecology at the Toledo Hospital. Dad called and asked me to come join him. I joined him in October of 1940 and had a successful father-son practice until he suffered a stroke.

My father was a trained surgeon. Even before I officially became a doctor, he taught me basic surgery. You could do that back then.

I returned to Celina in 1940 and have been here ever since.

I'm very lucky, very fortunate to have enjoyed good health all these years. You're just as good as your brain is. If you've got a good brain, you can get through anything. My brain is clear.

I'm still practicing medicine. Work day-in-and-day-out. I feel great working every day. I try to get to a golf course on Thursdays. Sometimes on Saturday afternoon.

211

Class of '68

When I was at Denison I was good enough to play on the varsity golf team. I had a seven handicap. As years went by, it got to be 13 and then 18. I thought I'd never get over 18. I'm a 22 now. I still hit some fine golf shots.

I'd like to think good athletes run in the Otis Family. Back in my Dad's college days, all of the schools had only one cheerleader. They called him 'The Yell Master.' Dad was that cheerleader at the University of Michigan.

He became very close to Michigan's famous football coach 'Hurry Up' Yost. That was 1912-13-14. Dad became famous in his own right.

My son Jim was Ohio State's starting fullback for three years [1967-1969], was named All-American as a senior and went on to have a fine professional career. His coach was my closest friend, Woody Hayes.

I've been blessed with three daughters and one son, 11 grandchildren and two great grandchildren. Jim and two of his sisters live in Missouri. One of my daughters lives right here in Celina.

Her son, P.J. is quite a track star. Jim's two boys are designed and ready for football. They're gonna be a fullback and a quarterback.

Woody and I were both born in 1913. As I said, I first met him when we were both sophomores at Denison. At that time, he was rooming with Bob Amos. Bob was a great guy. He was a Jeffersonian, a Democrat. Woody and I couldn't contend with that, but we had to.

Somehow, Woody and I decided to room together our junior year. We were roomies for two years.

Woody was an excellent athlete at Denison. He was a good offensive tackle on the football team. He was a good baseball player. I think he played second base.

Woody was a very good boxer. In fact, I was his second in the ring. I'd announce him. Then I'd be right with him all the time. I don't remember his being on the boxing team. I think he freelanced. As I remember, the bouts were very well organized.

Back then, he weighed between 175-185. He was pretty strong, muscular and had a good knockout punch. He was good. Why he'd knock people out.

Woody and I were involved in our studies, with our athletics, but we'd go out sometimes. We'd have a few beers. I'd get into some argument. I'd always call on Woody and he'd knock 'em out.

I was always interested in golf. Woody never golfed but he encouraged me to play. He'd say, 'Jim, play your golf because you're gonna work hard all your life. Play your golf. You like golf.'

He respected all kinds of sports. He was never one to ridicule because he thought it was a good thing to play a sport. After all, he was an all-round sports guy.

You couldn't help but like Woody Hayes. He was a loving man. He was a family man. He loved his parents. He had good parental training. He was real loyal and friendly to everybody. He was honorable. He was honest.

He liked to study and he became kind of a historian. Woody was a history major.

I met Woody's family when we were in college. His mother. His father. His brother. His sister. Woody's father was superintendent of schools.

212

Woody's brother, Ike, went to school in Iowa and became a veterinarian. I remember when we went to the Rose Bowl [1955], Ike said to me, 'Jim, can't you do something about Woody's weight?' At that time, Woody had gained weight. And by golly, one year later, Ike was the one that had a heart attack and died. Woody's family lived in Newcomerstown. I remember that quite well. He had a sister, Mary, who was quite a singer. She did a lot of operatic things in New York. Although I knew her, I didn't know her like I knew Ike.

Woody knew that I was directing myself into medicine, but I can't recall him telling me he wanted to pursue a career as a college football coach.

We graduated in 1935 and kinda went our own ways. I was fully involved in my medical studies. We kept in touch a bit. Before he joined the Navy, he became a high school coach at New Philadelphia.

It really didn't surprise me. After all, he was an excellent college player. He was a student of the game. We kept in touch while he was in the service, but it really wasn't until he left the service and returned to his alma mater in 1946 that we really began to renew our friendship.

Denison never had a good football team. I think Woody went something like 3-4 his first year. [It was 2-6]. But by golly, in his second year Denison was undefeated. He did it again his third year.

That made everybody take notice. He got the job down at Miami and did awfully well. In 1951, he was selected to come to Ohio State as head coach.

I'll never forget when Woody was selected. I thought to myself 'My God, Sakes Alive, what an honor.' There was a lot of publicity surrounding his appointment. In fact, Woody called me after it happened.

I said, 'Woody, I've heard you're getting the job or you have the job.'

He said, 'Jim, I've got it.'

I know that John Galbraith had high praise for Woody. I don't know if he was on the Board at Ohio State. He owned Darby Dan Farm. He highly recommended Woody. I know that was a big recommendation for him.

Back in Dad's heyday, we'd go on up to Ann Arbor to see a Michigan football game. We lived in a small town. We'd have Saturday night office hours. We'd drive to the game, then scoot all the way back home in time to open the office. Believe it or not.

You could say when Woody became head coach at Ohio State I became an Ohio State fan. In those early days, Woody'd come to see me on a regular basis because I'd do some physical checkups on him. He had some health problems even in those days.

I met Woody's wife before they got married. She was Anne Gross. Maybe he and Anne would come down and visit us once or twice a year. We'd have a nice dinner and they'd stay over. Or maybe we'd go to Columbus.

They had one son, Steve. Steve was born on my birthday, October 22. Woody's son is older than my Jim. Jim was born in 1948. The two boys would play together. Woody saw Jim from the time he was an infant. He saw him grow.

Woody always bragged about Jim. He said he was gonna be quite an athlete some day. Jim took trampoline, tumbling and all that. Woody saw him do all these things. Little did we ever know that someday Jim would be playing for Woody.

Class of '68

When Jim was doing so great in high school, people went to Woody and said, 'You'd better check on this Otis Boy.' Woody would tell them, 'I know about the Otis Boy.'

Until Jim went to Ohio State, the families somehow found time to socialize. But all that changed.

We didn't think it would be a proper thing, so we all agreed we wouldn't socialize. We didn't think it was the thing to do. Betty [Dr. Otis' wife] and Anne were real close. They talked all the time.

I didn't spend weekends with Woody from the time Jim was a freshman through his senior year, although we continued to remain close friends. Woody conducted himself as head coach.

Woody was tougher on Jim than anybody else because he was my son. I think Woody wanted it to be known that young Jim Otis got no favors just because he and his Dad had roomed together.

It was a pretty clarified thing. Jim was doing his thing. Woody was doing his thing. Jim's Dad was keeping out of it.

I praised my son and worked with him, stimulated him and did all I could as a father. But that was it. That was it.

I'll never forget his freshman year. When he went down to Columbus, Woody said to Jim, 'Jim, we have a fullback we think is a little better than you.' Jim said, 'We'll see, Coach.'

They made Paul Huff the freshman fullback and Jim the blocking halfback. Jim came to me and said, 'Dad, I think they've got their fullback.'

But my boy's a fighter. He worked so hard that he became the starting fullback as a sophomore. He was starting fullback as a junior and senior and led the team in rushing all three years.

As a sophomore, Jim had a bad game against Illinois. He fumbled on the Illinois eight yard line. That might have had something to do with the outcome of the game.

Jim cried to no end. He thought he let his team down. That's when Woody gave him some real going-over and benched him for the next two games.

Jim never told me that. I got it from the other players and observers. Then, of course, the press knew it and they called me from Cleveland. They thought I would make a big to-do about it. Well, obviously I wouldn't.

That would just about have been the worst thing I could have done. Naturally, I never would have complained to Woody about benching my son.

I remember The Associated Press reporter tried to bait me. I think they were hoping I'd say something like 'Hell, I'm not gonna put up with that.' What I said was 'Woody's the coach.'

When Jim was a sophomore at Celina High, the coach knew what kind of a guy I was. He said to me, 'Dr. Otis, we're gonna have a great team this year. We're gonna have Jim play offensive tackle and linebacker.'

Heck, he never played those positions. He wore Number 77 which is a tackle number. By the time the season ended, he was All-Western Conference fullback with the number 77. As the season wore on, the starting fullback got hurt or knocked out. His coach said, 'Jim can you play fullback?' Jim says 'Try me.'

214

It was one of the most electrifying things that ever happened in Celina athletics. We were behind 12-0 to Wapakoneta, one of our great rivals. Jim almost single-handedly helped win the game, 14-12.

The next year they gave him number 44 which is a backfield number. After his career was over, they took that number and retired it. Nobody at Celina High ever gets the number 44.

When Jim went to Ohio State his mother said, 'Jim, why don't you request 44?' Jim said, 'Mother, I'll get whatever number they give me.' They gave him jersey number 35 and he made that kinda a famous number. He wore that number throughout his college and professional careers.

Betty and I never missed a game while Jim played at Ohio State. When they went to Washington, we went to Washington. When they traveled to Minnesota, we went to Minnesota.

It didn't make a difference. When Jim played in the Coaches All-Star game at Lubbock, Texas [and was named MVP] we went to Texas.

Now in the pros, we didn't get to go every place.

My most memorable game?

That's an easy one. In 1968, Ohio State beat Michigan, 50-14. Jim scored four touchdowns to tie the great Hopalong Cassady for the most touchdowns in a game. Jim had high yardage in all of his games against Michigan.

Jim was out of the game after he scored his third touchdown. The score was 44-14. Woody wanted 50 points awfully bad. Ohio State looked like it was going in for another touchdown late in the game.

A little halfback ran the ball twice from the four yard line. Then Paul Huff, who was in for Jim at fullback, lost a yard. They didn't block or do anything.

Jim walked over to Woody and told him, 'Coach, I'll get that one for you.' Woody said, 'Go in.'

It was fourth-and-goal from the Michigan five when Jim went back in. He went in the huddle and looked right at sophomore tackle Dave Cheney.

'Dave, Coach wants me to call this play right over you.'

Woody didn't say that at all. Jim just wanted to pump up the guy a little bit. He made the touchdown to make it 50-14. That was the fourth touchdown that tied the record.

I've heard Jim say it so many, many times. Woody Hayes stimulated them or invigorated them so much that they could do anything on Saturday that they couldn't do on Wednesday.

I could see that greatness in a very young Woody Hayes. He was always a leader, never a follower. I could see it in how he studied. He gave it his all. He did that on the football field, in the boxing ring, on the baseball diamond.

He was a perfectionist. I don't know if that rubbed off on me or whether I felt that way too. I believe in perfection. He stimulated me to study and work hard. He knew how much I wanted to be a doctor.

Football was his life. Seven days a week. Morning-noon-and-night. He was determined to win and losing had a bitter taste. I don't remember what year it was, or who Ohio State lost to. It was something like 6-0.

The stadium was empty. There were only two people in the locker room.

Class of '68

Woody and me. Woody was upset with himself. He thought he hadn't performed well as a coach.

He said, 'Maybe I don't have it. Maybe I lost it?' That was his great modesty. He thought he had slipped.

And by golly, the next week he was back on top.

Woody would tear his cap and stomp on his watch during practice. Things like that. He did those kinds of things to stimulate exactness and better performance from his players.

As a young man, after I was in medicine, Woody was coming back-and-forth to see me. He had hypertension. He was getting diabetes mellitus. I saw it at the time. I advised him accordingly, whatever the treatments were in those days.

Diabetes is a notorious disease that causes vascular weakness and blood vessel weakness. At those times we didn't realize the things that cause plaque in blood vessels. We do know that diabetes is notorious for causing mental deterioration or vascular deterioration.

Diabetes can cause violent behavior. It can cause mood swings. Whether or not Woody took as good care of himself as he should have, I don't know.

By 1978 he was beginning to deteriorate. His health had worsened a bit. I happen to know team physicians were watching him. They would caution me that something was happening to Woody. You could see it. At that time, we didn't have the treatment for hardening of the arteries.

Woody suffered multiple-type strokes.

I really don't recall him ever saying 'I'm gonna quit.' That wasn't his style. I think he got a bad deal after the Clemson incident. Woody never told me anything that wasn't true and he told me, 'I didn't really hit that boy, Jim.'

That's what he told me. Unless his condition wasn't that keen, he never did. Woody was left-handed. If he really wanted to hurt that boy, he would have used his left hand. But he came at him with a right forearm.

Woody had become too great an individual. I would have counseled him. I would have had some kind of punishment. But I never, never would do what that school president did. Fire him like that. That was absolutely wrong.

They took away what meant most to him. Woody was saddened. He was down. I did all I could to try to build up his confidence. It was a sad, sad thing. From that point on, his health continued to be not so strong.

But Woody Hayes did rise from the ashes. He had an office in some building near the stadium. He could do his public relations and all that after Earle Bruce took over.

He would do his speeches. I remember he gave an address to a graduating function. It was at St. John Arena. I was invited to come to that and I heard it very well.

Woody would see the boys who played for him. I don't know what his formal position was. As years went by, he was honored more and more. It was kinda soon forgotten about his dismissal.

He never complained. He wasn't a cry baby. He had a wonderful life.

Woody died very sudddenly. My wife and I were enroute to Florida with our family when I learned of his death. I had a talk with Anne and Steve. They encouraged me to go ahead with the trip.

216

I had a conference call with some of the people at the funeral. I kinda regret that I couldn't get back to Ohio. It just so happens those were the dates we had chosen to go away.

I think I'll most remember Woody's kindness to humanity. He was a man who loved people. He'd literally give you the shirt off his back. He was a good man, a kind man. You couldn't say enough nice things about him.

The general public doesn't know the whole story. He was honorable. He never did anything to promote himself. That wasn't Woody Hayes.

There's not a day goes by that I don't think of him.

I loved him with all of my heart. I'll never forget him.

Chapter 32

THE MAN IN A FEDORA

Keith Piper was born-and-raised in Niles, Ohio. A three-year letterman at Niles McKinley High School in football, Piper was named All-Trumbull County and honorable mention All-Ohio. He interrupted his education at Baldwin-Wallace to serve in the U.S. Army Air Corps during World War II. Following his graduation, he kicked off a long and illustrious coaching career as line coach at his alma mater.

In 1951, he joined Jack Carl at Denison University. Three years later, he became head coach. Keith Piper produced 200 victories, including a perfect 9-0 season in 1985. Twice he was named Ohio College Coach of the Year. A 'rebel with a cause', Piper loved the old Single Wing. So much so that Denison's Big Red used that outdated formation during his last 15 years at Denison. Keith Piper retired after the 1992 season. He died of a heart attack while on a cruise in December of 1997. Keith Piper was 76 years old.

I played six years of junior high and high school football. I was 6-2 and weighed 175, played center on offense and linebacker on defense. In those days, you went both ways.

We played in a tough league with Warren, Canton McKinley, Massillon, Steubenville. In my three years we also played New Philadelphia. That was in 1937-39.

New Philadelphia may have been a smaller town than Niles, but those kids sure knew how to play football. They were big, and in those days, big meant about 235 pounds. They were very well coached.

In fact, they beat us all three years. They beat us 35-7 my sophomore year. They beat us 13-7 my junior year. And then in my senior year, and we had a great team, they beat us 14-0 in the snow and rain.

John Brickels was New Philly head coach in 1937. He left to become head coach at Miami of Ohio, later became the school's athletic director. He was also an assistant to Paul Brown at the Cleveland Browns.

He had an assistant coach who was stocky, about 5-9 or 5-10, and weighed about 200 pounds. He wore a hat with a wide brim. I think they call it a fedora. His name was Woody Hayes.

Things were a little different back then. You'd be warming up before the game, snapping the ball to the center. It was commonplace for the opposing coach to walk by, start to chat. And you'd be engaged in a little conversation.

That's actually how I first met Woody. He walked by, said something like 'Hey, Piper.' Then I'd respond. I haven't seen that for 30 years.

Woody Hayes became head coach at New Philly in 1938. As I said, New Philly pinned our ears back in '38 and '39. So, I had great respect for him way back then. I really didn't get to know him until I went to Baldwin-Wallace, through the stories of his players. Guys I competed against.

Gene Fellers, Bill Rodd and Dick Singerman always had those Woody Hayes stories. They'd say 'Woody would do it this way'...or 'He'd beat up on that guy.' Even back in my high school days, I could call him Woody.

They said Woody was known as the peanut-eating coach. I can't verify that. But that's what they told me.

There were so many stories.

For instance, one time someone was yelling at Woody from the stands, something about his team doing something wrong. Well, Woody went up into the stands to get the guy.

They idolized him. Consequently, I got to know Woody Hayes, and to love him. I never heard anything derogatory about him.

He was a tough guy, a street fighter kind of guy. He had that kind of reputation, but I didn't see any of this. Woody's former players all told me he'd been in several fisticuffs.

I was brought up during the Depression of the 1930s. Hell, you couldn't get enough money to go to a picture show. I used to watch football practice every night at the high school. It didn't cost anything.

That's when I fell in love with the Single Wing. That's what every team played. When I became a head coach, I wanted to put in the Single Wing, but my team wasn't ready for it.

In 1962 I installed it, more because of need than anything else. I just got rid of a quarterback for doing things he shouldn't be doing. In 1963, Tony Hall, from Dayton, became my first All-American. He was a tailback. But that's another story.

I played one year at Baldwin-Wallace before I was drafted. I got out in '46 and graduated two years later. When I returned, they retained me as a line coach and I stayed for three years. In 1951, I was hired at Denison.

I was the line coach, complete. What I mean is I had end-to-end on defense and end-to-end on offense. Jack Carl was a hell of a coach. He had a great record at Denison. It was a two-man staff in 1951. Later, they hired Kenny Meyers who would become head coach of the Los Angeles Rams.

Jack had played at Denison, had another year of eligibility left, but he took a commission in the Navy. He had quite a battle record in the South Pacific.

He came back as head coach of Hanover College in Indiana for two or three years. After that, he was hired at Denison to replace Woody Hayes.

I took over for Jack in 1954 and remained head coach for 39 years.

I knew of Woody Hayes' great record at Denison. I hired one of his ends from Denison's back-to-back [1947-48] unbeaten teams. Bob Shannon remained on my staff all those years. I got all the stories about Woody and those teams.

I'm sure there was pressure on Jack Carl, but you have to realize Denison is a little different type of school than what you typically read about in the papers.

Some of the administrators weren't head-over-heels in love with all the publicity and two consecutive unbeaten seasons. The attention going to football wasn't overly popular. Let's call it what it was. Jealous is that word.

We had a president who said the perfect season, one that would eliminate a lot of problems, would be five victories and five defeats. That was published in a lot of papers back in the early 1950s.

A. Blair Knapp was the name of the Denison president.

But I believe that stuff about 5-5 was strictly for public consumption. I'll tell you one thing. We had a heck of a team one year, the highest scoring small college team in the country. We went 9-1.

Except for me, there couldn't have been a happier guy than that same A. Blair Knapp.

I had a lot of excellent teams at Denison, but only one undefeated team. It's tough at a small college, or Division III. Your recruiting is limited. You have to wait for the cycle to come around.

One year you may have a great back, but no line. The next year it would be a great line, but no back. You had to wait until you got everything there at the same time. When you did, you had a great team.

The Ohio Athletic Conference was very tough. Wittenberg was knocking hell out of everybody. Baldwin-Wallace was always tough. In theory, there are no scholarships in Division 3. Our academic requirements are very, very high.

I'd like to think I wanted to win just as badly as Woody did. I wasn't afraid to follow Woody and Jack. I wasn't gonna lay down and take a few defeats to satisfy some administrators.

I learned from Earl Hooker, my high school coach. I learned from Jack Carl. I learned from Woody Hayes. Hooker was a very tough hombre. Compliments were never given out. I remember I intercepted a pass and went for a touchdown. In fact, it was the winning touchdown.

He said to me, 'I see you had a touchdown.' That was it. I respected him for it. He didn't shower anything on anybody. He just wanted the job done. I loved the guy. I really did.

Through the years, Woody Hayes never forgot his roots. I'm sure he was aware of what we were doing at Denison. He came to speak at our banquets. He'd drop by the school unannounced.

He was a character, but a positive force in my life. I idolized the guy.

Hard work and positive thinking. I think those were the elements that made him so successful. He recruited and wanted to have the best football players, and quite often he did. But if he didn't, he'd work their tails off until they became champions.

We all learned some things from him, with the type of mentality that he had.

He always had that real tough fullback. Even without blocking, he'd probably gain 2-3 yards. Woody'd always say, 'It's good enough for three.'

One coach at a clinic piped up, 'Well, Coach, that means at the end of three downs, it'd be fourth-and-one.'

Woody snapped right back. 'One of those we'd get over three yards. We'd get four-and-a-half.'

I know he was aware of what we were doing. One time we played Muskingum. We had a wrinkle on defense that we put in just for the game and it stopped 'em cold.

Muskingum was a very good football team at that time. Well, the newspapers celebrated this defense. Woody called me up and says, 'What the hell is that thing you're doing over there?'

I told him. Whether or not he used it, I don't know. But he most definitely wanted to know. We were close from that standpoint.

I tried to pick his brain. We were using the T formation at the time. This was when everybody was using the inside belly. That is a fake to the fullback and then give the ball to the halfback.

It was one of my visits to Columbus. Our season ended a week before Ohio State's. I'd go over and watch Ohio State practice for Michigan.

Woody was paranoid about opening up that practice to anyone. One year, I was the only guy watching the practice. He knew I wouldn't be giving away any secrets.

He was in a room with his assistants. He asked them to leave. Woody said, 'Now look, I'm gonna give you this way of blocking. Don't tell anybody I gave it to you.'

So he goes to the blackboard. It was a fantastic idea. We used it with great, great success. He was that type of guy.

Woody Hayes had been to my house several times. One time, the house was full. We'd had our banquet that night. We had a kid named Smits from Georgia there that particular night. His father had played for me.

The kid was a senior in high school. Woody was sitting on one of my captain's chairs in one of the rooms. He was talking to the kid, trying to recruit him.

Pretty soon the four legs went out. Woody's sitting on the floor. I'm embarassed, but it didn't bother him. He laughed a little bit. He enjoyed a good joke, especially on himself.

One time I went over to Ohio State to watch Spring practice. I was walking off the field with Tony Hall, who was on the football team.

Tony's older brother had played for me at Denison. I knew Tony and had tried to recruit him, but he went to Ohio State.

We're walking off the field together and jokingly I said, 'When are you gonna transfer over to Denison?' That was the extent of my conversation.

We went into Woody's dressing room and chatted a bit. We had a good time. When I arrived home, I got a phone call. It was Tony Hall.

He said, 'Were you kidding about transferring to Denison?'

I said, 'Hell, yes, I was kidding. But I can change real quick. I could become serious about it.'

I added, 'If you've got an inclination about doing this, you'd better talk with the old man [Woody]. I don't want to get involved. I'm not over there recruiting his players.'

So, Tony Hall went in and talked with Woody. Woody sat him down and wouldn't let him out for an hour. Woody said, 'You're an Ohio State type football player, far beyond Denison.'

Woody Hayes was right. Tony Hall was not small college caliber. He transferred to Denison and became small college All-American. With a player the caliber of Tony Hall, I could install the Single Wing with Tony as our tailback.

Woody knew me well enough. He never held a grudge.

I had a great assistant coach by the name of George Hill. He played fullback for me, later became my line coach. I think he was with me for five years. He's now defensive coordinator for the Miami Dolphins.

He left Denison for Cornell, then went to Duke. They all got fired at Duke and he was without a job. Somehow, Woody found out about George's situation. He needed a line coach.

So Woody calls me.

'I know he's a good football coach. I want to know some other things about him. Not his football. Don't give me any of that stuff.'

I said, 'Well, on weekends he's a meat cutter. He's a butcher. He's a house painter. Is this the stuff you want?'

'I'll throw out one other thing. With all the cameras we've got, we never send 'em out for repairs anymore. We just give 'em to George Hill and he fixes 'em. He can fix any camera as good as any professional.'

Woody asks, 'You mean he can fix a Kodak Analyst?'

I said, 'Yeah. You don't have to send 'em out.'

'That son-of-a-bitch is hired.'

That's a true story. That's how George Hill was hired by Woody Hayes at Ohio State.

Over the years I'd call Woody and ask him to come over and give my kids a pep talk before we played Muskingum. He'd come over and give 'em a hell of a talk, better than I could ever have done.

I never had great concern about Woody after he left coaching. He was tough. He was a survivor. He'd just set that jaw and looked straight ahead. Fullback right up-the-middle.

It was during the Fall of 1979. We're out on the practice field. I see this guy walking across the practice field. I think it's a cop for some reason. He had some pencils, or something, in his shirt pocket and I thought it was a badge.

I see it's Woody.

He just wanted to come over and be on the Denison campus.

We're talking on the sidelines. The offensive drills are going on. He says, 'Don't pay any attention to me. Damn it, look at the guy over there. He's offsides.'

Pretty soon I say to Woody, 'How about talking to the players.'

He says, 'Well, okay.'

I gathered up the team. We're in a semi-circle. Some guys are kneeling, some are standing.

Pretty soon the soccer team comes over. They'd been practicing on a field next to ours. There's a lot of students on campus. There's about 500 people out on the practice field. And there's Woody Hayes right in the middle, the ringmaster.

He proceeds to give a talk. There wasn't one word about football. 'How many of you people are taking Russian?'

Russian was more popular then than it is now. I think one person out of the whole crowd raised his hand.

He said, 'You've got to start thinking about this international problem we've got.'

It was a great speech. We were in awe. Everyone thinks in terms of the dumb football coach. Woody Hayes wasn't part of that. He was something else.

He died in March of 1987. The last time I saw him was at our football banquet the previous Winter. Woody was in a wheelchair and had to be pushed in by some of the players. He was fading out about that point.

Somehow, he still managed to give a hell of a speech.

After all, he was Woody Hayes.

Chapter 33

HERE COMES WOODY

John Hlay grew up in the hotbed of Ohio high school football. A two-time All-Ohio fullback at Niles McKinley, he came to Ohio State under the regime of Wes Fesler. A reserve as a sophomore in 1950, Hlay was on the scene when a whirlwind touched down in Columbus. His name: Woody Hayes. John Hlay was on Hayes' teams in 1951-52, leading the Buckeyes in rushing his senior year. Drafted by Green Bay, he played two seasons in the NFL with the Packers and New York Giants. He is now a sales rep in Columbus, Ohio.

Comparing Wes Fesler and Woody Hayes is like talking about night and day. Two entirely different people. One who led two different lives. One who was consumed by only one thing.

Fesler was an excellent college coach. His 1949 team went to the Rose Bowl. In 1950, Vic Janowicz won the Heisman Trophy as the best college player in the country.

But to him, being head coach was a business. It was an eight hour a day job. Once he went home to his family, football took a back seat.

He was able to separate his job from his family. His assistant coaches led a regular life. Coach Fesler was a real gentleman, on-and-off the field.

We didn't win a national championship, but we didn't have bad teams. But at Ohio State 'pretty good' isn't good enough. You win big or you're gone.

I can remember the famous Snow Bowl game of 1950 against Michigan. It was a blizzard-and-a-half. I sat on the bench, drinking bouillon soup. We tried about half-a-dozen different types of gloves to keep our hands warm.

We tried surgical gloves, workman's gloves, leather gloves. Nothing really worked. We lost something like 9-3 or 9-6.

As I recall, there didn't seem to be any indication that Fesler's job was in jeopardy. I certainly didn't think 1950 would be his last year at Ohio State.

I think the pressure came down from above, and from downtown. He didn't succeed enough. At that time, Woody Hayes was head coach at Miami. Before that, he was at Denison.

I can't say for sure if Wes Fesler was fired or quit. When Woody came in, he said, 'I'll make you a winner. I will make you a winning team my first year.'

He gave a spiel. He convinced the Board that he was gonna come in and immediately make Ohio State a winning team.

And why not? Woody had coached back-to-back unbeaten teams at Denison. His Miami Redskins lost only one game his last season and won the Tangerine Bowl.

As I said, Wes Fesler looked at his job as a business. He had a life when he left the field. He put in his time.

But as far as putting his heart-and-soul into it. As far as a man who lived-and-died football. That wasn't Wes Fesler...at least not to me.

That was Wayne Woodrow Hayes.

223

Woody Hayes knew the situation when he went to Ohio State. He knew it was 'The Graveyard of Coaches.' He was willing to accept the challenge. If he got it done, fine. If not, they could fire him.

He would do it his way. He expected no less of himself than he did his staff. There were no days off during the season for anyone. He was a tyrant, a barbarian.

I was born-and-raised in Niles, Ohio. I came from a poor family. My brother was a pretty good football player. He went to Baldwin-Wallace.

I was fortunate enough to be named All-Ohio my junior and senior years. I was 6-foot and weighed about 185. I managed to get up to 200 in college.

Believe it or not, Niles McKinley played a straight-T back in my days. As I recall, Canton McKinley and Barberton also used the T. Most of the other schools, however, used the old Single Wing.

I had some 45 schools interested in me. I visited the University of Georgia, Notre Dame, Michigan, all of the Big Ten schools. In those days, Wally Butts of Georgia was one of the top coaches. Out of Youngstown came two great players—Frankie Sinkewicz and George Poster.

I damn near went to Purdue. My high school coach was supposed to go with me, but at the last moment he changed his mind. I became good friends with head coach Stu Holcomb and Jack Mollenkopf, who was then Purdue line coach.

Instead of Purdue, I decided to go to Ohio State.

Freshmen weren't allowed to play varsity when I came in 1949. But three years later, the rule was changed and I got to play in the same backfield with Howard [Hopalong] Cassady.

I played the T in high school. Ohio State played Single Wing. I had a little difficulty making the transition to a Single Wing fullback.

The fullback was a spinning fullback who handled the ball. He was the one who would take the ball, do the spin, hand off.

Curly Morrison did most of the running from the fullback spot my sophomore year [1950]. Janowicz was the glamour boy at tailback.

When we reported for the first practice in 1951, Woody Hayes held a team meeting. He really came into a tough situation.

He had been a Commander in the Navy. When he came to Ohio State, he was dealing with two different age groups. He had young people like myself and he had a lot of World War II veterans.

He's dealing with two types of personalities, two competing forces. I wouldn't have wanted to have been in his shoes.

We had a new coach and a new formation. That didn't bother me. Not even Woody's style bothered me. But what he wanted to do with me, however, sure did.

It may have been after the third day of practice. He took me aside and said, 'Hlay, I'm thinking about making you a running guard.'

I thought to myself, 'My God, I've never played the line in my life.' I took it upon myself to make sure that never happened.

I worked my ass off. I'd show him I was a fullback. Believe me, it was fear that drove me, that motivated me. It looked like I was going to start at fullback on offense and at linebacker on defense when I did this real dumb thing.

I got involved in a barroom brawl. First of all, we shouldn't have been there.

But when one of my fraternity brothers got in trouble, I had to defend him. To put it mildly, Woody Hayes wasn't too pleased with me. I had put him in a tough situation. He's trying to maintain discipline and I get myself involved in a scuffle.

He called me into his office.

'Hlay, you're through here.'

And he meant it.

I told Woody 'I've got two more years here I'm not going anyplace.'

As it turned out, my suspension lasted only four games.

At that time his son, Steve, was a young man. Now he's a judge in Columbus. One day Woody Hayes called me back into his office.

'I've got a young man, my own son. He's made mistakes, but I've always given him another chance. I'm gonna give you another chance, but I'll tell you something. Whatever those guys do once, you're gonna have to do twice.'

He allowed me to stay. My penalty was I would only play on defense. I was happy to accept those terms. At least I was back on the team. I was an outside linebacker.

We go to Wisconsin. I get sideblasted and get my leg injured. I'm out 2-3 weeks, then return for the Pittsburgh game and get hurt again. I played three games my junior year, all out of town, and got hurt each time. I never set foot on Ohio Stadium soil that season.

It was a long season. We went 4-3-2.

Before the start of my senior year, Woody set the same ground rules for me.

'Hlay, you know the same thing goes for you. What these guys do once, you're gonna have to do twice.'

During my Summer at home, I worked harder than ever. I worked on the railroad and worked out every night. As far as conditioning, I was hard-as-nails.

But I had this crazy idea that I was gonna try out for Golden Gloves. I thought I could make a hell of a boxer. Anyway, one day I get a call from the office. It's Woody Hayes.

'Understand you're going out for Golden Gloves?'

I told him I was.

'Well, I'll tell you what,' he said. 'You're either gonna be a football player or a boxer. Let's you and me go down to the gym and put some gloves on. Then you can decide if you want to be a football player or a boxer.'

That's the truth. Woody wanted to go downstairs and mix it up with me. And believe me, he was dead serious. His brother was a fighter. Woody boxed when he was in school.

I made up my mind in an instant.

'I'm gonna be a football player.'

That was that.

I'd seen the man in action. I'd seen him in practice when we'd run the same play 25 times. He'd throw that cap down and stomp on it. He'd bark 'I'll make this goddam play work.' And we'd run it until he was satisfied.

I played in all nine games my senior year [1952]. We went 6-3. I was a two-way starter. Although I was an excellent blocker, I was fortunate enough to lead the team in rushing.

225

I probably had my best game against Purdue. In those days, very few people got 100 yards in a game. I gained 135 yards.

I didn't have a lot of touchdowns that season. I think 4 or 5.

I played with Janowicz and Cassady. While Vic was a good all-around player, Hopalong was spectacular. First of all, he was a cocky kid. But he backed it up.

He probably broke more ballgames than any player I was involved with. I saw him break up a Wisconsin game with an 80-yard pass interception.

He wasn't a power runner. He could jitterbug. He was a game breaker, both offensively and defensively. Hoppy won the Heisman as a senior in 1955. Given a choice between these two Heisman winners, I'd take Cassady hands down.

Janowicz wasn't the same player in the T as he had been in Wes Fesler's Single Wing. I don't think he was too fond of Woody, but when Janowicz was very ill years later, Woody Hayes was right there to help the guy.

Every player that went to Ohio State to play football was talented. I believe the coaches tried to give everyone a chance. Sometimes it was just one chance. The day that you're called upon you'd better perform because if you don't you could get lost.

The turning point for me was a scrimmage we had my senior year. Woody was there in the huddle, calling the plays. For some reason he called my name four straight times.

Once to the left, once to the right, once up the middle. Something like that. Each time I had a very good run. I had one hell of a scrimmage that day. That's how I got to play nine games.

One thing Woody couldn't tolerate was fumbling. You don't fumble. That was everybody's fear. You fumble and you're gone.

That's what I probably feared the most, but I didn't let it drive me crazy. You have to stick it in the back of your mind.

We lost to Purdue, the game I gained 135 yards. In fact, I fumbled once and lost the ball. But he didn't jerk me out and put me on the bench. I think what probably saved me was my blocking ability. I wasn't afraid to give up my body.

I can remember one boy who played fullback. He was one of my rivals. Bob Kepne came out of Dayton. He was a hell of a highly-recruited fullback.

He and Jack Wagner took over my fullback spot when I sat out those four games. Anyway, we're playing Freddie Benner and SMU.

We're on their 35-yard line and marching in for a score. But Bob Kepne fumbled and we lose the ball. SMU goes on to win, 7-0.

Check the record. That was the opening game in 1951. That was the last time Bob Kepne played in a varsity game. Not even one down. We were both juniors.

The guy [Woody Hayes] was a madman sometimes. When he spoke, you jumped. You bounced when he told you to bounce. He cracked the whip.

But you know what, I can't think of any other coach who had more heart. He had 200 percent love for the game of football.

There's never been, as far as I'm concerned, a more dedicated, more intense, more involved individual. And sometimes that got him in big trouble.

Like when he grabbed that Clemson kid in the 1978 Gator Bowl. He just wasn't thinking. It was an honest mistake. I don't think he should have been fired for it.

I think Woody would have liked to have been athletic director in his later years. His name would be put up for nomination.

But he knew he'd never get the job. No one would have been able to control Wayne Woodrow Hayes. As far as I'm concerned, that kind of guy doesn't get the AD job at Ohio State.

Sure he was hard. But he was fair and you can't ask more than that. I loved the man.

Saturday's Standout --- By Getchell

OHIO STATE'S 205-POUND BLOCKBUSTING FULLBACK, WAS HERO EVEN IN BUCKEYE DEFEAT BY PURDUE LAST SATURDAY. THIS BRUSING NILES SENIOR BLASTED BOILERMAKER LINE FOR 135 YARDS IN 22 TRIES, A 6.1 YARD AVERAGE.

Big JOHN HLAY

IN TWO GAMES, JOHN HAS POUNDED OUT 196 YARDS IN 35 TRIES. UNFORTUNATE RHUBARB MINIMIZED HIS EFFORTS LAST YEAR AND HIS LITTLE PLAYING TIME WAS CONFINED TO DEFENSE.

HE'S THE HUSTLINGEST GUY ON THE SQUAD NOW AND HAS MORE THAN VINDICATED HIMSELF, MAY YET BECOME ONE OF OSU'S FINEST FULLBACKS. HE STARTS FAST, HITS LIKE A BULL-DOZER AND USUALLY CARRIES THE DEFENSE ON HIS BACK.

Chapter 34

'THE INCIDENT'

In one moment of anger or frustration, the course of football history at Ohio State was altered. No longer would Woody Hayes prowl the sidelines. No longer would he lead his beloved Buckeyes in combat. No longer would the media have old Woody to kick around anymore. After all, he was 65. Time to simply fade away.

The date: December 29, 1978.

The place: The Gator Bowl at Jacksonville, Florida.

The opponents: Ohio State vs Clemson.

The setting: One minute and 58 seconds to play. Ohio State trails, 17-15, but the Buckeyes are on the move.

The incident: Clemson's Charlie Bauman intercepts Art Schlichter's pass. As he is chased out of bounds, Woody Hayes steps up and hits Bauman with his right forearm.

The penalty: Ohio State athletic director Hugh Hindman fires Woody Hayes.

A 33-year coaching career is over. An institution at Ohio State, Woody Hayes will never coach a 29th season.

A general without an army, Wayne Woodrow Hayes would never speak ill of Ohio State University. He would rise from the ashes and continue to spread his own kind of personal magic for almost nine more years until his sudden death on March 12, 1987.

The pass interception spoiled a dazzling performance by Schlichter, a freshman, who completed 16 of 20 attempts for 205 yards.

Trailing 17-9, the 20th ranked Buckeyes moved to within two points of tying Clemson on Schlichter's two-yard touchdown run. But Schlichter was dropped by Clemson's Jim Stuckey and Eddie Geather as he attempted a two-point conversion.

Then came the late interception.

Then came 'The Incident.'

All hell broke loose. Both benches cleared.

Tom Levenick, a freshman recruit from Peoria, Illinois, was standing on the sideline when the play unfolded.

According to Levenick, Bauman waved the ball at the Ohio State team after making the interception. The next thing he knew, his coach was swinging at everyone.

"I have never been so embarassed in my life," he said. "I was frozen for a second. I turned and tried to shield Coach (Woody Hayes) from the television camera. I just didn't want anyone to see what was going on.

"When the game ended, we kind of knew it was the end. We felt it. The athletic director (Hugh Hindman) walked in and was tight-lipped. He seemed angry. He never came into our locker room after a game. I knew something must have been really wrong."

Levenick paused, then sighed. "I just hope no one saw what was going on. I tried my best to get the cameraman out of there. Woody should be allowed to go out the right way."

The Gator Bowl attracted a crowd of 83,000 at Jacksonville, Florida. Millions more watched the Ohio State-Clemson night clash on television. ABC telecast the game.

The problem was, not everyone saw Hayes hit Bauman the first time and no one watching the telecast saw it again. ABC was deluged with phone calls.

Bob Goodrich, who produced the telecast, said he did not see Woody Hayes attack Bauman. Don Bernstein, an ABC publicist, said "The interception wasn't on tape.

"So that means that we didn't have the sequence that followed. Our replay cameras were isolating on another pass receiver. This kind of thing is bound to happen sometimes."

After the game Bauman said "I was hit. I don't know by who."

But a few minutes later, he was asked that same question. This time his only comment: "I'm not saying anything."

Jonathan Brooks, a Clemson defensive end, said "A lot of players said Woody hit him. It looked like he did. I was in the middle of a whole bunch of people trying to get out of there."

It took officials several minutes to clear the field.

Woody Hayes was assessed an unsportsmanlike conduct penalty. He did not appear at the post-game press conference. Instead, Ohio State defensive coordinator George Hill went in his place.

Said Hill:

"I didn't see it. I was there, but still couldn't see. Whatever it was was certainly unfortunate."

Clemson head coach Danny Ford refused to criticize Woody Hayes. "I've got an idea of what happened, but I'm not saying. I think my players conducted themselves on the field with class."

Ohio State Athletic Director Hugh Hindman, who played for Woody Hayes at Miami of Ohio and later served as an assistant coach, went into the locker room.

He told Hayes he would consult with OSU president Harold Enarson and for Hayes to "expect the worse." Hindman left the Gator Bowl and found the university president at a nearby villa.

Hindman recounted the incident and the details. Enarson endorsed Hindman's yet-to-be-announced decision.

Hindman twice consulted with Big Ten commissioner Wayne Duke in the early hours of Saturday, December 29, 1978.

Said Duke:

"It is not my intention to comment on the text of these conversations, except to say that on the second occasion at approximately 6:30 this morning, Hindman advised me that Coach Hayes had been relieved of his coaching duties and that this information has been released to the press."

He called Hayes' firing "very regrettable, the termination of a great, great career in my opinion."

By eight o'clock in the morning, Hugh Hindman told Woody Hayes of his decision. But even then, it turned out to be messy.

In Woody Hayes' mind, he would be allowed the honorable way out. He would be allowed to retire.

Before accompanying his team on the long flight back to Ohio, Hayes called long-time friend and Columbus Dispatch sports editor Paul Hornung. He telephoned to keep a promise. Hayes had told his old friend that he would be the first to know when he had resigned.

The conversation was brief. Woody Hayes said, "I'm resigning as of now."

Woody Hayes never thought he'd be fired. He once said, "No alumni and nobody else, even you members of the press, fire a coach. The players fire a coach and as long as I'm on the same wavelength with them, I can coach as long as I want to."

The Gator Bowl story initially ran in the Dispatch sports section. The headline read: "Hayes Incident Adds To Defeat."

But what had been 'an incident' escalated into the paper's lead story in the later edition. After Woody Hayes had called the highly-respected sports editor.

The two-inch headline on Page One blared "WOODY HAYES RESIGNS."

Woody Hayes remained in the Ohio State dressing room long after the game had ended. Then, he was escorted to the team bus by three special duty policemen.

However, the protection really wasn't necessary. Only a few fans lingered.

When the plane touched down, a silent Woody Hayes grabbed the intercom and spoke to his players.

He appeared tired. He wore sunglasses. He told the players to go home and study because a lot of them were failing.

Then, according to Tom Levenick:

"He simply put his head down and told us that he wasn't going to be our coach next year. He got off the plane and that's the last anyone had seen of him."

Grim-faced and tight-lipped, Hayes was one of the first off the plane. He ignored a horde of reporters and was escorted into a waiting police car.

Shortly after Woody Hayes had left Jacksonville, Hindman called a press conference to announce "Coach Hayes has been relieved of his duties as head football coach."

Then he added, "This decision has the full support of the president of the university. I told him [Hayes] this morning at the hotel about the decision."

In a terse statement he said, "It was the toughest decision I ever will have to make. I still have great admiration for him [Hayes]."

OSU president Harold Enarson sat alongside Hindman during the press conference. "There is not a university of an athletic conference in this country which will permit a coach to physically assault a college athlete," he said.

Enarson said he had mixed feelings. "One thing cries to be said. I, along with many, many people, feel a great sadness that a coach with such an illustrious record for a quarter century should leave the business in this tragic fashion."

He admitted this wasn't the first time Hayes' stormy behavior had grabbed his attention. "We talked one-to-one, on a man-to-man basis. I'm not prepared to go beyond that," meaning he had had previous talks with Woody Hayes.

At the press conference Hindman confirmed that he had asked for Woody Hayes' resignation before the abrupt firing. He recalled the conversation when he went to Hayes' motel room early Saturday morning.

Hindman quoted Hayes as saying, 'Do I have the opportunity to resign?' Said Hindman: "Yes, you do have that opportunity." Hindman then quoted Hayes as saying 'I'm not going to resign. That would make it too easy for you. You just go ahead and fire me.'

According to Hornung's published story, Woody Hayes' version differed sharply. While Hayes admitted he was angry when he fired back at Hindman, he regained his composure.

Hayes told Hornung, 'That's when I called you. I had resigned at that moment.'

Historians can battle it out: Did he quit or was he fired?

Would it have made a difference had Woody Hayes swung and missed? One report said Hayes struck Charlie Bauman three times.

In one insane moment, the reputation of a great university had been tarnished. It had gone way past the point of 'forgive and forget.'

Reaction was immmediate:

Tom Osborne, head coach, Nebraska: "He was a victim of his own emotions. I think what happened last night was unfortunate. College football is supposed to be something more than win at all costs. People want to win. If you lose you feel like somebody died pretty close to you for awhile."

Barry Switzer, head coach, Oklahoma: "I didn't react that way. I can't see myself doing that. But we haven't coached for 40 years."

Bo Schembechler, head coach, Michigan: "I'm saddened by it. I hate to see something like that happen. None of us who have been closely associated with him as a player or coach wanted to see it happen this way.

"I only hope you people [the press] look on the great things he's done as a coach, not dwell on his indiscretions. I think you ought to take into consideration the enormous pressure of coaching football today. Sometimes you do things that if you had second thoughts you wouldn't do. I'm not condoning what happened, just saying there's enormous pressure."

John Robinson, head coach, Southern Cal: "I would think little of those who would gloat over it. Tragedies happen to all of us in our lives. When you decide to judge anyone you've got to measure the good he's done in his life with the bad. People judging a situation like that can become very cruel. I know this man has done a lot of great things."

Don Canham, athletic director, Michigan: "I think we all feel the same all over the country. It's the passing of an era. I hate to see it happen that way. People who know him are sad about it. I guess it's an argument for retirement at 65. That's bad for the coaching profession. I think Ohio State handled it properly. It's the first time I've ever heard of a coach hitting an opposing player in any sport."

John Fuzak, former NCAA president and faculty athletic representative at Michigan State: "It's really too bad. Woody's had a great career as a coach. You hate to see this kind of thing happen."

Joe Paterno, head coach, Penn State: "I don't want to comment without knowing all the facts, except to say it's a sad end to a great career."

Bear Bryant, head coach, Alabama: "I am saddened by the circumstances because he is a class person who has given his entire life to football. He is a warm personal friend and has meant so much to football over the years."

Class of '68

Margaret Griffin, mother of Archie, Ray and Duncan. All played for Woody Hayes. Archie Griffin was the only two-time Heisman Trophy winner in college history: "He used to come into our kitchen and sit down just like regular folks. He was a good man. It makes you cry to think what happened. He shouldn't have gone out that way.

"I just wish there was some way he could have retired gracefully. Not this way. I feel so badly. I liked him and all my sons liked him. I don't think there were too many players who didn't like Coach Hayes."

Rev. Francis W. Park, senior pastor at the Covenant Presbyterian Church. It was only a few blocks from Woody Hayes' home: "I thought about giving my sermon today about Woody. I thought about it a long time. But it just seemed so tangential to other matters.

"You'll find that people will talk about it. Some will be sad, others will be joyful. Others won't care. But I just don't think people really wanted to hear about it in church. Everyone knew it. Everyone expected it. Everyone in church today seemed resigned to the fact it had to come sometime. He has been having problems right along. He is 65, and he was perhaps ready to retire anyway. People just seem sorry that it had to come this way."

John Boothe, reporter for WBNS Radio, Columbus: "A lot of people said he was completely right in punching out that guy. But most are saying he was a disgrace to the university and that he should have retired a long time ago."

A neighbor who knew Woody Hayes for 25 years. He asked not to be identified: "I've known Woody ever since he came to Columbus. I just came here with my wife to find him. He needs help now. He needs all the friends he can get.

"I just didn't want to see him go out this way. I have been watching him for years now and I saw all this coming. I really think he's a sick man inside. Things are churning up inside him. All the frustrations are built up. In the end all he could think about was winning. And it started to boil over. That's what got him. I'm going to keep looking. He needs friends."

Clemson head football coach Danny Ford regretted Hayes' dismissal.

"He has been a great football coach. I would have settled for an apology from Coach Hayes, the Ohio State administration and the Big Ten. I didn't expect this big an apology."

It was a stressful time for the Ohio State players, the coaching staff.

Tony Mason, a member of Woody Hayes' staff for one year, put it best: "I don't know what's going to happen. You hear a lot of rumors. We're really in a state of limbo."

He and the other coaches "were all sad the incident happened. We were somewhat in a state of shock when we realized what had happened. In a way, it seems like a bad dream. You really hate for a guy who has all these accomplishments to end this way.

"Coach Hayes is a demanding guy, a hard worker. I'm 30 and he's 65 and it was very hard for me to keep up with him. I've never worked for anyone who cared for the players, their well-being, and their schoolwork as much as Coach Hayes."

Art Schlichter, the 18-year-old freshman quarterback from Miami Trace, wished he had not thrown that interception.

232

"I shouldn't have thrown it. I was throwing to Ron Springs. He wasn't open for a moment, but when I rolled out I saw him come open and I came back to him. I didn't see the linebacker [Charlie Bauman].

"I enjoyed playing under Coach Hayes. He's a great coach and a legend. He does tremendous things for Ohio State football. Things fell the wrong way. What more can I say."

Senior defensive end Brian Cato said some of the players were crying."It affected everybody. It's going to be a deep loss to Ohio State. He's brought a lot of great players here. He started the Ohio State tradition of winning as far as I'm concerned."

Two-time All-American linebacker Tom Cousineau was stunned.

"I'm very, very sad. He was a great coach and a great man. If I had the chance I would play for him again."

Almost immediately the speculation began.

Who would replace Woody Hayes?

And just as quickly, Lou Holtz' name popped up. Holtz had served one season [1968] as backfield coach under Woody Hayes. He left in 1969 to become head coach at William and Mary. At the time of Hayes' firing, he was head man at Arkansas.

Contacted in Honolulu, Hawaii where he was preparing for the Hula bowl, Holtz said, "As far as Lou Holtz is concerned, I'm at Arkansas. I've always wanted to coach at Ohio State but I'm extremely happy at Arkansas. As long as the people want me here I'll be here."

But then he seemed to leave the door open.

"I think Ohio State's a great job, a great school, a great state. I went to school there, grew up there. I'm from Ohio. My wife's from Ohio. I think you can't possibly have the background I have without having strong feelings for Ohio State. It's the first score I look for in the newspapers."

Red-lettered bumper stickers suddenly appeared in Columbus: "It's gotta be Lou."

Hugh Hindman "hadn't seem them. I'm sure we'll have a lot of that sort of stuff."

Hindman planned to meet with university president Harold Enarson to establish a process for selecting Ohio State's 20th head coach.

On January 2, 1979, Enarson named a commmittee to conduct what he called "a national search" for a new football coach.

In a prepared statement, Enarson said he had asked William Nester, Ohio State vice president for student affairs, and Hindman to recommend a successor to Woody Hayes "at the earliest feasible time."

Enarson and Nester headed a search committee that also included the school's four athletic councilmen and three assistant athletic directors.

The 'short' list would included Holtz, Ohio State defensive coordinator George Hill, Ohio State quarterback/receiver coach George Chaump, plus:

*Earle Bruce of Iowa State, who coached defensive backs, centers and guards at Ohio State from 1966-1971. His Cyclones finished the season at 8-3, losing to Texas A and M in the Hall of Fame game.

Class of '68

*Bo Rein of North Carolina State, a former Buckeye halfback and graduate assistant whose team beat Pitt in the Tangerine Bowl.

*Rudy Hubbard of Florida A and M, Hayes' backfield coach from 1968-1973. His team went 12-1 and won the National Collegiate Division 1-AA championship.

*Ralph Staub of Cincinnati, Hayes' offensive coordinator who left Ohio State in 1977 after seven years.

*Bill Mallory, former Colorado coach who was Ohio State defensive tackle coach from 1966-1968. He took Colorado to the Big Eight title and the Orange Bowl in 1976, but was dismissed after a 6-5 season in 1978.

On January 7, 1979, Lou Holtz repeated denials that he was a candidate to replace Woody Hayes. "I have made a commitment to Arkansas and that's a commitment I'm going to honor. I have a good situation at Arkansas and I haven't accomplished what I want to there."

Four days later the Ohio Senate adopted a resolution honoring Woody Hayes for his "many years of dedicated service" to Ohio State University.

The resolution, sponsored by Sen. Thomas A. Van Meter, a Republican from Ashland, called Woody Hayes a "brilliant strategist and dedicated football theorist" and noted he ranked behind only Glenn [Pop] Warner and Paul [Bear] Bryant in career victories.

"However, more important than this is his influence over all those with whom he has come in contact—fellow coaches, players, supportive staff, fans and friends," read the resolution.

"Tough, aggressive and temperamental on the field, fiery and belligerent during the heat of competition, Coach Hayes is just as fervent in his dedication, compassion and concern about the physical, emotional and intellectual well-being of his friends, colleagues and young charges both in and out of the sports arena."

On January 11, Iowa State athletic director Lou McCullough admitted "I'm afraid I've lost him." Meaning that head football coach Earle Bruce was about to jump ship to Ohio State. "He's got the inside track."

The 47-year-old Bruce, a former assistant under Hayes at Ohio State, admitted he had been interviewed by OSU athletic director Hugh Hindman. "I guess I'll hear from them when they get through the interviews."

The next day, Ohio State confirmed it would name Earle Bruce as head coach. The official, who asked not to be named, said Bruce would officially resign from his coaching post at Iowa State and would be introduced at a news conference the next day.

On January 13, 1979, Bruce, a 1953 Ohio State graduate, succeeded his former coach. "It's really a dream come true," he said and called the Ohio State job "the epitome of college coaching."

Because of an Ohio law, he would sign only a one-year contract at a salary between $35,000-$45,000. "I'm not worried about my contract. I'm smart enough to know winning football keeps a coach in his contract.

Bruce said he talked to Woody Hayes. "He said he would support me in any way."

Thus, the Woody Hayes Era was over.

THE COACHES

Woody Hayes had the great ability to surround himself with talented and dedicated assistant coaches. His 1968 crew certainly possessed those attributes. A perfect blend of youth and experience. Esco Sarkkinen, an Ohio State All-American in 1939, was the 'old man' of the group. He was chief scout and also handled the defensive ends.

Hugh Hindman and Lou McCullough would later carve out their own niches as athletic directors at major universities, Hindman at Ohio State and McCullough at Iowa State. 'Baby' of the group was Rudy Hubbard. In 1967, he was a running back at Ohio State. A year later, he would take over as backfield coach.

Bill Mallory, Earle Bruce and George Chaump rounded out the coaching staff. All would go on to successful careers as head coaches. In fact, Bruce, who played for Hayes at Miami of Ohio, would succeed his mentor as Buckeyes' head honcho in 1979.

Holtz, now a TV football analyst for CBS, would become the second winningest head coach in Notre Dame history. Second only to Knute Rockne.

Wayne Woodrow Hayes could sure pick 'em.

235

Chapter 35

FROM HIGH SCHOOL TO 'THE BIGS'

George Chaump was born in Scranton, Pennsylvania and raised in West Cittson. He played football and track in high school, gaining all-conference honors in football. He went to Bloomsburg State, played football but was injured. At age 22, he joined his ex-high school coach as an assistant, thus launching a 20-year coaching career that covered the full gamut—high school, college and the National Football League as backfield coach for the Tampa Bay Buccaneers.

He began his college career as assistant to Woody Hayes at Ohio State, and remained at that Big Ten school for 11 years. He then became head man at Indiana [PA], Marshall and the United States Naval Academy [1990-1994]. If the right opportunity came along, he would love to return to coaching.

When I was a junior in college, Tom Dean, my former high school football coach, called me and gave me a nice little pep talk. He then sent me a nice letter saying I was the type of guy he'd like to have on his coaching staff.

In other words, if I kept up my grades and graduated, he'd hire me as an assistant. I was pretty thrilled. I didn't play my senior year because of injuries so that job offer kept me from feeling sorry for myself.

At age 22 I began my coaching career as assistant coach at William Penn High School in Harrisburg, Pennsylvania. I remained as an assistant for three years at two schools and then was named head coach at John Harris which was William Penn's arch rival. I thought that was kinda ironic.

I was head coach at John Harris for six years. During that time, we won six straight conference championships and believe it or not, went undefeated my last four years.

It was common for college recruiters to attend our games. Earle Bruce was chief recruiter for Ohio State in our area. Earle had been head coach at Massillon High School. He would later become Ohio State head coach.

I got to know Earle. I also got to know Ohio State head coach Woody Hayes. Woody was a great recruiter.

Certainly I had heard of him. Who in the football business hadn't. I heard him speak at football clinics. He was very, very impressive.

As a big-time coach, he spent a lot of time with high school coaches. He spent a lot of time with this small-time coach. I was in awe. I was flattered.

He'd come up and talk football. We'd go out to dinner. He gave me a lot of time and a lot of attention. Little did I realize that he was auditioning me for a spot on his staff.

I'll never forget it. It was February of 1968. I got a call about 7:30 in the morning. Woody told me there was a plane leaving Harrisburg and 'I want you on that plane. We've already called and made arrangements.

'Your tickets are at the airport. C'mon down to Columbus.'

You bet I made that flight. I had to wait a little to see Woody. He was out recruiting. The position was for quarterback and receiver coach.

Harvey Shapiro

I felt I could do it. I never lacked in self confidence. I went to the clinics. I worked with the quarterbacks, in fact, I was coaching probably the finest high school quarterback in the country, a young man named Jimmy Jones. We used a balanced attack. We mixed the run with the pass. But mainly, we had great passing. Jimmy Jones set a state record with 35 touchdown passes in one season, eight in one game. Heck, that was more touchdown passes than Woody's team would throw in two years.

We also had a great wide receiver in Jan White. Jan was not only an All-American in football but in track and field as well. He was a record-setting hurdler.

As it turned out, Jan went to Ohio State and was a three-year starter for Woody. I never promised Woody I could deliver Jimmy Jones. I said I'd try. Ironically, Jimmy went to Southern Cal. He didn't want to go to Ohio State.

When I was at Ohio State, I always kidded Woody. I said 'Don't worry about it. You got the better of the two.'

Woody had a temper. Everyone knows that. He didn't get into too many arguments. Early on, I tried to sell him on a great fullback. He got mad and said, 'Get the hell out. Right now!'

I didn't get out. I was with Woody for 11 years.

Crazy thing about the whole deal. I didn't seek the job. It sought me. I wonder how many college coaches would have jumped at the opportunity to be on Woody's coaching staff. I was really naive about money. That wasn't even a factor. Woody matched my yearly high school salary which was something like $11,500. We took the Rose Bowl, won the national championship and I had a part in it.

And even when I began my second season at Ohio State in 1969, it was for the same amount of money. As I said at that time, it was more the opportunity than it was the money.

I was lucky. In high school, I had Jimmy Jones at quarterback. At Ohio State, I had Rex Kern. Kern, Ron Maciejowski and Billy Long were all quarterbacks on our '68 championship team. As a group, it was the strongest I ever had.

When I got to Columbus, I didn't know much about the moods of the people. I knew Ohio State was a great school, a great team and Woody Hayes as a great coach.

But I found out there was a lot of talk of criticism. I'd get asked 'What are you coming here for.'

'Woody's not gonna make it. He's hanging on.'

I remember going down High Street and seeing a sign in the window of a beer garden. It said 'Bye, Bye, Woody Hayes.' I distinctly remember seeing that.

Until then I never realized the pressure of a big-time coach. After all, Woody Hayes was quite a hero. He had won a national championship. It's not like he had a losing record. His 1966 team went 4-5.

It was a big-time football program. The Buckeyes played in an 80,000 seat stadium which was awesome. So all the pluses in my mind outweighed the negatives. That's how I started.

Woody was a hard, stubborn sort of person and the football field was just a laboratory for his personality. You talk about the stubbornness. His robust offense. His lack of imagination and creativity. That was Woody. That was his personality.

237

Class of '68

It wasn't wrong. It wasn't bad because you win with that toughness. He was just a tough guy. He said what he believed in and that's what made him a great coach.

I'd like to think I had a role in Woody inserting the I formation in '68. He reluctantly agreed to a whole new offensive approach. We installed it in time for our Spring practice.

When the Fall came, Woody wanted to ditch the whole thing. But the coaches talked him out of it. We had invested too much time in the new look.

He went to Bruce Jankowski at wide receiver, moving Jan White from wide receiver to tight end. And we went to the I.

After a lot of arguing and fighting Woody said, 'Dammit, I'll do it my way too. We're also gonna run this [robust T] because I know this is gonna fizzle.'

We opened up against SMU and scored 35 points. Then he began liking it. When we played Purdue and won [13-0], he got to like it pretty good.

Woody wanted to run the I as an insurance policy to his T. We ended up using the robust T because it was a great shortage offense. Not only did we use it in short yardage situations, but also when we got down inside the 20.

Once we got down to the 20, we shifted to Woody's stuff. It was great. You're really in four down territory. We scored just about every time we got inside the 20. Statistics were amazing. I think we failed to scored only four times inside the 20.

When I arrived at Ohio State, I met Kern and Maciejowski. Before Spring training began I watched films on Kern and Billy Long. Billy had been starting quarterback the past two seasons.

Billy was a good athlete. He was the starting shortstop on the baseball team, so Woody excused him from Spring practice. I didn't have him for the 20 Spring practices.

But I had Rex Kern and Ron Maciejowski.

Before we began practice, Woody asked me for my evaluation of Kern and Long. I told him 'I think Kern's gonna be a great quarterback. Billy Long is gonna have a hard time playing. I think Rex is gonna overtake Billy...especially since he'd miss most of Spring practice.'

Woody said 'You're nuts.'

I said 'We'll see.'

After he saw Kern all Spring, I think Woody came around. 'You're right. That kid is a great one.'

Kern was a fabulous quarterback, an All-American. He was the main reason for our success during that three-year span. They were competitors. They all wanted to play. They were great supporters of each other. They were men. They had good character. It was a friendly rivalry.

At Lancaster High School, Kern was an All-American in football, baseball and basketball. In fact, he played basketball his first year at Ohio State. He was a hell of a point guard. I think he could have made a major league baseball player.

He was a humble kid, very religious, but a little devilish. Rex liked to play jokes. He wasn't a weakling. Far from it, but he was fragile. For some reason he was injury-prone. He had all kinds of injuries.

He had back surgery after his freshman year. He had a disc removed. He was really beaten up as a sophomore. He had a concussion. The Friday before our big

238

game with Michigan in 1969, we worked out on the artificial turf. It was icy. Rex was along the sideline and his feet went out from under him.

He went into a rolled-up tarp and strained his back. He could hardly move. That morning they worked and worked on him. Kern had trouble getting out of bed. He played in that game. We lost that one [24-12] and along with it the national championship.

Right after the Rose Bowl against Stanford his senior year, Kern separated his shoulder during practice. We went to an option attack so that he didn't have to pass. Lo and behold, we got beat by Stanford [21-17].

I honestly believe to this day as far as the 1968 team is concerned that everything revolved around Kern. When he was at his best I think we had a better chance of winning and that team could probably have been national champs three years in a row.

Kern was as fast as the other guys. What he had was a cat-like balance. I remember during the Northwestern game he went back to pass but took off running. He got hit on a hell of a tackle.

He went right up in the air, did a flip, came back down on his feet and kept on running. Like a cat in the air, he always seemed to land on his feet. He had great balance. He had great vision, seeing what's happening and then reacting. He was quick.

As a passer, Rex Kern was better than they gave him credit for. Maciejowski had a stronger arm, but Kern had a very good touch. He had a feel.

We were very conservative passing. We didn't really pass as much as the other major powers, because we could do it without passing. We had Leo Hayden, [Larry] Zelina, [John] Brockington, [Jim] Otis. We had Kern and the option game, so we didn't have to go to a full-fledged passing attack.

However, had we had to do it, Kern did have the ability to throw the ball. He had a big league arm for baseball. He had a better arm than most quarterbacks in college football.

If we threw 20 times a game it was a lot. Woody's philosophy was simple. He said 'You win running the football.' He believed in that. We had good backs and a good offensive line. When you have that type of talent you're gonna run.

But the passing game certainly played a part in our success. We did introduce the threat of a pass and the pass did bail us out of a lot of games.

Ronnie Maciejowski was a little bigger than Kern. He was stronger and tougher physically, but he wasn't as nimble as Rex. He was a very strong runner, more like a fullback. Yet, he had the quarterback talent and ability. He certainly was no slouch.

Mace could have been starting quarterback at a lot of schools. Certainly it was tough on him. It was tough on Billy Long. I really sympathized with those two quality kids.

Mace was a little quieter than Kern. He was a great competitor. He was smart. They were all very smart.

Billy Long was the type of guy you couldn't help but love. He was the son of a coach down in Dayton. He was just a great team player, a super guy.

We're playing Purdue and leading, 6-0. We got to the Purdue 14. Kern is hurt. Woody put Billy Long in. The fans started booing. I don't believe it was directed against Billy Long. I think they were booing Woody for not going with Mace.

So Billy Long goes into the game. Woody calls a pass, believe it or not. Billy went back to pass but all his receivers were covered. He took off right up the middle and scored.

I'll tell you. I've never seen such an emotional, dramatic thing. The people gave him a standing ovation and I was so happy for him. Billy was too great a kid to be booed.

Over the years I've kept in touch with all of them. I remember talking to Billy during one of his visits. He told me, 'Hey, I couldn't beat him out. He was quicker. He was just better. It was the right thing to do.'

That's the kind of character you win with. He was very, very honest in his evaluation.

As quarterback coach I spent a lot of time with them. You live with them when you work with Woody. Meeting. Meeting. Meeting. Practice. Practice. Practice. You have your periods for your individual work. I'm always with the quarterbacks.

Woody's philosophy was to get to know your players, be close to your players. I worked for other people and their philosophy was different.

I left Ohio State to become backfield coach for the NFL Tampa Bay Buccaneers. Head coach, John McKay was the guy who hired me. Incidentally, we beat McKay's team in the 1969 Rose Bowl.

Well, John McKay didn't get too close to his players. He said, 'don't fall in love with them.' As a head coach, I tried to find a balance.

Navy head (1990-1994) coach George Chaump began his career as an assistant to Woody Hayes at Ohio State. Phill Hoffmann photo

Chapter 36

A PARTY TO REMEMBER

Lou Holtz was born in Follansbee, West Virginia but moved to Ohio as a youngster. He graduated from East Liverpool High School [1955] and Kent State University [1959] and kicked off his long coaching career as an assistant at Iowa in 1960. Eight years later, at the age of 31, Holtz served one season as backfield coach under Woody Hayes at Ohio State. It was a stepping stone for things to come.

A year later, he was named head coach at William and Mary. For almost 30 years, Lou Holtz was one of the most colorful and successful head coaches in college football history. After the 1996 season, he resigned at Notre Dame after 11 campaigns and 130 victories. He was the second winning coach in Irish history behind the legendary Knute Rockne.

Eight of his teams finished in the Top Ten. His '88 edition was unbeaten and untied [12-0], beat West Virginia in the Fiesta Bowl, 34-21, and claimed the national title. Holtz signed on as a CBS television football commentator in 1997. Will it be a pit stop or a long-term commitment? Only time will tell.

In his own words:

I wanted to coach Ohio State, being from Ohio. A guy named Rick Forzano arranged for me to have lunch with a guy by the name of Esco Sarkkinen. That was in January of 1967. I was coaching at South Carolina.

I was to meet him for lunch at one o'clock. He didn't show up until approximately 2:15. He was shopping and got tied up. I waited that hour and 15 minutes and was still there when he came. We then talked. I knew nobody on the Ohio State staff. We talked and we talked and we got along very well. The following December, a guy by the name of Harry Stroble retired as offensive line coach [at Ohio State].

Coach Hayes decided to revamp his staff and asked for coaches to put up recommendations for position, including defensive backfield coach. He was going to take Earle Bruce, who had coached at Massillon, Ohio and who was coach of the defensive secondary, and move him to the offensive line.

Esco Sarkkinen remembered me and put my name up on the board. There were many names up on the board, including Lou Holtz.

Now we go to the coaches' convention in January the following year [1968]. On January 5th, I was working for a guy by the name of Paul Dietzel. He was coaching in the Hula Bowl.

I recorded the minutes for the American Football Coaches Association. I was Recording Secretary. Coach Hayes was a member then. After the meeting, they had a dinner and cocktail party for the members of the Board. They asked me to stay. I was sorta off on the side at the cocktail party. You have Rip Engle [Penn State], Darrell Royal [Texas], Bear Bryant [Alabama].

You've got all the top coaches. I'm on the side. Woody Hayes came over to me. I introduced myself as Lou Holtz. The name rang a bell. I don't know it, but

241

it rang a bell. So for four hours, Coach Hayes talked to me about defensive backfield play.

He asked me to stay and sit down with him during dinner. After dinner, he kept me with him. I had no idea he's interviewing me. On the next day—January 6th—which was my birthday, I had an offer to go to Georgia Tech for a guy named Bud Carson.

Carson, who replaced Bobby Dodd, was head coach of the Cleveland Browns and defensive coordinator with the Philadelphia Eagles. He offered me a job at Georgia Tech which was very lucrative.

But that same day Hayes called and offered me a job as defensive backfield coach at Ohio State. I was going to go to Georgia Tech rather than Ohio State. I didn't think it was fair to Coach Dietzel to interview for both.

My relatives found out I had a chance to go to Ohio State.

They called. I decided to go to Ohio State. I spent two days there. Coach Hayes spent a lot of time with me. The only assistant coach I had a chance to meet there was freshman coach Tiger Ellison. I knew nobody else on the staff but Esco Sarkkinen, but Coach Hayes convinced me that Ohio State was the right place to go.

That's how I ended up at Ohio State University.

Looking back, I have no regrets whatsoever. I came to Columbus the year after Ohio State had a rather mediocre year at best. I think they were 5-4. We were going to play all those sophomores in 1968. We had no idea we had that kind of talent.

We opened up against a very good SMU team. They had [Chuck] Hixson and [Jerry] Levias. They opened up by beating Auburn at Auburn. I scouted that game which was a week before our opener.

We beat 'em, 35-14, but they threw for about 476 yards. I think Hixson threw 76 and completed 40. I think we had five interceptions, so we beat a good team.

Next game we played was against Oregon. We didn't play that well but we won [21-6]. Then our first Big Ten conference game was against Purdue.

They beat us quite handily in 1967. They had a quarterback by the name of Mike Phipps, a tailback by the name of Leroy Keyes and a wide receiver by the name of Jim Bierney.

Purdue was ranked No. 1 nationally before our meeting. We shut 'em out, 13-0. Boy, you talk about a great victory. They'd just beaten Notre Dame.

They utilized Keyes in a lot of different ways. They did certain things with him as a tailback. They did certain things when they split him out.

That summer I bet Coach Hugh Hindman one hundred dollars that we would shut Purdue down. I had a drink. That's probably the last time I ever had a drink.

But if you go back and look at that game, Purdue moved the ball very well in the first half. We gave 'em the ball in poor field position. They would move down and make a mistake. A penalty. A turnover. A lost-yardage play.

At halftime, it seemed like they had 200 yards but no score. It wasn't a case where we stopped them from moving the ball.

They came out in the second half and we kicked off. They threw a pass out into the flat that Jack Tatum should have intercepted and ran back for a touchdown. But he dropped it. They came out and ran a curl cut. We had put in a little extra coverage for 'em. Ted Provost picked it off and ran it back for a touchdown. We missed the extra point.

The next time they got the ball, we dropped off [Jim] Stillwagon, our middle linebacker or middle guard, and he intercepted a pass. He ran it back to about their eight-yard line.

Rex Kern went in and got injured. They put in Billy Long who ran a quarterback draw, I think, for a touchdown. We beat 'em, 13-0.

The longer they went, the more inept they became on offense. It wasn't a case where they just got a little frustrated the more the game went on because they'd had such great success against us the year before.

There isn't any doubt that game gave us confidence, but we were still young. We go to Illinois later in the year. We had a 24-0 lead, blew it and had to come back. They scored 24 points the second half, predominantly just running the ball and made three two-point conversions following each touchdown.

Kern got hurt and Mace came off the bench and led us to a 31-24 win. He completed a key third-and-18 pass.

We beat Michigan State. It was rather close [25-20]. Northwestern gave us a hard game. Iowa had a good football team. Probably the only game that wasn't close was Michigan which we beat, 50-14, in the last game.

We beat O.J. in the Rose Bowl. By that time, we were a great football team and we were getting better. The guy who really played a fine game was [defensive halfback] Timmy Anderson. We had Jack Tatum to the wide side. They ran into the short field a lot and Tim was there for us.

It was hard to keep your focus at the Rose Bowl. We lived in the Huntington Sheraton Hotel. It was hard to be out there for that long and keep your focus. Woody Hayes could do it.

It was a wonderful time for me. I was from Ohio. I went to school in Ohio. To win when nobody expected it was really special. It was just a wonderful year.

You don't realize how special it is at the time. But throw in the Big Ten, the Rose Bowl, the national championship, unbeaten and untied, and do it with so many young players. You look back and you have to say that was a very special time.

This was a very special team. You don't find many like the Ohio State football team of 1968. But when you do, you usually find a national champion.

Lou Holtz coached at Notre Dame for eleven seasons and scored 130 victories. He was the backfield coach for the Ohio State Buckeyes 1968 team under Woody Hayes.

Photo courtesy University Notre Dame

Chapter 37

WOODY CAME A CALLIN'

Bill Mallory has spent most of his life involved in football, both as a player and a coach. That amounts to 47 years, including 40 on the high school and college coaching level. As head coach at Miami of Ohio, Northern Illinois, Colorado and Indiana, Mallory compiled a record of 168-129-4. His Miami Redskins posted an 11-0 record, which included a victory over Florida in the Tangerine Bowl. All told, Bill Mallory-coached teams made a half dozen bowl appearances. His longest tenure was 13 years at Indiana that ended in 1996. From 1966-1968, he was defensive tackle/nose guard coach at Ohio State.

BILL MALLORY, Bloomington, Indiana.

I was born in Glendale, West Virginia but raised in Ohio. My father was a coach and a teacher who later got into administration and then into business. My mother was a teacher. We moved around a lot in Ohio. I graduated from Sandusky High School.

I played end, both in high school and in college. I think in my last year of high school, I played at 190-195 pounds. In college, I played at 205-210. Back then that was solid size. I went both ways.

I was recruited by Ara Parseghian at Miami of Ohio. I went to school there, played there and graduated there. My last year I played for Johnny Pont.

I was named to the Mid-American Conference team, both as a junior and as a senior. I was team captain my senior year. Back then freshmen were eligible to play. We lost only two games during my three-year career.

I majored in physical education and social studies and there was no question that I wanted to coach. My father had been a coach. I had grown up involved in athletics. I really enjoyed it. There was never any question as to what I wanted to do.

My secret dream was to one day return to Miami as head football coach. Fortunately, I was able to fulfill that dream.

When I finished college my Dad gave me some advice. 'The thing you want to do is get your Master's. You can always begin teaching and coaching. Just make sure you're well prepared. Get in somewhere as a grad assistant. Work under a person you know you're going to learn from.'

I took his advice. I applied and got in as a grad assistant under Doyt Perry at Bowling Green. Doyt really had tremendous success at Bowling Green. He had been a great coach at Upper Arlington High School. He was one of Woody's first assistants at Miami of Ohio. He came to Bowling Green in 1951.

I stayed as a graduate assistant for one year, then I got the head coaching position at East Palestine High School, outside of Youngstown. In fact, Doyt helped me tremendously in getting that position. Johnny Pont helped as well. I was about 23 years old.

I had good success. I was there for one year. We went undefeated and were ranked in the state.

Doyt Perry contacted me and I returned to Bowling Green as defensive

244

coordinator. I was there for six-and-a-half years. Then he retired.

My next stop was at Yale under Carmen Cozza. It was Carmen's first year at Yale. He had also played under Woody Hayes. Carm replaced Johnny Pont who went to Indiana. I went there as defensive coordinator.

I really had no intention of leaving Yale. I was happy there. I never went after any coaching position, except for my first job at East Palestine. The jobs came after me.

That's how I accepted the position of defensive line coach at Ohio State. I was 31 years old. Woody tracked me down and called me. I think Doyt Perry had something to do with it. I was on the road, recruiting at the time.

Certainly I was familiar with Woody Hayes and his program. I'd go down to Ohio State and attend Spring practices, along with Doyt. We went two or three times.

I came down and spent a day with Woody. We didn't really talk much about football. He was more interested in learning about me, my recruiting, what kind of a person I was.

We went out to dinner that night. It was relaxing. I never felt like I was under pressure. He offered me the position at that time.

I told him I'd like to talk it over with my wife. I told Woody I'd also like to discuss it with Carmen Cozza. I wanted to break the news to him personally. Woody agreed.

But when I came home, somehow the news of my appointment had already been carried by the news services. We rented a U-Haul, packed all our stuff and moved from Connecticut to Ohio.

I was making $12,000 a year at Yale. I went to Ohio State for the same amount of money. So money wasn't the deciding factor. One time my wife figured out I was making 25 cents an hour.

The first year was tough. We had a losing record [4-5] and the wolves were howling. Woody was on the spot. Although we went 6-3 in 1967, it was not a great team, but that set the tone.

Woody's salvation was the '68 team which was a good blend of seniors and juniors along with that very talented sophomore class. This was an exceptional group of young players. They were winners. They had an attitude.

Actually, they matured a year early. We knew they'd be good but we didn't expect it to happen so early. Everything just seemed to come together that season.

It all began against Purdue. That 13-0 win over the No.1 rated team in the country really raised our confidence level. We got the hell kicked out of us the year before and Woody pointed to that game for a whole year.

I can't tell you how much film the coaching staff saw in preparing for that one game. By the time practice was over, I think we knew the Purdue offense as well as they did. We knew their tendencies on a given situation. But knowing and stopping can be two different things.

Purdue had a big offensive line. Defensively, we were small. But we were quick. We were tenacious. We knew we had to control the line of scrimmage. We had to contain their running game. We had to stop them up front.

One scheme depended on our quickness. We used a 5-2, but switched to an eight-man front at times. That seemed to confuse Purdue. I worked with Esco [Sarkkinen] on our pass rush. We put an awful lot of pressure on their fine quarterback Mike Phipps. Occasionally, we'd blitz. We liked to angle our tackles and nose guard quite a bit.

Class of '68

We had great activity up front all the way across the defensive line. They were quick and very feisty. We had flexibility as a team.

Our biggest defensive tackle didn't go over 225. Our great nose guard, Jim Stillwagon, went maybe 215-220. Jim was the key. We'd move him around. They'd usually try to double-team him. That's how good he was.

The flexibility with Stillwagon allowed us to get into an eight-man front. Purdue had trouble blocking us. Then we'd stunt. We'd blitz Jack Tatum from the corner.

It was a coordinated effort. Our people up front did a tremendous job. They teed off on 'em, really out quicked 'em. Our defenders did a great job.

Leroy Keyes never caught a pass all afternoon. He tried one last attempt and Tatum made a one-handed knockdown. We covered their pass patterns very well.

Of the players I coached, Jim Stillwagon was our most talented defensive player. He was a great athlete. Jim had been a linebacker in high school. We made him a nose guard.

We needed a real good athlete, someone who was very active and he was perfect. He was everything you could want in a nose guard. He had the speed, the size, the quickness. He was cocky, very competitive. Jim Stillwagon gave me 110 percent every time he took the field, whether it be at practice or during a game. He really wanted to be a great football player. He worked at it.

Tackles Paul Schmidlin, Bill Urbanik, Ralph Holloway, Brad Nielsen, all went about 220. They weren't what you'd call real gifted athletes. They were good program athletes. They were great attitude kids. They worked hard. They were tough.

The team got better and better as the season progressed. They played with more confidence and greater purpose. The team matured.

We ran their tails off, particularly at the end of the season. They ran a lot of 40s for conditioning. They ran a lot for stamina. We were out in California almost three weeks preparing for the Rose Bowl.

We took a lot of pride in stopping the other team's premier running back. We worked hard on pursuit. We worked hard on shaking off blocks.

O.J.[Simpson] caught a crease against us in the Rose Bowl and broke it for 80 yards and a touchdown. That was early in the game. We didn't make the same mistake again.

Ron Johnson of Michigan was a great ball carrier. He broke one for 39 yards against us.

Those were the two longest runs of the season against us.

I was at Ohio State for three years. When Bo Schembechler left Miami of Ohio to take over at Michigan, I was asked to be head coach. It was my alma mater.

I went with Woody's blessings. He would never hold anybody back. Those were great times. They were great kids.

Bill Mallory coached for 13 years at Indiana University and recorded a lifetime career record of 168-129-4. He was a defensive coach at OSU in '68.

Chapter 38

THE PERFECT QUESTION

Lou McCullough was born-and-raised in Florence, Alabama. He played football, basketball, baseball and tennis in high school. Upon graduation, he joined the U.S. Army Air Corps and served three years. At Geneva Military College and Wofford College, he played and lettered in five sports—football, basketball, baseball, track and tennis. McCullough earned his Master's at Columbus University. It was one of the few schools in the country which taught how to become an athletic director. His long-and-distinguished career in athletics spanned 46 years and included coaching assignments at Wofford, Wyoming, Indiana, Iowa State and Ohio State. He was also national scout for the NFL Dallas Cowboys.

McCullough served as athletic director at Iowa State for 12 years and as commissioner for the Trans America Conference for 10 years. He is now enjoying retirement in Athens, Georgia. Lou McCullough came to Columbus Ohio in 1963 as offensive backfield coach and was promoted to defensive coordinator a few years later. He was architect of the Buckeyes' tenacious defense.

LOU McCULLOUGH, Athens, Georgia.
I'd played sports all of my life, but until I got to college I wasn't sure if I would devote my life to athletics. I was also considering pre-dentistry. I started coaching in 1949 at my alma mater, Wofford College in Spartansburg, South Carolina. I was a teacher and assistant coach, with a starting salary of $2,400.

But, heck, I never went into athletics for the money. I loved what I was doing. The most I earned as an assistant coach was $19,200. But that was after nine years at Ohio State.

After Wofford, I went to the University of Wyoming. I coached the backfield on offense and the defensive ends. In fact, I coached both the offense and defense for 15 years in college.

I left Wyoming after four years and went to Indiana University for about a year-and-a-half. Then I went to Iowa State University with Clay Stapleton as assistant head coach.

Iowa State played in the Big Eight Conference against the likes of Oklahoma and Nebraska. We beat Nebraska two or three times during the five years I was there. We beat Oklahoma back-to-back and that's the first time Iowa State had beaten them in 33 years.

In 1959, Iowa State had a team we called 'The Dirty 30.' It was probably their best team in those days. We played Oklahoma for the right to go to the Orange Bowl. We had 27 players on scholarships and three others who came from the student body.

I had to make a decision when I came to Iowa State. The first year we didn't go out of state very much. But there weren't enough quality high school players, so we had to go looking for them.

I always enjoyed recruiting, as tough and competitive as it was even back then. When I was at Wyoming, I had to go on the road sometimes for six or seven weeks at a time.

The second year at Iowa State, the decision was made to become more aggressive in recruiting. I had a choice betweeen Ohio and Pennsylvania, both real hotbeds for high school football. I chose Ohio because it was closer. There are more cities of 50,000 or more population in Ohio than any other state in the country. So there's a great talent pool. Man, if you could just get the Catholic high school players out of Dayton, Cincinnati and all those other places, you'd have some great players.

The best league in the country in those days was Steubenville, Canton McKinley, Niles, Massillion, Alliance. Those kids were well coached. I mean well coached.

One of those coaches was Earle Bruce who was named Coach of the Year at Salem, Sandusky and Massillon. [McCullough and Bruce later coached together at Ohio State].

We collected newspapers from Dayton, Columbus and all-around Ohio. I had several friends in different cities in Ohio that I had cultivated. They would keep me informed on the best players.

I would send out a questionnaire to the high school coaches, asking them to list what players they thought were good enough to play in the Big Eight.

I'd head for Ohio at the end of the season. I covered the entire state of Ohio, with the exception of the Toledo area. A man named Arch Steele scouted the area for us.

I had a man develop a little film container that could fold. I would take these containers on my first trip to Ohio after the football season. My address was on it so the high school coaches could put two films in it for me. Nobody was doing that in those days. That gave us a good advantage. We got the film on the players real early.

Had I been recruiting today, all my information would have gone into a computer. I put all of the information into books.

It took quite awhile, but you learn the shortcuts. I didn't fool around long. I had a system. When I went into a home I made a decision in a hurry as to whether or not the kid would be interested in our school.

I said to the parents 'I don't want your son coming out here just for the trip. We don't have the money. If your son would like to play and get a good education, that's fine.' I eliminated a lot of freeloaders that way.

We had good success recruiting. We had over 50 players from Ohio, some really good ones. I never did try to compete against Ohio State.

We got a player from Troy, Ohio named Tom Vaughn who made All-American for us. He probably was the top recruit in Ohio. He narrowed it down to Michigan and Iowa State. We were fortunate enough to get him.

You got to know the coaches. Some coaches will spook you. Some will tell you they've got a great kid. He's 6-4. He looks good. He's got a nice crew cut. He shakes your hand, almost breaks it. He's a good student. But then you get the film and he hasn't hit anybody. So, a lot of coaches take kids that they shouldn't take. You've got to judge a football player on what he does when the ball is snapped until the whistle blows.

What did the kid do from the snap of the ball until the whistle blew is still the most important thing.

As I said, I'd been at Iowa State for five years. I was happy. One day Woody

Hayes just called and told me I'd had some really good recommendations from some of his former coaches. He said he would appreciate if I would come to Columbus and visit him.

While I wasn't expecting the call, on the other hand it didn't surprise me. I wasn't a mystery. You get to know coaches and they get to know you. You get to know coaches that know football.

Right now there aren't many college coaches out there that know football because they've only played one position. They haven't played offense and defense, or coached offense and defense. They have a defensive coordinator and coaches to do the job that they should know how to do.

I had met Coach Hayes a couple of times. I knew one thing about him. He was fair. Ohio State had such a great tradition. They're the only school in the state that has all that tradition. Everybody knew about Ohio State, that is if they knew anything about football.

As it turned out, Coach Hayes had checked me out with John Pont [Miami of Ohio], Bill Hess [Ohio University] and Doyt Perry [Bowling Green] to see if I was honest in recruiting. Those three gave me a fine recommendation.

I spent two days with Coach Hayes. After two days, he learns a lot about you. He checks out your character. He checks out your background. Don't worry, he checks a coach out. He knows what he's doing.

I didn't try to form an opinion in two days. I knew he was a hard worker and a great football coach. I didn't ask him many questions. He asked most of the questions.

I was at the blackboard most of the time. He asked me about offense, about defense and everything else.

What happened after those two days was kind of an oddity. He asked me what I wanted to coach. He said, 'Do you want to coach offense or defense? You can coach either one of them.'

He didn't ask for my answer right then. He said he'd call me at 6 o'clock Wednesday night. 'I'd like you to give me your answer then.'

Believe it or not, by five o'clock on Wednesday, I still hadn't made up my mind. And he was calling at six.

Here's his approach when he called me promptly at six: 'Hello, Lou, this is Coach Hayes. You're coming with us, aren't you?'

I said 'Yes.' If he had said 'Whaddya think?' I'm not sure I would have said 'Yes.' I probably would have said, 'Well, I don't know.'

That was a good approach. I'll always remember it.

I decided I wanted to be the offensive backfield coach because they had Matt Snell and Paul Warfield. I went to Spring practice as one of three new assistant coaches. Tiger Ellison was freshman coach and Hugh Hindman coached the offensive guards and tackles.

Coach Hayes really ran the offense, so I didn't have much to do in that capacity. But I had every duty you could think of. I was in charge of the Summer operations when Coach Hayes was gone. I was in charge of recruiting. Whenever anything went wrong and there was blame to pass on, it would be me. Ha.

I changed the entire recruiting program when I got there. They really didn't have an established recruiting program. I still did a lot of the recruiting in Ohio.

Ohio State didn't pay the assistant coaches very well. The average yearly salary at the time I came in 1963 was $9,300. I didn't say anything about it my first year because I came for $11,500.

The next year, after getting to know Coach Hayes, I told him he oughta give the coaches a raise. They worked hard, day and night.

He asked me 'Do you think they really deserve a raise?'

I said, 'Yeah, we all deserve it.'

Coach Hayes didn't think much about money. He was making $22,000 a year and I think he didn't take a raise for several years.

As I said, recruiting was very, very competitive, even back then. We had everybody coming to Ohio, including the Michigans, the Penn States.

After three years as offensive backfield coach, I became defensive coordinator. I also coached the linebackers. In 1968, Lou Holtz joined us as defensive backfield coach. Esco Sarkkinen, who had been an All-American at Ohio State back in 1939, coached the defensive ends. Bill Mallory coached the defensive line. It was a four-man defensive staff.

Woody primarily ran the Oklahoma [5-3] defense. They also kept 'The Monster' to the wide side. That's what they wanted to do. But I had to change that when I took over because we couldn't handle motion, the spreads, and things like that with a 5-3.

When I coached the backs and we were facing a team that ran a multiple defense, I had to prepare a quarterback for three different defenses.

Conversely, we ran three different defenses. We ran the Oklahoma as a basic defense. We ran a '63' [6-3] which was like the Notre Dame Split 6 to stop the run. We used the 4-3 primarily on passing downs.

For instance, if we were playing Northwestern and we're using a 5-3, they'd run all over us. So we shifted to the 6-3 and we could stop their running game. We could keep our passing lanes better with the 4-3. With the 5-3, your passing lanes aren't as good. What I'm talking about is rushing the passer.

We ran the multiple defenses and we'd shift which gave us an advantage. We'd line up in a 5-3, for instance, and quickly shift into a 4-3. They always thought they'd catch us in our shift. They only caught us once in five years and it didn't hurt.

I called the defenses from upstairs. I'd always call 'em to Bill Mallory. We'd use sign language. We spent a lot of time working on those signals.

Sometimes we might go a quarter and let the second-string linebacker send it in so people wouldn't catch on. We gave our linebacker the right to change. Sometimes you have to change the defense.

If you were in a defense and couldn't change, that could be fatal. I remember one time we lost a game because of it. A team came out unbalanced and we weren't ready for it.

Michigan once came out with an unbalanced line and we shut them down. In fact, they thought we knew their plans. We had worked hard on it.

[Linebacker] Mark Stier would call 'Move' and we made the shift. We had a color scheme, too. We used a lot of colors. Say we'd call an off defense, an Oklahoma, but it wasn't a good defense against that offensive set. So our linebacker could call 'Blue 43' or 'Red.' Then he'd say 'Move', and we'd shift. We had a very, very good defensive scheme in those days.

Defensively, we were small. We were very, very quick and I firmly believe we were in better physical shape than any of our opponents.

We had various programs for our defensive people. We did a lot of different things that the offense never did physically. I'd say we worked 10 times harder than the offensive people. We just felt we should do that. We used quick, quick drills. We used very similar things that the University of Alabama did in those days. We tried to be quick, move laterally, take the proper pursuit angle.

We had some average seasons before 1968. One game I remember, they had a plane that flew over Ohio Stadium. It was the Northwestern game. I don't know exactly the year, but it flew the entire game.

I remember Woody wanting to shoot it down. It said 'Goodbye, Woody.' It just circled the stadium the entire game. At Christmas time, Mrs. Hayes sent out a Christmas card that was very unique. It showed the stadium. It showed a little airplane flying and it said 'Merry Christmas. We're still here.'

Coach Hayes lasting almost four decades at Ohio State was a miracle. You don't last long there. Just look at Earle Bruce who succeeded Coach Hayes. He was the winningest coach in the Big Ten, yet he was fired. There's a power struggle everywhere.

Although we had a losing season [4-5] in 1966, the seeds were planted for the best recruiting class I've ever seen. We had several legitimate All-Americans from that class. I'm talking about kids like [quarterback] Rex Kern, [noseguard] Jim Stillwagon, [Monster Back] Jack Tatum, [defensive backs] Tim Anderson and Mike Sensibaugh. They were all sophomores in 1968. They were the backbone of our national championship team. In the Rose Bowl, 16 of the first 22 were sophomores.

Rex Kern could have had a scholarship in football, basketball and baseball. He was kinda an overachiever in school. Later, he got his Ph.D. His Dad was a barber. If you get to know the background of a Rex Kern, you find out he came from really strong parents. Woody was very careful about that. I think it was one of his best assets. He would turn down some great players because he felt they didn't have the character to play at Ohio State.

I felt we were gonna have a good year [in 1968]. We had a lot of talent and a lot of character. We played some close games. We were much better defensively in 1969 and 1970 when this sophomore group became juniors and seniors.

In 1968, we made mistakes that a national championship team shouldn't make. We really had great defenses the next two years. That's what comes with maturity. We shouldn't have lost to Michigan and Stanford, but that's another story.

Normally, Coach Hayes shied away from starting young players, but he couldn't ignore this exceptional group. They were just better athletes.

Rex Kern was a better athlete than Billy Long who had been our starting quarterback in 1967. Billy Long was a good quarterback and a fine young man. His Daddy was a high school coach. I liked him as well as any kid we ever had, but Rex had a little spark in him. He was a good passer, too. We threw the ball an awful lot that year.

We didn't have that 'three yards and a cloud of dust' mentality that so many have associated with Ohio State. Sometimes, I thought we threw too many times.

I'm proud to say that eight All-Americans came out of that 1968-69-70 group. I'm talking about Stillwagon, Tatum, Anderson, Sensibaugh, Kern, defensive back Ted Provost, offensive tackles Rufus Mayes and Dave Foley.

Class of '68

How I got Tatum and Sensibaugh on defense is worth telling. Tatum was a great running back in high school. He turned out to be one of our greatest players. Well, he and John Brockington were both sophomores. They were both fullbacks.

What we did was Woody would take a player for offense and then I'd get my choice of a player for defense. Coach Hayes took John Brockington at fullback. That gave me Jack Tatum.

Woody took Rex Kern as quarterback and that gave me Mike Sensibaugh [at safety]. Sensibaugh was recruited by everybody as a quarterback. So, that's what we did.

Everybody won.

Tatum was quick as a cat. He could really unload on you. He could hit you like a 250-pounder. Good tacklers don't arm tackle. They use their leg drive. That's where they get their strength. I'd say Jack Tatum was probably the strongest tackler in the open field that I've ever seen.

Jim Stillwagon was the best defensive player I ever coached. He played at a small high school in Ohio. Usually the coaches send you 16 MM movies. That is except Jim Stillwagon. The only thing I had on him was 8 MM. I got the film and not many other folks could get it.

He made All-American his junior and senior years [as did Jack Tatum], but Stillwagon should really have made it three years in a row.

He won every defensive honor that could be bestowed on a college player— Vince Lombardi Trophy, Outland Trophy—and they were well deserved.

When a player is a star his sophomore year you wonder how he's gonna turn out in Spring practice the next year. Is he gonna loaf? Does he think he has it made?

This is a true story. We're scrimmaging one day in the Spring. It's Jim Stillwagon's junior year. We had a loudspeaker and we're filming the practice session.

I stopped practice and said 'You know this is a very,very unique team that we have. Raise your hand. How many people here named Stillwagon?'

Obviously, one of 'em raised his hand.

Then I said, 'Well, this is odd because in the last 10 plays Stillwagon has made all the tackles. I thought we had several players named Stillwagon.'

He always worked hard. The last day he played for Ohio State, he was full speed. And I mean he was strong. We used to put him on the center's nose when they punted. He would hit the center so hard that sometimes he'd go past the fullback.

He could play pass defense, too. We used him in the 4-3. He could play a lot of places because he was so dedicated, a team man.

Jack Tatum went on to have a great pro career with the Oakland Raiders. I advised Jim to go to Canada because they offered him a much bigger signing bonus. I told him 'You could get hurt and you'd lose the money. Take what you can get.'

He took my advice.

Lou McCullough called the defensive plays for OSU from upstairs. He was the architect of the Buckeye defense that won the National Title in 1968.

Section V

Game by Game

Photo courtesy Ohio State University Archives

GAME ONE

Rex Kern #10 in his first varsity start.

Chapter 39

GUNFIGHT AT THE 'BUCKEYE CORRAL'

OHIO STATE 35, SOUTHERN METHODIST 14

September 28, 1968...at Ohio Stadium.

Ohio State nervously awaited 'The Gunslinger'...alias a tall, tough Texan named Chuck Hixson.

A 6-2, 188-pound sophomore quarterback with a golden right arm. A lethal weapon that had repeatedly hit the target in his impressive college debut.

Ohio State chief scout Esco Sarkkinen and backfield coach Lou Holtz were on hand for the SMU-Auburn opener. The Buckeyes were to meet the Mustangs the following Saturday in their 1968 season debut.

SMU shocked the favored Auburn Tigers, 37-28, behind the deadly combination of Hixson to-Jerry Levias.

A redshirt in 1967, Hixson connected on 27 of 48 passes for 283 yards against Auburn. All told, SMU attempted 52 passes. Levias, a 170-pound senior receiver, was his favorite target.

SMU, however, showed more than one dimension, running off 91 plays utilizing a wide variety of offensive formations.

As Lou Holtz put it: "They threw from both one-yard lines...and everywhere in between." Including a 'trick' pass from Levias-to-Hixson.

SMU faked a back into the line, handed off to Levias who showed reverse but then suddenly pulled up and found an unguarded Chuck Hixson on the opposite end of the field.

Tongue-in-cheek, Holtz added "That's when they were still being conservative. They opened up a little bit after that."

Sarkkinen was likewise impressed with Hixson. "At halftime a newspaperman mentioned that Hixson was a sophomore, but had been red-shirted. I told him 'He must have been red-shirted by the Dallas Cowboys' because he looked like he'd walked right out of their camp."

Holtz called Levias "a truly tremendous athlete. He can beat you in so many ways. It's going to be one helluva football game."

Following his team's loss to SMU, veteran Auburn head coach Shug Jordan warned "SMU is a vastly underrated team. Future opponents look out."

The loss could have been even more embarrassing for Auburn had not the secondary picked off four Hixson passes.

There was some concern about another quarterback...Ohio State's Rex Kern.

An All-American in three sports at Lancaster [Ohio] High School, Kern had undergone back surgery in the Spring of 1968 and had been withheld from contact during most of the Fall pre-season practice.

While he had been sharp in practice, playing under fire could be entirely different.

"If the doctors give us the OK," said Ohio State head coach Woody Hayes "he'll be in there. He's been in there all Fall."

Class of '68

History records that Rex Kern was given the go-ahead to play.

History also records that the talented redhead would not play in anyone's shadow, not even the huge shadow cast by Chuck Hixson.

Ohio State survived the 'wild west show', 35-14.

Hixson, cut from the same cloth as SMU legends Don Meredith and Fred Benners, threw a then-record 69 passes, completing 37 for 417 yards and two touchdowns. Levias wiggled loose for 160 yards on 15 pass receptions.

All told, SMU completed 40 of 76 attempts for 437 yards. The attempts stood as an NCAA record for quite some time.

Ohio State, on the other hand, kept the gun in the holster for the most part. Kern and senior backup quarterback Billy Long fired only 17 times for a modest 145 yards.

Kern's eight completions in 14 tries totaled 139 yards. But more important, they accounted for two touchdowns. He also scored a third on a quarterback keeper. In his own way, he was just as exciting as Hixson in a brilliant varsity debut.

Kern's TD tosses of 18 and 20 yards both went to junior halfback Dave Brungard of Youngstown, Ohio. Kern's 44-yard completion to sophomore halfback John Brockington [Brooklyn, New York] set up his own touchdown scamper.

With the cool demeanor of a riverboat gambler, Rex Kern settled the issue with a key 16-yard keeper on fourth-and-11. He simply took matters into his own hands by calling the play so quickly that punter Mike Sensibaugh couldn't even get onto the field.

That gutsy run around right end kept the drive alive. Moments later, Kern fired an 18-yard scoring strike to Brungard to give Ohio State an unsurmountable 26-7 lead.

SMU lived by the pass and literally died by the pass.

The Buckeyes picked off five Hixson aerials, including two by junior linebacker Mark Stier of Louisville, Ohio. Sophomores Tim Anderson, Mike Sensibaugh and Doug Adams also joined in on the fun. The interceptions blunted five SMU scoring drives.

Ohio State's defensive strategy was simple but effective. Both ends dropped off, as did linebackers Stier and and Dirk Worden as well as middle guard Jim Stillwagon.

Bend but don't break. Give up the short-to-medium range passes but not the 'bomb.' Keep Jerry Levias out of the end zone.

Buckeyes' head coach Woody Hayes was elated with the defensive effort. "Seventy-six passes and only 14 points has to be close to a record. And say, we scored as many times as they did with the pass."

Not one of Ohio State's 17 passes fell into enemy hands.

Yet, it was far from an easy victory.

At halftime, Kern had engineered Ohio State to a 26-7 bulge. The crowd acknowledged his performance with a standing ovation shortly before intermission.

After a scoreless third period, the Buckeyes tacked on nine more points in the final stanza. The offense managed 92 yards after intermission, primarily on the ground.

SMU made a major adjustment in the second half and it worked. That coupled with Ohio State's conservative game-calling.

The Mustangs bunched eight players on the line of scrimmage. SMU head coach Hayden Fry figured, and correctly so, that Ohio State would not risk a costly mistake.

Basically, it was run three plays and punt. Sensibaugh was more than up to the task. During the seemingly endless game, the sophomore safety [Cincinnati, Ohio] punted a total of 11 times.

Cagey old Woody Hayes knew the danger of the forward pass.

As he would so often preach: "Only three things can happen when you pass and two of them are bad."

"Ohio State is going to have one of the better teams in the country," Fry predicted. "They've got great personnel. They've got an outside attack to go with their inside attack.

"We did an extremely poor job of defending their outside attack in the first half, or maybe if you turn it around, Ohio State did a very excellent job of running it.

"We stopped their inside attack in the first half and I thought our boys did a fine job in the second half. I'm extremely proud of my team. I think we showed enough today. They could become a fine club. All our youngsters learned a lot."

Fry discussed his team's huge offensive output this way:

"We ate up a lot of grass, but we didn't get it across. They did a great job of coming up with the ball. They came up with great plays, particularly on defense."

Ohio State played a Jekyll-and-Hyde kind of game.

Said Hayes: "We were about as sharp as a wet donut in the second half. We tried not to open it up too much. We've become quite a passing team," he noted with a grin. "They widened their ends in the second half, made it tough for us.

"We are more explosive on offense [this season]. We have more people who can do things with the ball. We just have to make sure we utilize them. We used a lot of people in the game, but I would have liked to get them in earlier.

"I guess you would say it was a typical opener at that, even with all the passing. Our first touchdown was a cheap one, but we did have some breaks go our way.

"We never would have won without those five interceptions. We figure you have to intercept about one for every 14 passes thrown against you. We got one of 15. That's close and we really did pretty well defensively.

"They are a splendid pass protection team and they keep you honest with the screen pass. They're a passing team and they know it.

"We were sort of hanging on in the second half. Our first quarter was pretty good football. Then Kern's run [for a first down] sort of iced it for us. Maybe it iced it too much. We were that cold in the third quarter."

Ohio State gained only 39 yards rushing, 52 passing the second half. Game total: 372 net yards.

Ohio State forged out to a 20-7 lead. It was fourth-and-11 on the SMU 41. "I was about to punt," pointed out Hayes. "That's when Kern took matters into his own hands for a dazzling 16-yard sortie down the sidelines. Three plays later, Kern hit Brungard for the clincher. Kern is just one hell of a kid. He has great enthusiasm."

Had Kern not succeeded, would Hayes have been so kind?

During the opening half, Hixson completed 22 passes for 249 yards and one touchdown. Afterwards, he had no memory of the opening 30 minutes. "I don't know exactly when I got hit or on what play, I think it happened early in the game. I just can't remember anything in the first half."

With everything back in focus, Hixson brought his team to within 12 points of Ohio State, 26-14, in the fourth quarter. That was as close as SMU came. "I was impressed with their defense," noted Hixson. "I didn't throw it to them [five interceptions]. Ohio State went after it aggressively."

Chuck Hixson and his golden right arm felt fine after the game. "The most I ever threw in a game was 48 last week."

Despite the constantly defensive pressure, Ohio State got to Hixson only four times, most of that punishment taking place late in the game when SMU tried to play 'catch up.'

Although Jerry Levias caught 15 passes, the Buckeyes succeeded in keeping him out of the end zone.

Brungard, a 5-10, 184-pound junior, accounted for 139 total yards...101 yards rushing and 38 yards as a receiver.

On his 41-yard scoring burst, Brungard crashed over left tackle, bounced backwards, slid to the outside and dashed down the sidelines untouched.

Junior fullback Jim Otis [Celina, Ohio] added 63 yards, including a nine-yard TD blast to open the scoring. Kern added 45 net yards.

Rex Kern survived one anxious moment during the game. He was slammed to the turf in the second half after making a handoff. He got up slowly. He was OK. "It had nothing to do with the [back] operation," he said. "I was hit higher up on the side of the back. It hurts some, but it's nothing serious. Everything is fine. Couldn't be better."

Kern would suffer eight injuries during his sophomore season. He was knocked out of several games and didn't play against Wisconsin. But he would prove resilient during his brilliant three-year college career.

Hixson tried to make it interesting after Kern had engineered a 15-play, 82-yard scoring drive in the waning moments of the first half.

After a scoreless third period, Hixson climaxed a long drive with an eight-yard scoring strike to tight end Ken Lemming. It was now OSU 24, SMU 16.

The momentum had changed. Southern Methodist was surging, Ohio State back pedaling.

Following the kickoff, Kern was nailed for a 14-yard loss. Mike Sensibaugh's booming punt got the Buckeyes out of trouble, but Hixson moved his Mustangs from their own 36 to the Ohio State 18. Hixson fired on fourth down. However, senior linebacker Dirk Worden knocked down the pass. OSU had 'dodged the bullet.'

Unable to move the ball, Ohio State was once again forced to punt. The offense was clearly gasping for air. It was time for the defense to take control.

Sophomore defensive end, Mark Debevc of Geneva, Ohio, playing in place of injured senior Nick Roman, trapped Hixson on his own 23. A major penalty then moved SMU backwards, to it's own six yard line.

On the next play, Debevc tackled Hixson in the end zone for an important safety. That meant SMU wouldn't win with two touchdowns and two conversions.

The clinching TD came with 6:45 to play as Kern guided Ohio State 43 yards—in four plays— to pay dirt. He completed a 23-yarder to soph tight end Richard Kuhn.

The 'ice cool' sophomore quarterback then calmly whipped a 20-yard TD strike to Brungard.

Rex Kern tried to get a good nights sleep on the eve of his first collegiate start. Sleep did not come easy.

"I was pretty nervous Friday night. And yes, I'm a little tired and beat up, but nothing serious. It's just great to win."

OHIO STATE 35, SMU 14

	OSU	SMU
First downs	18	27
Rushing Yardage	227	50
Passing Yardage	145	437
Return Yardage	49	88
Passes	9-17-0	40-76-5
Fumbles Lost	1	3
Yards Penalized	61	51

SMU	0	7	7	0-	14
OSU	14	12	0	9-	35

OSU—Kern, 3 run [Merryman kick]
OSU—Otis, 9 run [Merryman kick]
SMU—Fleming, 8 pass from Hixson [Lesser kick]
OSU—Brungard, 41 run [kick failed]
OSU—Brungard, 18 pass from Kern [kick failed]
SMU—Fleming, 6 pass from Hixson [Lesser kick]
OSU—Safety, Hixson tackled in end zone
OSU—Brungard, 20 pass from Kern [Merryman kick]

RUSHING
OSU— Brungard 14-101, Otis 18-63, Kern 18-45, Gillian 2-24, Hayden 2-6, Long 1-1, Greene 1-minus 1, Maciejowski 1-minus 3, Brockington 4-minus 5; **SMU**— Richardson 11-62, Livingston 1-5, Lesser 1-3, Clements 1-2, Levias 2-2, Hixson 6-minus 24.

PASSING
OSU— Kern 8-14-0-139, Long 1-3-0-6; **SMU**— Hixson 37-69-5-417, Carter 3-7-0-20.

RECEIVING
OSU— Brockington 2-54-0, Brungard 2-38-2, Kuhn 1-23-0, Otis 2-16-0, Jankowski 1-8-0, White 1-6-0; **SMU**— Levias 15-160-0, Fleming 9-104-2, Richardson 5-61-0, Holden 4-55-0, Clements 3-32-0, Stringer 1-11-0, Jordan 2-10-0, Floyd 1-4-0.

Chuck Hixson flashed a golden arm during his career. As a sophomore, Hixson hit on 37 passes against Ohio State for 417 yards and 2 TDs

Chapter 40

'POOR KID FROM SAN ANTONE'

Chuck Hixson was born-and-raised in San Antonio, Texas. An All-City and All-State selection from Highlands High School, he played in the annual 'Big 33' game pitting the best preps from Texas against the best from Pennsylvania. A three-year starter at SMU, Chuck Hixson set a bevy of NCAA school and Southwest Conference passing records during his collegiate career. He had a brief NFL career, playing backup to Lenny Dawson on the Kansas City Chiefs. He is now a commercial real estate asset manager. On weekends, he's a soccer referee. Chuck Hixson lives in Dallas.

I'm a fourth generation Texan, born-and-raised in San Antonio. I think my best accomplishments took place off of the football field.

I married my high school sweetheart some 30 years ago. In fact, our first daughter, Shelley was born just a few weeks before our 1968 battle against Ohio State.

I have three daughters. My youngest, Natalie, is a great soccer player on scholarship and playing for The University of Oklahoma.

Highlands High School was a big school. We had 650 in my graduating class. Our high school attack was pass-oriented and wide open for that era.

I was fortunate to be selected to play against Pennsylvania in the 'Big 33' game and against Oklahoma in the 'Oil Bowl.' I also played in the Texas High School All-Star game.

Believe it or not, I wasn't inundated with college offers. I received about 15-16 scholarship offers. My choice narrowed down to SMU or Arkansas.

I chose Southern Methodist because of Dallas and the opportunity to throw the football. And for a poor kid from San Antone, this memory remains with me. I'm talking about my visit to Dallas.

It seemed like all the cars were new, everywhere I looked. And yes, I was familiar with such former SMU greats as Doak Walker, Kyle Rote and Don Meredith.

I played on the freshman 'Pony' team in 1966, as did all the freshman of the day. I was red-shirted in '67 since Mike Livingston was a solid starter at quarterback. Mike and I were later re-united as backups to Len Dawson at Kansas City.

'68' was the marketing slogan on billboards and on ad spots for the Mustangs' season. We had strong senior leadership with both running backs, wide receiver Jerry Levias and a few senior defenders mixed with new guys.

I was one of 6-8 redshirt sophs. We had true sophomores and juniors.

We started strong, upsetting Auburn. We finished the season at 8-3, beating Oklahoma in the Bluebonnet Bowl.

Our three losses were to national champion Ohio State, No. 2 Texas and Sugar Bowl champion Arkansas. We had a good year.

In addition to Levias, there was Mike Richardson at running back. He rushed for more than 1,000 yards that year and caught more than 50 passes, as did tight end Ken Fleming.

Class of '68

Our 1968 team set numerous records for yardage, total plays, etc. Coach Hayden Fry was the offensive mastermind.

The SMU-Ohio State game was 30 years ago but it seems like only yesterday. It was a picture-perfect day inside that massive horseshoe called Ohio Stadium.

I was greatly impressed with Ohio State's size and speed. When the captains went to the center for the pre-game coin toss, OSU's massive offensive tackles Dave Foley and Rufus Mayes towered over our captains.

We laughed and tried to 'outquick 'em.' Foley and Mayes played as fabulous as they looked.

How many teams, ever, had such an assembly of great running backs competing for two positions? Imagine... John Brockington and Leo Hayden were second teamers. Their defense was new to each other as a unit, but bursting with talent. Three future NFL stars in the same secondary...[Jack] Tatum, [Mike] Sensibaugh] and [Tim]Anderson.

They played zone for most of the game, stayed back and reacted [fast] to the ball. We exploited short passing lanes and perimeter areas by flooding their zone with receivers. But not for long and not for much profit.

They were hard-hitting and well coached. Lou Holtz was secondary coach. What a combination.

I did manage to throw five interceptions, two, as I recall in Ohio State's end zone.

Two defensive players stand out in my memory. Jack Tatum with his great range delivering hits and Jim Stillwagon's fierce activity along the line of scrimmage.

Ohio State and Texas were the best teams of 1968, as evidenced by the polls, and certainly from my standpoint.

Believe it or not, I'm glad that SMU played them both.

HIXSON'S SOUTHWEST CONFERENCE NCAA RECORDS

Most passing attempts one game—69, Ohio State, 1968.
Most passing attempts season—468, 1968
Most passing attempts career— 1115, 1968-70 *
Most passes completed one game—37, Ohio State, 1968
Most passes completed season— 265, 1968
Most passes completed career— 642, 1968-70*
Most yards passing one game—417, Ohio State, 1968
Most yards passing season—3103, 1968
Most TD passes one game— 4 [tie], Arkansas, 1968
Most TD passes thrown season — 21, 1968
Most rushing/passing plays one game—75, Ohio State, 1968
Most rushing/passing plays season—556, 1968
Most rushing/passing plays career— 1358, 1968-70*
Most yards rushing/passing season— 2995, 1968
Most yards rushing/passing career— 6874, 1968-70
Most TD passes thrown career— 40, 1968-70
*NCAA record

GAME TWO

Rufus Mays #73 throwing a block during the Oregon game.

Chapter 41

A WIN IS A WIN

OHIO STATE 21, OREGON 6

October 5, 1968...At Ohio Stadium

Woody Hayes couldn't hold back his anger.

For the second consecutive game, his starting quarterback, sophomore Rex Kern has been bruised-and-battered.

"This is open season on quarterbacks," snapped Hayes.

Kern was leveled in Ohio State's 35-14 opening season triumph against Southern Methodist. It was called a cheap shot by one writer. "Remember you said that," cautioned Hayes.

But he had seen enough after Kern suffered a mild concussion and what at first was suspected as a broken jaw in Ohio State's 21-6 win over Oregon.

X-rays, however, proved negative.

"We're not out there to butcher kids," continued the Ohio State head coach. " I don't know how I could tell my team to go out and get a player. This is too great a game played by great kids.

"We've got to get rid of it [dirty play]. It's up to us to improve it. Little things can be sophisticated and improved. We can work on it.

"A few years before," he pointed out, "we had trouble with players piling on, didn't we?"

Kern gained 40 yards on eight carries and completed 11 of 19 passes for 113 more yards in his second varsity start. He would be hurt three times during the game. The 'big hit' would take place in the second quarter.

Kern caught a headgear in the face after a pitchout to junior halfback Dave Brungard. His battered body finally wore out in the final stanza.

It only hurt when he laughed, cried, breathed, or barked out signals.

Rex Kern would have a week to prepare for No.1-ranked Purdue.

He would wear a red-cross shirt during that week, meaning 'HANDS OFF.'

"This is not a game for the offense," added Hayes. "A lot of yards [288 rushing, 168 passing] that didn't add up to a damn thing...except the big ones."

The 21-6 verdict before 70,191 at Ohio State wasn't beautiful, but a win is a win is a win.

Hayes conceded his Buckeyes didn't have Oregon on their minds. "Don't take that as an alibi. There is no question Purdue is the best team in the country. The sportswriters and coaches agree. I'm not telling you anything new.

"Like Michigan State a couple of years ago, it seems as though they [Purdue] can become just as strong as they need to be. They showed that against Notre Dame last week. If we are to make it a contest [next Saturday] at Ohio Stadium, we'll have to get a lot better."

The combination of Ohio State's offense—"we were sloppy today"— and the

Kern injury turned Woody Hayes into an unhappy camper. Just two days earlier he was almost in a giddy mood. 'The General' watched practice from a two-story tower erected at the Buckeyes' practice field. Notre Dame had it's version. It was nothing new to college football. Woody Hayes enjoyed his first view from the top. "You can see a lot from up here," he said. "You can sure see if they run their pass cuts right or wrong."

It was Thursday and he was very pleased. "Our kids were pretty snappy." That means sharp, ready-for-combat. But would Ohio State keep that edge on Saturday?

After all, the Buckeyes were fresh from their opening season conquest of pass-happy SMU. Oregon, on the other hand, fell 28-7 to Colorado in the season opener.

A week later, the Ducks fell victim to Stanford, 28-12. Stanford quarterback Jim Plunkett hit on three TD passes.

After only one varsity appearance, Rex Kern already had a big fan in 1955 Heisman Trophy winner, "Hopalong" Cassady.

"Rex Kern is really an exciting player," said the all-time Buckeye great. "I love to watch this kid. I can hardly wait for the next play to see what he's going to do. He's just a natural great athlete."

Ohio State hardly looked like the No.5-ranked team in the country against Oregon despite amassing 456 total yards. At halftime, the Buckeyes held a scant 7-6 lead, and that first period touchdown was defense-generated.

In a move that would pay huge dividends, 5-10, 168-pound junior Mike Polaski was given the starting nod at safety over Mike Sensibaugh.

Defensive halfback coach Lou Holtz explained it this way. "It's nothing against Sensibaugh. Polaski did a better job against SMU."

Forced to punt deep in it's own territory, Oregon couldn't stop the floodgates. The Buckeyes called for a three-man blitz. Polaski, the gritty little pest from Columbus [Ohio] Brookhaven High School, not only blocked Alan Pitciathley's boot, but caught the ball on the fly.

The end zone was only nine yards away. Just a nice stroll on a Saturday afternoon. Jim Merryman, a junior walk-on, added the extra point. It was 7-0 after just 82 ticks of the game clock.

Later in the first stanza, a Kern-to-fullback Jim Otis pass-run play amassed 52 yards to the Oregon 44. However, that drive stalled, as did three others on the Oregon 41, 27 and 18 yard lines.

It would be that kind of frustrating afternoon.

Upstart Oregon simply refused to fold. Picking off four Ohio State passes, the Ducks scored their own touchdown in the closing moments of the first half.

Reserve quarterback John Harrington connected on a perfect 10-yard scoring strike to end Denny Schuler. Harrington, subbing for Al Pitciathley who was injured, found Schuler on the goal line. Ken Woody's extra point kick, however, sailed wide.

Oregon's only TD of the game came with only 55 seconds left in the opening half.

Woody Hayes shifted gears after intermission, reverting back to his power-running game. Otis was the plow horse and rushed for a game-high 102 yards on 17 attempts, including a 35-yard scoring burst in the third stanza. Admitted Otis, "We were looking ahead to Purdue. You can't help it. But now we can really look to Purdue."

Senior Billy Long, Ohio State's starting quarterback in 1967 and soph Ron Maciejowski saw action when Kern had to leave the game.

Maciejowski, a home-grown product from Bedford [Ohio] High School, teamed up with sophomore wide receiver Bruce Jankowski on a 55-yard scoring play in the fourth quarter.

'The Bomb' was actually a flare pass thrown to a sprinter with 9.8 speed. Jankowski simply turned on the after burner.

Offensively, Ohio State ran 95 plays. That normally should have resulted in a runaway, a laugher.

On a day when the offense self-destructed, the tenacious defensive unit stepped front-and-center.

Defensive coordinator, Lou McCullough didn't mind crowing. "It was our best effort yet—they were all great."

Polaski, for instance, prevented an Oregon touchdown when he broke up a long pass with an over-the-shoulder deflection.

Dave Whitfield, a 184-pound junior defensive end, was nursing a knee injury that kept him sidelined for most of the SMU game. Although not quite fully recovered, he was all over the field. Twice Whitfield nailed Oregon backs for losses totaling nine yards. Twice his rushes forced the Oregon quarterback into throwing wildly for OSU interceptions. His big hit caused a fumble. The Massillon [Ohio] native not only recovered a fumble but assisted on seven tackles.

Junior defensive tackle Brad Nielsen had six solo tackles and four assists. Soph noseguard Jim Stillwagon had seven unassisted stops, four assists. Senior linebacker Mark Stier intercepted a pass.

Ohio State's defense was so tough in the second half, Oregon never got beyond it's own 38 until the Ducks intercepted Maciejowski's last pass. That was on the Oregon 41.

Oregon registered only six first downs for the game, totaling a paltry 140 yards. The Ducks were forced to punt 13 times.

Second-year Oregon head coach, Jerry Krei called it a combination of his team's poor offensive showing, coupled with Ohio State's unyielding defense.

"We didn't get a first down in the second half. It's a reverse cycle. Last week it was good offense and poor defense. This week the defense played well and the offense played poorly. The defensive unit did every bit it could do.

"Ohio State's a fine football team. They're a heck of a defensive team. We obviously didn't block well, or they had a soundly conceived defense for our offense."

In the final two periods, Oregon netted only seven yards on the ground.

He had high praise for the 19-year-old Kern. "He's a very fine football player. He certainly has the ability to make the big play. You think you've got him cut down and all of a sudden he's still running with the ball."

Oregon picked off four Ohio State passes, two thrown by Long, and recovered two fumbles. Twice Oregon forced the Buckeyes to settle for field goal attempts. Both tries were unsuccessful.

Despite a woeful offense, Oregon managed to stay close until late in the third period. That's when Ohio State wingback Larry Zelina [Cleveland, Ohio] fielded

a punt on the OSU 39, then twisted and dodged 26 yards to the Ducks 35.
On the next play, Otis burst over left tackle and rambled for a touchdown. Ohio State moved out to a 14-6 lead.

Less than four minutes later, Maciejowski, a third-string quarterback, combined with soph wide receiver Bruce Jankowski [Fair Lawn, New Jersey] on a 55-yard scoring play.

Jankowski caught the short sideline pass and outraced the Oregon secondary. It wasn't very pretty, but the young Buckeyes were 2-0, extending their modest win streak to six over two seasons.

The stage was set.

Bring on big, bad Purdue.

OHIO STATE 21, OREGON 6

	OSU	ORE
First downs	22	6
Rushing Yardage	288	62
Passing Yardage	168	78
Return Yardage	94	84
Passes	12-25-4	8-21-2
Fumbles Lost	2	1
Yards Penalized	33	5

ORE	0	6	0	0-	6
OSU	7	0	7	7-	21

OSU— Polaski, 9, interception [Merryman kick]
ORE— Schuler, 14, pass from Harrington [kick failed]
OSU— Otis, 35, run [Merryman kick]
OSU—Jankowski, 55, pass from Maciejowski [Merryman kick]

RUSHING
OSU— Otis 17-102, Kern 8-49, Brungard 18-35, Maciejowski 4-30, Brockington 7-25, Coburn 2-8, Zelina 1-6, Hayden 5-3, Huff 6-3, Long 1-2, Gillian 1-0; **OREGON**— Welch 21-49, Pitcaithley 5-9, Olson 1-9, Camplin 2-5, Marshall 7-4, Veruti 1-3, Harrington 4-minus 17.
PASSING
OSU— Kern 11-19-113-1, Maciejowski 1-4-55-1, Long 0-2-0-2;
ORE— Olson 1-1-40-0, Harrington 5-12-36-1, Pitcaithley 2-8-1-2.
 RECEIVING
OSU— Jankowski 4-75-1, Otis 3-40-0, Brockington 2-27-0, White 3-26-0.
ORE.— Lindsey 1-40-0, Schuler 4-29-1, Kantola 1-6-0, Welch 1-3-0, Smith 1-0-0.

GAME THREE

Photo Courtesy Mark Stier

Mark Stier was one of the keys to stopping Purdue.

Chapter 42

'GREATEST SHOW ON EARTH'

OHIO STATE 13, PURDUE 0

October 12, 1968...At Ohio Stadium

They called him "THE Golden Mr. Do-Everything" at Purdue. And the nickname fit Leroy Keyes to a T.

As a sophomore in 1966, the 6-3, 205-pounder from Newport News, Virginia played primarily as a defensive halfback. In his second varsity game against Notre Dame, he intercepted four passes, plucked a fumble in mid-air and raced 95 yards for a touchdown.

He also played a bit on offense, carrying the ball 12 times for 101 yards [8.4 yards average], caught two passes, threw for two touchdowns on the halfback option play and averaged 26.1 yards on seven kickoff returns. Purdue posted a gaudy 9-2 record for a share of the Big Ten title, then nipped Southern California, 14-13, in a Rose Bowl thriller.

In 1967, head coach Jack Mollenkopf switched his do-everything back to offense. Keyes rushed for 986 yards and 13 touchdowns, caught 45 passes for 758 yards and six more TDs. His 19 touchdowns led the nation in scoring as he became the first Big Ten performer to do so since the pre-World War II days of Michigan's Tom Harmon.

One of those victories was a 41-6 laugher over Ohio State. Keyes didn't have to strut his stuff in this romp. He gained 39 yards on six attempts, including a 21-yard TD to pad the Boilermakers' halftime cushion to 35-0. He also caught four passes for 64 yards.

As the 1968 season began, Leroy Keyes was rated as a genuine Heisman Trophy threat. He would finish second in the balloting to O.J. Simpson of Southern Cal, then carve out a successful eight-year NFL career with the Philadelphia Eagles and Kansas City Chiefs. He would be named Purdue's greatest football player ever.

Purdue was not only favored to capture the outright Big Ten title but was the pre-season pick to snare the national championship.

On the other hand, the sophomore-dominated Ohio State Buckeyes were a mystery. The raw talent was certainly there, but would the lack of battlefield experience prove to be their 'Achilles heel?'

The Boilermakers proved the pundits right by steamrolling past their first three opponents—West Virginia [44-6], Notre Dame [37-22] and Northwestern [43-6]. That's an average of 41 points per game.

Following it's impressive manhandling of Notre Dame, a national magazine called Purdue "coldly professional."

Ohio State bypassed SMU and Oregon. Thus, the stage was set for the October 12, 1968 meeting at Ohio Stadium.

Veteran Purdue head man Jack Mollenkopf was expecting a war. He knew Woody Hayes.

Class of '68

"I know Mr. Hayes and how much he's been after my hide. Woody used to be after my hide in other ways. But now I know he's been working on us ever since last year. That's gonna be a helluva game."

Woody Hayes was looking forward to the confrontation. "It's amazing what a great draw a great team has. Everyone wants to see this great Purdue team. I'm a little anxious myself. And if you sometimes wonder if it's really that good, just study the pictures of them in action like I did all Sunday night [the day following Purdue's 43-6 drubbing of Northwestern].

"It's a splendid football team, with splendid personal, extremely well coached. They have good plans and make then happen. They're big and agile. Any team that can stay in the ball game with them deserves a real high compliment."

Ohio State super scout Esco Sarkkinen had this to say about Purdue: "Most impressive is the fact it's a very good first down team...78 in three games. They have the ability to eat up first downs.

"This is a credit to Bob DeMoss, [offensive coordinator], a shrewd analyst. You've got to stay ahead of him because of his ability to diagnose your defense and pick them apart."

He made special mention of Leroy Keyes and sophomore quarterback Mike Phipps. "The running and passing of Keyes and Phipps is sheer classical form, but the unsung feature is Phipps in that he's an outstanding blocker. He's the guy who springs Keyes on many of his sweeps."

'Sark' was well aware of Keyes' least publicized, ability. "He's a remarkable decoy. Whenever he's flanked, he takes quite a bit from the defense since you've got to double cover him.

Purdue, he noted, runs from 10 different sets. "If you concentrate on Keyes and Phipps, they'll hurt you with Bob Dillingham at split end and Jim Kirkpatrick at wingback.

Dillingham, a 6-2, 192-pound junior from London, Ohio took over for the graduated Jim Bierne, a player Mollenkopf said couldn't be replaced.

"I've heard people say Bob couldn't do the job," snapped, DeMoss. "Well, all Dilly does is get open and catch the ball."

Dillingham set a school record 11 receptions for 147 yards and two TDs against Northwestern.

Northwestern head coach Alex Agase witnessed the Purdue juggernaut up-close-and-personal. "They have everything we thought they would, but they did it better than we expected."

While he was duly impressed with the elegance of Leroy Keyes, Agase noted, "Everybody overlooks Mike Phipps. And they've got a defense that's every bit as good as their offense."

Keyes began the '68 season modestly enough against Virginia. He picked up the tempo against Notre Dame and Northwestern.

Against Notre Dame, he ran for two touchdowns of 16 and 18 yards, gaining 90 yards in 15 carries. He threw a 17-yard TD pass on a halfback option play. He also caught three passes for 33 yards, two on vital third down situations.

Inserted at cornerback when Notre Dame was forced to pass, Keyes draped a blanket around Irish All-American end Jim Seymour. It was an all-around effort befitting a Heisman candidate. "Winning this game is more important than the Heisman," he said after the game.

270

"Lots of guys win the Heisman Trophy and you never hear of them again. But if you play on a championship team, they remember."

Jack Mollenkopf couldn't contain his joy. "Our kids rise for Notre Dame. They know the only way to get recognition is to beat the Irish. I didn't realize until now what a great thing it is to beat them."

Now ranked No.1 nationally, Purdue could have basked in the glow of the Notre Dame upset and simply gone through the motions against Northwestern. Instead, the Boilermakers kicked it into high gear in the second half, scoring five touchdowns enroute to their 37 point win.

Keyes scored the 'hat trick', all three touchdowns on runs of six yards. He carried 22 times for 96 yards, caught four passes for another 46 and then relaxed on the bench for much of the second half.

Starting out slowly, Purdue led 13-0 at halftime. The verdict was sealed during the opening series of the third period. Northwestern's Bob Doyle fumbled the kickoff. Purdue recovered on the Wildcats' 25.

Four plays later, Keyes rolled in for his second TD and it was 21-0.

Northwestern had lost to Southern Cal and O.J. Simpson the previous week, 24-7. Simpson carried 34 times for 189 yards. Northwestern coach Alex Agase considered Purdue the better team and Keyes the better all-around player.

After three games, Purdue ranked fourth nationally in scoring [41.3 points per game], 11th in total offense [437 yards per game average]. Ohio State's stingy defense ranked fourth against the run, allowing just 56 yards per game in two outings.

By midweek, Woody Hayes wasn't happy with the defense. "Fair" was his description. Defense coordinator, Lou McCullough was a bit more satisfied despite the fact that Cincinnati frosh Harry Howell, imitating Leroy Keyes, had run rampant at times during practice and even completed a 'bomb' to split end Dick Wakefield who was imitating Purdue's Bob Dillingham.

"We're getting better," he promised.

A highly partisan home crowd of 84,000-plus had a front seat on history and a prelude of wonderful things to come. Seemingly unbeaten Purdue could be beaten. Beaten far worse than the final 13-0 score really indicated. A team that hadn't been shut out in the last 28 games would limp out of Ohio, hoping to regroup for the battles that lie ahead.

Ohio State chewed up the clock as well as the natural turf, out gaining Purdue, 411-186 yards. Led by junior fullback Jim Otis, the Buckeyes marched for 335 yards on the ground, including 144 yards on 29 carries by the Celina, Ohio battering ram.

Soph halfback John Brockington added 69 yards on 10 carries in the second half. Junior Dave Brungard had 41 on 10 solos.

Ohio State's tenacious defense made life very uncomfortable for Mike Phipps, Purdue's usually very accurate-throwing quarterback. Phipps pulled the trigger 28 times but fired blanks on 18 occasions. That added up to 106 yards. Two of his passes were intercepted...one for a 35-yard touchdown gallop by junior defensive back Ted Provost. In fact, it got so bad for the shellshocked Phipps, he had to be replaced by Don Kiepert who missed four of six attempts. He gained only 23 yards.

It was simply TOTAL DOMINATION!

Ohio State coach Woody Hayes called it "the greatest defensive effort I've ever seen." And who would disagree with him?

Class of '68

While the Buckeyes chalked up big yardage in the first half, you couldn't tell that by merely looking at the scoreboard. It was scoreless at the break.

Junior placekicker Jim Roman should have sued his right leg for non-support. He missed two short field goal attempts while a third kick was blocked.

Twice Ohio State advanced to the Purdue 11 yard line, only to be pushed back by a pair of 15-yard penalties. Believe it or not, it happened during the same series.

The Buckeyes eventually made it to the Purdue four. What should have been a 'gimme' field goal turned out to be a misfire. Another drive stalled on the Purdue 22. Again, Roman couldn't split the uprights.

With only seven seconds left and Ohio State camped at the Purdue seven, Billy McKey blocked Roman's field goal try. Purdue kicker Jeff Jones wasn't any better. Twice the Boilermakers managed to advance to the Ohio State 14. Jones attempted field goals from the 21. He missed both.

That's how you end up with a scoreless opening half.

Unable to move the ball on the ground, Purdue desperately tried the air lanes after intermission. Phipps and Keyes combined for a nine-yard gain deep in Purdue territory. Jim Kirkpatrick plunged for a first down.

Phipps then threw a pass into the flat. Incomplete.

So he tried again. This time Ted Provost stepped in front of intended receiver Bob Dillingham and ran to daylight. A 35-yard TD and it was 6-0. The extra point kick failed.

By the second half, Purdue had given up on it's running game. Running into a brick wall just ain't much fun.

Midway in the third stanza, Purdue took position deep in it's own territory. Phipps tried a pass up the middle. He 'connected' with Ohio State noseguard, Jim Stillwagon, a 6-0, 220-pound sophomore from Mt. Vernon, Ohio.

Stillwagon picked it off on the Purdue 25. Otis banged out 16 yards on two attempts. Things were lookin' good. Only nine yards away from pay dirt. However, the Purdue defense stiffened, throwing Rex Kern for a five-yard loss.

Shaken up on the play, Kern had to leave the game.

Enter Billy Long, the deposed starting quarterback, a 6-1, 186-pound senior from Dayton Ohio.

It would be a long, long season for Long who would slip back to No.3 on the depth chart behind Kern and Maciejowski. Not exactly the way he had hoped to end his career. But for one shining moment, Billy Long was THE MAN.

It was third down on the Purdue 14. Long faded back to pass, but couldn't find a receiver. But he did see an opening up-the-middle.

Billy Long took off. He met no resistance until he reached the goal line. Four Purdue defenders tried to stop him in his tracks, but Billy Long refused to go down.

Touchdown. Fourteen-yards and a cloud of smoke.

Jim Roman salvaged something out of a miserable kicking day by adding the PAT [point-after-touchdown]. Ohio State's lead had 'swelled' to 13-0 with 19 minutes left to play.

Ohio State kicked off, but it was the same story for Purdue's punchless offense. Three downs and punt.

Starting on their own 47, the Buckeyes immediately coughed up the ball as Don Webster recovered on the OSU 48. However, Ohio State's unyielding defense more than met the challenge. Another futile offensive series for Purdue. Another punt.

Larry Smith's sixth punt of the game pinned the Buckeyes back on their own 10 yard line.

Sticking to the ground, Ohio State appeared on the move when 'fumblitis' struck for the third time. Purdue's Lenny Wirgowski recovered on the OSU 34.

While Purdue recovered two fumbles and it's defense played a gritty game, the offensive unit simply couldn't deliver a 'knockout punch'.

Following that fumble recovery, back-up quarterback Don Kiepert replaced Mike Phipps and seemed to infuse new life into the lifeless offense.

Kiepert connected on two passes for 23 yards. Purdue was on the Ohio State eight yard line. First-and-goal. But as the old saying goes, 'When the going gets tough the tough get going.'

In this case, the Buckeyes were very, very tough. In four downs, Purdue managed to gain only one yard. There was still 10 minutes left to play. In theory, plenty of time to suddenly come to life.

But realistically, it was all over.

Ohio State had waited an agonizing year to avenge the 41-6 shellacking. Now it would be Purdue's turn to count the days for the next meeting.

Purdue's Jack Mollenkopf tried to reduce the impact of the decisive setback. "This isn't the entire season. We've got six big games to go. Now we're going to find out just how tough we are. If one defeat ruined everything, we wouldn't have gone to the Rose Bowl two years ago. Nor would Indiana have gone last year.

"How many major teams were unbeaten last year? Just one and it was beaten on New Year's Day. So, we've got to start all over. We're going to find out how tough we are. We're going to find out if the students and the fans are behind our team, or just behind the No.1 ranking.

"I still think we have a great team. Now it's up to us to prove it the hard way by coming back from a great disappointment."

Mollenkopf was frustrated by his team's lack of offense.

"We weren't ready. Give the blame to me, but don't blame the boys. I over-estimated our offense, or underestimated their defense. In any event, we didn't do the things I thought we would be able to do.

"We had a lot of near misses and this had to be their [Ohio State's] best day. Sometimes it goes like that. It did for us on the same field last year.

"But whatever you do, don't fault our defense. The defense did a good job all day, and especially when it was backed up against the goal line. The defense gave up only one touchdown.

"Our offense just put too much on the defense all day long. Nearly everyone who played on offense made some mistakes. You just can't score without concentration and we didn't have that."

Mollenkopf added, "Woody out-coached me."

However, the veteran Ohio State coach would have none of that.

"Only thing wrong with me being a big shot and answering all these questions is that I don't do the job my coaches do. I don't monkey with the defense one bit any more."

So how did the Buckeyes dominate what Jack Mollenkopf had called "the best Purdue team I have ever coached?"

Class of '68

Hayes said early in the week "we can stop Keyes running. We're sure of it." Purdue cued it's offense. Leroy dotting the I and he'd run; Leroy flanked and Mike Phipps passed or the other backs—Perry Williams or Jim Kirkpatrick— ran.

In 1967, Purdue used Keyes as a decoy. Phipps went wild, completing 14 of 19 passes for 210 yards and rushing for 49 more. The Buckeyes never laid a hand on him.

A year later, Phipps literally had to run for his life. He missed 18 of 28 tries, had two intercepted, was thrown for 58 yards in losses by a relentless pass rush.

Keyes gained only 19 yards on seven carries, caught four passes for 44 yards...only one in the second half.

Mollenkopf explained the strange use of Keyes. His coaches in the press box said Ohio State "was taking away his running game with their ends and good linebackers."

Woody Hayes called that "the finest compliment I've ever had because nobody else stopped Leroy."

Hayes rated this game right up with a 17-0 shutout of Michigan in 1955 as an all-time best. Delighted Ohio State publicist, Bill Snypp said "it deserves a special Oscar...replaces Ringling Brothers as the greatest show on earth."

OHIO STATE 13, PURDUE 0

	OSU	PUR
First downs	22	16
Rushing Yardage	335	57
Passing Yardage	78	129
Return Yardage	30	11
Passes	8-16-0	12-34-2
Fumbles Lost	2	0
Yards Penalized	96	43

Ohio State	0	0	13	0-	13
Purdue	0	0	0	0-	0

OSU—Provost, 35, interception [kick failed]
OSU— Long, 14, run [Roman kick]

RUSHING
OSU— Otis 29-144, Brockington 10-69, Kern 11-45, Brungard 10-41, Huff 4-17, Long 1-14, Zelina 2-3; **PUR**— Williams 11-29, Keyes 7-19, Kirkpatrick 4-17, Phipps 12-minus 4, Kiepert 1-minus 4.
PASSING
OSU— Kern 8-16-78-0, Brungard 0-1-0-0; **PUR.**— Phipps 10-28-106-2, Kiepert 2-6-23-0.
RECEIVING
OSU— Jankowski 2-23, Otis 3-22, White 1-16, Zelina 1-11, Kuhn 1-6; **PUR.**— Keyes 4-44, Dillingham 3-34, Williams 2-26, Kirkpatrick 2-16, Engelbrecht 1-9.

Chapter 43

ANATOMY OF AN UPSET

In 1967, Purdue humbled Ohio State, 41-6. The Boilermakers enjoyed a 35-0 lead at halftime. It was the Buckeyes' worst defeat in the last 36 games. Woody Hayes would plot and plan revenge for a year. Short in patience but long on memory, he entrusted the 'battle plan' to defensive coordinator Lou McCullough.

On paper it figured to be a mismatch, Ohio State's sophomore-dominated team against the top-ranked powerhouse in the country. A veteran juggernaut triggered by quarterback Mike Phipps and do-everything back Leroy Keyes. The result: a stunning 13-0 upset victory, a springboard to an unbeaten, untied season and Hayes' second national championship.

LOU McCULLOUGH, In his own words:

I'll never forget the 1967 Ohio State-Purdue game. They killed us. In fact, they scored twice while I was coming out of the press box. I couldn't believe it; I was furious. We shouldn't have thrown the ball. That's another story. They beat the daylights out of us. We were determined it wouldn't happen in '68. And you do that by knowing the enemy as well as you know yourself. You do that with long-range planning.

I got all their films from the 1967 season and had 'em duplicated. I took their 10 best passes and 10-12 best running plays and made a film.

I made several copies and sent it around all Summer long to our defensive people, to let them look at and study. Each one of our linebackers had a copy.

Don't ever give 'em something unless you test 'em. I would send various situations and various formations. I would include at least 15 questions on the test.

I started this procedure about the middle of July. I sent out the tests once a week. I spent a lot of time on the phone, quizzing each one of our defensive players.

We had scouted 'em so much and seen 'em so much. It seems like a thousand times. I'd study the films every night.

I knew what they could do and what they couldn't do. We knew their tendencies. We knew Purdue was smart. Very smart.

Bob DeMoss was their offensive coordinator. He called the plays. He was very, very good. So we figured if we took away something, he's gonna see it and he's gonna counter. That's how good he was. We figured on him being that smart.

And he played right into our hands. That's how we intercepted the pass to score our first touchdown.

If we took a certain pass away with a defense, we figured he would see that and he'd call a quick out-and-cut to Leroy Keyes.

We figured when he would call that outcut pass, we're gonna have a 'Robber' on. We even told Coach Hayes we would do it. It's in his book.

I believe Lou Holtz and Earle Bruce had a bet. I know in the press box we told the offensive coaches 'We're gonna intercept this one for a touchdown. Here it comes.'

Class of '68

It was our third game of the season, our first Big Ten game. And here we're playing the No. 1 team in the country.

We opened up against SMU and they threw a lot of passes. That was good because it gave us a crash course on pass defense. We learned an awful lot.

SMU had that little old Levias kid. Boy, he was good.

Our second game was at Oregon. We dedicated their stadium.

Next was powerful and seemingly unbeatable Purdue.

It must have been second down because Purdue had thrown a pass right before the big play. We put 'The Robber' on, figuring he—Phipps—was gonna throw the outcut.

And he did. That left a man free. Ted Provost could come up, gamble, cut right in front of Leroy Keyes and take the pass away. He went 35 yards for the touchdown to give us a 6-0 lead.

Jim Stillwagon intercepted another Phipps' pass around the 25-yard line, and ran it to the Purdue 14. Billy Long came in to replace Rex Kern, and ran up-the-middle for our second score. We beat 'em, 13-0.

Our offense played a fair game. Our defense was the difference.

Chapter 44

AN OLD RIVAL

Bob DeMoss enrolled at Purdue in 1945. He came to play basketball. Instead, he carved out a fine career on the gridiron. He quarterbacked the Boilermakers from 1945-48. After a short stint in the NFL with the New York Bulldogs, he returned to his alma mater and remained until 1993. DeMoss began his career as quarterback coach, then held positions as freshman coach, backfield coach/ offensive coordinator, head football coach—1970-1972—and assistant athletic director until his retirement. He still maintains close ties with Purdue as game manager during the home football season.

BOB DeMOSS. West Lafayette, Indiana.
I was born-and-raised in Dayton, Kentucky. Population about 5,000. I played basketball and football in high school.

We played the Single Wing back then. I wasn't a runner, believe me. I was tall—almost 6-3—and skinny—150 pounds. I really considered myself more of a basketball player than a football player when I came to Purdue.

As fate would have it, football would hold the key to my career.

I was starting quarterback for four years, from 1945-1948. I played against some darned good teams. Michigan was national champion. Notre Dame was national champion.

I started as a freshman against Ohio State which was ranked as No. 1 in the country.

We went over to Columbus, and in front of 78,000, we upset 'em 35-13. I was scared to death. I'm playing against all the guys that were my heroes two years before that.

Heck, I was a basketball player. I didn't know what I was doing. But anyway, we beat 'em. Head Coach Cecil Isabel did a great job. They had a great football team. I go back a long way against Ohio State.

After my college career, I was drafted by the New York Bulldogs of the National Football League and by the Baltimore Colts of the rival All-American Conference.

My professional career lasted all of five exhibition games and four regular season games with the Bulldogs. I was backup quarterback to Bobby Layne. Bobby would pick me up in his Cadillac for practice every day. It was great. He was great.

After the fourth game, the Bulldogs dropped me. The New York Yankees of the All-American Conference were a very good team. All they needed was a quarterback. They invited me to practice with them. I did that, but I wasn't allowed to sign. The Colts held my draft rights. I was caught in the middle. I was shut out.

So, I went back home to Indiana. I was a spectator at our next-to-last home game when Stu Holcomb talked to me. He was my coach in 1947 and 1948.

Class of '68

He said 'I want you to come back. I've got four freshmen quarterbacks next year. I want you to coach the quarterbacks. What do you think?' I said 'I'll be there.' So that's how it all started.

Jack Mollenkopf had been our defensive coordinator from 1947-1955. He became head coach in 1956. That was Len Dawson's last season. Over the years Purdue has been blessed with a series of great quarterbacks. Guys like Dale Samuels, Bernie Allen, Ross Fichtner, Mike Phipps, Ron DiGravio, Bob Griese and Gary Danielson. I had some good guys to work with.

For years the Big Ten had a rule. Only the Big Ten champion could go to a Bowl game...and that was the Rose Bowl. And you couldn't go in consecutive years.

It's a totally different story nowadays. It seems like 5-7 schools gets various bowl invitations every year. In my last year as head coach—1972—my team finished third in the Big Ten. We had a 6-5 record. That would have been good enough.

Bob Griese's last year was 1966. He led Purdue to a 14-13 victory over Southern Cal in the Rose Bowl. That was an excellent team. Unfortunately, we had to play both Notre Dame and Michigan State who were co-national champions.

In 1967 we had nine starters back from that Rose Bowl team. The only major replacement we had to make was at quarterback, and we had a young man from Columbus, Indiana named Mike Phipps.

In Mike's three years, Purdue went 8-2, 8-2 and 8-2. He finished second in the Heisman Trophy voting his senior year. We never lost to Notre Dame during that span.

As I said, league rules prevented us from going back to the Rose Bowl. Mike was a sophomore and Leroy Keyes a junior in 1968. Leroy had played in the Rose Bowl as a defensive back.

In '67 we went to Columbus, to the lions' den, and whipped Ohio State, 41-6. After our last practice before that game I said to myself 'we're not ready to play.'

At halftime we had a 35-0 lead. We go into the locker room and everyone's jumping up-and-down. A lot of the assistant coaches had the feeling the game was over. They were ready to get on the bus.

Not me. I've been in that stadium many times and I've seen Ohio State come back and kick the daylights out of people when the game appeared to be over at halftime.

I'm looking for Jack Mollenkopf, and I can't find him. He's back in the intramural locker room sitting there. He said to me, 'Tell me I'm not dreaming.'

I said, 'You're not dreaming.' I told him about the atmosphere and he said, 'We'll go in and take care of this.'

I replied, 'We take the kickoff in the second half. Let's see what happens and we can go from there.' Mollenkopf agreed.

We got the kickoff and scored in five plays to make it 41-0. At that point, Coach Mollenkopf pulled his first unit off the field. We played the rest of the game with the second team which was a good thing to do.

It was just one of those days. We could have scored 80 points. I think we could have scored any time we wanted to. We had no reason to do that. Life is too short for all that stuff. After the game, Woody thanked him for calling off the dogs.

In the 1968 pre-season polls, we were picked No. 1 in one poll and Notre Dame No. 1 in the other poll. Both teams lived up to their billing to set up a Purdue-Notre Dame clash at South Bend.

We sure as heck looked like a Number One team that day as we beat Notre Dame, 37-22. We kicked the heck out of 'em.

278

You never dominate Notre Dame. You outguess 'em sometimes. That's what happened in '68.

We had a guy catch 11 passes that day, a kid named Bob Dillingham. They were doubling up on Leroy Keyes. We hurt 'em with Leroy the year before by putting him out wide as a flanker and throwing the ball to him one-on-one. Notre Dame remembered that, so we went back to the weak side and kept throwing the ball to Dillingham.

That made us the undisputed No. 1 team. We knew Ohio State was coming up in two weeks, but in this game you don't look ahead. You go week-by-week, game-by-game.

We easily won our third game against Northwestern. We were averaging 41 points a game and looked unbeatable. Offensively, we'd use a little bit of everything. We went with two tight ends and three strong backs. We spread out the field. We went with doubles on one side. We did the same thing the year before.

In 1967, we scored 291 points. We scored 291 points in '68.

If anyone would have told me we would hold Ohio State to 13 points, I would have been delighted. Certainly we felt our offense was capable of scoring at least 13 points.

We knew Ohio State was talented. They had a wonderful group of sophomores. I knew they were still smarting over the 35-point loss the year before. But we thought we were still good enough to win even though we had to replace three interior linemen, a good wide receiver on offense, and had to replace seven starters on defense.

After all, we were 3-0 and had disposed of Notre Dame.

Our offense hadn't changed much from 1967-to-1968. We saw no reason to change what had been working so well for us. As Woody used to say 'You win with people.' We had good people.

We thought we were ready to play. I wasn't worried about Ohio State. I was concerned only with our team. Your staff is concerned about the mentality of your own ball club.

The first half was scoreless. Our offense couldn't generate anything. Ohio State was marching up-and-down the field, but our defense was holding on.

On several occasions during the first half Ohio State's defense really stuffed us. I'm talking about third-and-one, and third-and-two situations for a first down.

Ohio State met the challenge.

Everyone knows that Ohio State had a potent offense in 1968 with that young Rex Kern at quarterback, Jim Otis at fullback and a group of very talented backs such as Leo Hayden and John Brockington. When Brockington is playing backup to Otis you know Ohio State is loaded offensively.

To me, the key to their wonderful season was the defense. They were so quick. Jim Stillwagon was very, very hard to handle playing noseguard. And that Jack Tatum was a force at strong safety. I could go on-and-on.

At halftime we're just trying to find out what's going on. We're going through our normal routine. The head coach says 'Get your offense together, get your defense together. Let's see what's going on.'

We talk to our players. I'm the offensive coordinator and we haven't scored a point. I remember asking Perry Williams, our fullback, 'What's wrong?' He said, 'I don't know.'

We decided to stick with the game plan the second half and try to do better.

But it didn't do any good. They just outplayed us. Ohio State seemed to run against us with ease. They really took it to our defensive unit. The only touchdown their offense could generate was a scamper by their backup quarterback, Billy Long, on a busted play.

They scored their first touchdown on a pass interception. I think Ted Provost picked it off on an automatic.

All the credit goes to Ohio State. They did their homework. They knew our game plan as well as we knew it. There was no shame in losing 13-0 to the national champions. You're gonna win some, you're gonna lose some. We won a lot more than we lost.

The statistics show that Leroy Keyes gained only 19 yards rushing on seven carries. He never was a factor. Truth is Leroy got dinged in the game. He got hurt. That's why he didn't play that much.

I remember he went off tackle one time and we had to take him out of the game. But I honestly don't believe it would have made a difference with a healthy Leroy Keyes. Ohio State simply deserved to win the game.

Leroy Keyes and Mike Phipps were exceptional players, exceptional young men. Believe it or not, Leroy wasn't a highly sought-after player. Out of Virginia, his team beat schools like Hampton Institute and Norfolk State.

Fortunately, we had a coach on our staff —Bernie Miller— who was from that area. Leroy was a very versatile athlete. He wasn't a horse. He was a thoroughbred.

As a sophomore, he played safety. We used him on offense as a tailback, a wide receiver. He even ran back kickoffs.

Mike Phipps was a local boy who made good. He was a wonderful quarterback. In his senior year he carried a young football team on his back. We went 8-2 and beat Notre Dame again.

Let me tell you how good Mike was. Leroy Keyes ran crazy against Illinois for 295 yards. You know who the lead blocker was? Mike Phipps on the toss.

Our quarterbacks always led the toss. Mike Phipps sprung him about four times for big gains. He was very unselfish, a good, tough football player.

Mike finished second in the Heisman Trophy voting in 1969. I think he lost it when Ohio State buried us 42-14. Woody poured it on. I'll never forgive him for it.

He was running Otis the last two minutes of the game, getting another touchdown. That made it 42-7. We scored late, but by then the game was long over. I didn't like it considering we called the dogs off early in the second half—1967— after we had a huge lead.

I go a long way back with Woody Hayes. I recruited against him from 1952-1972. He was hard to beat. He was a charmer. As a coach, he did a good job. He took his talent and used it well.

His kids loved him. Randy Hart played for Woody, played tackle for him. He was one of our assistant coaches when Jim Young was named head coach. Randy thought the world of Woody.

One thing for sure, Woody's kids sure knew how to block. I coached a couple of 'em in All-Star games. Allan Jack was recruited as a fullback, but they made him an offensive guard at Ohio State. He was a good one. In the All-Star game he was telling me how to block on certain plays. I said 'That's a pretty good idea,' so we blocked that way. They were well coached.

Chapter 45

THE GREATEST EVER

Leroy Keyes was born-and-raised in Newport News, Virginia. A three sports star in high school—football, basketball, track—he attended Purdue University. Concentrating on football, Keyes was a do-everything performer, an All-American who finished second to O.J. Simpson of Southern Cal in the Heisman Trophy balloting.

Keyes went on to play five years in the NFL with Philadelphia and Kansas City. For more than a quarter century, he served in the Philadelphia, Pennsylvania school system. He returned to Purdue as running back coach in 1995. He now serves as administrative assistant for football operations.

Number 23 was named Purdue's greatest football player.

LEROY KEYES. West Lafayette, Indiana.

I grew up in the segregated South. That's how it was in the 60s. I went to George Washington Carver High School which was an all-black school with a student enrollment of about 230.

I played football, basketball, and ran track. I guess I was born little, but by the time I was in ninth grade, I reached my full height of six-three-and-a-half.

As an eighth grader, I was on the junior varsity basketball team. As a ninth grader, I started in basketball. I was a forward. I averaged 19.2 points as a freshman, 23 as a sophomore, 25 as a junior and 29.2 points, seven assists and 12 rebounds a game in my senior season.

I was a starting safety and punter for the varsity football team my freshman year in high school. For my first two years I was also quarterback, but I didn't like it so I moved to running back my last two years. I also did the kickoffs.

I ran the relays in track. I was a sprinter, but I was kinda lazy. My best event was what they called the broad jump back then. It's now called long jump. I set a state record of almost 25 feet which may still stand today.

The blacks played in their own league. The whites played in their league. They were front page news in the Sports section. We were back page news.

But all that changed because of a guy named Charlie Karmosky who did a lot of writing for the daily paper. He knew of my exploits, and he became a 'revolutionary' by getting us onto the front page.

I was a C-plus, B student in high school. I know I should have done better, but I didn't fully realize the importance of good grades. I thought my athletic skills would take me anywhere I wanted to go.

I had my share of college overtures. For instance, I had feelers from Notre Dame, Penn State, Syracuse and Illinois for football, UCLA in basketball, New Mexico State in track.

Admittedly, I didn't do too well in my college entrance board exam. The night before I took the exam, I attended my senior high school prom. In fact, I was still wearing my tuxedo when I went to Hampton College to take the test.

Class of '68

When the results became known, almost every school jumped ship on me. But not Purdue. Purdue still wanted me to visit and re-take the exam as well as the SAT. They said they'd pay for it. I said, 'Fine.'

So, I went to Purdue and took both tests. I scored 1,300 in the college entry board the second time and passed the SAT test. All of a sudden, I get a call from Buddy Young of Illinois, Joe Paterno of Penn State, Ben Schwartzwalder of Syracuse. I even got a call from Army.

But I said to each and every one of them, 'Thank you gentlemen. But where were you when I was down?'

Purdue had been loyal to me. I knew I had to be loyal to Purdue.

A coach named Bernie Miller was the one who recruited me for Purdue. Even though he was at Iowa State, he was recruiting the Virginia area. When he left Iowa State for Purdue, he was allowed to continue to recruit in Virginia.

There was another reason I decided to go to Purdue. It may sound crazy but it's true. When Purdue flew me out on my visit, I was wined-and-dined, so to speak. Strictly first class treatment.

I met a football player named Jim Long. Jim was big. I'd say 6-5 and 265-270 pounds. Here I was a pretty darned good basketball player, so going a little one-on-one against Jim wasn't at all intimidating. I'd met a lot of big bodies in high school.

Well, he beat me up physically.

I knew I had to come back to Purdue and get even with this guy. He owed me something. When I told my friends that story after I returned to Virginia, they all said 'That couldn't be the reason why.'

It was one of the reasons.

Jim was a senior. We became very good friends. When I returned to Purdue after all those years, Jim was one of the first people to contact me.

I could have played both football and basketball in college. But I promised myself I'd graduate in four years and I didn't think I could do that by playing two sports. So, basketball had to go.

I played on my fraternity team. We'd have an exhibition game between the football team and the freshman basketball team. I guarded the great Rick Mount and held him to eight points.

Oh yes, about Jim Long. We played against each other. The next time, I took him to school.

We didn't play any games as freshmen. We'd just practice and play on the scout team. Let's say the varsity was going to play Michigan State.

I'd imitate Gene Washington because we were both about the same height. They'd give me jersey Number 84 and I'd run his pass routes. Like a 12-yard drag, a 15-yard deep curl, or whatever.

I got a lot of experience as a freshman.

Purdue had a long history of recruiting blacks that went back to the early 1950s. I was one of four black football players. As sophomores, we were all varsity starters.

As a sophomore, I was the No. 2 flanker and the starting left cornerback. The only spot that Purdue needed to fill was at the left corner.

We tied for the Big Ten championship and won the Rose Bowl. The highlight for me was my second start. It was against Notre Dame. I recovered a fumble in mid-air and went 95 yards for the touchdown. I had 11 solo tackles as well. We played a lot of man-to-man that game. My job was to shadow Nick Eddy, their tailback/flanker. I did OK.

People seem to think that when Purdue shifted me to offense my last two years, I was primarily a tailback. Not really. I was a flanker.

Whenever we ran what we called 'Student Body Right, Student Body Left,' I'd line up as the I-back, or tailback in the I formation, Perry Williams was fullback. Jimmy Kirkpatrick was the running back, Mike Phipps the quarterback. They just tossed me the ball. The guard, quarterback and fullback would block for me. I'd sit back there, accelerate a little bit and explode. It worked.

Very seldom was I running what I call ISO-PLAYS between guard and tackle. It was off tackle and wide. But in my senior year they found out I had a little more power so they gave me the ball and I ran wherever they wanted me to run. But I was still a flanker. I probably averaged 15 carries a game. Guys like O.J. Simpson of Southern Cal, Ron Johnson of Michigan and Iowa's Ed Podolak ran the ball a lot more than I did.

I carried a max 198 at Purdue. I was tall and slim.

We were a veteran team going into the 1968 season. We were solid across the board. The only thing I can say 30 years later is that the only thing that beat us that season was ourselves.

We took two teams too lightly and it taught us a lesson. We should have won the national championship. Instead, we lost to Ohio State and Minnesota and finished 8-2.

Two weeks before we met Ohio State we went to Notre Dame in the battle of the unbeatens. We were ranked No. 1 in two different polls. We went to South Bend with confidence. We knew we could beat Notre Dame.

We just outplayed 'em. We just did what we had to do. We tackled that day. We hustled for the ball. Offensively, we sustained our drives, got the first downs when we needed the first down. We took it to 'em strong.

In that game, I went both ways. I played cornerback on defense and wide-out on offense. I did a little shadowing of Notre Dame's great receiver, Jim Seymour. Wherever he went, I went. They were more afraid to win than we were.

When you play against Woody Hayes and Ohio State you know his team is prepared, especially since we gave them a real pasting the year before.

On paper, we were the stronger team. We were the seasoned, veteran team. Although we were warned not to take any team for granted, we might have been a little cocky. After all, we beat Notre Dame. We were No. 1.

Football was my first love. That's why I gave up a chance of playing major college basketball. I just enjoyed the exhilaration. I enjoyed making the impact on 10 other players. I got a great satisfaction of having the guys looking up to me.

I'm not trying to take anything away from Ohio State. They played their game and we didn't. I felt that I was personally a major part of our failure in that game. I wasn't able to perform up to my usual standard. I wasn't able to be Leroy Keyes. Going into that game I'd say I was 35 percent healthy. My back had gone out. I don't know how it happened.

Class of '68

I couldn't bend over. I couldn't get into a two-point stance. I could hardly move it was so bad. I couldn't feel my feet. It was a sciatic nerve. I'd never experienced the problem before.

I can't remember getting hurt in the Notre Dame game. Sometimes when you're walking you take a wrong step. Maybe you slip on a rainy day. Your body sends you a message. It says 'No, No.'

I told my coaches I'd give it a try. But anytime there's something physically wrong with you, you're not playing at 100 percent efficiency. I don't know what football player can go onto the field at 50 percent or 75 percent and still do the things he normally does. I don't recall how much of the game I played. It seems like I'd go in for a play and then come out. I'd be on the sidelines trying to get back in shape so I could get back in and help my team.

We missed two field goals in the first half. We couldn't generate any offense and yet it was scoreless. Ohio State ran up-and-down the field at will, particularly their big fullback Jim Otis. And yet the game was scoreless.

And when Ohio State finally scored on a 35-yard run off an intercepted pass, Mike Phipps put the ball exactly where he wanted. The pass was intended for me. I just couldn't get to it on time.

Hey, the guy read it, stepped in to make a great catch and took it the distance. Mike goes back and plants. It looks like he's going to throw right, but he comes back to the left, to the wide side of the field. It was a 15-yard curl.

When you throw a curl route or an out to the wide side of the field, if the defensive back or linebacker picks it off the only thing between him and the end zone is the yard markers.

That's what happened.

It felt like I was running in cement boots. You're trying. The adrenalin is flowing. You're upbeat. But nothing is happening. It felt like I was going in slow motion, but I wasn't going anywhere.

If you're healthy, you can flat out clear a zone. You can drive the linebacker or defensive back off, cut on the ball, catch it, turn around and make something happen.

Or you can get a toss, plant your feet on the ground and accelerate into a hole. But I could do none of those things.

I got a shot before the game. At halftime you put ice on the back, get a massage. I took painkillers. I would go in for a play, carry the ball, get tackled and leave the field.

As I look back at the game by looking at the game films, and by word that came back from Columbus, they may have assigned Jack Tatum, their outstanding rover back, on me. I believe he shadowed me.

I think Ohio State did a great job scouting Purdue. They took us out of our offense. Basically, they rushed for monster yards, but they didn't score anything on the ground.

Outside of the interception and the quarterback scramble for the second touchdown, the game could have gone either way. They got those two breaks and capitalized on it. We couldn't sustain anything.

After the game we were kinda downcast. We looked at each other and said, 'We let this one get away.' But there was still a bunch of games left on our schedule.

284

We had only one conference loss and we felt we could still win this thing. We felt destiny was in our own hands. That was before our stinker at Minnesota.

We went up to Minnesota, and for some reason we just weren't ready to play football. It's as simple as that. I think we went there with the attitude 'This team doesn't belong on the same field with us.' We went up there and they taught us a real lesson.

We were down 34-0 at halftime. We rallied in the second half. We were playing on emotion. We were playing on pride. We knew we were better than them. We gave Minnesota quite a scare, but we just couldn't go ahead.

We ended up losing something like 34-31. We would have liked to have gone unbeaten that season. We still were one of the better teams in the country.

We came up short two games that we could have and should have won. The Minnesota loss was three times as painful as the 13-0 loss to Ohio State.

Photo courtesy Purdue University

Leroy Keyes Career Achievements

*Inducted into Virginia Sports Hall of Fame.

*Inducted into Hampton Roads Hall of Fame.

*Inducted into Collegiate Football Hall of Fame.

*National Football Foundation Hall of Fame (1990).

***Chosen by public vote as the Greatest Player in the
100 year history of football at Purdue University.**

GAME FOUR

Woody called sophomore tight end Jan White a gem. "We haven't had one this strong, not even Jim Houston."

Chapter 46

TO SKIN A WILDCAT

OHIO STATE 45, NORTHWESTERN 21

October 19, 1968...At Ohio Stadium

Ohio State's herd of talented running backs rumbled for more than 300 yards in the Buckeyes' 13-0 blanking of top-ranked Purdue.

Jim Otis and Company simply took advantage of offensive tackles Dave Foley and Rufus Mayes great blocking ability to virtually gain at will.

Hugh Hindman, OSU's offensive line coach, oozed praise for his 'Twin Towers', these 6-5, 250-pounders."They did an outstanding job against the huge Purdue defense. Rufus graded 80 percent and Dave 77 percent. The way we grade, anything over 70 percent is a fine job.

"Each played his finest game. This is the first time they've been physically healthy. Rufus started the season with a sprained ankle. Dave hurt his knee against Oregon."

Considered prime pro prospects, Foley and Mayes had different styles. Explained Hindman:

"Dave is more an inside type blocker. Rufus is geared more to pass blocking and outside blocking. That's why we flip-flop our line to better utilize their special abilities."

Foley, an All-Ohio tackle at Cincinnati [Ohio] Bacon High School, was a three-year starter [at tackle] for Ohio State. Mayes, on the other hand, played tight end for two years. He was shifted to offensive tackle during Spring drills.

"Considering the things he's had to learn, he's come along very well," added Hindman. "He will improve greatly."

Hindman compared Foley and Mayes to Ohio State tackles Bob Vogel and Daryl Sanders who played in the early 1960s, "If they continue to play like they did Saturday [against Purdue]." Both Vogel and Sanders became NFL starters in their rookie seasons.

Their assignment against Northwestern would be to face-off against two smaller but quicker defensive tackles in 240-pounders Bill Galler and Frank Mullins.

While Ohio State stunned Purdue, defending national champion Southern Cal bounced back into first place in the United Press International Board of Coaches poll.

USC, unbeaten in four starts, received 21 first place votes and 329 points. Ohio State vaulted from fifth to second place, receiving eight first place votes and 296 points.

Purdue slipped from first to fifth place.

Woody Hayes' Buckeyes were immediately installed as 20-point favorites against visiting and winless Northwestern [0-4].

Despite a commanding 10-3 career record against Northwestern, Woody Hayes knew it usually didn't come easy against the pesky Wildcats.

Only twice had Ohio State enjoyed a laugher—49-0 in 1955 and 47-6 in 1957. Enroute to a 6-3 season record in 1967, Ohio State clawed out a 6-2 decision. That's right. Six-to-two.

Class of '68

"Northwestern's always been tough on us. We studied films of the Northwestern-Purdue game all Sunday evening," said Hayes "and this made us realize what an amazing job our defense did against Purdue.

"Northwestern's always had a good defensive team, but couldn't contain Purdue nearly as well as our defense did."

This pointed out the perils of winning to Woody Hayes.

"Whenever you win you get a lot of friends...and a lot of dedicated enemies. They all shoot at you as we did against Purdue last Saturday."

In 1967, Northwestern won the battle of statistics. It wasn't even close. The 'Cats had a 17-11 bulge in first downs and a 243-173 total yardage advantage.

It took a 44-yard second half kickoff return by Dave Brungard to set up the game's only touchdown. Ohio State deliberately gave up the two-point safety to keep Northwestern at bay.

"Last year we did everything against Ohio State except score," said Northwestern head coach Alex Agase."Son-of-a-gun, we're meeting another No.1."

Not yet.

Ohio State super scout, Esco Sarkkinen discounted the Wildcats' winless record. "Northwestern no longer is awed by its opposition. Agase is a wily coach. He has good game plans against us. His players are aggressive, competitive type of athletes.

"And if you're looking for signs of Northwestern being demoralized, they're not. They hang in there."

Maybe it was all rhetoric. Ohio State buried Northwestern, 45-21, before 83,454 roaring fans at Ohio Stadium.

What a perfect Saturday afternoon.

Ohio State piled up a school record 565 yards in keeping pace with Michigan and Minnesota for the early Big Ten lead, all at 2-0.

To punctuate the perfect day, even Woody Hayes got into the act. He fielded a Northwestern quick-kick cleanly. " I failed to call for a fair catch," he quipped, "so that I could show my players how easy it is to catch a football."

Rex Kern, Ohio State's exciting soph quarterback, accounted for 291 of those record 565 yards. The previous team record had been 526 yards enroute to a 51-15 rout of Illinois in 1962.

Kern collected 121 yards in 20 rushes and 170 yards passing on eight of 14 completions. He came within 22 yards of equaling the single-game yardage record set by John Borton in 1952 against Washington State. All of Borton's yardage came through the air.

Battered in Ohio State's three previous games, particularly in the Oregon slugfest, Kern's jaw managed to stay hinged to the rest of his body.

Kern teamed up with soph tight end Jan White for a 72-yard touchdown as well as a 23-yard TD pass to another sophomore, wide receiver Bruce Jankowski.

Kern's more-than-capable understudy, Ron Maciejowski completed two of three passes, including a 37-yard touchdown strike.

The Buckeyes rushed for 347 yards and added 218 through the air in amassing 28 first downs.

Agase called Ohio State "the best of the five teams we've met. Kern's the guy who really hurt us most when he was still in the game."

288

Said Hayes, "Our offense was much better, but our defense was not sharp. We had about 10 sophomores in there and I didn't want to hide them. The difference between me and other coaches is you give me good football players and I'll letcha know about it. This is the best squad in depth we've ever had."

He was well aware of the pitfalls that could lie ahead. Especially with a young team.

"When a team is up that's when players get fatheaded...and that's where a mean old coach comes in. I worried more about Northwestern than I did Purdue. I thought we'd do well against Purdue, but against Northwestern I wasn't sure. I thought we'd be soft."

Woody Hayes had reason to be concerned.

Ohio State took the opening kickoff, charged down to the Northwestern 14 but had to give up the ball on downs. Kern romped for 23 and 17 yards. On a fourth down sweep, however, he was stopped for only a yard gain.

The Buckeyes quickly regained possession. This time, they would not be denied. Kern fired and soph tight end Jan White snared the pass on the Wildcats' 47, then outdistanced two defenders to complete the electrifying 72-yard play. Jim Roman's PAT failed and it was 6-0.

On the ensuing kickoff, Tim Anderson's boot went out of bounds on the Northwestern 47. 'Cats soph quarterback Dave Shelbourne spearheaded an 11-play scoring drive with a 15-yard TD pass to Pat Harrington. Dick Emmerich's kick gave underdog Northwestern a 7-6 lead. It marked the first time in the 1968 season—a span of 17 quarters—that Ohio State had trailed an opponent.

Northwestern tried to pull out all the stops, including a quick kick. The 'Cats second quick kick in as many quarters paid off as Ohio State took over on it's own 26. Kern found Jankowski for gains of 10 and 15. He hit White for nine. Kern let his feet do the talking with a twisting 20-yard scamper up-the-middle to the Northwestern 7.

The Buckeyes then displayed their own kind of razzle-dazzle. Junior fullback Jim Otis vaulted over the line on what appeared to be a direct handoff from Kern.

Northwestern went for Otis' excellent fake. All Rex Kern had to do was to tuck the ball on his sweep and sweep into the end zone untouched. Ohio State 12, Northwestern 7.

A one-point conversion kick was the normal thing to do. But on this day, Ohio State wrote it's own script. A left-handed heave by 'kicker' Larry Zelina to holder Billy Long caught the Wildcats by surprise.

In fact, Ohio State would try this Zelina-to-Long connection again. It would fail only because Long slipped and fell on his way to the end zone. Northwestern, however, refused to fold.

Shelbourne flipped a screen pass to fullback Bob Olson, in the 'Cats 45. Only a touchdown-saving tackle by soph 'Rover back' Jack Tatum [Passaic, New Jersey] prevented the touchdown.

It was first-and-goal on the Ohio State four-yard line.

Shelbourne scored on the next play. Emmerich kicked the ball through the uprights and the game was tied at 14-14.

Time was running out in the first half.

Kern hit junior wingback Ray Gillian for 19 yards. Another Kern-to-Gillian

289

pass added up to 25 more yards. On the ninth play of the drive, Otis crashed across from the six. Roman's extra point kick gave Ohio State a hard-fought 21-14 edge at halftime.

Northwestern kept on clawing in the second half, moving from it's own 29 to the OSU 36. But on fourth down, Shelbourne's quarterback sneak fell just inches short of a first down.

Northwestern tried a quick kick for the third time in the game, but this time the maneuver backfired. The punt went out-of-bounds on the Northwestern 41. In fact, Woody Hayes caught it in front of the Ohio State bench.

Following three rushing plays for 18 yards, Kern fired a 23-yard TD strike to Jankowski. Roman's kick failed. OSU had a 27-14 lead.

The Wildcats, however, had one more growl. Once again, Shelbourne was the triggerman, engineering a 72-yard scoring drive. He found soph end Jon Hittman for gains of 21 and 14 yards, plus the final six. Emmerick converted and the gap was narrowed to six points, 27-21.

Sophomore tailback Leo Hayden ran back the kickoff 17 yards. Kern and White teamed up for another 17. Fading back to pass again, Rex Kern appeared trapped.

But like a cat with nine lives, he wiggled loose and found Hayden for 16. However, Kern was shaken up on the play and replaced by Billy Long.

Long, who had scored a 14-yard TD against Purdue, again displayed his running ability with a 15-yard jaunt around left end. Otis ended the long march with a six-yard TD run. It was 33-21.

By the time the game ended, Ohio State had exploded for three touchdowns in the final quarter to turn a nail-biter into a romp.

Kern gained 121 yards rushing [20 attempts] and added 170 passing on eight of 14 completions for two touchdowns.

Otis gained 48 yards on 15 tries and scored twice.

All told, eight different Ohio State ball carriers had some fun. Also included were Dave Brungard [16-56], Hayden [6-51, 1 TD], Gillian [5-21], Horatius Greene [4-18], Zelina [2-17] and Long [1-15].

Soph backup QB Ron Maciejowski also had a profitable day, hitting 2-for-3 for 48 yards, including a 37-yard touchdown to Ed Bender.

Northwestern's Alex Agase called Ohio State "The best I've seen in recent years. They've got depth and what every good team needs—athletes with wonderful skills.

"Their offensive team is so much improved. The obvious reason is speed and that includes Kern who is no slowpoke. You can't cope with it for 60 minutes.

"We were tiring in the fourth quarter and those kids he put in made us look like we were in cement. They were fresh, besides fast.

"They would not help us with fumbles, interceptions or other mistakes. When you don't make mistakes, they're tough to stop. Usually teams help stop themselves some."

It certainly wasn't a typical Ohio State-Northwestern game.

"That's almost as much scoring as Ohio State scored in the last six games we've played. They never averaged over one touchdown in the last six encounters."

Alex Agase was proud of his team.

"We were in the ball game quite awhile and had a chance to win. We scored three times and that's the most we've scored all year and against a defense I have a lot of respect for."

Said Woody Hayes:

"Funny thing about football games. Last week our defense won the ball game. This week it was the other way around. Give Northwestern a lot of credit and I'm not just saying that because I'm supposed to.

"For two-and-a-half quarters they moved the ball against us better than anyone. We did not especially wear them down, but our offensive yardage was very efficient today where it had not been before. We hammered at the offense all week.

"This is a good, rugged Northwestern team. It reminds you of Ohio State in years gone by. They tried to stack us up in the middle like they did last year. We didn't want to make the same mistakes that we did then.

"We figured to go out wide and go deep. Pass more than we have. Later on, we ran the middle. Things work that way. This is as much passing as we have done in a long time."

Hayes then discussed Kern's injury. His super soph twice had to leave the game.

"The doctor explained to me that Rex's shoulder is something like a 'crazy bone.' If he's hit a certain way it becomes numb. Eventually it clears up...we hope by the next series of downs. He also has a tenderness about the hinges of his jaw where he was hit two weeks ago."

At one point in the game, Ohio State had 16 sophomores in the starting lineup."This is the best squad in depth we have ever had. I didn't say it was the best.

"I said the best in depth. Our coaches are doing a great job of getting these young people ready to play. This was a game with few mistakes. Our sophomores did not make the big mistake today."

OHIO STATE 45, NORTHWESTERN 21

	OSU	NU
First downs	28	18
Rushing Yardage	347	104
Passing Yardage	218	184
Return Yardage	65	115
Passes	10-19-0	16-31-2
Fumbles Lost	0	0
Yards Penalized	78	40

Northwestern	7	7	7	0-	21
Ohio State	6	15	6	18-	45

OSU—White, 72 pass from Kern [kick failed]
NU— Harrington, 15 pass from Shelbourne [Emmerich kick]
OSU—Kern, 7 run [Long pass from Zelina]
NU— Shelbourne, 4 run [Emmerich kick]

OSU— Otis, 6 run [Roman kick]
OSU—Jankowski, 23 pass from Kern [kick failed]
NU— Hillman, 7 pass from Shelbourne [Emmerich kick]
OSU—Otis, 6 run [pass failed]
OSU—Hayden, 3 run [kick failed]
OSU—Bender, 37 pass from Maciejowski [kick failed]

RUSHING:
OSU—Kern 20-121, Brungard 16-56, Hayden 6-51, Otis 15-48, Gillian 5-21, Greene 4-18, Zelina 2-17, Long 1-15; **NU**—Olson 10-38, Kurzawski 10-24, Adamle 8-16, Shelbourne 12-15, Smeeton 2-6, Emmerich 2-5.
PASSING:
OSU—Kern 8-14-170-2, Maciejowski 2-3-48-1, Long 0-2-0; NU—Shelbourne 15-29-176-2, Kurzawski 1-1-8-0, Adamle 0-1-0-0.
RECEIVING:
OSU— White 3-97, Jankowski 4-53, Bender 1-37, Gillian 2-31; **NU**— Olson 1-60, Hubbard 2-25, Emmerich 2-21, Hittman 2-20, Kurzawski 1-15, Adamle 2-11, Smeeton 1-11, Shelbourne 1-8.

GAME FIVE

Ron Maciejowski rescued the Buckeyes several times during the '68 season.

293

Chapter 47

'MACE' TO THE RESCUE

OHIO STATE 31, ILLINOIS 24

October 26, 1968...At Champaign, Illinois.

Winless Illinois vs. unbeaten and No.2-rated Ohio State.

It appeared that this David would need two sling shots to fell mighty Goliath.

Illinois had managed to score just 39 points in five games, allowing a whopping 194 in losses to Kansas [47-7], Missouri [44-0], Notre Dame [58-8], Indiana [28-14] and Minnesota [17-10].

Those five opponents had amassed a total of 2,256 yards...or 451.2 per game.

On the other hand, Ohio State's 'hurry up' offense was averaging 87 plays, up from 74 in 1967.

As Woody Hayes put it, "We're running our plays so fast, I can't even get in a play anymore." Complaining? No sirree.

Part of the increase was due in part to a new rule change. Prior to the 1968 season, the clock kept on ticking while the chains were moved following a first down. Now, the clock would stop.

Ohio State was coming off a record 565 yard effort against winless but spunky Northwestern.

Illinois, on the other hand, had lost by 50 to Notre Dame.

Ohio State's Esco Sarkkinen was at that rout. "Notre Dame was devastating Saturday," he said. "They were really sharp. They had gained 530 yards by the end of the third quarter and ended up with 673 yards."

Sark' had been around the block a time or two. He preferred to approach this Big Ten game with caution. "We always feel Illinois does better against Big Ten opponents."

It was also Homecoming at Illinois. Another reason to expect the unexpected.

Illinois was battered and bloodied. Fullback Rick Johnson, the Fighting Illini's leading rusher, was listed as doubtful. Quarterback, Bob Naponic had a bad knee.

In addition, Dave Jackson was out for the season. A speedster, Jackson had supplied the offense spark for Illinois' 17-13 conquest of Ohio State in 1967.

A team blessed with depth at virtually every position, Ohio State could survive a key injury. But surely not Illinois.

The Buckeyes were relatively healthy offensively. Defensively, "we're hurting", said defensive coordinator Lou McCullough. Two starters would miss the game because of injuries—right end Mark Debevc and halfback/safety Mike Polaski. The two did not accompany the team to Illinois.

Debevc was suffering from tendonitis, brought on by an ankle sprain. Junior Mike Radtke, a converted linebacker, would take his place. Polaski was bothered by a hip pointer. Former quarterback Jerry Ehrsam, a senior, was penciled in for the start.

While senior linebacker and co-captain Dirk Worden made the trip, sophomore

Doug Adams [Xenia, Ohio], would once again take his place in the lineup. Worden, the team's MVP in 1967, had a knee injury. In addition, the status of soph noseguard, Jim Stillwagon, was up-in-the-air. He lasted only five plays against Northwestern before his knee, injured in the Purdue game, gave out. If Stillwagon couldn't make it, senior, Vic Stottlemyer would get the nod.

Despite the growing medical casualty list, there was no panic. After all, inept Illinois had been averaging less than eight points a game.

McCullough didn't have to go back too far in his memory. Illinois had beaten the Buckeyes two in a row on late heroics.

In 1966, Ohio State held a 9-3 lead but the Fighting Illini went on a late drive and got a touchdown. A year later at Ohio Stadium, Illinois repeated the fourth quarter feat.

Same script. Same result.

Soph back John Brockington had a tender ankle, but Leo Hayden, another talented sophomore, was ready for more playing time. Against Northwestern, the Dayton, Ohio tailback proved he could sweep around end, explode over tackle and catch passes.

Despite the still tender jaw, Rex Kern would start at quarterback. Junior Dave Brungard would start at left half, ahead of Hayden. He would be joined by soph wingback Larry Zelina, and bruising junior fullback Jim Otis.

Of most concern to Illinois was Kern, a scrambler who seemed to make good things happen. As Illinois scout, Brodie Western put it, "Kern presents as many problems to an opposing team as any signal-caller in the nation."

After just four varsity starts, the Lancaster, Ohio magician had rushed for 260 net yards and passed for 500 more. His completion average was a highly-respectable 55.5 percent.

Upset by the continual battering of Kern, Woody Hayes once again cried out for heavy penalties against players and coaches guilty of 'get-the-quarterback' tactics. When Hayes failed to reach Big Ten commissioner Bill Reed to once again voice his protest, he decided to send a film illustrating his charges.

"This is getting out of hand," he snapped. "The word is obvious...underline that...obvious. I say piling on is always obvious.

"You can avoid it when no more than that far [holding his hands less than a foot apart] from an opponent. I'm disgusted with what's being done to passers after the pass.

"This has no place in football. From the films I see—and not all are games involving Ohio State— it is not an accident.

"When these things are done obviously and purposefully it has to be ruled upon, the same as piling. We have five officials; one of them should watch for it. This is getting out of hand.

"Some coaches must say to their players, 'Let's teach him it's a rough game.'

"Well, I say kick a player out of the game if he does it once; kick him out for the season if he does it twice. Suspend his coach—not necessarily the head coach—for a week, and it will stop.

"This seems to be the way some coaches try to stop the option play—get the quarterback. I am not referring to any single specific instance. I see it in films from various sources. I see far too much of it."

Rex Kern had been wearing a special enlarged face mask to protect a jaw injury sustained in the Oregon game. That was the second game of the season.

"We're lucky his jaw is not broken," Hayes said bitterly. "One of these days it will be shattered."

Ron Maciejowski entered the Illinois game with 3:30 to play, replacing an injured Rex Kern.

One sophomore replacing another.

Ohio State was in deep trouble. What had once been an easy 24-0 halftime cushion had evaporated into a 24-24 tie. Winless Illinois had clearly gained the upper hand, erupting for three touchdowns and converting all two-point after-touchdown plays.

The Buckeyes faced a second-and-16 on their own 30.

Woody Hayes had the choice of either veteran Billy Long or little-used Ron Maciejowski, a sophomore.

Call it a gut feeling or whatever. Hayes called for Maciejowski "because he's a better runner. I felt he could run us out of trouble."

'Mace' didn't disappoint his coach. He delivered big time. Moving into the huddle, the 6-2, 185-pounder was told it was second-and-16. He was stunned. "No kidding. Boy, I didn't know what it was."

On the first play he whipped a 10-yarder to soph wingback Larry Zelina. It was now a critical third-and-six.

Give up possession and the highly-favored Buckeyes faced the real possibility of a shocking defeat. Settle for a tie and an outright Big Ten title could slip away.

A tie-breaking field goal or go-ahead touchdown was the only acceptable alternative.

To get within field goal range, Ohio State had to move within the shadow of the Illinois goal line. Place kicker Jim Roman didn't have the 'cannon' for a long-range field goal.

On the next play, Mace rolled right for 12 yards and a crucial first down. "It was supposed to be a pass over the middle to Otis," he said, "but the linebacker played Jim so tight I ran."

First-and-10 on the Illinois 48. "On the next play I lined up and saw where their safety was. I couldn't believe it.

I knew the play [a deep pass to Larry Zelina] was wide open. All I could think of was the coach's words, 'Whatever you do, don't overthrow.' So I underthrew the ball. Boy, that Larry is great. What hands."

Zelina caught the pass on the Illinois 27 and muscled his way to the four-yard line, completing the 44-yard play.

First-and-goal on the Illinois four.

Said Zelina, "I'm supposed to go at the safety, cut, give him a head fake and go. I was surprised to see the safety playing so far right. I just cut up the middle and forgot the fake. I knew I'd be caught from behind, but I just wanted to carry them inside the 10 to give us better field position."

Three plays later, Otis followed Zelina and tackle Rufus Mayes into the end zone. Zelina took out the linebacker, Mayes the inside defender.

Ohio State had dodged the bullet, 31-24, to extend it's unbeaten streak to 10 in a row over two seasons. Only Yale, with 14 victories, had a longer streak.

Woody Hayes was a bit shaken by the scare.

"That's what can happen when a team comes out all fired up like Illinois did in the second half...when we had five defensive starters out, a real problem.

"Right now they're [his Buckeyes] just another team and they'll find out about it Monday."

Ohio State's road to Pasadena and the Rose Bowl suddenly looked like a treacherous journey. Michigan seemed to have the inside edge, the softer challenge.

Michigan's remaining opponents had a combined 6-17 record. Ohio State's opponents were 11-13. Ohio State's next hurdle would be Michigan State, followed by Wisconsin and Iowa.

Michigan State would not fall easily. The Spartans [4-2] upended Notre Dame, 21-17, in their last outing.

Thus, it appeared the November 23rd collision between Ohio State and Michigan would settle the Big Ten title picture. And with that, a trip to the Rose Bowl.

Michigan's 'road to Pasadena' could be impeded by Northwestern, Illinois or Wisconsin. But not likely.

It looked so easy for the Buckeyes at Champaign-Urbana. They took the opening kickoff and roared 72 yards in 19 plays. The seemingly relentless drive consumed eight minutes.

However, that drive ran out of steam on the Illinois six.

Would it be a harbinger of things to come?

It didn't seem so, at least not in the beginning. On it's next possession, Ohio State drove 45 yards on seven plays to set up Jim Roman's 21-yard field goal.

Relying on the power of junior fullback Jim Otis, the Buckeyes moved 65 yards on five plays. Otis bulled over from the one.

Otis literally carried his team on his strong back during that series with runs of 17 and 32 yards. He finished the game with 72 yards on 11 carries and two touchdowns.

Kern strutted his stuff in engineering the second TD drive. He hit Otis for 17 yards and soph tight end Jan White for nine on a crucial third down play. He climaxed the nine play, 58-yard drive with an 11-yard TD scamper up-the-middle.

The Lancaster, Ohio field-general passed and ran the No.2 ranked Buckeyes to a seemingly unsurmountable 24-0 halftime bulge.

During the five play, 52-yard march, he completed key passes of 5, 22 and 9 yards to Bruce Jankowski, White and Zelina. His second TD of the game came on a 16-yard keeper.

For the game, Ohio State amasssed 453 yards, but it would take the last minutes heroics of Ron Maciejowski to pull it out.

Soph tailback Leo Hayden gained 77 yards in 14 attempts, including 62 yards in the first half. Zelina played a solid game, totaling 137 run-catch yards. He rushed for 61 yards [8 carries] and caught five passes for 76 yards.

Illinois failed to register a first down in the opening 24 minutes against Ohio State, resembling the same team that had been buried 58-8 by Notre Dame the previous week.

Class of '68

But two interceptions by Kern, one ending the first half and one starting the third quarter, seemed to infuse new life into the over matched Fighting Illini. Illinois' defense stopped the Ohio State game in the second half. The one-two punch of Rich Johnson and reserve Ken Bargo, plus the scrambling antics of quarterback Bob Naponic suddenly found holes in Ohio State's solid defense.

Johnson plunged two yards for a touchdown, climaxing a six-play, 30-yard drive; Naponic dove two yards to cap an 18-play, 86-yard march; Bargo slashed two yards to end a 14-play, 80-yard series.

And to add insult-to-injury, Illinois converted on all three two-point conversion plays. The momentum had clearly shifted. Illinois was relentless, Ohio State battered and dazed.

Woody Hayes had felt his Buckeyes had grabbed a 27-16 lead late in the fourth quarter. Roman tried a field goal attempt from the Illinois 21.

"The field goal definitely was good," he fumed."Referee [Howard Wirtz] hasn't called it either way yet. I saw her go over and rules are if any part of the ball goes over it's good. The whole damn ball went over and you may quote me."

He didn't stop there.

Hayes wondered why the officials stopped the clock on a late Illinois drive and kept the clock running instead of calling for the first down measurement of Ohio State's winning TD drive.

"Our captain [Dave Foley] had to ask for a measurement and it was a first down. Boy, those were two great calls," he said facitiously.

On a high note, Hayes said "Zelina had a doggone good day...and Maciejowski too."

Illinois coach Jim Valek said his Illini goofed on the 44-yard Maciejowski-to-Zelina pass play. "We got into the defense alright, but we missed a defensive backfield assignment and that left Zelina wide open."

Despite the dramatic comeback, Valek didn't consider it a moral victory, "I wasn't satisfied with our play. You've got to win to be satisfied. I told the team "You can't expect to win playing 35 minutes of football. You've got to go all out for 60 minutes."

Valek said his game plan didn't change in the second half.

"We had a chance to begin moving the ball late in the second quarter and it seemed to give us confidence. We used the same offense, the same plays in the second half. The execution was a lot better and that was the difference."

Woody Hayes said tongue-in-cheek, "Maybe it was good for us to play a game like this." He admitted "the momentum had started to change in the last five minutes of the first half.

"It was fine. We won and showed me we could come back. Otis went into that end zone, didn't he? That means something."

The only casualty was soph defensive back Tim Anderson, who left the game in the second quarter with a back injury. Despite a less-than-healthy knee, noseguard Jim Stillwagon saw action.

"The biggest hero we can have this week is the doctor," said Hayes."We've got to get 'em back.We should have Worden, Polaski and Debevc back this week. We might have to go without Anderson."

298

OHIO STATE 31, ILLINOIS 24

	OSU	ILL
First downs	25	21
Rushing Yardage	290	200
Passing Yardage	163	102
Return Yardage	135	106
Passes	14-23-2	9-23-3
Fumbles Lost	1	0
Yards Penalized	29	45

Ohio State	3	21	0	7-	31
Illinois	0	0	16	8-	24

OSU— Roman, 21, field goal
OSU— Otis, 1 run [Roman kick]
OSU— Kern, 11 run [Roman kick]
OSU— Kern, 16 run [Roman kick]
ILL.— Johnson, 2 run [Johnson run]
ILL— Naponic, 2 run [Naponic run]
ILL— Bargo, 2 run [Bargo run]
OSU— Otis, 2 run [Roman kick]

RUSHING
OSU— Kern 14-57, Brungard 5-12, Zelina 8-61, Otis 11-72, Hayden 14-77, Maciejowski 3-11; **ILL.**— Naponic 14-36, Johnson 16-69, Bess 1-1, Bargo 17-82, Kmiec 3-12.
PASSING
OSU— Kern 12-21-109-2, Maciejowski 2-2-54-0; **ILL.**— Naponic 9-23-102-3.
RECEIVING
OSU— Zelina 5-76, White 5-50, Jankowski 3-20, Otis 1-17; **ILL.**— Bess 2-4, Kmiec 2-24, Burns 1-9, Dieker 4-65.

GAME SIX

One of Ohio States most versatile backs, Larry Zelina made a key paly in the win over Michigan State.

300

Chapter 48

TOUGH WHEN IT COUNTS

OHIO STATE 25, MICHIGAN STATE 2

November 2, 1968...At Ohio Stadium.

Notre Dame trailed underdog Michigan State 21-17 with just three minutes to play and the ball deep in it's own territory. But with dangerous Terry Hanratty throwing to a crop of talented receivers, headed by All-American end Jim Seymour, it ain't over till the final gun sounds.

Methodically picking Michigan State apart, Hanratty calmly completed seven straight passes. It was now first-and-goal at the Spartans' three-yard line.

Sixty-seven seconds left to play. Plenty of time for another storybook Irish come-from-behind victory.

This time, however, it was not meant to be.

This time, gritty Michigan State would repulse the attack.

'Ironman' Allen Brenner, a two-way player at wide receiver and safety, would knock down an apparent Hanratty-to-Seymour touchdown pass.

Middle guard Bill Dawson would stop Ron Dushney after a one-yard gain.

That man Brenner would put the collar on Hanratty for no gain. In fact, the 6-1, 196-pounder would be credited with three TD saves in the thriller.

Game over.

Irish eyes are crying.

During the battle, Michigan State stopped Notre Dame five times in four-down territory.

Twice in the final period, the Spartans stuffed Notre Dame inside the three. Once in that stanza, the Irish fell 12 agonizing inches shy of a touchdown.

One week later the stage was set: Ohio State's potent offense Versus Michigan State's gutsy defense.

While Michigan State, at 4-2, had been eliminated from Big Ten title contention, veteran head coach Duffy Daugherty wanted nothing better than to derail the unbeaten Buckeyes on their fantasy trip to the Rose Bowl.

Duffy would like nothing better than to beat his old rival Woody Hayes.

Ohio State, ranked fourth nationally in total offense, appeared healthy for this key game. Starting soph quarterback Rex Kern, knocked out of the Illinois game, was pronounced fit for combat. Sidelined with a sprained ankle for the last two games, running back John Brockington was rarin' to go.

The defense was also basically sound. While senior linebacker Dirk Worden had suffered a knee injury against Purdue which would limit him to only token appearances, soph Doug Adams was now becoming a fixture.

When defensive back Timmy Anderson was sidelined, versatile Mike Polaski stepped right into the starting spot.

That's what happens when a team is blessed with depth and virtually at every position.

Class of '68

Michigan State didn't overwhelm anyone, but the Spartans were sure darned pesky.

Six backs had gained 100 or more yards rushing, led by 195-pound sophomore Tommy Love with 548 yards. All told, the Spartans had gained 1,399 yards rushing and scored 15 touchdowns.

Soph quarterback Bill Triplett wasn't exactly a slouch as a passer, accounting for 722 yards and three touchdowns. A Rex Kern-type of slashing runner, he averaged 4.0 yards on 56 carries, even with pass-play losses.

Brenner, the team's leading receiver [16 for 271 yards] and fourth leading tackler [39 stops, 2 interceptions] averaged 55 minutes a game on the field.

Soph defensive end Rich Saul, twin brother of offensive guard Ron Saul, led the Spartans with 75 solo tackles.

As far as defensive coordinator Lou McCullough was concerned, Ohio State was giving up too many points. The Buckeyes had yielded 21 and 24 points in their last two games to two Big Ten cellar-dwelling teams, Northwestern and Illinois.

Head coach Woody Hayes was also concerned, especially after he had called Ohio State "a truly great football team."

He always seemed to find the perfect moment to apply just about any comment to his favorite essayist, Ralph Waldo Emerson.

"Blame is safer than praise. I hate to be defended in a newspaper. As long as all that is said is said against me, I feel a certain assurance of success. But as soon as honeyed words of praise are spoken for me, I feel as one who lies unprotected before his enemies."

A record crowd of 84,859 jammed into Ohio Stadium for the annual event called Parents Day. They didn't go home disappointed.

Despite the loss of Kern early in the game, 'super sub' Ron Maciejowski staked Ohio State to a 19-7 halftime lead. Just when it appeared as if it would all slip away, Ohio State's defense toughed to preserve a 25-20 decision.

It would be the second consecutive game that 'Mace' had replaced the injured Kern and directed a victory. In the waning moments at Illinois, he moved OSU 70 yards to pay dirt in the final three minutes to produce a shaky 31-24 verdict, after blowing a 24-0 halftime lead.

In the hectic and scoreless fourth quarter, the tenacious Ohio State defense forced Michigan State to punt twice, recover two fumbles and trapped Spartan runners six times.

"Once again," said Daugherty, "we beat ourselves. You can't turn the ball over that often [four lost fumbles, three pass interceptions]. When you turn the ball over seven times to a team like Ohio State, it's a wonder you don't get beat worse than that.

"Our kids played hard. We're not going to be a great team until we stop beating ourselves. If we put together two halves like the second half"...He didn't finish the sentence.

However, Daugherty fell short in labeling Ohio State a "great team" as he did during his pre-game rhetoric. "Ohio State has a fine team. All our opponents are good."

Said Woody Hayes, "These were two pretty good football teams. About all I can say is that we won by five points and that is just about all."

Was Michigan State the Buckeyes' toughest opponent to date?

302

"Sure it was the toughest because we played it most recently. It seemed to me that in the first half we were never stopped, unless by a penalty. The second half started to even up a little bit."

Ohio State surprised Michigan State with it's 'sneak attack' the first half. "We decided to cross them up from the very start of the game," noted Hayes, "running plays in sequence [without a huddle] or having quarterback Rex Kern call them from the line of scrimmage."

Surprisingly, the Buckeyes used the air route most of the way in their first TD drive because "we've been running on first down and they knew it."

"We also felt their defense against running was better than their pass defense and still I believe it was. The thing that impressed me about the game was that our offense had to protect our defense. It did it. And when the defense late in the game had to protect the offense, it also did it.

"They came at us real hard, put pressure on our passer. We'll work on that this week. We'll have to protect our passer better. Say, we gained 225 yards passing, didn't we? I guess we didn't pass enough," he said with a chuckle.

Regarding Kern's injury:

"Kern appears to have a severely sprained ankle. I don't know yet if it's anything worse. But I guess Maciejowski will be starting next week [against Wisconsin]."

"Woody Hayes didn't know exactly how Kern was hurt. He told me he did not feel he would be able to run the plays if we put him back in the game."

Maciejowski entered the game with five minutes left in the first half and Ohio State nursing a 13-7 lead. He promptly guided a 13-play, 83-yard scoring drive. Junior fullback Jim Otis bulled across from the three. In a typical fashion, Ohio State came out throwing.

Taking possession on the OSU 17-yard line, Kern found soph wide receiver Bruce Jankowski in the flat for a seven-yard gain, then connected with soph tight end Jan White for 10 more. Kern's third straight pass, however, was knocked down.

On the next play, Kern faked a handoff to tailback Leo Hayden then circled right end for 15 yards. After Hayden gained one, Kern went back to the air game.

He hit Hayden for seven, Jankowski for 39 to the Michigan State one-yard line on a broken play.

The 185-pounder started scrambling to his right, circled back to the other side with Spartan defenders in hot pursuit. Yet, he had the presence to spot Jankowski wide open. Two plays later, Otis muscled over from the one. Ohio State had a 6-0 lead. The game was but 113 seconds old. Jim Roman added the extra point kick.

Two plays after Michigan State gained possession, OSU sophomore safety Mike Sensibaugh picked off a Triplett pass returning it for 21 yards to the Michigan State 37.

However, the drive fizzled. Roman's 50-yard field goal attempt barely missed clearing the crossbar.

Ohio State recovered an MSU fumble on it's own 36 to set the stage for the second touchdown. Triplett completed a pass to Frank Foreman who lost the ball after a hard hit. The ball squirted forward and was inadvertly booted by a Michigan State player. Several Ohio State players had a shot at recovery before Sensibaugh finally corralled the slippery pigskin.

Eight plays later, Kern unloaded. Jankowski stretched out his 6-2 frame in the right corner of the end zone for a spectacular 14-yard TD catch. Roman's PAT attempt failed and it was 13-0 in favor of Ohio State.

Key play in the drive was Larry Zelina's 34-yard gain onf a short Kern pass. Zelina was actually tackled on the MSU 28, shook off the defender, and willed his way down the sidelines for 14 more yards.

That set the stage for Jankowski's sprawling fingertip grab.

The game's most controversial play kept a Michigan State drive alive, just when it appeared Ohio State had forced a punt. An offside penalty called against OSU on a trick play breathed new life into a sputtering Michigan State march.

On the 19th play, Triplett slipped across from the one.

This is what happened: Facing a fourth-and-two, Michigan State came out in a scrimmage formation with a man under center, but then shifted into punt formation. An Ohio State lineman charged across the line with the first motion.

Offsides. Five yard penalty.

First down, Michigan State.

After the game, Woody Hayes was livid. He blasted the 'sucker shift.'

"The rule states that any motion which simulates a play is a violation. When the quarterback started out from behind the center...that simulates a play.

"If that one didn't I never saw one that did although the officials don't always agree with me. We'll have to go back to the rules committee this Winter and straighten it out. The purpose was so obvious...to draw us offside."

Naturally, Duffy Daugherty disagreed.

"There was absolutely nothing wrong with it. I told the officials before the game we were going to use it.There are times when I'm not too happy with the call. But I'll never criticize an official publically.

"They are human just like everybody else. They have to make split-second decisions on the field, the same as a coach or a quarterback."

Triplett completed nine of 15 passes for 137 yards in the third period, including a 13-yard TD pass to Foreman. Gary Boyce's PAT cut the gap to 19-14. There was 9:14 left in the period.

Ohio State took the next kickoff with Brockington returning to his own 38. A personal foul against Michigan State on the play tacked on an additonal 15-yards. It was first down on the MSU 47. Mace hit Jankowski for five, then pitched out to Zelina for a 12-yard gain.

Avoiding a strong pass rush, Maciejowski managed to turn a negative into a one-yard gain. On the next play, he found Hayden for 26 to the Michigan State three.

First-and-goal.

Otis managed only two yards on two cracks.

Third-and-goal.

On the next play, Mace appeared to be trapped on the three. A Spartan defender actually had a grasp of his jersey. However, Maciejowski managed to break free, continued around left end for the important touchdown to pad the OSU lead to 25-14.

Ohio State gambled on a two-point conversion, but Mace's pass was picked off in the end zone.

Michigan State again rallied in the closing minute of the third period after receiving a punt on the Ohio State 31. Triplett and Tommy Love moved the ball to the six. After three rushes, Love punched it over from the one. At that point, the Buckeyes' defense took over.

Junior linebacker Mike Radtke caused two Triplett fumbles with junior defensive tackle David Whitfield recovering both. That last fumble came with 90 seconds to play. Radtke turned in another outstanding play in the fourth quarter. He nailed Triplett for a 14-yard loss on a third-and-six at mid field.

Soph linebacker Doug Adams also recovered a fourth quarter fumble. The defensive unit forced Triplett to a net loss of 18 yards with a relentless pass rush. Mike Sensibaugh, Ted Provost and Mike Polaski each intercepted a Triplett pass.

Before being forced to leave the game, Rex Kern became only the fourth Buckeye to gain 1,000 yards in a season though he played less than two quarters in his sixth varsity game.

He amassed 158 yards, including 138 on nine of 12 pass completions. He now had 1,084 total yards.

Kern called all of the plays before his injury. But when Ron Maciejowski took over, all the plays came in from the sidelines.

Said Woody Hayes, "Ron didn't have more than 20 minutes of action until this game. It wasn't fair to have him call the plays."

OHIO STATE 25, MICHIGAN STATE 20

	OSU	MSU
First downs	24	18
Rushing Yardage	214	134
Passing Yardage	215	137
Return Yardage	94	80
Passes	16-26-1	9-15-3
Fumbles Lost	1	4
Yards Penalized	71	26

Ohio State	7	12	6	0-	25
Michigan State	0	7	13	0-	20

OSU— Otis, 1 run [Roman kick]
OSU— Jankowski, 14 pass from Kern [kick failed]
MSU —Triplett, 1 run [Boyce kick]
OSU— Otis, 3 run [pass failed]
MSU— Foreman, 13 pass from Triplett [Boyce kick]
OSU— Maciejowski, 2 run [pass failed]
MSU— Love, 1 run [pass failed]

RUSHING: OSU Kern 5-20, Otis 18-52, Zelina 7-63, Hayden 10-47, White 1-2, Maciejowski 12-30, Kuhn 1-0; **MSU**— Triplett 24-minus 18, Love 21-59, Berlinski 1-2, Wedemyer 7-71, Highsmith 6-20.
PASSING: OSU— Kern 9-12-138-0, Maciejowski 7-14-77-1; **MSU**—Triplett 9-15-137-3.
RECEIVING: OSU— Jankowski 8-88, White 4-46, Hayden 2-33, Zelina 2-48; **MSU**— Foreman 7-123, Bowdel 1-8, Love 1-6.

GAME SEVEN

Mace #18 looks downfield. Leo Hayden #22 is set to throw a block and big Dave Foley #70 is behind Maciejowski ready to do his thing.

Chapter 49

RUN, RONNIE, RUN

OHIO STATE 43, WISCONSIN 8

November 9, 1968...At Madison, Wisconsin.

When Ohio State starting quarterback, Rex Kern gets hurt or can't move the potent offensive unit, relief is just a heartbeat away.

Relief is spelled R-O-N M-A-C-I-E-J-O-W-S-K-I.

One sophomore taking over for another with the same impressive results. Throw another "W" into the victory column.

With Kern hobbled by a sprained ankle, head coach Woody Hayes gave Maciejowski, a 6-2, 186-pounder from Bedford, Ohio his first varsity start.

'Mace' simply ran for three touchdowns and passed for a fourth score in turning a ho-hum 10-0 lead into a 43-8 rout before a chilled 40,927 at Randall Stadium.

The air temperature read 30 degrees. It would get a lot hotter on the field.

The Big Ten match started off modestly enough. Jim Roman's 28-yard field goal climaxed Ohio State's opening drive. It was 10-0 on Maciejowski's eight-yard scoring strike to soph wingback Larry Zelina and Roman's PAT.

For the first 30 minutes, the underdog Badgers had been playing over their heads. Fueled on emotion and a gritty defense led by Ken Criter, the gas tank would run empty after intermission.

Ohio State had survived a 25-20 scare against Michigan State the previous week. Maybe the Buckeyes were looking past Wisconsin, to their next opponent— powerful Iowa led by one-man wrecking crew Ed Podolak.

It was only human to take Wisconsin for granted. Despite all the upset warnings. A football game is a marathon and not a sprint. Cream usually rises to the top. Talent wins out.

ENOUGH CLICHES, ALREADY.

"We were a little lazy in the first half after getting 10 points so easily," opined Woody Hayes. Then he added, "Wisconsin played good defensive football." Hayes admitted he 'saw red' the first half.

"Yes, we adjusted a little between halves, but nothing really important. Yes, we saw something. It was a lot of red shirts coming up the middle." And it was Ken Criter leading the 'blitz brigade.'

"That No. 33 [Criter] did a good job. Wisconsin ought to be proud of him," said the Ohio State coach." I don't usually congratulate a kid after a game, but I did him. He's a real good hitter and not as big as I thought."

To counter Wisconsin's blitzing, Ohio State turned Maciejowski loose on sweeps. 'Runnin Ron' gained 124 net yards on 23 carries [5.4 per carry average] and scored touchdowns on runs of 5, 1 and 10 yards. He also completed 13 of 19 passes for 153 yards and one TD.

Not a bad day for this 'Super Sub.'

Class of '68

When Mace didn't ramble wide, junior fullback Jim Otis banged straight-ahead for 94 yards on 18 attempts. He scored second half TDs on 2 and 3 yard plunges. Ohio State rushed for 225 of it's 301 total yards in the second half.
The Buckeyes registered 27 first downs, compared to only eight by Wisconsin. For the day, they gained 468 net yards. Total: 86 plays [61 rushing 25 passing.]
Other offensive standouts:
Soph wingback Larry Zelina totaled 157 yards. He rushed for 37 on only four carries, snared five passes for 120 yards. That's 24 yards per catch. Jankowski and Zelina caught five passes each. Jankowski's added up to 37 yards.
Ohio State played a Jekyll-Hyde kind of game. Mr. Hyde was far more effective. The Buckeyes began with a steady air barrage. Mace came out throwing.
After being trampled on the first play of the game by a Wisconsin blitz, he completed 37 and 14 yard passes to Zelina and Jankowski. However, the drive bogged down on the Badgers' 13. Enter senior Jim Roman who booted his 18-yard field goal with 11:21 left in the opening period.
Ohio State owed a big 'Thank You' on that drive to Wisconsin safety Tom McCauley who dropped a sure interception.
Moments later, Ohio State had the ball. The end zone was 70 yards away. Mace hit Zelina for 32 yards, Jan White for eight more. He climaxed the aerial bombardment with an eight-yard TD pass to Zelina with 5:08 left in the first period.
It was a good day for Roman [Canton, Ohio]. He added his fourth point of the game after the Zelina end zone catch.
Maciejowski pulled the trigger 15 times in the first half, completing nine for 110 of his 153 yards.
Uncharacteristically, Ohio State rushed for only 76 yards in the opening half.
After intermission, Woody Hayes changed strategy. RUN...RUN...RUN. What had been a relatively close game turned into a blowout.
The Buckeyes exploded for three touchdowns in the third period. Winless 'David' simply couldn't stop unbeaten 'Goliath.' It was just that simple.
Ohio State rambled 67 yards to paydirt after receiving the second half kickoff. Maciejowski gained 55 of those yards on five solos, including the last five. Roman's kick made it 17-0. Time of possession: 4 minutes 22 seconds.
Less than four minutes later it was 24-0. The short drive [49 yards] required only seven plays. Otis punched it over from the two.
That man Zelina set up Otis' off-tackle plunge with a 17-yard burst up-the-middle on a counter.
The third scoring drive consumed 51 yards and again Mace and his 'crazy legs' proved too much for overmatched Wisconsin.
His 25-yard rumble around right end moved the sideline chains to the Badgers' 20. Otis scored from the three. Roman, however, missed the extra point. It was 30-0.
Wisconsin scored it's only touchdown in the third period, marching 68 yards on 11 plays. Quarterback John Ryan had his one shining moment of glory during that drive.
His 37-yard 'bomb' to the Ohio State 14 highlighted the march. Ryan took it over from the one, then flipped a two-point conversion to wingback Stu Voight, the Badgers' top receiver.

Wisconsin immediately lined up for an onside kick. The Buckeyes' put their 'best hands' up front.

Recover the squibber and who knows what can happen?

But it was not meant to be. Ohio State recovered Jim Johnson's short kick on the OSU 47. The subsequent scoring drive took just five plays. Maciejowski pushed across from the one. A bit earlier, Mace sprinted around right end for 27 yards.

Roman's second misfire of the game didn't matter. It was 36-8 with 9:56 left to play. And even when Wisconsin intercepted a pass in the end zone to seemingly blunt another Ohio State drive, a penalty nullified that play.

Senior quarterback Billy Long, the forgotten man, had been bumped down to No.3 behind OSU's super sophs Rex Kern and Ron Maciejowski. His game appearances had been few-and-far-between.

With a fourth down situation, Long threw into the end zone. Wisconsin's Tom McCauley picked off the pass and ran it back to his own 20.

The officials, however, called a roughing-the-passer penalty on Wisconsin, nullifying the interception. It thus became first-and-goal for Ohio State at the Badger 10.

Woody Hayes then inserted Mace back into the starting lineup quicker than you could say "TOUCHDOWN." He rambled around left end for his third rushing TD of the day.

Jim Roman added insult-to-injury with his fourth PAT of the game.

Ron Maciejowski had turned in a game-of-a-lifetime.

Wisconsin's Ken Criter was just as brilliant in defeat. He made 16 solo tackles and assisted on 11 other stops.

Despite the bone-chilling temperature, Woody Hayes glowed in his Buckeyes' 11th straight victory over a two-year period.

"We like to establish our pass attack early and we can pass this year. Maciejowski did a good job. I think Kern is quicker and makes better use of his speed, but I think Maciejowski is a stronger runner.

"That's a nice problem to have. We have a lot of good players. This is the best squad we've had in a long time. We have a lot of speed and quickness in both units and at a lot of positions. Wisconsin did a great job in the first half with the material they have."

He praised the officials and even the artificial turf at Randall Stadium.

"The officials did an excellent job. You can quote me on that. That was a clean game. A game like this could get rough but they kept it under control."

Concerning the Tartan Turf: "The field was just great. All we got was a bumped elbow. I give it my unqualified endorsement. It can't help but make for better football. If it cuts down one injury, it is worth the price.

"If you don't want it, send it down to Ohio State and I'll take up a collection and give you some money for it," he joked.

Did Ohio State take Wisconsin too lightly?

"Did we have trouble getting up for Wisconsin?" Hayes repeated. "No. We studied movies of the Indiana game and we almost wore out the pictures. Wisconsin all but won and Indiana is a good team."

The victory was Ohio State's seventh straight of the season and fifth in the Big Ten. The loss was Wisconsin's eighth in a row and 0-17-1 under head coach John Coatta.

Class of '68

Commented Coatta, "They're a real good, balanced football team. If you stop them one place they can hurt you someplace else. They can go inside, outside, or pass. "They just ran at us in the second half. They have a lot of personnel and they do a job. They have the type of backs who just don't go down very easy."

OHIO STATE 43, WISCONSIN 8

	OSU	WIS
First downs	27	8
Rushing Yardage	301	88
Return Yardage	24	5
Passes	15-25-1	6-15-1
Fumbles Lost	1	3
Yards Penalized	25	75

Ohio State	10	0	20	13-	43
Wisconsin	0	0	0	8-	8

OSU—Roman, 21 FG
OSU—Zelina, 8 pass from Maciejowski [Roman kick]
OSU—Maciejowski, 5 run [Roman kick]
OSU—Otis, 2 run [Roman kick]
OSU—Otis, 2 run [kick failed]
WIS— Ryan, 1 run [Voight, pass from Ryan]
OSU—Maciejowski, 1 run [kick failed]
OSU—Maciejowski, 10 run [Roman kick]

RUSHING
OSU—Maciejowski 23-124, Otis 18-94, Zelina 4-37, Brungard 3-16, Brockington 2-10, Sensibaugh 1-7, Long 2-7; WIS.—Todd 13-47, Smith 12-44, Voight 4-12, Crooks 2-5, Richardson 3-minus 1, Ryan 11-minus 19.
PASSING
OSU— Maciejowski 13-19-153-1, Long 2-6-14-0; WIS.— Ryan 6-15-99-0.
RECEIVING
OSU— Zelina 5-120-1, Jankowski 5-37-0, Rusnak 1-10-0, White 2-9-0, Brockington 1-4-0, Otis 1-minus 13-0; WIS.—McCauley 1-37-0, Isom 1-28-0, Voight 2-21-0, Reddick 1-8-0, Smith 1-5-0.

GAME EIGHT

Sophomore quarterback Rex Kern of Lancaster, Ohio provided the magic to a 10-0 Dream Season with his golden arm, fast feet and plain old guts. He went on to a pro career with the Baltimore Colts.

311

Chapter 50

RABBIT BY A HAIR

OHIO STATE 33, IOWA 27

November 16, 1968...At Iowa City, Iowa.

Ask Woody Hayes if he'd rather be the greyhound or the rabbit?

He'd answer without hesitation: "I would rather be in the position of playing stay-ahead football instead of catch-up football. Given a choice, I would prefer the former."

In reeling off eight consecutive victories in 1968 and 12 over a two-year period, Ohio State had blown leads against Illinois and Michigan State, only to find a way to win.

That way was backup quarterback Ron Maciejowski.

The Buckeyes had squandered a 24-0 halftime lead against winless Illinois. Mace' re-lit the engine. The result: 31-24.

The Buckeyes had forged ahead, 19-7 against Michigan State, then held on, 25-20. Again, Mace replaced the injured Rex Kern and stopped the bleeding.

And for the third time in this magical 1968 season, prosperity almost turned into tragedy. And for the third time, Ohio State took a deep breath, regrouped and displayed the resiliency of a champion.

The Buckeyes, forged a 12-0 lead at halftime against potent Iowa, increased that margin to 26-6 before the pass-happy Hawkeyes made it very interesting.

Ohio State survived a 33-27 scare to set up a 'winner-take-all' battle for the Big Ten championship against Michigan. Along with the title would be a trip to the Rose Bowl.

This time, however, Ron Maciejowski wasn't needed.

This time an injury-prone Rex Kern would survive the pounding.

The 'name of the game' was to put a muzzle on Iowa senior tailback Ed Podolak. That the Buckeyes did in limiting the 6-1, 193-pounder to a paltry 45 yards in 15 carries.

Just a week before, Podolak had exploded for a Big Ten single-game rushing record of 286 yards in only 17 attempts. He scored on TD runs of 60 and 32 yards as Iowa humiliated Northwestern 68-34.

In the process, the Hawkeyes shattered two Big Ten records.

Podolak's 286 yard effort eclipsed the two-year old conference record of 208 yards by Clinton Jones of Michigan State.

Iowa's 639 total yards moved to the top of the honor role. And why not? The Hawkeyes were the most potent offensive team in the conference.

Iowa's resurgence was due in large part by moving Podolak from quarterback to tailback.

For two full seasons, Ed Podolak was a pretty darned good quarterback. A guy who combined passing and running skills. A genuine double threat.

As a sophomore in 1966, Podolak passed for 1,041 yards [77-191] and five touchdowns. He added 450 yards rushing and three more TDs.

As a junior, he combined for 1,337 yards [1,014 passing, 323 rushing] and eight touchdowns.

When the 1968 season began, Podolak was back at the controls. In Iowa's 21-20 opening season squeaker against Oregon State, Podolak scored on runs of 3 and 10 yards.

However, an injury would knock him out of the lineup. When he re-emerged, it was as Iowa's starting tailback. Junior, Mike Cilek and Sophomore Larry Lawrence took over the quarterback duties.

A quarterback who occasionally runs is one thing. A full-time ballcarrier is another. History shows he was more than up to that new role.

In four full-time starts prior to the Ohio State meeting, Podolak rambled for 129 against Wisconsin, 104 against Purdue, 112 against Minnesota and the record-smashing 286 against Northwestern. That's 631 yards in four Big Ten games.

Ohio State's Woody Hayes put it simply:

"Our defense has a great challenge this week."

OSU head scout Esco Sarkkinen elaborated.

"He's [Podolak] even more effective now because he doesn't have to drop back before he runs. When he starts on a sweep the defense doesn't know whether he'll run or pass.

"They called about six passes Saturday with Podolak doing the throwing, but he actually threw only two. He picked up 98 yards exercising the option. He made his 286 yards on just 17 carries. That indicates his big-play ability."

Sark believed "Lawrence is to them what Rex Kern is to us." Indeed high praise for Iowa's 6-2, 221-pound sophomore. He scored four touchdowns against Minnesota to tie a Big Ten record and had accounted for eight other scores.

For the season, Lawrence had completed 62 of 119 pass attempts and four touchdowns. While his net rushing total was only 70 yards [he lost 164 on pass plays] Lawrence led the Hawkeyes with eight rushing TDs. "Not all quarterback sneaks either," added Sarkkinen.

"That gives them two exceptionally fine football players in the same backfield...and both of them can run or pass."

And then there was Mike Cilek backing up Lawrence. Cilek hit on 12 of 17 attempts for 240 yards, but more important, six of those completions went for touchdowns.

Raved Iowa PR honcho, George Wine, "I don't think I ever saw a team with so many kids who can throw and run. We've got so many good players in the skilled positions. Our blocking has been fantastic. Podolak has added dimension to our offense. He's a heckuva threat."

But Iowa was far from a two-man wrecking crew.

Junior fullback Tim Sullivan entered the Ohio State game averaging 5.6 yards per carry. He had 507 yards. Dennie Green, Berry Crees and Bill Powell had combined for 615 yards.

All-Big Ten receiver Al Bream led Iowa in receiving with 24 catches, 432 yards. He was followed by tight end Ray Manning [27-357] and Crees [17-322].

Despite a deceptive 4-4 record, Iowa was indeed a very dangerous team. The Hawkeyes were enjoying a two-game winning streak, scoring a gaudy 103 points in romps over Wisconsin and Northwestern.

So, who's afraid of those big, bad Buckeyes?

For most of the game, it was all Ohio State.

OSU scratched out a 12-0 halftime lead, increased the bulge to 19-0 and 26-6. That should have been enough to discourage any opponent.

But not Iowa.

With the ground game virtually non-existent, the Hawkeyes mounted an aerial assault and almost shot down the Buckeyes.

A rally of 21 points in the final quarter just fell short.

Ohio State had clearly escaped by the hair of it's chinny-chin-chin.

Defense coordinator, Lou McCullough called it "the sorriest defense I've seen in 20 years".

Iowa head coach Ray Nagel had a slightly different perspective. He praised the Buckeyes' defensive effort.

"Ohio State is strong on both offense and defense. I would say their greatest strength is on defense. They really put pressure on our passers and did a good job of holding up on our receivers at the line. They also took our outside game away from us."

A rain-soaked 44,131 at Iowa City had little to cheer about for most of the game.

Ohio State took a hard-fought 12-0 halftime lead on two long scoring marches.

Larry Zelina ran the opening kickoff back 21 yards to the Buckeyes' 28. They then banged out 17 more, utilizing the upfront blocking ability of tackles Dave Foley and Rufus Mayes and the slashing runs of junior fullback Jim Otis.

Soph quarterback Rex Kern then crossed up Iowa with a pitch to Zelina, a soph wingback from Cleveland. Zelina danced down the sidelines to the Iowa 29.

Kern gained 10 on two carries. Zelina added six. Ohio State was camped on the Iowa seven.

Otis rammed it over on the next play and it was 6-0. Jim Roman's PAT kick, however, sailed wide.

While the 14-play, 73-yard second touchdown drive featured Otis' off-tackle antics, Kern's fancy feet accounted for the final 18 yards.

First, he scooted around left end for 16. On the next play, Kern worked his ball handling magic. Faking a hand off, Kern calmly directed his blockers and 'waltzed' into the end zone.

Iowa threatened three times in the opening drive, but came up empty each time. Marcos Melendez missed an 18-yard field goal.

Next time, Iowa marched to the OSU 38, only to run out of gas as the Buckeyes stiffened on fourth down.

Soph noseguard Jim Stillwagon pounced on an Al Bream fumble on the Ohio State 12 to blunt another Hawkeyes' scoring drive.

Iowa also showed a gritty defense by stopping an Ohio State drive with a pass interception.

Had not a critical 15-yard holding penalty nullified Kern's electrifying 18-yard TD run during that same series, there would have been no need to throw the ball.

Following the interception, Ohio State held Iowa and regained possession. This time nothing would stand between the Buckeyes and the Iowa end zone.

Kern climaxed the nine-play, 79-yard march with a two yard sweep. Otis' 25-yard off-tackle burst keyed the drive.

It was 12-0 with little time left in the first half. The Buckeyes went for the two-point conversion but failed.

At halftime, Ohio Stated had piled up 195 yards, mostly on the ground. Otis led the way with 63 yards, followed by Zelina [43] and Kern [41]. With Podolak shackled, Tim Sullivan cut loose for 71.

Ohio State spent most of the second half operating from the old-fashioned tight T. Iowa spent most of the time firing and re-loading.

The Hawkeyes completed 18 of 24 passes after intermission and outgained Ohio State, 253-225.

Ohio State rumbled 55 yards in six plays for a 19-0 cushion. Otis, who led both teams in rushing with 166 yards [29 carries], bolted across from the one.

Lawrence moved the Hawkeyes 73 yards in 10 plays accounting for 59 on three completions, including a 29-yarder to Ed Podolak and the OSU four.

Podolak made a leaping catch between two defenders to set up Lawrence's TD sneak. It was 19-6.

Mike Cilek took over at quarterback and made it real interesting for Ohio State, almost overcoming a 33-13 deficit.

Woody Hayes was happy to escape with a "W."

"Iowa is a team that is getting better. Their second half attests to that. Their first half doesn't. Our defense did a good job of containing them in the first half.

"We figured they would pick up some in the second half, but not that much. Iowa really didn't get going offensively until that new quarterback [Mike Cilek] came into the game.

"He almost had to pass. We knew that Iowa was almost forced by the clock to pass. I never saw a clock stop so frequently in the last six-to-eight minutes. It must have taken a half hour to play. Everything seemed to be either a first down or an incomplete pass and the clock would stop."

Hayes admitted the poor weather conditions played a role in Ohio State's game plan.

"We anticipated weather like this even as far back as September 15 when we scrimmaged in rain and mud. Actually the field was in very good shape for this time of year. It rained very little after they took the tarp off. My shirt isn't even wet.

"I will say the weather caused us to run more from a closed formation than we might like." That was fine-and-dandy with Jim Otis.

Iowa's Ray Nagel was "proud of the team but disappointed that we didn't win. I really don't know if we can play better than we did. I didn't feel we were out of the game until it became obvious in the last few seconds."

In the final nine seconds of play, and trailing by six points, Iowa tried an on-side kick. In fact, it was the second straight time the Hawkeyes had tried the same tactic. And just as before, Ohio State fielded the bouncing ball.

"Yes, I'd try the on-side kicks again if given the situation. We had to take a chance and gamble a little bit. I felt we needed some breaks if we were going to win.

"We didn't get them. Instead, the breaks went against us and Ohio State played almost errorless ball. You have to credit Ohio State with what it did."

Ohio State played the game under less-than-favorable conditions without committing a fumble. Nagel credited Ohio State's hard-running backs, especially

Otis, with making Iowa's tackling look "shoddy. Gosh, I'm impressed with him. He's a fine, fine runner."

Kern had a busy day, rushing for 66 net yards on 24 tries. In addition, he completed five of 12 passes. Two, however, were intercepted.

Soph tailback John Brockington added 62 yards [10 carries] and Zelina 50 on only six attempts.

Sullivan's 103 yards on 17 attempts led losing Iowa.

Ohio State junior linebacker Mark Stier led the defensive unit with eight solo stops and one assist. He also intercepted an Iowa pass, returning it for seven yards.

Soph 'Rover back' Jack Tatum had seven unassisted tackles and one pass interception.

All told, the Ohio State secondary had to make 20 tackles. The linebackers were almost as active with 13 unassisted stops.

It was that kind of crazy day.

OHIO STATE 33, IOWA 27

	OSU	IOWA
First downs	22	23
Rushing Yardage	337	141
Passing Yardage	83	246
Return Yardage	34	49
Passes	5-12-2	20-32-2
Fumbles Lost	0	1
Yards Penalized	29	45

Ohio State	6	6	14	7-	33	
Iowa	0	0	6	21-	27	

OSU—Otis, 7 run [kick failed]
OSU—Kern, 3 run [pass failed]
OSU—Otis, 1 run [Roman kick]
IOWA—Lawrence, 1 run [kick failed]
OSU—Kern, 1 run [Zelina kick]
IOWA—Podolak, 3 run [Melendez kick]
OSU—Brockington, 22 run [Roman kick]
IOWA—Manning, 12 pass from Lawrence [Melendez kick]
IOWA—Reardon, 9 pass from Lawrence [Melendez kick]

RUSHING: OSU— Otis 29-166, Kern 24-66, Zelina 6-50, Brockington 10-62, Huff 1-2, Sensibaugh 1-minus 9; **IOWA**— Sullivan 17-103, Podolak 15-45, Lawrence 9-minus 2, Crees 3-1, Cliek 1-minus 6.
PASSING: OSU— Kern 5-12-83-2; **IOWA**— Lawrence 13-20-178-1, Podolak 0-1-0-0, Cilek 7-11-68-1.
RECEIVING: OSU— Zelina 4-67, White 1-16; **IOWA**— Mannin g 4-42, Bream 2-36, Sullivan 2-12, Podolak 3-35, Crees 4-66, Wallace 1-4, Reardon 4-51.

GAME NINE

Ohio State pounded "that team up north" 50 to 14 with the tremendous play of fullback Jim Otis.

Chapter 51

GIVE THE BALL TO OTIS

OHIO STATE 50, MICHIGAN 14

November 23, 1968...At Ohio Stadium.

It seemed as if destiny had written the perfect script.

Ohio State and arch-rival Michigan squaring off for the Big Ten championship and the opportunity to 'smell the Roses.'

Each power boasting identical 6-0 conference records. Unbeaten and No. 2-ranked Ohio State [8-0] against once-beaten Michigan [8-1].

A sell-out crowd at Ohio Stadium.

A national television audience.

Who could ask for anything more?

There was a feeling of unrest in the Ohio State camp. A queazy kind of feeling. The engine was chugging on seven cylinders. Not just the great escape at Iowa, a fourth down horror show. Also 'near death' experiences against Illinois and Michigan State. On the other hand, Michigan was chuggin' on all eight cylinders.

After a stunning 21-7 opening season upset loss to California, Michigan had reeled off eight straight victories. The Wolverines were hot. Ron Johnson was even hotter.

For the second straight game, the Buckeyes defense would be severely tested by a literal 'one man gang.' Two super running backs who had shattered the Big Ten single-game rushing record on consecutive weekends.

First, Iowa's Ed Podolak rambled for 286 yards to put his name in the record book.

No sooner had the ink dried than Ron Johnson of Michigan turned on the jets for an astronomical 347 yards on 31 carries. He scored touchdowns on runs of 1, 35, 49, 60 and 65 yards. A five-bagger.

As fate would have it, Ohio State faced Podolak a week earlier. And as fate would have it, Johnson was anxiously waiting in the wings. The Buckeyes had stifled Podolak, limiting him to 45 yards on 15 rushes.

Johnson, for one, was hoping Ohio State would concentrate it's defensive effort to 'cut him off at the pass.'

"I just hope Ohio State does overplay one phase of our offense. We can beat them with our balance."

Ohio State chief scout, Esco Sarkkinen agreed.

"Michigan is a well-drilled team. It has shown great offensive consistency. Dennis Brown is a big play quarterback. He's a fine passer, has good legs and moves well on the sprintouts. He's hit 95 of 205 passes this year with only seven interceptions.

"Michigan is much, much better [than the team that lost to Ohio State, 24-14, at Ann Arbor in 1967], mainly because Brown and Johnson have improved on their 1967 performances and because their line blocking is so effective.

"They have also got a much better defense. They're very opportunistic. The defense has recovered 11 fumbles, intercepted 24 passes. The defense is well-balanced. The 4-3 gives you a 6-1 look and the defensive secondary is extremely good and experienced."

In it's last three games, Michigan's stingy defense had allowed only nine points. Sark wasn't nieve enough to think Ron Johnson was just an ordinary running back.

"He has the size [6-1, 196], speed, agility and balance that characterizes all good backs, but he has a couple of other characteristics that makes him even better.

"He's bull-shouldered, strong in the upper torso. He shrugs off high tackles. Unlike those who run to daylight, he positions himself to his closest downfield blocker and makes his cut off them.

"He particularly likes to run off tackle, using the blocks of tight end, Jim Mandich [215], tackle Bob Penska [225], fullback Garvie Crew [218] and wingback John Gabler [208]. I guess you'd have to say that Johnson is the best back in the league right now."

Mandich called Johnson "a fantastic runner." Crew said "he makes a good blocker out of me. I can make a bad block and Ronnie will read it right and break for a big gain. And if I can give the linebacker a good lick, he's gone."

While Ron Johnson's clocking for the 100 yard dash was a seemingly human 10 seconds, Michigan head coach Bump Elliot couldn't "remember anybody ever catching him from behind. I can't ever recall."

As for Johnson, "carrying the ball is the enjoyment of football. I never tire of it. I'd carry on every play if they'd let me."

Then he passed on some friendly advice to Ohio State.

"If I were Ohio State I'd be more worried about Michigan's defense. It's gotten better every game."

Ohio State entered the showdown ranked fifth nationally in running offense [292.1 yards per game] and sixth in total offense [446.8]. Contrast that with Michigan which rated 19th in rushing [236.6] and 19th in total offense [404.7].

The Wolverines, however, held the edge defensively.

Michigan held opponents to an average 11.7 per game to rank ninth nationally. Ohio State rated 27th in scoring defense, allowing 15.0 points per game.

On paper, it figured to be a titanic battle.

On the battlefield, it turned out to be a rout.

The Buckeyes proved that possession is indeed nine-tenths of the law. They controlled the clock for 38 minutes and 49 seconds as compared to 21 minutes, 11 seconds for Michigan. That included less than eight minutes of ball control in the second half when Ohio State turned a slim 21-14 lead into a debacle.

Not since 1946 had a traditional Ohio State-Michigan game turned into an embarassment. But then it was Fritz Chrysler's Wolverines taking a big bite out of Ohio State 58-6.

Giddy with the sweet taste of a 50-14 victory, Woody Hayes delighted in using a verb for a noun. "It helps to be able to possession that football."

There was little solace for Ron Johnson in defeat even though he re-wrote two Big Ten records. He scored both of Michigan's touchdowns to finish the season at 19 and a Big Ten single-season scoring mark of 92 points. He also set a single-season rushing mark of 1,017 yards in seven games.

Class of '68

Johnson managed a tough 91 yards on 21 attempts. Both of his TDs were on one-yard plunges. His longest run of the day, 39 yards, set up Michigan's second score. That means Ohio State limited his 20 other thrusts to an unimpressive 52 yards. That's 2.7 yards per carry.

For the first time in his brilliant three-year college career, Ron Johnson was caught from behind. Soph defensive back Jack Tatum did the catching.

"I had to catch him," explained Tatum, "because we had a 'fire game' [rush] on. I guessed wrong and he whizzed right past me."

During the storybook 1968 regular season, no opposition running back ran for 100 or more yards against Ohio State's small but quick defensive unit.

In fact, three Buckeyes gained more yards than the heralded Johnson. Fullback Jim Otis not only scored a career-high four touchdowns but bulldozed his way for 153 yards on 34 attempts.

In the process, Otis broke the school's single-season and scoring records. His 19 TDs were one more than Heisman winner 'Hopalong' Cassady had compiled in 1955. Otis' 96 points were four more than Gene Fekete had accumulated way back in 1942.

Soph quarterback Rex Kern [19-96] and soph wingback, Larry Zelina [8-92] also outgained Ron Johnson.

Zelina would have done a lot better had he not been kayoed on Ohio State's first extra point attempt. Exit Zelina. Enter junior wingback Ray Gillian.

Gillian pranced for 66 yards on only five solos.

Ohio State ground out 421 yards rushing on 79 attempts and added 46 more passing on six of nine completions. That added up to 467 net yards against one of collegiate football's best defenses. Michigan rushed for 140 on 41 attempts and added 171 yards through the air on 14 Brown completions in 24 throws. Three of his passes resulted in interceptions by Tatum soph, Doug Adams and junior Art Burton. Adams and Burton were linebackers. Woody Hayes called it "the best game ever played by the best football team I've ever had. It deserves to be No.1."

His offensive game play was simple.

"We wanted Jim Otis to carry about 30 times. We're a better football team when he's running. If you told him to run into the Lincoln LeVeque tower, he'd do it and he'd probably move it a little bit.

"Otis is just one helluva football player, so quick even I can't believe it. I never saw a kid so sure of himself. He's never given us a bad practice yet and he'd only missed three in two years."

As a sophomore, Otis led the Buckeyes in rushing with 530 yards on 141 carries. As a junior, Otis again was the most productive runner, piling up 884 yards on 189 bull-rushes.

And he still had one game to play this season...the Rose Bowl.

Affectionately dubbed J.O. by his teammates [as opposed to O.J. as in Simpson], the 6-0, 208-pounder enjoyed the accolades but was quick to heap credit where credit was due.

"All I know is I had some great blocking all day...really great. [Offensive tackles] Dave Foley and Rufus Mayes are really something."

Otis was tired of carrying the albatross around his neck. Meaning the long-time relationship between his father and Woody Hayes.

320

"I get sick-and-tired hearing people say I'm the starting fullback because my Dad and Woody Hayes were college roommates."

Woody Hayes seconded the motion.

"I get sick-and-tired hearing people say I start Jim Otis because his Dad was my best friend. Otis is in there because he's the hardest working guy I've ever seen. He's in there every single day taking a fierce beating. I've never seen a guy like him, a remarkable worker.

"He played last year with a broken thumb and a broken toe. He got cracked on every single play running, blocking or carrying out a fake, but he never complains. And because he's in there every day, Jim Otis doesn't make mistakes."

Nothing has come easy for Otis.

"I guess I've always had a tough time proving things myself. I was a tackle my sophomore year at Celina when our fullbacks got hurt and I volunteered for the job. Otherwise, maybe I'd never been a fullback."

As a soph at Ohio State, he started the season sharing fullback duties with Paul Huff, another sophomore, but quickly began asserting himself.

After he fumbled against Illinois, Otis found himself buried in Woody Hayes' doghouse.

"I was the sickest guy you ever saw after we lost that game. I didn't play much [four minutes] the next game at Michigan State and not at all against Wisconsin.

"Woody doesn't take kindly to fumbles and I don't blame him. But I got my chance again. I tried to make the best of it."

In the final two games of the '67 season, Jim Otis exploded for 149 yards on 35 carries and one TD against Iowa, then responded with a 114-yard effort [26 attempts] against Michigan.

He was at fullback to stay.

Michigan's Bump Elliot was short and to the point.

"We expected Ohio State to be a heckuva team and they were. They have a lot of weapons and use them well. But I'd have to say Rex Kern is the greatest. There are other good ones, but he's really something."

Michigan grabbed an early 7-0 lead, capped by Johnson's one-yard plunge. His 39-yard burst keyed the drive.

Facing a fourth-and-inches situation on the Michigan five, Otis rumbled over left tackle for his first TD of the game.

Kern's five-yard keeper up-the-middle early in the second stanza, coupled with Jim Roman's second straight extra point, provided Ohio State with a 14-7 lead.

Momentum seemed to be walking the Buckeyes' sideline. Unable to move the ball, Michigan was forced to punt. However, sure-handed Mike Polaski, who would become an All-American shortstop, muffed the punt. Michigan recovered on the OSU 28 and scored eight plays later on Johnson's one-yarder. The conversion kick tied it at 14-all.

At that point, it had all the makings of a typical Ohio State-Michigan dogfight. And even when Ohio State scratched out a 21-14 at halftime on Otis' two-yard run with 36 seconds it still seemed like anyone's game.

Ohio State continued to chew up large chunks of real estate in the third period. Soph wingback Larry Zelina took it wide for a six-yard touchdown. Roman's kick failed. It was 27-14 with 15 minutes to play in the Big Ten title clash.

Class of '68

It would be an unforgettable 15 minutes for Ohio State, an agonizing and endless 900 ticks of the second hand for Michigan.

Ohio State erupted for 23 unanswered points in the final stanza. No doubt to the delight of a record 85,371 at Ohio Stadium. Roman's 32-yard field goal at the 2:35 mark opened the scoring floodgates. The Buckeyes had forged out to a16-point cushion at 30-14.

Despite unfavorable wind conditions, Michigan had no other choice but to pass. The Wolverines' ground game had been neutralized.

It was squarely in the hands of quarterback Dennis Brown.

Ohio State's relentless defense was anxious to face the challenge. Two interceptions would set up two more touchdowns.

Soph linebacker Doug Adams [Xenia, Ohio] picked off a Brown toss to set up Kern's three-yard keeper at 4:46.

Subbing for the injured Zelina, junior wingback Ray Gillian [Uniontown, Pennsylvania] rambled for 50 yards to set up Otis' third TD of the game. That came at 11:23.

Still more than three minutes left to play.

Junior linebacker Art Burton's pickoff set up the final score.

The task fell on reserve fullback Paul Huff. But he lost a yard on the play. So Jim Otis was inserted back in the game. Otis banged across from the one. Ohio State had scored 50 points against 'that team up North.'

Emotions surfaced in the closing minutes of play, resulting in jostling near the Michigan bench after Wolverines' tackle Tom Stincic nailed Kern on a keeper.

Ohio State felt the tackle was made out-of-bounds. Michigan maintained the stop took place on the playing field.

Kern seemed unperturbed. He ran the next play straight at Stincic. The play after that. And the play after that.

Stincic finished the game with eight solo tackles and 15 assists.

When the rout finally ended, the record crowd swarmed onto the field and managed to tear down the steel goalposts.

Both Woody Hayes and Bump Elliot agreed on the game's turning point. That came in the final 36 seconds of the first half when Ohio State punched across a touchdown to snap the 14-14 tie.

"It put them in fine position," said Elliot.

It also put the unbeaten, untied and No.1 rated Ohio State into the Rose Bowl against O.J. Simpson and formidable Southern Cal.

They had muzzled Ron Johnson. But could they squeeze 'The Juice'?

OHIO STATE 50, MICHIGAN 14

	OSU	MICH.
First downs	28	17
Rushing Yardage	421	140
Passing Yardage	46	171
Return Yardage	62	15
Passes	6-9-1	14-24-3
Fumbles Lost	2	1
Yards Penalized	37	43

Ohio State	7	14	6	23-	50
Michigan	7	7	0	0-	14

MICH—Johnson, 1 run [Killian kick]
OSU — Otis, 5 run [Roman kick]
OSU — Kern, 5 run [Roman kick]
MICH—Johnson, 1 run [Killian kick]
OSU — Otis, 2 run [Roman kick]
OSU — Zelina, 6 run [kick failed]
OSU — Roman, 32 FG
OSU — Kern, 2 run [Roman kick]
OSU — Otis, 3 run [Roman kick]
OSU — Otis, 1 run [pass failed]

RUSHING
OSU— Otis 34-143, Kern 19-96, Zelina 8-92, Gillian 5-66, Brockington 10-20, Hayden 1-4, Long 1-1, Huff 1-minus 1; **MICH.**— Johnson 21-91, Craw 8-25, Werner 1-19, Moorhead 1-11, Brown 10-minus 6.
PASSING
OSU— Kern 5-8-41-1, Long 1-1-5-0; **MICH.**— Brown 14-24-171-3.
RECEIVING
OSU—Jankowski 3-22, Brockington 2-19, R.Smith 1-5; **MICH.**—Mandich 7-78, Harris 2-34, Staroba 1-28, Johnson 3-18, Imsland 1-13.

Chapter 52

HE'S A 'ONE MAN GANG'

When you have a workhorse, run that critter!

Run, O.J., Run.

O.J. Simpson, Southern Cal's super tailback, combined style and stamina. A 207-pound senior who took a licking and kept on ticking. And ticking. And ticking.

Simpson came into the USC-Oregon State Pack 10 title game averaging 37 carries and 181 yards per game. He was a shoo-in for the coveted Heisman Trophy.

Comprehend these stats:

In two seasons at USC his team had posted a gaudy 19-1-1 record. In the process Simpson scored 35 rushing touchdowns and set 11 school records. During the 1968 season he accounted for 22 of Southern Cal's 23 rushing touchdowns.

Southern Cal had gained 2,195 yards rushing on 550 attempts...and one nicknamed 'The Juice' had accounted for 1,709 of those yards on 355 carries.

How could a running back carry the ball 355 times without sustaining a serious injury?

Reasoned Simpson, "I think it's running hard. If you run hard you'll be bringing the force to the tackler."

Interjected starting quarterback Steve Sogge, "I think the reason O.J. doesn't get hurt is that he's so quick they never get a good shot at him. When he comes back to the huddle I ask him to tell me if he's ready. He's always ready. I like to hand off, stand back and watch the greatest runner in the country."

A world class sprinter, the 207 pounder had reeled off a 9.4 clocking in the 100-yard dash some 17 times. In addition, he was a member of Southern Cal's record-setting 400-yard relay team.

He would need all of those skills against upset-minded Oregon State.

An expected victory over the Beavers would propel USC to it's third straight Rose Bowl appearance against the Ohio State-Michigan survivor. That battle was seven days away.

Despite the underdog role, Oregon State thrived on the challenge. After all, the Beavers had shut out O.J. and Southern Cal 3-0 the previous year.

And for most of the 1968 clash, it looked like deja vu all over again.

O.J. Simpson couldn't dig a foxhole deep enough to hide in from the 59,236 fans at the Los Angeles Coliseum. Sure he had gained 84 yards on 21 attempts the first half, but he did more harm than good—fumbling at the Trojans' 23 yard line, dropping two passes and bobbling a pitchout.

Not exactly the stuff living legends are supposed to be made of.

After a scoreless first half, Oregon State clawed out a 7-0 lead on 230-pound Bill Enyart's one-yard smash and Larry Rich's PAT.

Following the ensuing kickoff, Southern Cal moved to the Oregon State 35 but Simpson fumbled again. The Beavers recovered.

O.J. Simpson simply shook off the bad luck. He was mentally tough and that began to show. Carrying the ball on six of seven plays, Simpson moved USC to the Oregon State 22. On a third-and-eight situation quarterback Steve Sogge faked a handoff to Simpson and passed to flanker Terry Dekralis who somersaulted into the end zone. Rich Ayala's kick tied it at 7 all with 13 minutes left to play.

Eight minutes later, Ayala's 27-yard field goal pushed Southern Cal into a 10-7 lead. Simpson's slashing runs and Sogge's rollouts spearheaded the drive.

USC cornerback Sandy Durko then picked off a Steve Preece aerial setting the stage for the game's most spectacular play.

Simpson described his 40-yard touchdown jaunt, "Dan Scott (fullback) took care of the end and Bob Chandler (flanker) cracked back on the back coming up. All I had to do was turn the corner and keep running."

Clearly, stopping O.J. Simpson would be the Buckeyes' primary concern. They had silenced Leroy Keyes of Purdue, Iowa's Ed Podolak and Ron Johnson of Michigan. Just one more herculean effort.

Would Jack Tatum, Ohio State's super sophomore roverback, shadow 'The Juice' as he did Leroy Keyes?

Maybe yes. Maybe no.

As Ohio State defensive coordinator Lou McCullough put it, "We always play our rover to the wide side of the field. Tatum was on Keyes so much because Keyes was a flanker most of the time."

As tailback in Southern Cal's I formation Simpson can run in any direction. Tatum hoped Simpson would come his way. "I've been thinking about O.J. quite a bit."

Would Ohio State go on the assumption that O.J. would get his 180 yards and therefore put extra pressure on USC's quarterback, Steve Sogge?

Woody Hayes was well aware of Sogge's passing and scrambling ability. "We have great admiration for him. He's a competitor."

Sogge, a 5-10, 175-pounder, had completed 103 passes for 1,268 yards and eight touchdowns. His accuracy percentage was a highly-respectable 58 percent.

Said McKay, "He's one of the real keys to our ball club. He's a kid who wasn't big enough, or fast enough, or a good enough passer; but we're 19-1-1 with him and the only game we lost was 3-0 in the mud to Oregon State last year.

"He has great confidence in himself and the team has great confidence in him. He's calling the shots. O.J. has said because Sogge is 50 percent improved, it's made it easier for him.

"Sogge completed 103 passes this year and our school record is 109, so you can see we're putting the ball in the air even though everybody considers us primarily a running team."

Simpson felt the Rose Bowl winner would be determined on emotion. "If we can be up emotionally, we can beat these guys. If we're emotionally ready, we can beat anybody."

He sure was 'up' for Oregon State.

O.J. Simpson carried the ball 47 times for 238 yards. Earlier in the season, he had carried 47 times against Stanford.

In 1966 Don Fitzgerald of Kent State University set a single-season record with 294 carries during that season. 'The Juice' was just three attempts shy of erasing Fitzgerald's name from the books and he still had a regular season game to play against Notre Dame before the Rose Bowl.

In the last two games Simpson would carry the ball 63 more times.

Ohio State linebacker Mark Stier couldn't wait to prove the Buckeyes were truly the best college football team in the country. "There's a lot more at stake than just the Rose Bowl. McKay said we shouldn't be No. 1 because we only played nine games and didn't play Notre Dame (USC and Notre Dame played to a 21-21 tie). We've got to prove that we're No.1."

All-American offensive tackle Dave Foley added, "I think we've already proved we're No. 1. It's a matter of pride. We've got to prove it to these people out here."

Ohio State left Columbus on December 20th for California. While Woody Hayes put his Buckeyes through grueling two-a-day drills, there was a little time to relax. Like a trip to Knotts Berry Farm.

A week before the Rose Bowl senior linebacker Dirk Worden went down in practice. His dream of an appearance crumbled in just one play.

Dr. Bob Murphy examined Worden and told him the bad news. "You've torn the ligaments again."

After practice, all of his teammates tried to console Dirk Worden. "Football has been good to me and..." but his voice broke.

Stier had a bum shoulder and soph wingback Larry Zelina bruised ribs. Injury-riddled soph quarterback Rex Kern had been kept out of contact drills.

All would start against Southern Cal.

GAME TEN
The Rose Bowl

Ray Gillian replaced the injured Larry Zelina at wingback. He was superb.

Chapter 53

A GAME TO REMEMBER

OHIO STATE 27, SOUTHERN CAL 16

Rose Bowl: January 1, 1969

It was a football fan's fantasy...the top two college teams clashing head-to-head. Unbeaten, upstart Ohio State against once-tied Southern Cal and it's one-man scoring machine.

They simply called him O.J.

He would win the coveted Heisman Trophy, symbolic of college football's top player. He would break loose for a spectacular 80-yard touchdown run before a live audience exceeding 100,000. Millions more watched on national TV.

On any other given day against any other given team, it would have been enough. But not on this day. Not against this very special team.

Spotting the Trojans a quick 10-0 lead, Woody Hayes' Buckeyes would reel off 27 unanswered points, then coast to only the schools' second unbeaten/untied season in 78 years.

Ohio State sophomore quarterback Rex Kern hobbled by a shoulder injury which had sidelined him for the team's first 10 days of Rose Bowl practice, was named the game's Most Valuable Player by a panel of writers covering the game. [He would dislocate that same shoulder during the Rose Bowl.]

Two days before the matchup, junior linebacker Mark Stier sustained a separated shoulder. A question mark before game time, Stier would lead the brilliant defensive unit.

And yes, O.J. Simpson rushed for 171 yards on 28 attempts in the losing effort. One burst of 80 yards, 91 more yards on 27 thrusts...3.3 yards per try.

The game started out looking like Ohio State's worst nightmare.

Three scoring chances ended in frustration and failure. All three involved sophomore wingback Larry Zelina.

Kern unleashed an apparent TD pass. Zelina was behind the secondary. All the soph quarterback had to do was deliver. But he overshot his receiver.

A few minutes later, Kern's pass bounced off Zelina's fingers at the one-yard line.

Zelina could have provided the Buckeyes with a 3-0 opening period lead, but his 17-yard field goal attempt was wide. It would be his last play of the game.

Zelina cracked a rib on a punt return earlier in the game. It was too painful to continue.

Southern Cal field-general Steve Sogge, a catcher on the baseball team, displayed his throwing accuracy by completing 19 of 30 passes for 189 yards and one touchdown.

He completed four clutch third-down passes to spearhead an apparent TD march, including three passes to Simpson. In fact, O.J. caught eight passes for 85 during his very, very busy day.

A 16-yard Sogge-to-Simpson completion moved the Trojans to the Ohio State three. Only a key play by soph defensive back Jack Tatum kept Simpson out of the end zone. Tatum knocked him out-of-bounds.

It was first-and-goal. Four cracks to score a touchdown.

However, it was not meant to be.

Ohio State soph safety Mike Sensibaugh dropped Simson for a yard loss. Second-and-goal.

Sensibaugh and Tim Anderson, another soph defensive back, then combined to drop Simpson in his tracks.

No gain.

Third-and-goal.

Trying to fool Ohio State, Simpson attempted his first of two halfback passes. The result: one incomplete, one intercepted.

Fourth-and-goal.

Southern Cal played it safe as place-kicker Ron Ayala booted a 31-yard field goal for a 3-0 lead.

Ohio State breathed a big sigh of relief. It could have been worse.

What was worse was Simpson's 80-yard touchdown run. The play started out harmless enough. O.J. took a handoff and headed around left end behind his blockers. He broke a couple of tackles. At that point, the gain was for 10 yards.

Then he reversed direction. Nothing but daylight ahead of him. Nothing but a 10-0 Southern Cal lead.

At that point, a large Ohio State rooting section estimated between 18,000-20,000 had little to cheer about. The majority of the 102,063 fans, however, delighted in the long gallop.

Ohio State took the ensuing kickoff, showed the stuff of champions, and marched 69 yards for it's first touchdown. There was 1:45 remaining in the first half.

The drive took 13 plays and was climaxed by junior fullback Jim Otis' one-yard dive. Jim Roman added the PAT and it was 10-7.

Two plays highlighted the drive. Soph tailback Leo Hayden banged 13 yards to the Southern Cal 21. Then junior wingback Ray Gillian made a leaping grab of a Kern pass, good for 18 yards.

It was first-and-goal at the Trojan three.

Twice the Buckeyes gave the ball to Otis. He scored on his second attempt. Momentum was starting to swing the other way.

Sogge went back to pass. Defensive ends Dave Whitfield [junior] and Mark Debevc [soph] dropped him for a 13-yard loss. Instinctively, Southern Cal called time out.

All that did, however, was to give Ohio State time to tie the game in waning moments of the first half.

Ohio State took over with 1:04 left...just 64 ticks of the clock.

Kern hit soph tight end Jan White for 17 yards. Another completion to Gillian added 13.

With fourth down and time running out, Ohio State called time out. Senior Jim Roman calmly booted a 26-yard field goal to the score at 10-all.

In the first half, O.J. Simpson was a hero. In the second half he fumbled twice. Ohio State recovered twice. His second miscue would prove fatal.

A poor 26-yard Southern Cal punt gave the Buckeyes excellent field position in the third quarter. Starting from their own 46, they scratched out enough yardage to set up Roman's second field goal, this one a 25-yarder.

That kick gave Ohio a 13-10 lead. A lead that would only increase.

On second down following the kickoff, OSU junior defensive end Paul Schmidlin unloaded on Steve Sogge, forcing a fumble. Senior middle guard Vic Stottlemeyer recovered on the Southern Cal 21.

A jack-rabbit kind of runner, Rex Kern turned a broken pass play into a brilliant 14-yard scamper to the Trojans' four yard line. On the next play he sprinted to his left and tossed a touchdown pass to the awaiting Leo Hayden. Roman's PAT made it 20-10.

There was plenty of time left on the scoreboard for Southern Cal to mount one of it's patented comebacks. There was 13:52 left to play. On the first play, Sogge flipped a short pass to Simpson in the flat. But before O.J. could turn the corner, Mark Stier blasted Simpson, jarring the ball loose. Junior defensive back Mike Polaski recovered on the USC 16.

Kern didn't waste much time. In fact, he didn't waste anytime to break the game wide open.

On first down, he threw over the middle to Gillian who took the ball in full gallop at the Southern Cal 12 and raced into the end zone. There was 10:05 left to play. Roman's extra point kick padded the lead to 27-10.

Simpson's final embarassment came when his option pass from the Ohio State 11 was picked off by Anderson in the end zone.

Southern Cal managed to score with 45 seconds left to play as Sogge connected with Sam Dickerson on a 19-yard play. A two-point conversion pass, however, failed.

It made no difference to Woody Hayes that his team still had an 11-point lead. Victory seemed certain. Southern Cal would have to score a touchdown and field goal to pull off a miracle.

However, the volatile Ohio State coach didn't see it quite that way. He stormed out onto the playing field to protest the touchdown.

If appeared as if Polaski had intercepted the pass. He had his back to the end zone. Dickerson had his arm wrapped around Polaski as they both went out of bounds.

The officials ruled that both players had possession of the ball and ruled touchdown for Southern Cal.

But it really didn't matter.

Ohio State had won the Rose Bowl and with it the undisputed national championship.

As expected, there was bedlam in the Ohio State locker room.

"Now let them vote," shouted Rex Kern.

"Yeah," responded a dozen teammates.

Woody Hayes sat on a bench, the game ball tucked under his arm. The players quickly gathered around their coach, each shaking his hand.

Then the chant began."ONE...ONE...ONE." Hayes screamed out "ONE", holding up one finger.

Then, the battle cry became "ROSE BOWL...ROSE BOWL."

In the midst of the celebration, the imposing figure of O.J. Simpson entered the room. He was still wearing his red-and-gold No. 32 jersey.

One of the Ohio State players barked "Hey guys, quiet. O.J., O.J."

Several other players relayed the news.

'The Juice' extended his hand, and in a loud clear voice said, 'You're the best ball club in the country and don't let anybody else tell you you aren't. Congratulations."

The Ohio State players grabbed his hand. Woody Hayes came over. He and Simpson shook hands. "Thanks, thanks," the veteran Ohio State coach muttered.

OSU assistant coach Hugh Hindman rushed into the room, carrying a silver trophy to be awarded to the game's outstanding player. "This year," he said, "it goes to Rex Kern."

Kern waved the trophy. "Every part of this belongs to you guys, the greatest team in the nation."

Then things got serious for the moment. Woody Hayes led his team in prayer. It was a long prayer. Then he headed towards the interview area. Once a policeman opened the door, the awaiting press began to chant "We want Woody."

Why did Woody Hayes run out onto the field with the issue already settled?

"I knew I was taking a 15-yard penalty," he said afterwards."I wanted to find out [why] and I still don't know. The official said he'd tell me later. And if he does, I'll tell you. But it's the first time I ever saw a touchdown called with the ball on the ground."

After his first of three previous Rose Bowl victories, Hayes incurred the wrath of West Coasters by saying four or five Big 10 teams were stronger than Southern Cal.

The same question popped up more than a decade later.

"I'll be doggoned if you're going to catch me again. I'd put Purdue, Michigan and this team on just about par. All these are great football teams. Maybe I'd better put it that way and nobody'll be mad."

Was this his best Ohio State team ever?

"Our '54 team was a fabulous team. We had some great runners on that team too; maybe not as many as we do now and not as much speed on the line. Our '61 team was awfully good too."

Was this his biggest victory?

Woody pondered the question for a moment.

"I suppose it was.

"Pretty convincing, wasn't it?

"I was a little worried. We weren't sharp and we had Stier hurt—and Rex's shoulder. But Mark played the whole game and Rex's shoulder went out again but popped back into place."

Defensive coordinator Lou McCullough echoed Woody's words of praise concerning the 202-pound senior linebacker. "The world will never know what Mark Stier did today unless you tell them."

What Mark Stier did was probably play his greatest game as a Buckeye. He called the defensive signals, was all over the field. He had 4 solo tackles and assisted on 2 other stops in the 81 degree heat.

"It hurt quite a bit," he admitted, "but they did a pretty good job of padding it up. "The Rose Bowl victory was a fitting climax to his career." It was a good way to go out."

"Kern's shoulder went out in the third quarter. The arm was stretched and the shoulder put back in place during a time out."

"Really it wasn't my best [game]" said Kern. "My passing was awful. I overthrew Larry Zelina and I overthrew Bruce Jankowski. They were both open in the end zone."

Kern passed for two TDs, ran for 35 yards. He played the game wearing a harness that didn't prevent a dislocated shoulder from popping out of it's socket. "I felt pretty good. The shoulder bothered me only in the third quarter."

Southern Cal's 10-0 lead only served as a wake-up call," Said Kern. "When the No.2 team's got you down 10-0 what do you do? You fold up or you come back like champions."

Fullback Jim Otis agreed. "When O.J. made that run the offense got together on the sideline and had a little meeting. We decided that now would be the time. We decided we'd better wake up or this guy was going to blow us off the field.

"Our game plan was simple. We felt we could do the same thing against Purdue [13-0] and Michigan [50-14]. We felt that now if the same material failed we would truly be losing to a better team.

"As it was, O.J. was the greatest back we'd seen and USC was the best team we'd played. It was our defense that did the job. It kept giving me the ball in great field position. The defense won the game."

Despite his one-yard touchdown plunge and 101 yards rushing, Jim Otis was still a bit critical about his performance. "Personally, I don't feel I ran that well. But then I suppose the Trojans had something to do about that. The USC defense is the toughest I've played against."

Dave Foley and Rufus Mayes, Ohio State's massive offensive tackles, had high praise for Southern Cal.

Said Mayes: "The Trojan defense was one of the best we'd met this year. That Al Cowling really impressed me."

Added Foley: "By far, USC's defensive line is the largest we've played. They controlled our sweeps, but we ate them up inside."

Jack Tatum, Ohio State's super soph 'Rover back' made only four tackles in the game. It clearly demonstrated USC's respect for this future All-American and NFL star. They shied away from him.

"I was honored and I was thankful. I don't know what you can say about O.J. He is simply great. You stick him hard, he gets up and congratulates you."

As they say, Mark Stier met O.J. Simpson 'up close and personal.'

"O.J. Simpson deserves the Heisman Trophy. He was always looking to cut back, but we did a pretty good job of stopping him. On that long run he cut back behind about eight guys."

Woody Hayes was in a very talkative mood after the game. He was still in the locker room when he instructed defensive halfback coach Lou Holtz to send the bus load of happy warriors back to the hotel.

Holtz had dashed into the room and shouted to Woody, "The boys are getting awfully restless [on the bus]. They'd like to get going."

Replied Woody Hayes, taking a shower: "Don't wait on me. I'll get back to the hotel."

He would linger on for a few more moments.

A reporter asked him how he was feeling.

"Happy?" Woody repeated the question."Why sure I'm happy. Say I've got to get back to the hotel. The President of the United States is going to call. That's the word they got to me. I don't want to miss that."

Woody Hayes did not miss THAT call. He admitted he was a little worried, "We weren't sharp and we had Stier hurt and Rex's shoulder. But Mark played the whole game and Rex's shoulder went out again but popped back into place.

"I thought we'd win. Hell, yes. Oh sure.

"Why? Because I felt we could move the ball on them. They took away our wide game but to do that they put eight men up front and we hurt them with our passing and we could run inside. I felt if we just played our football we could win.

"The biggest factor was our defense in the second half. O.J. broke loose for that big one in the first half, but we did a good job of stopping him in the second half.

"We did a good job of rushing Sogge. We forced them into two fumbles and two interceptions. That's four turnovers and the biggest thing was that we had no fumbles and no interceptions.

"It takes a great back to cut back, but that son-of-a-gun [Simpson] sure did it. That's the biggest play we've had broken on us in 10 games."

Then it was time to leave. It was time to return to his hotel and await President Richard Nixon's congratulatory phone call.

Woody Hayes let his team stay in California for a few days. He would leave for Vietnam to meet American combat troops. To tell them about the Rose Bowl. To bring messages back from young men waging another kind of war.

OHIO STATE 27, SOUTHERN CAL 16

	OSU	USC
First downs	21	19
Rushing Yardage	260	177
Passing Yardage	101	189
Return Yardage	65	119
Passes	9-15-0	19-32-2
Fumbles Lost	0	3
Yards Penalized	53	51

Ohio State	0	10	3	14-	27
Southern Cal	0	10	0	6-	16

USC— Ayala, 21 FG
USC— Simpson, 80 run [Ayala kick]
OSU— Otis, 1 run [Roman kick]
OSU— Roman, 26 FG
OSU— Roman, 25 FG
OSU— Hayden, 4 pass from Kern [Roman kick]
OSU— Gillian, 16 pass from Kern [Roman kick]
USC— Dickerson, 19 pass from Sogge [pass failed]

Class of '68

RUSHING
OSU—Otis 30-101, Hayden 15-90, Kern 12-35, Zelina 1-9, Gillian 6-14, Brockington 2-6, Huff 1-5; **USC**— Simpson 28-171, Sogge 8-minus 19, Scott 5-16, Lawrence 1-9.
PASSING
OSU— Kern 9-15-101-0; **USC**— Sogge 19-30-189-1, Simpson 0-2-0-1.
RECEIVING
OSU— Gillian 4-69-1, Zelina 1-5-0, White 1-17-0, Jankowski 1-2-0, Hayden 2-8-1; **USC**— Simpson 8-85-0, Dickerson 3-50-1, Lawrence 3-16-0, Klein 4-31-0, Chandler 1-7-0.

Chapter 54

ANATOMY OF AN 80-YARD RUN

Mike Polaski was a junior when Ohio State faced Southern Cal in the 1969 Rose Bowl. He was a 5-10, 158-pound defensive halfback...soaking wet., He was one of four players who had a shot at nailing O.J. Simpson as the 207-pound senior tailback weaved his way down field enroute to a spectacular 80-yard touchdown run.

In his own words:

I'm playing the wide side halfback. I'm lined up on Sam Dickerson. He's split out about 17 yards from the offensive set. The play starts out as a pitch, a sweep by O.J. to the opposite side of the field. To the closed side.

O.J. starts going to the closed side of the field, to his left. Mark Debevc, who's our defensive end, has a shot at him but can't make the play.

Mark Stier, who's playing linebacker, has a chance to get him. But he can't. (They both had hands on him). O.J. doesn't go down.

In the meantime, Dickerson has come out. His job is to block me. I start in my pursuit going to the opposite side of the field. I'm just trying to keep him [Dickerson] away from me and at the same time get an angle on O.J.

As I'm watching O.J. weave his way through the line of scrimmage, Debevc had his chance. Stier had his chance.

Mike Sensibaugh's playing safety. He comes up and gets a shot at O.J.'s legs. He kinda makes him stumble, but O.J. doesn't go down. I'm just three yards away from him. O.J. is just regaining his feet.

He's on the hashmark which gives him 17 yards to make a move, go to the closed side of the field. The guy weighs 207 and is a 9.3 sprinter. I can tell you I'm not a 9.3 sprinter now and I wasn't back then. I still have to maintain an angle on him in order for him not to outrun me.

I also know that most backs like to operate on the wide side of the field because they have more room to maneuver. I know that I have to guard against him cutting back to get to the open side of the field.

I decide I'm gonna try a 45 degree angle. If he tries to outrun me to the sideline, I still have an angle on him. If he tries to cut back I'm gonna get a hand on him. If nothing else, slow him down so pursuit can get to him. He's gaining his footing. He makes a 90 degree angle cut and I don't even touch him. I turn in my tracks and start chasing him.

Timmy Anderson and I follow him down the sidelines. We get within five yards of him, but we can't close the gap. He just outruns us the rest of the way into the end zone.

After the touchdown, I get to the sidelines and one of our student managers has the telephone. He tells me 'Holtz wants you in the press box.'

I don't want to talk to him.

But the kid wouldn't take no for an answer. So I get on the phone.

'Yeah, Coach.'

'What the hell is going on down there?'

'It was the greatest move I've ever seen. The guy made a great move.'

'Son, I don't care how you get it done. We've just gotta get it done. We can't have this. This can't happen. I don't care how you get it done. You've just gotta get it done.'

I get off the phone. There was a game to play.

We put the hit on O.J. the rest of the day. The guy is a great college back, the best I played against while at Ohio State.

Later in the game I did get some sticks on him. One hit caused a fumble and Mark Stier recovered. Mark Stier put another hit on him, caused a fumble that I recovered. Tatum, Sensibaugh and Timmy Anderson all got real good sticks on him at the goal line.

O.J. had power. When he wanted to stick it to you he had a package there to deliver that blow. But he didn't really want to do that all the time.

He always seemed to be bobbing-and-weaving coming through the line. His head and shoulders always seemed to be looking like he was avoiding punches or something. He was looking for a way to slide.

He never gives you an opportunity to put a good shot on him. He never got a lot of punishment because he was always able to move one way or the other, to make a blow a glancing blow rather than a head-on collision.

Here's a guy who had a ton of moves and absolutely great speed for a running back.

He knew what his strengths were. He was gonna pick-and-choose the places where he put his head down to take a shot or give a shot.

Section VI

For the Record

Woody's Record

NEW PHILADELPHIA HIGH SCHOOL (1938-1940)

1938			1939			1940		
19	Akron East	0	34	Brookfield	0	0	Brookfield	7
26	Zanesville	0	33	Zanesville	7	13	Zanesville	26
6	Lorain	14	7	Lorain	7	0	Lorain	54
33	Collinwood	7	20	Mansfield	0	0	Mansfield	7
32	East Liverpool	0	41	East Liverpool	18	0	Liverpool	34
33	Wooster	0	38	Springfield	6	13	Springfield	28
35	Niles	6	14	Niles	0	0	Niles	27
7	Akron South	0	6	Bellaire	2	7	Bellaire	53
21	Dover	6	28	Struthers	7	7	Struthers	6
212		**33**	23	Dover	0	0	Dover	19
			244		**47**	**40**		**261**

Won 8 - Lost 1   Won 9 - Tie 1   Won 1 - Lost 9

DENISON UNIVERSITY (1946-1948)

1946			1947			1948		
13	Otterbein	18	48	Rio Grande	0	38	Otterbein	7
7	Wash & Jeff	12	19	Wash & Jeff	14	54	Capital	0
0	Wooster	21	50	Beloit	7	40	Beloit	6
13	Muskingum	14	28	Wooster	0	27	Wooster	0
12	Oberlin	19	33	Oberlin	0	38	Oberlin	13
14	Capital	13	24	Muskingum	14	7	Muskingum	6
0	Ohio Wesleyan	39	56	Capital	7	32	Wittenberg	6
31	Wittenberg	0	18	Ohio Wesleyan	6	41	Case	7
90		**139**	12	Wittenberg	6	**347**		**45**
			228		**54**			

Won 2 - Lost 6   Won 9 - Lost 0   Won 8 - Lost 0

MIAMI of OHIO (1949 - 1950)

1949			1950	Mid-America Champions	
23	Wichita	6	54	Bowling Green	6
18	Virginia	21	0	Xavier	7
19	Xavier	27	35	Western Mich	0
26	Pittsburgh	35	42	Butler	7
26	Ohio U.	0	28	Ohio U.	20
34	Western Mich	20	39	Wichita	13
46	Western Reserve	7	27	Dayton	12
53	Dayton	20	69	Western Reserve	14
6	Cincinnati	27	28	Cincinnati	0
251		**163**	34	Arizona State*	21
			356		**113**

*Salad Bowl

Won 5 - Lost 4   Won 9 - Lost 1

Woody's Record

OHIO STATE (1951 - 1978)

1951

7	Southern Methodist	0
20	Michigan State	24
6	Wisconsin	6
10	Indiana	32
47	Iowa	21
3	Northwestern	0
16	Pittsburgh	14
0	Illinois	0
0	Michigan	7
109		**104**

Won 4 - Lost 3 - Tied 2

1952

33	Indiana	13
14	Purdue	21
23	Wisconsin	14
35	Washington State	7
0	Iowa	8
24	Northwestern	21
14	Pittsburgh	21
27	Illinois	7
27	Michigan	7
197		**119**

Won 6 - Lost 3

1953

36	Indiana	12
33	California	19
20	Illinois	41
12	Pennsylvania	6
20	Wisconsin	19
27	Northwestern	13
13	Michigan State	28
21	Purdue	6
0	Michigan	20
182		**164**

Won 6 - Lost 3

1954   Big Ten Champions

28	Indiana	0
41	California	13
40	Illinois	7
20	Iowa	14
31	Wisconsin	14
14	Northwestern	7
26	Pittsburgh	0
28	Purdue	6
21	Michigan	7
20*	Southern California	7
249		**75**

Won 10 - Lost 0   *Rose Bowl

1955   Big Ten Champions

28	Nebraska	20
0	Stanford	7
27	Illinois	12
14	Duke	20
26	Wisconsin	16
49	Northwestern	0
20	Indiana	13
20	Iowa	10
17	Michigan	0
201		**97**

Won 7 - Lost 2

1956

34	Nebraska	7
32	Stanford	20
26	Illinois	6
6	Penn State	7
21	Wisconsin	0
6	Northwestern	2
35	Indiana	14
0	Iowa	6
0	Michigan	19
160		**81**

Won 6 - Lost 3

Woody's Record

OHIO STATE (1951 - 1978)

1957   Big Ten Champions

14	Texas Christian	18
35	Washington	7
21	Illinois	7
56	Indiana	0
16	Wisconsin	13
47	Northwestern	6
20	Purdue	7
17	Iowa	13
31	Michigan	14
10	Oregon*	7
267		**92**

Won 9 - Lost 1   *Rose Bowl

1958

23	Southern Methodist	20
12	Washington	7
19	Illinois	13
49	Indiana	8
7	Wisconsin	7
0	Northwestern	21
14	Purdue	14
38	Iowa	28
20	Michigan	14
182		**132**

Won 6 - Lost 1 - Tied 2

1959

14	Duke	13
0	Southern California	17
0	Illinois	9
15	Purdue	0
3	Wisconsin	12
30	Michigan State	24
0	Indiana	0
7	Iowa	16
14	Michigan	23
83		**114**

Won 3 - Lost 5 - Tied 1

1960

24	Southern Methodist	0
20	Southern California	0
34	Illinois	7
21	Purdue	24
34	Wisconsin	7
21	Michigan State	10
36	Indiana	7
12	Iowa	35
7	Michigan	0
209		**90**

Won 7 - Lost 2

1961   Big Ten Champions

7	Texas Christian	7
13	UCLA	3
44	Illinois	0
10	Northwestern	0
30	Wisconsin	21
29	Iowa	13
16	Indiana	7
22	Oregon	12
50	Michigan	20
221		**83**

Won 8 - Lost 0 - Tied 1

1962

41	North Carolina	7
7	UCLA	9
51	Illinois	15
14	Northwestern	18
14	Wisconsin	7
14	Iowa	18
10	Indiana	7
26	Oregon	7
28	Michigan	0
205		**98**

Won 6 - Lost 3

Woody's Record

OHIO STATE (1951 - 1978)

1963

17	Texas A&M	0
21	Indiana	0
20	Illinois	20
3	Southern California	32
13	Wisconsin	10
7	Iowa	3
7	Penn State	10
8	Northwestern	17
14	Michigan	10
110		**102**

Won 5 - Lost 3 - Tied 1

1964

27	Southern Methodist	8
17	Indiana	9
26	Illinois	0
17	Southern California	0
28	Wisconsin	3
21	Iowa	19
0	Penn State	27
10	Northwestern	0
0	Michigan	10
146		**76**

Won 7 - Lost 2

1965

3	North Carolina	14
23	Washington	21
28	Illinois	14
7	Michigan State	32
20	Wisconsin	10
11	Minnesota	10
17	Indiana	10
38	Iowa	0
9	Michigan	7
156		**118**

Won 7 - Lost 2

1966

14	Texas Christian	7
22	Washington	38
9	Illinois	10
8	Michigan State	11
24	Wisconsin	13
7	Minnesota	17
7	Indiana	0
14	Iowa	10
3	Michigan	17
108		**123**

Won 4 - Lost 5

1967

7	Arizona	14
30	Oregon	0
6	Purdue	41
6	Northwestern	2
13	Illinois	17
21	Michigan State	7
17	Wisconsin	15
21	Iowa	10
24	Michigan	14
145		**120**

Won 6 - Lost 3

1968   **Big Ten & Nat Champs**

35	Southern Methodist	14
21	Oregon	6
13	Purdue	0
45	Northwestern	21
31	Illinois	24
25	Michigan State	20
43	Wisconsin	8
33	Iowa	27
50	Michigan	14
27	Southern California*	16
323		**150**

Won 10 - Lost 0   * Rose Bowl

Woody's Record

OHIO STATE (1951 - 1978)

1969	Big Ten Co-champions	
62	Texas Christian	0
41	Washington	14
54	Michigan State	21
34	Minnesota	7
41	Illinois	0
35	Northwestern	6
62	Wisconsin	7
42	Purdue	14
12	Michigan	24
383		**93**

Won 8 - Lost 1

1970	Big Ten Champions	
56	Texas A&M	13
34	Duke	10
29	Michigan State	0
28	Minnesota	8
48	Illinois	29
24	Northwestern	10
24	Wisconsin	7
10	Purdue	7
20	Michigan	9
17	Stanford*	27
290		**120**

Won 9 - Lost 1   * Rose Bowl

1971		
52	Iowa	21
14	Colorado	20
35	California	3
24	Illinois	10
27	Indiana	7
31	Wisconsin	6
14	Minnesota	12
10	Michigan State	17
10	Northwestern	14
7	Michigan	10
224		**120**

Won 6 - Lost 4

1972	Big Ten Co-champions	
21	Iowa	0
29	North Carolina	14
35	California	18
26	Illnois	7
44	Indiana	7
28	Wisconsin	20
27	Minnesota	19
12	Michigan State	19
27	Northwestern	14
14	Michigan	11
17	Southern California*	42
280		**171**

Won 9 - Lost 2   * Rose Bowl

1973	Big Ten Co-champions	
56	Minnesota	7
37	Texas Christian	3
27	Washington State	3
24	Wisconsin	0
37	Indiana	7
60	Northwestern	0
30	Illinois	0
35	Michigan State	0
55	Iowa	13
10	Michigan	10
42	Southern California*	21
413		**64**

*Rose Bowl
Won 10 - Lost 0 - Tied 1

1974	Big Ten Champions	
34	Minnesota	19
51	Oregon State	10
28	Southern Methodist	9
42	Washington State	7
52	Wisconsin	7
49	Indiana	9
55	Northwestern	7
49	Illinois	7
13	Michigan State	16
35	Iowa	10
12	Michigan	10
17	Southern California*	18
437		**119**

Won 10 - Lost 2   *Rose Bowl

Woody's Record

OHIO STATE (1951 - 1978)

1975	**Big Ten Champions**	
21	Michigan State	0
17	Penn State	9
32	North Carolina	7
41	UCLA	20
49	Iowa	0
56	Wisconsin	0
35	Purdue	6
24	Indiana	14
40	Illinois	3
38	Minnesota	6
21	Michigan	14
10	UCLA*	23
384		**102**

Won 11 - Lost 1   * Rose Bowl

1976	**Big Ten Champions**	
49	Michigan State	21
12	Penn State	6
21	Missouri	22
10	UCLA	10
34	Iowa	14
30	Wisconsin	20
24	Purdue	3
47	Indiana	7
42	Illinois	10
9	Minnesota	3
0	Michigan	22
27	Colorado*	10
305		**149**

*Orange Bowl
Won 9 - Lost 2 - Tied 1

1977	**Big Ten Co-champions**	
10	Miami (Fla.)	0
38	Minnesota	7
28	Oklahoma	29
35	Southern Methodist	7
46	Purdue	0
27	Iowa	6
35	Northwestern	15
42	Wisconsin	0
35	Illinois	0
35	Indiana	7
6	Michigan	14
6	Alabama*	35
343		**110**

Won 9 - Lost 3   *Sugar Bowl

1978		
0	Penn State	19
27	Minnesota	10
34	Baylor	28
35	SMU	35
16	Purdue	27
31	Iowa	7
63	Northwestern	20
49	Wisconsin	14
45	Illinois	7
21	Indiana	18
3	Michigan	14
15	Clemson*	17
339		**217**

*Gator Bowl
Won 7 - Lost 4 - Tied 1

Woody Hayes' career as a college head football coach spanned four decades. It began at Denison and ended in 1978 at Ohio State. He compiled an overall record of 238-71-10, including 205-61-10 at Ohio State.

Woody's Year by Year Record at Ohio State

YEAR	W	L	T	%
1951	4	3	2	.555
1952	6	3	0	.667
1953	6	3	0	.667
1954	10	0	0	1.000
1955	7	2	0	.778
1956	6	3	0	.667
1957	9	1	0	.900
1958	6	1	2	.778
1959	3	5	1	.389
1960	7	2	0	.778
1961	8	0	1	.944
1962	6	3	0	.667
1963	5	3	1	.611
1964	7	2	0	.778
1965	7	2	0	.778
1966	4	5	0	.444
1967	6	3	0	.667
1968	10	0	0	1.000
1969	8	1	0	.889
1970	9	1	0	.900
1971	6	4	0	.600
1972	9	2	0	.818
1973	10	0	1	.954
1974	10	2	0	.833
1975	11	1	0	.917
1976	9	2	1	.791
1977	9	3	0	.750
1978	7	4	1	.625
	205	**61**	**10**	**.760**

Woody's All Opponent List at Ohio State

SCHOOL	W	L	T
Alabama	0	1	0
Arizona	0	1	0
Baylor	1	0	0
California	4	0	0
Clemson	0	1	0
Colorado	1	1	0
Duke	2	1	0
Illinois	22	4	2
Indiana	22	1	1
Iowa	20	5	0
Miami (FL)	1	0	0
Michigan	16	11	1
Michigan State	9	7	0
Minnesota	11	1	0
Missouri	0	1	0
Nebraska	2	0	0
North Carolina	3	1	0
Northwestern	18	4	0
Oklahoma	0	1	0
Oregon	5	0	0
Oregon State	1	0	0
Penn	1	0	0
Penn State	2	4	0
Pitt	2	1	0
Purdue	10	4	1
SMU	7	0	1
Stanford	1	2	0
Texas A & M	2	0	0
TCU	3	1	1
UCLA	2	2	1
USC	5	4	0
Washington	4	1	0
Washington State	3	0	0
Wisconsin	25	1	2
	205	**61**	**10**

ALL-AMERICANS Under Woody Hayes

ENDS

Dean Dugger	1954
James Houston	1958-1959
Jan White	1970
Van DeCree	1973-1974
Bob Brudzinski	1976

TACKLES

James Marshall	1958
James Davidson	1964
Douglas VanHorn	1965
David Foley	1968
Rufus Mayes	1968
John Hicks	1972-1973
Kurt Schumacher	1974
Pete Cusick	1974
Chris Ward	1976-1977

GUARDS

Mike Takacs	1952
James Parker	1955-1956
Aurelius Thomas	1957
James Stillwagon	1969-1970
Ted Smith	1975
Aaron Brown	1977

CENTERS

Ray Pryor	1966
Tom DeLeone	1971
Steve Meyers	1974

LINEBACKERS

Dwight Kelley	1964-1965
Jack Tatum	1969-1970
Randy Gradishar	1972-1973
Tom Cousineau	1977

OFFENSIVE BACKS

Howard Cassady	1954-1955
Robert White	1958
Robert Ferguson	1960-1961
Rex Kern	1969
Jim Otis	1969
John Brockington	1970
Archie Griffin	1973-1974-1975

DEFENSIVE BACKS

Arnold Chonko	1964
Ted Provost	1969
Mike Sensibaugh	1970
Tim Anderson	1970
Neal Colzie	1974
Tim Fox	1975
Ray Grffin	1977

PUNTER

Tom Skladany	1974-1975-1976

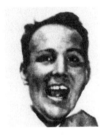

Howard Cassady   *Jim Stillwagon*

Rex Kern   *Jack Tatum*

Other Books Written
by
Harvey Shapiro

"Faster Than Sound"
The quest for the land speed record.
Published by A.S. Barnes & Company (U.S.A)
&
By Thomas Yoseloff Ltd. (London)

"Sports Stars Cookbook"
Published by
Carl Hungness Publishing, Speedway, Indiana

"Where Eagles Fly"
Published by
Witness Productions, Marshall, Indiana

"Man Against The Salt"
Pubished by
Minerva Press, London